Sunny Jacobs is now a free woman. She teaches yoga and tours the world raising awareness about the death penalty with her Irish partner, Peter Pringle. Her story is the focus of the award-winning play *The Exonerated*, in which she has starred as herself. Sunny and Peter live in Ireland.

D1344592

STOLEN TIME

The Inspiring Story of an Innocent Woman Condemned to Death

Sunny Jacobs

BANTAM BOOKS

LONDON • TORONTO • SYDNEY • AUCKLAND • JOHANNESBURG

TRANSWORLD PUBLISHERS
61–63 Uxbridge Road, London W5 5SA
A Random House Group Company
www.rbooks.co.uk

STOLEN TIME
A BANTAM BOOK: 9780553818284

First published in Great Britain
in 2007 by Doubleday
a division of Transworld Publishers
Bantam edition published 2008

Addresses for Random House Group Ltd companies outside the UK
can be found at: www.randomhouse.co.uk
The Random House Group Ltd Reg. No. 954009

The Random House Group Limited supports The Forest Stewardship
Council (FSC), the leading international forest certification organization.
All our titles that are printed on Greenpeace approved FSC certified paper
carry the FSC logo. Our paper procurement policy can be found at
www.rbooks.co.uk/environment

Typeset in 10.5/15pt Giovanni Book by
Falcon Oast Graphic Art Ltd.
Printed in the UK by CPI Cox & Wyman, Reading, RG1 8EX.

2 4 6 8 10 9 7 5 3 1

I dedicate this book to all the people who suffer from circumstances they cannot control and who need to know there is hope. I dedicate this book to all the people who made a difference in my life at times when I couldn't do it on my own. I dedicate this book to the knowledge that there really is something out there that can help us if we so choose.

Finally, I dedicate this book to you, the reader, with Peace and Love.

ACKNOWLEDGEMENTS

This book began with the recording of the torn and crumpled bits and pieces of a shattered life written on scraps of whatever paper I could find, sometimes even toilet paper. A miasma of pain, fear, anger, hopes, dreams and memories with the occasional glimmer and glow of humour became the raw material from which I reconstructed myself and the circumstances that served as the crucible from which a new life was forged.

There was a time when I thought I might leave the material for this book to my granddaughter for her to work with some day. I have been largely unremarkable, and totally devastated, and extremely blessed in this lifetime that seems like at least three lifetimes. And it seemed important to me to leave that legacy – to show that an ordinary person can come through extraordinary circumstances and be OK. And now, with the help and guidance of a number of good people, and some Grace, I have the opportunity to share it with many others. I am very grateful.

Special thanks to my agent, Caroline Michel of the William Morris Agency, London; the gentle genius of Jo Micklem, editor; and Francesca Liversidge, senior publishing director at Transworld, whose love for her dog, Max, convinced me of her sensitivity. Thanks to Rosie for shepherding me through the first draft; Jackie for the push I needed; Deborah for her good sense; and Peter for his steadfast support. Thanks to all those whose work went into the production of this book. Thank you to all those involved in *The Exonerated*. And to all my family and friends, I thank you for your part in my life and mine in yours.

And to all those who are no longer here, I hope you are happily observing from somewhere and smiling.

STOLEN TIME

1

T HEY CAME FOR ME in the middle of the night. The girls all woke up to wish me well. I was the only passenger in a police car with two male officers in front and one female officer in back with me. We had an escort riding behind us. At each county line they changed, like in a relay race. There was a helicopter overhead as well. They drove at 80 mph and I wondered if we would make it there safely. The trip took approximately seven hours.

No one knew what death row would be like for me because I was the only woman in the state of Florida under a sentence of death. Since there was no death row for women, I hoped they would take me to the men's death row, in Starke, Florida, where Jesse was. But that wasn't to be the case. We arrived at the women's prison in Ocala in the early hours of the morning, making the trip without any stops. Florida Correctional Institution for Women, a dome of greenish yellow crime lights glowing

11

eerily in the blackness of the Everglades like an alien spacecraft, was many miles from where the eighty-six men on death row were housed.

The first step in the process of commitment to the state prison system was to be fingerprinted, again, and have my picture taken, mugshot style, by a dried-up-looking old man, who turned out to be one of the women inmates. Hair cut short like a man's in an old-style ducktail with the point in the back. Skin like rawhide draped over a bone-thin frame. Her hands, though, were very delicate and her movements were fluid and precise, like those of an artist. Her speech was soft, and clear, although the voice could have belonged to a man, mid-range and slightly nasal. She was straight up and down in her blue prison work shirt and jeans that had been pressed and starched and sharply creased with obvious care.

The guard, a nondescript white woman with short curly hair, stood aside, allowing the inmate to take over. She led me to a stool in front of a blank white screen where she positioned me for the full-faced shot with a small easel in front of me on which a set of numbers and letters had been placed – FO4015. She went to her camera, focused the lens and asked if I wanted to have my glasses on or off. I chose to keep them on. Then she repositioned me for the side view. Little did I realize then that my new identity was being created. From that moment on, I would be known as Female Offender 4015.

From the ID room, I was taken to a doctor for a brief examination, which consisted of a pulse and blood pressure check, and a dentist who X-rayed my teeth. Then I was escorted to the clothing room. Another work-shirt-clad inmate stood behind a counter with stacks of shirts, pants, pyjamas and underwear behind her on floor-to-ceiling shelves. Although she was dressed identically to the photographer, she didn't look masculine. She studied me for a moment, obviously sizing me up with a practised eye. 'Five two, one hundred and ten pounds, right?'

I was issued a set of white cotton pyjamas, underpants and bras in sizes as close to mine as were available, a towel, washcloth and rubber shower shoes. The underpants were a size large. The inmate said she would try to do better next week. I didn't really care. I didn't expect to be here very long. She told me her name as she pushed the pile towards me on the counter.

'Thank you,' I said in a voice that sounded small and not my own. I looked at the guard again.

'Let's go. Grab that pile and follow me.' I don't know which of us was most alien, the guard, the inmate or me. I felt trapped in the space between them. I picked up the clothing and followed the guard out on to a path which led between the buildings and on to a grassy hillside.

We were met by a male guard who was to be my escort from that point on. The woman guard handed him my paperwork and, after a brief glance at my face as if trying to see what I was thinking, she turned and walked back into the building.

He indicated with a movement of his head that we should go. I walked slightly behind him, keeping my eyes on the hat he was wearing, like the ones the state troopers wore. He wasn't a bad-looking man, and he didn't seem to have any animosity towards me. He never really looked at me at all.

We walked for quite a way, passing buildings on either side that looked like dormitories. There was an occasional woman entering or leaving but for the most part the paths were empty. I was carrying my clothing along with a small box of toiletries – my toothbrush, hairbrush and hair ties, cigarettes and the few pictures I had brought with me from the jail. I clung to my little pile as if my life depended on it, each object contained within becoming like a talisman of security and hope.

As we approached each building, I thought to myself, This must be the one. We crested the hill, leaving all the dormitories behind. On the other side of the hill there was only one building. It was a U-shaped cement block, a single-storey building with a flat roof. Tightly girdled by two separate fences topped with massive tangles of barbed wire, it was separated from the rest of the compound by about fifty yards of empty space. We approached it, the guard and I, a sad little procession. And although there was no one in sight, it felt as if hundreds of eyes were upon me.

The guard paused at the first of the two gates through which we would have to pass. Selecting the key from the large metal ring he carried, he opened the first gate. I waited as he locked it behind us and selected the key to the second gate. Same procedure. There was a woman guard waiting in the entrance. I looked at the guard who had escorted me to this point. He looked back at me, then turned to the woman in the doorway. 'Here she is.'

'I'll take her from here. Thanks.'

I looked from one to the other. I didn't want him to leave and lock me in here alone with her. His eyes slid towards me, just briefly, and then he turned and left, locking the gates behind him.

'You can come with me now,' she said firmly, putting a hand on my arm.

'They said I could keep my box of stuff.'

'Well, why don't you come in and we'll see what's in it and go over the rules.'

I went in. She closed and locked the big wooden door behind us.

'They call this the Flattop,' she began, 'and this will be your new home . . .'

I wondered if she meant it was the place where I was to await my death. I looked at her more closely now. She was a big woman, very dark-skinned, with her hair done neatly in a twist at the back of her large, round head. But her face was kind, and she seemed to want to put me at ease. We were in what appeared to be the front office. There was a barred door behind her that led into the back of the building.

'Here, put your things down, and take a look at this list of rules. You can smoke here in the office if you like.'

She tapped me out a cigarette from the pack I had and lit it for me, placing the cigarettes and matches in her desk drawer afterwards.

I skimmed the rules quickly. Towel, soap, toothbrush, toothpaste, one pair rubber shoes, one pair white pyjamas, no cigarettes. 'But this isn't what I was told. I was

15

told I could have these things. In jail, they told me . . . and when do I get to smoke? It says here that I can't smoke in my cell.'

'You'll be allowed to smoke every time you are out of your cell. And you can smoke here in the office. I'll take you to your cell now. You can leave your things here for the time being.'

'There's a picture in there I'd like to have . . .'

'You'll take the state-issued items with you to the cell for now.'

I accepted the small pile without comment.

'We'll see that you have everything you need, and you can talk to the superintendent later today about any questions you might have concerning the rules.'

She picked up the phone and requested an escort to take me to the cell. The guard must have been right outside because he was at the door in a moment.

'OK. Let's go now.'

There was no use in protesting at this point and I didn't want to start off on the wrong foot with this woman on whom I would have to depend for my every need. She let the guard in and, together, they led me down the corridor beyond the barred door.

It was like a dungeon – dark, shadowy, still as death. The concrete walls smelled of dampness. Our footsteps reverberated down the hallway. We passed four cell doors as we made our way to the very last cell at the end of the corridor. She opened the door with a large key on a large ring full of keys just like you see in the movies. There were no words spoken. What would one say that could possibly suit the occasion? 'Enjoy your stay! Welcome to death row!' I looked from one face to the other. They were waiting. I took a breath and held it as I turned towards the open door to my cell. This was to be where I would await my death.

2

IN THE EARLY 1960S, nice Jewish girls were supposed to be virgins, or at least not to get pregnant outside marriage. If you did, you would go into seclusion to have the baby and give it up for adoption, or have your parents adopt it, or, as a last resort, have an abortion. When I got pregnant, I knew I had to have my baby and keep it. I was horrified at my parents for suggesting abortion and didn't appreciate that they were in fact trying to protect their child, me.

My mom took me shopping for a dress to wear to the wedding. It would be a formal religious service with the rabbi and the four-poled chupa under which we would stand, and the traditional breaking of the glass, and the throwing of the bridal bouquet. But my mom said it wouldn't be appropriate for me to wear white. I could wear beige, she said. Only slightly off-colour, like me. I chose a green silk dress to wear. Green being the colour of fertility, I thought it was more appropriate. No one else seemed to get the symbolic connection.

I was in my fourth month of pregnancy when Kenny and I were married. The wedding was held in a small hall in Manhattan. Uncle Ed, my father's brother, and my brother sat in the front row laughing because I was nervous and the bouquet in my hands was shaking. Kenny had trouble breaking the glass and, at the end, when I threw the bouquet it landed on the floor. I was too nauseous to eat when we went to the Tavern on the Green in Central Park. But the deed was done, all legal and proper.

I told myself it was an act of devotion but it was more an act of defiance. I wanted my baby. I dropped out of university. Eric Stuart was born just before my nineteenth birthday.

Kenny and I tried being grown-up parents for a few months but we were too immature, and I showed up at home one day with the baby. Kenny moved back in with his family and I lived with mine. Neither of us was prepared for the responsibilities of adulthood.

When Eric was two, my parents sent me to live in Florida 'so I could be on my own' and grow up.

When I first met Jesse Tafero in 1973, Miami was a warm, friendly place where young people could live a carefree lifestyle on very little money. It was a life of sand, surf, sun and fun. There were war protesters, soldiers, immigrants, retirees, jet-setters and hippies. I was twenty-four years old and a 'flower child', which is how hippies thought of themselves in those days. At the time, I was in a long-term, monogamous relationship with Irish John, a laid-back kind of guy who was very good with Eric, my now five-and-a-half-year-old son. We had a house in North Miami surrounded by tree nurseries. I called it the Ranch. It was a sweet old house with a stream running behind it and a family of ducks that would come to the door for their daily feed of dried corn. You could walk outside and collect your breakfast of oranges, grapefruits, bananas and coconuts fresh from the trees in the morning. It was a kind and gentle way of life. A happily married old couple had lived in the house for many years and their scent lingered like a fond memory. There was something very warm about it. Late at night I would go out with my cats and run through the trees and bushes. I knew the yard like the back of my hand so I didn't need my glasses and we'd come in smelling of night-blooming jasmine. It had been a very happy time.

The landlord had given us notice that he was selling the place, but on the salary from my part-time telephone sales job I couldn't afford to make the down payment so we were in the process of moving. Packing, carrying, wrapping. I wasn't in a good mood. Everything was in disarray. One of John's friends pulled up in a red Porsche with someone he wanted us to meet.

John entertained the guys on the floor in the living room while I continued to do the work of getting ready to move.

I was passing by with a box full of things from the bedroom. They were rolling joints, which was what you did in those days when a friend came over. You offered them coffee, tea, a bottle of beer, a joint, in about that order. I would have liked to sit down and smoke a joint and find out who this stranger was too. There was something disturbing about him. Sort of upset my electrons or something. I wasn't sure what it was. They were just sitting there watching me as I went back and forth, which began to annoy me. And when John asked for more rolling papers, I responded uncharacteristically, 'You want papers? Get them yourself.' My own voice sounded strange in my ears. John looked up at me in disbelief. I picked up something as if to throw it. I was losing my temper and even at that moment I thought, what's wrong with you, Sunny? I looked from one face to the other. The stranger was grinning at me like the Cheshire Cat. At that moment I felt as if I had been hit in the stomach. It knocked the air out of me. He looked as if he was proud of making me feel like that. I turned and left in a confused rush.

For the rest of the time they were there, the stranger sat there silently observing. He radiated an energy that touched me in a place where I had never been touched before. It was like discovering I had another sense organ inside my body. And it began sensing. When our eyes met, it was as if he could see inside. And he knew it – he did it consciously and he saw me react to it. When Jesse left that day, he told his friend that I was going to be his wife.

'She's John's old lady. They've been together a long time.'

'She's going to be my wife.'

John and I moved to another house in the same neighbourhood. It had French doors in the living room and a big backyard. Right after we moved in, a lot of dope business started to come John's way that required him to go on business trips. And it wasn't just the usual marijuana peace and love crowd. He developed a cocaine

21

habit, which he'd never had before. I had my own rules about this because I had a child. You could have a beer, smoke pot, but nothing more than that in my house. John started getting really bad. It became a daily thing and he needed more and more. One day, he came back from a trip and I had his bags packed. I told him when he came in, 'Don't unpack. Here's the rest of your stuff.' It was hard for me, and I cried a lot. At that time in my life the only thing I wanted in the world was to find a husband for myself, and a father for my son.

At first, Jesse and his friend in the Porsche came over just to see if I was OK. Although Jesse's presence was still disturbing in its intensity, the strength of it attracted me. We spoke a little just to be polite. He didn't make any moves on me at that time but there were others who did. Suddenly I was very much in demand, I guess because I was considered what Jesse would call a 'good old lady'. Honest, loyal, dependable – and I could cook. So all of a sudden I had suitors. There were three of them. One was a very eccentric character who owned a paramilitary vehicle and used to go out into the Everglades with it. He was kind of weird but he did own a house that had been left to him by some relatives. Then there was John, who was trying to clean up his act. And there was Jesse. If one came and brought flowers, the others would see and the next time they would bring flowers. If one brought a bottle of wine, the next time the others did too. In theory it was wonderful, but all the time I cried my heart out and decided there just wasn't 'that one special person' for me. I had given up on that idea. And it was over that idea that I cried, more than I did over losing John, really, although I truly loved him. So I decided that, since I wasn't going to find the one for me, I might as well just enjoy them, one by one, for whatever their qualities were, and be independent.

Two of my suitors were very polite. If one was there and another came the first one would say, 'OK, I guess I'd better go now.' But when Jesse was there and one of the other guys came by he would say, 'Come on in. Have a seat. Hey, how you doin'?' He would entertain them as if he were the man of the house. And he would stay until they finally left. And then one day he just didn't leave. He didn't really have anywhere to go. He had been sleeping at his friend's house on the sofa.

Jesse was soft-spoken and gentle. He enjoyed playing with my son and he was polite and well-mannered. I felt that reflected his upbringing, although his recent past was still mysterious to me. It would be years before I realized that Jesse had systematically set up the circumstances that caused me to break up with John. When he said I would be 'his', he set about making it happen by getting his friends to involve John in their courier business, carrying and indulging in cocaine. Sooner or later, Jesse knew, it would destroy our relationship. Everyone knew my feelings about hard drugs and not having them around my child or my house.

Jesse respected no boundaries. Boundaries existed to be breached in the hard, violent world he had come from only three months prior. I was a peace and love vegetarian. Violence was anathema to my life. Our worlds were

23

magnetic opposites. But Jesse was also very passionate and expressive. Besides having this aura of power, he knew about meditation and yoga and music and painting. Jesse became my teacher. I wanted to know everything he was willing to teach. Jesse was the most fascinating human being I had ever met. And he was so beautiful to look at – the way he moved, the way he'd drape himself into a chair. He had that lean and hungry look and seemed to operate on a more intuitive level than other people I had known. He was sensitive to every nuance of what went on around him. And he had this funny way of smiling, a sort of jaunty, cockeyed grin that I found irresistible.

One evening after Eric was asleep, we were on the couch, talking. Jesse said something that made me laugh, and then he suddenly went very quiet. He looked so serious. I wondered if something was wrong. He passed his finger over my lips like a butterfly kiss, tracing the outline over the top, out to the corners, across my bottom lip, bringing his fingers to rest against my cheek. I stopped breathing. He lifted my hand and kissed each finger, placing a kiss in the palm and closing the fingers around it, never moving his eyes from mine. I was lost. He was the light and I had to follow the light. I wanted to become as much a part of his life and his world as I could.

With Jesse I discovered a dimension I didn't know was there. Colours became very bright; sounds felt like warm liquid in my ears. It changed my life.

Now we both slept in the little room at the other end of the house from Eric so he wouldn't hear. I had put a mattress on the floor, which filled the room, and we stayed in there the better part of a week. I only got up to fix Eric breakfast and send him to school and to pick him up afterwards, or to receive him at the door when he came home on the bus, and be with him until bedtime. Jesse and I made our own world in that room. We talked, and we had sex, and I'd bring in a snack and we'd eat in there, or we would smoke a joint, and we'd have more sex, and we'd talk. We lived in our bubble and we stayed that way. After that first week we became a family. We just fell right into it. Finally, there was someone to teach Eric how to play ball and do things like a man. A husband for me and a father for my son. My dream come true. I was not sure it was Eric's dream come true, although he seemed happy enough as long as I divided my time between them and gave Eric some one-on-one time before bed.

The extreme sensitivity that made Jesse so attentive almost felt like paranoia sometimes, when he would react to the least little noise as if we were in a war zone. But with some small assurances from me he was soothed and that pleased me. I didn't know about Jesse's past until months later when a mutual friend told me about it. If I had known when I first met Jesse that he had been in prison for seven years for robbery, it definitely would have made a difference. I had a young child to think about. I didn't say anything to Jesse about it. But it helped me to understand some of his odd habits, like not hanging up his clothes and his aversion to using plastic utensils. And Eric was already calling Jesse 'Dad'.

Jesse had a job working for a used car salesman who

was a friend of his dad's. As it turned out, his parents lived not far from me. He was very closed about his life, what he did, where he went. I attributed everything to his having been locked up at an early age. This self-imposed naïveté of mine was not something new. And it wasn't just about him. It was about the world in general. I didn't get involved in the Vietnam War. I didn't want to see that. I was under the erroneous impression that I could avoid the negative things in life by only acknowledging the positive ones. The only thing about the Vietnam War that impressed itself on my consciousness was the monk who burned himself to death. Self-immolation. I will never forget that picture. How could anybody have that much devotion and self-control? Devotion and self-control seemed to me to be the ideal for a human being.

Jesse didn't actually tell me about his past for months. And then not until he had to. We were parked outside an office building in North Miami. He had said he had to see somebody and I was waiting in the car. When he came out he told me, with some difficulty, that he was on parole. The parole officer had said to tell whoever had given him a ride to leave. To Jesse that meant they were going to take him into custody and we had to get out of there.

That was when he told me about his past and his time in prison. I thought, he's been with me for months and I have never seen him do anything wrong. Why would they do such a terrible thing to him? I didn't understand it, but I was going to help him.

What had happened was that the FBI was looking for

26

a man who had escaped from prison and was considered extremely dangerous. He had been Jesse's protector and mentor, the sensei. The authorities had kept coming to Jesse's job. His boss was upset about this constant flow of parole officers, police and detectives, which he said was beginning to affect his business. So Jesse quit the job. But when you are on parole you can't do that. You have to have permission to change jobs, or residences. Apparently the parole officer was going to work with him to straighten things out. But Jesse had made his decision. And I made mine.

We left Miami the next day. I gave my favourite desk to John's mom, who was still a friend, to keep for me. The rest of my possessions went into storage or got left behind along with the life I had known and the path I had been travelling. Jesse, Eric and I packed up the car and headed for my parents' house in Charlotte, North Carolina, and a life and path away from all that had been familiar. We lived under a cloud from then on.

My parents never really liked anybody I brought home. They always thought I could do better. And Jesse wasn't even Jewish! He made them uneasy. His presence in my life made them very uncomfortable. 'What does he do?' 'He doesn't work?' We stayed at my parents' house for a while, sleeping together, which they didn't like. At first we slept in different rooms. My mother said, 'It's not *nice*, we hear him sneaking down the hall every night.' So I said, 'Well, why don't you just let us stay in the same room so we don't have to sneak? Nobody is getting fooled here.' So we stayed in the same room. And Eric would come in each morning and sleep in between us, the whole family together.

Eventually, we got our own place. We had our difficult times because Jesse had never lived with anybody but his parents and the men in prison. So whatever it was that he needed to do, I allowed him the space to do it. Which meant that sometimes he even went out with other women. I tried not to think of it as cheating. I told myself he needed to do this in order to grow up and grow out of it. He had been deprived of the natural course of development. I had to allow him these extremes or he'd be kind of crippled. He needed to feel he was macho, like they had taught him in prison. It was a notion I would be unsuccessful in dispelling.

If we had quarrelled, he would not sleep in the same room with me because he had been told by his mentor, 'Don't ever sleep with a woman if you've argued with her because she'll stab you while you're asleep.' I had a hard time convincing Jesse that we're not all like that. And it broke my heart. He was so wounded. It was just awful to think of how much he had suffered, being put in prison at such a young age, and what he'd missed in life. I wanted to give it all to him . . . even if it made me unhappy. So if he needed to be with women to build up his ego and make him feel like a man then I let him. I let it happen. I'd just ask him to please be honest with me and tell me. Loyalty and devotion to what I believed in – self-immolation.

Our sex wasn't just physical and it wasn't just emotional. There was this extra element where we weren't

28

even in our physical forms any more. It was as though we had exchanged personas. It was total.

We traded in my car for an old bread truck that we reincarnated into a camper van. We painted the outside light blue. Inside, we draped green taffeta over bamboo poles to line the walls in the back, added a Salvation Army mattress supported by plywood laid over the wheel wells for a bed, and covered the floor with linoleum in a tile pattern. We spent most of the summer camping in the Cherokee National Forest. Neither one of us knew how to build a fire, or put up a tent. And we didn't have the proper clothing. But it was great fun. Eric and Jesse would go out hunting bats at dusk, and raft down streams in inner tubes. We read stories together at night. And we had a box full of instruments for a family band. Jesse bought Eric his own guitar. We did Eric's lessons as we drove – spelling, maths, English and life in general. If we passed a field of cows, that was the day's lesson. And there was always time to pick berries, or run through fields of flowers, or climb a hill to see what was at the top.

Sometimes Eric and I had to go back down the mountain and live at my parents' house so I could earn some money working for my dad. When we were in town we always got together with my brother, Alan, and his family. He had married a hometown girl in Miami after high school and his stint in the army. They had a little boy and would later have a little girl. He and John were still good friends and we talked about John a lot – how he was doing, who he was with, where he was living. He was still struggling with drugs but he was managing to work and he was still as loyal and good-hearted as ever. He always asked about me and about Eric. My brother was working for my dad at his factory. Dad had moved his business from New York to Charlotte to avoid the high costs, and they had bought a house there. It was a hard move for my mom. She was a New York girl, out of place in the South. She didn't mind watching Eric during the week while I did secretarial work for my dad. And then the weekend would come and we'd go back up the mountain.

It was on one of those trips up the mountain that I got pregnant. At the time, Jesse and I had been together a year and some months.

Towards the end of that summer my parents sent Eric to camp. It was fun for him to be with other children. Jesse and I used the child free time to go to New York. The only incident to mar the idyllic summer of 1974 was when we were stopped on the road by a policeman who searched the van and found a marijuana cigarette. Upon further inspection of the van at the police station, we were charged with the contents of Jesse's party pack – a selection of tablets and good smoke – a gun, which was a misdemeanour. But, things went back to normal and we enjoyed the remainder of the summer in our blissful bubble. When we got back to Charlotte we were broke again, I stayed with my parents while Jesse went on a trip. When he came back we got an apartment. For a while, Jesse made a living painting portraits. But he was afraid to apply for a steady job because of his past. We talked about the possibility of his doing freelance work painting murals. My pregnancy was becoming advanced. Eric needed stability. And with a new baby coming we would need a regular source of income. He promised to try.

I lived for his approval and to help him to fulfil what I saw as his potential to become someone great. He was the one with the Destiny and I was the one with the Fate. I was on this earth to help him to achieve his Destiny. I was nothing but for that. How sad! How tragic! How mistaken I was. As it turned out, he was the one with the Fate and I was the one with the Destiny. But hindsight is 20/20, and love is blind.

Jesse went on another trip just before I had Tina, and when he came back I was in labour. I had been desperate to reach him. I had called the numbers he had given me but the people hadn't seen him; they said they'd give him a message whenever he got in touch. I was frantic.

He got back just in time and we left for the hospital. I went with my mother in my parents' car and he followed. At that point, you want to be with your mother. You want your partner around but when you're having a baby you definitely want your mommy to be there with you. Mom was worried it would happen on the way. When we got to the hospital my mom helped to get me registered. Jesse was furious because she used my real name, which he feared could be linked with his own. His paranoia about being found was a driving force in our lives, and the main consideration in all decisions. He was living in fear and we were ruled by it. But, as he stood there in his Chicago trench coat and fedora, his concerns about not being conspicuous seemed a bit ridiculous. I told him I was sure it would be OK, and I told my mom he was just nervous about the baby coming, and we managed to get me upstairs to get on with the business of having a baby.

I had taken Lamaze classes. Jesse had started taking them with me but then he wouldn't go. So I went by myself, just me and my pillow. At the hospital I wrote down that he had taken the class too so he could get this green outfit, the doctor outfit, and come to coach me. He was going to be my breathing coach. No one would be allowed into the labour room who hadn't taken the course. When Jesse stopped coming I should have had my mom come instead, but I hadn't wanted my parents to have another reason to be angry at him. Now, that meant my mom would not be allowed into the labour room with me.

I was trying to be calm, trying to breathe like they taught me in the class. I had written out all the instructions for Jesse so that he could help me through it. Then a whole group of student nurses filed into the room and crowded around. I was in major labour by this time, and they were looking at me and poking at me and I couldn't do my breathing. It was really upsetting me, so I turned to Jesse and said, in between puffing and blowing, 'Could you get them out of here?' This was something Jesse didn't need Lamaze training to accomplish.

'Get out!' He turned into a madman! They ran from the room. He literally chased them. 'Are you OK, baby?' He was very protective. I said, 'I'm OK. It's OK. It really didn't bother me that much.' Then I started going into the final stages of labour and I told him, 'Go get somebody. Go get somebody, it's coming out. I can't hold it! It's going to come out.' He ran, and came back literally dragging someone.

She looked and said, 'Yes, it's time for the doctor.'

They were wheeling me into the delivery room and he was just standing there, frozen. I said, 'Jesse, come on, come on!'

He said, 'I can't do it. I just can't.' He didn't move.

And I said, 'You have to come, you promised. You have to be there to watch your child be born. I need you there.'

'Sorry, baby, but I just can't.'

With only a moment to regret not having taken my mom to the Lamaze classes, I turned to the nurses now surrounding my bed.

'OK, get me to the delivery room.'

They were saying, 'Don't push! Don't push!'

They got me to the delivery room and put my feet in the stirrups and then they said, 'Now push. Now push.'

I had gone through all this so that I could see my baby born. But the round mirror above me was askew. 'Fix the mirror!'

'Just push. Push!'

'I'm not pushing until you fix the mirror.'

'The baby is coming. Push!'

'Somebody fix the mirror.'

So they fixed the mirror. And she was born. It was amazing. They cleaned her up and held her so I could see.

'She didn't cry yet. She didn't cry yet.'

They laid her on my chest, and told me it was OK. She looked just like Jesse in miniature. She was fine. It wasn't necessary to cry.

They took me to recovery. But it was so crowded they put me in the hall next to the broom closet. Jesse had stayed at the hospital. He was waiting for me in the hall. He apologized. 'I'm so sorry. I just couldn't do it.'

I said, 'It's OK. It's OK.'

I had always been told that women were stronger, emotionally, than men. Yet, for a long time, I wanted somebody on whose strength I could depend. I now know from hard-earned experience that each of us, male or female, must at some point take responsibility for ourselves and our lives. That's the way it is.

We couldn't take Tina home at first because she was only five pounds when she was born. She was too small, too weak, to breastfeed, so they tried to feed her in other ways and I had to go home without her.

She was in there for a week. I had to pump out my breast milk and bring it to the hospital in little plastic sacks for them to feed her because she did better on the breast milk. And I was bursting. I felt like I had footballs on my chest. I called the La Leche society and they finally told me what to do. They said, 'Get in a hot shower and just stay there until the milk starts flowing out. It will start pouring out like somebody opened a faucet. You just need to relax.' So I did. And it started pouring out. It was like an orgasm! So I'd do the breast pump in the shower. I learned how to express the milk by hand and I could aim right across the room and getcha! It was funny. And then, finally, Tina came home. And we were happy.

My parents came over to the apartment to help me. My dad, especially, was having trouble accepting the baby. My parents were upset with Jesse for not being there for me during the last part of my pregnancy. I hoped it would work itself out in time. Up until now, Jesse had been earning a sporadic income painting murals and doing portrait work at the annual Golden Gloves boxing event in Kentucky. He had made a couple of trips to Chicago, where some friends were arranging something for him. I didn't want to know about it. He had an interest in guns, the mechanics and aesthetics of them. He thought that if he could buy damaged guns and repair them, he could sell them back to the travelling dealers and make a living. Jesse asked me to buy them in my name because he had a record. I felt a little nervous about this because I had never seen a real gun, except for the one my uncle Joe had brought home from the war as a souvenir. Guns were not a peace and love kind of thing. But it was legal for me to buy them, like art objects to be restored, and it was something he could do. My parents asked what Jesse would do now that we had a new baby to take care of and Eric, who was nine years old, needed to remain in school and in one place. I told them that Jesse was going to get a job. They were sceptical, but they accepted what I told them, saying, 'We'll have to wait and see.' My dad played with Eric and my mom helped me with the baby. Tina was a good baby, with a sweet face and a sweet disposition too. I was sure everything would work out.

3

J ESSE HAD BEEN OFF on a trip to Florida to do some work with his friends. At the time, we had been living together for three years. Tina was ten months old and Eric was in the fourth grade. We had just got an apartment in town and still didn't have a phone. After this trip, Jesse was going to paint murals for a living. But he just needed to make a little money first to get us started.

I was waiting at the pay phone outside Dunkin' Donuts on Independence Boulevard like I did every night, with the kids in the car. Although it wasn't the best place to be at night, the parking lot was well lit. There was no one around, no houses, no people. I kept the doors locked and we didn't stay long. This night the phone rang.

'Mommy will be right back. Eric, watch the baby.' I jumped out of the car and caught it on the third ring.

'Hello?'

It was Jesse. He had no money and was staying with some woman and her Dobermann. She wanted to go into the clothing business with us. He wanted me to get some material from my dad's factory. I asked what had

36

happened to the deal with his friends. I did not want to know anything that might not fit into my peace and love world view but I knew things with his friends didn't necessarily turn out as planned.

'It fell through. Are you gonna come?'

'I'll leave tomorrow. Tell me where to find you.'

And so a chain of events was set in motion that would change all of our lives for ever. I could have told him to stay there until he had the money to come home to us. I could have told him to go jump in the ocean with this woman and her Dobermann. I could have said, 'You got yourself into this mess, now you get yourself out.' I could have gone to work for my dad for a couple of weeks and sent him the money to come home. But Jesse was the sun and I was the moon, and I had no light but that which was reflected from him. I had to be with him. I was afraid I would lose him. I had thought having a child of his own would make a difference.

I called my parents and asked them to keep an eye on the apartment for me until we got back. They said it was an irrational plan and they would worry about the kids on such a long drive. North Carolina to South Florida was quite a distance for a young woman with two small children by herself in an old jalopy. But my weakness was stronger than their rational arguments.

The children and I left the next morning after stopping by my dad's place for the bolts of taffeta material Jesse had requested, and picking up a case of oil at the gas station so I could keep the car running till we got to Florida. The thought of Jesse with that woman drove me on throughout that day and all through the night. I never cheated on him. I loved him.

I look back at that young woman and ask myself, what if she had left the children with her parents? What if she hadn't been so blind? I guess you could even say she was selfish – not thinking of the children's welfare above her own needs and the fulfilment of her own dreams. I think it would be more accurate to say she was desperate.

When we got to Florida, Jesse had pretty much worn out his welcome. The addition of a partner and two children was the final touch. We had to find somewhere else. The car we had come down in had died. It was a miracle that it had made the trip all the way from North Carolina to Florida in the first place. Jesse arranged for one of his friends to drive us around and we ended up staying at the guy's apartment. His name was Walter Rhodes. He called himself Rusty; I called him creepy. We stayed at his place for two nights. The first night Jesse stayed in the bedroom with the kids and me. The second night he said that he had to spend time with Rhodes. He didn't return to the bedroom till morning.

By the third day, I'd had enough. I couldn't stand to stay in Rhodes's apartment any longer. It just felt like the wrong place to be, especially with the children. I told Jesse how I felt. And Eric was upset by a terrible dream about something bad happening to us.

Jesse managed to arrange for us to go to the home of another friend in West Palm Beach, where we could wait for my parents to wire us enough money to get home. Rhodes would drive us to West Palm in his Camaro. We

38

had put the attaché case he had acquired with the collection of guns in the trunk because Jesse was hoping to sell one or more for cash.

It was late, maybe two in the morning, when we left. We got on the freeway but it was too late to go knocking on someone's door. Jesse and Rhodes argued about it because Rhodes didn't want to be stuck with us for the rest of the night. We ended up pulling into a rest area off the interstate. Jesse and Rhodes finished the argument and we settled in to sleep until it got light. I was in the back with the children. Eric was sleeping with his head resting on my right shoulder and the baby was cradled in my lap after nursing. Jesse had his arms folded across his chest with his head leaning against the passenger side window. Rhodes was hunkered down in the driver's seat with his head tilted back. I slipped into a dreamless sleep.

I was startled awake when the driver's door was jerked open suddenly and a man reached into the front seat, bent over like he was getting something from the floor.

'Get out! Keep your hands where I can see them and get out.' It was a highway patrolman. What was wrong, I wondered. We were just resting in a rest area, parked legally.

Rhodes got out of the car with his hands loosely raised.

I knew Rhodes was trouble from the first time I saw him. Maybe the car wasn't registered properly? Maybe the car was stolen?

He asked Rhodes for ID and told him to stand in the front of the car. There was another man with the trooper.

I hadn't seen him before. He wasn't wearing a uniform, just white T-shirt and dark trousers, so I couldn't tell who he was or why he was standing there watching. The trooper had taken something out of our car and he was getting his radio from the police car.

'What's happening, Jesse?'

'I don't know. He found one of the guns I sold to Rhodes.'

'When did you sell him the guns?'

'Yesterday, for riding us around and for stuff he's gonna do for me. We'll get some money out of it too.'

'He's going to go back to prison for having those guns, isn't he?'

'Let me handle this, OK?'

The trooper finished his transmission and was back at the driver's door of the Camaro.

'OK. You too.' He was leaning in, talking to Jesse. 'Get out of the car.'

'I can't. The door doesn't open on this side.'

'Let's see some ID from you.'

Jesse hesitated, digging into his back pockets as if he was having trouble locating his wallet. He was not going to show ID. I knew we were in for trouble now. Jesse had already violated his parole. He would almost surely go back to prison.

The trooper was getting angry and impatient. He ordered Jesse out of the car again, this time reaching in and grabbing him by the shirt, trying to pull him out across the front seat. I looked at Eric's face. He was scared. So was I.

Jesse and the trooper appeared to be almost dancing, arms locked around each other, swaying side to side in between the cars, turning this way and that. Finally, the trooper wrestled Jesse around against the side of the Camaro and told him to empty his pockets. Then he asked about the attaché case that was up front on the floorboards. Jesse liked carrying an attaché case. Status symbol, I guess. Releasing his grip on Jesse, the trooper reached back into the car for the attaché case, demanding that Jesse open it. Jesse claimed it wouldn't open.

The trooper was looking at me now. He asked for ID. I fumbled around in my purse. He grabbed my purse, completely out of patience. Digging around, he came up with a parking ticket and went to the phone to call it in.

Rhodes appeared at the passenger-side door. The window on that side was open and he reached into the front seat for something. Withdrawing his hand, he lit a cigarette, watching what was going on with the trooper and Jesse through the car window. The other man with the trooper was just standing there. Rhodes's head disappeared from the window. He seemed much calmer as he left. Maybe a cigarette was what he needed. Jesse was saying he had to take a leak and went to a nearby tree to pee. This was chaos. I couldn't see where Rhodes had gone. Jesse came back to where the trooper was once again trying to open the attaché case. He wanted Jesse to open the attaché case and Jesse was refusing. Oh, no! They were arguing over the case!

There was some sort of transmission coming in on the trooper's radio. He and Jesse began scuffling again. The trooper was yelling for the other man to help him. Together, they wrestled him towards the police car, forcing him face down over the hood. The other man now had Jesse's arm twisted up behind his back. The trooper was yelling at Rhodes to go back over to where he had been. He was pumped full of adrenaline, pulling out his gun and waving it from side to side, trying to cover the whole area, Rhodes, Jesse and me.

The children and I stayed perfectly still. I was holding Tina and I gave Eric's leg a squeeze with my right hand. We were frozen in the moment . . . and then . . . Jesse was struggling to free himself from the grip of the man who had him pinned over the front of the police car in an arm-lock. The trooper, still waving his gun around in between the cars, was shouting:

'The next one to move is a dead motherfucker!'

And then—

The sudden blast of gunfire erupted, filling the world with deafening force.

BANG!

I threw myself over the children, clutching them tightly to me.

BANG, BANG, BANG, BANG, BANG, BANG!

We were consumed by the gunfire.

It all happened so quickly and yet it seemed as if time had been drawn out like a fine wire, slowly beginning to sag in the middle. When the shooting stopped, real time began again. My mind began to function, penetrating the fog and the smell of gunfire that filled the morning air.

Silence. Darkness. A vague consciousness. A thought . . . are we dead? Is this what it is like to be dead? Does it hurt? Hurt would probably be a sign that we were alive, but I felt nothing. Could a bullet have passed through my body and killed us all without my knowing it? I took a breath. I must be alive. I opened my eyes. I felt alive. I wondered if my body was thick enough to have shielded the children. But there was no movement beneath me. The children lay motionless. They hadn't made a sound throughout the entire ordeal. I raised myself just enough to see.

Expressionless faces, still frozen in time, stared at me through fear-glazed eyes that used to be the windows of their little souls.

'Eric, are you OK?'

'Yes, Mommy.'

I felt my own heart start beating again. I looked at the baby. Her eyes were wide open. She blinked. It was only then that I dared raise my head to look out at the scene beyond the shattered window of the car. Where was Jesse?

Rhodes was running from in between the cars around the front of the police car. He had a gun in his hand and he was shouting:

'Come on! We're taking the police car!'

Jesse was standing there in between the cars. He still seemed frozen. Rhodes was shouting something else and waving the gun. Jesse moved towards us now. He was telling us we had to get out of the car and go with Rhodes.

'Can't we just stay here?'

Jesse shook his head no. I saw the same face I'd seen

43

when I first looked at the children. Expressionless, except for the eyes.

'Come on. We've got to go.'

It was an effort to string together a whole thought. It was as if the atmosphere had become thick with blood and adrenaline and I was trying to think through Jell-O.

We are going somewhere, so I will need to bring diapers.

There was a brown paper bag full of our stuff on the seat next to Eric. I reached over to rummage through it for whatever I thought we would need. Finding comfort in the familiar feel of the children's clothing, the scent of the disposable diapers, I could feel the edges of my consciousness again.

Maybe, if we didn't move fast enough, Rhodes would just leave us. I began to gather diapers and things.

'Come on! Come on!' Rhodes called again.

Jesse began to get nervous and said we'd better go, now. He took the bag of diapers and clothes and helped me out of the car with the baby in my arms. He reached back in for Eric but didn't have a good enough grip on his arm. Eric slipped and fell into a pool of blood at our feet!

'Oh, my God!' My stomach almost heaved, but I reached out and helped Eric up, saying, 'It's all right. Come on, let's hurry now,' trying to stay calm outwardly so he wouldn't get upset. I looked up into Jesse's eyes and saw the same fear and confusion that I was feeling. We didn't speak. He opened the back door of the police car, threw the bag in and then helped me and the kids in, closing the door behind us. Jesse got in the front and

Rhodes drove off down the road, leaving the bodies of the wounded men and the Camaro in a pool of blood and dust.

So that was it. We were the hostages of a man in desperate flight from an act of violence that would define all our lives from that moment onward. What would happen to us now? Nobody said a word. We sped along the interstate in silence, each frozen within the adrenaline-induced fear and confusion of having been so close to violence and death. I had the feeling that we were fleeing from death rather than rushing towards something. There was no plan, no refuge. There was only the silence in the interior of that police car racing through the foggy morning air into oblivion. Even the children were silent. We pulled off at an exit where Rhodes threw out some papers and handed the gun he had been carrying to Jesse, picking up the other one from the seat of the car where the trooper had placed it earlier. Then we continued on.

'We've got to get rid of this police car,' Rhodes said as he turned into the Century Condominium complex. There was a convenience store on the corner and I suggested that I could call us a cab. It was the only thing I could think of to try to get away from him with my kids. But he didn't respond. I didn't want to draw further attention to myself because he might decide to kill us too. Why hadn't I left the children at home with my parents, I thought fleetingly. Now we were all being driven around by a madman who would probably use us as hostages! I gave Eric's hand a squeeze and tried to reassure him.

As we drove up the main drive, there was a man walking through the parking lot to the right. We pulled in and parked at the far end of the lot. Rhodes told Jesse they would tell the man we had a sick child and needed to borrow his car to take the child to the hospital, because Rhodes said that we needed something less conspicuous than a police car.

Rhodes got out of the police car and headed over towards the man. Jesse hung back for a moment, looking over his shoulder at me, trying to be reassuring. Then he got out and followed Rhodes, who had already approached the man. This was my chance to get myself and my babies away. I tried to open the door but it would not budge. Desperately, I tried again, not realizing that the back doors of a police car cannot be opened from the inside. We were trapped. Maybe they would just leave us here and go on? Maybe not. Jesse seemed to be signalling to us and then came back to get us.

I was made to transfer our belongings and the children into an orange Cadillac. Rhodes again elected to drive, placing Jesse in the back with the car's owner, who was now a hostage along with us. He was an older man with white hair, kind of chubby. I hoped he wouldn't have a heart attack. He looked like I felt. The kids and I rode in the front this time. I kept the baby on my lap and Eric was next to the door. Where was he taking us now? Where could we go? I heard the old man saying he was scared and Jesse telling him not to be scared, that no one would hurt him. That brought images of the morning to my mind. So much blood. The smell of it was still in my nostrils, as was the picture of when Eric slipped in the blood and I saw it, and I saw the man lying there. I wondered if he was dead or alive but I had to close my eyes against the memory and focus on the present because we were still not out of danger. It wasn't over yet.

During the whole ride in the police car as Rhodes drove us away, the thing that occupied my mind was how oddly slow and distorted time had been during the shooting. It was as if everything was happening in slow motion. And yet it all happened so quickly. There was nothing anyone could have done to stop it. The event had taken on a life of its own. I looked at Eric. What must have been going through his young mind? How would all this affect the baby? She was only ten months old but Eric was nine and aware of everything that had happened. We seemed to be crawling along in the morning rush-hour traffic. It was bumper to bumper, especially on our side of the road.

I heard a helicopter overhead. Maybe a traffic reporter? It seemed to be hovering above us. And then I heard a small plane. I knew then that it was almost over. We would be saved. I glanced at Rhodes, who was intent on the traffic ahead. He didn't seem to notice the sounds of the helicopter or the plane. He seemed locked in on that one channel in his mind like he had been before. Some cars were leaving the line and driving down on the shoulder of the road. Up ahead I could see what the delay was now. There were trucks parked sideways across the road with only a small opening between them for traffic to pass through.

As we got closer, you could see a whole line of

47

policemen forming to the left of the lanes of traffic. They all had rifles. My heart was racing and my breath was coming hard. Rhodes saw it too and after a moment of deliberation he floored the car, accelerating around the traffic towards the opening between the trucks. At the last minute, he swerved to the left. We went into a skid and were heading straight for one of the trucks parked on the side of the road. I put my arm out to keep Eric from being knocked forward, trying to brace myself at the same time. Holding Tina close into my body, I tried to fold myself over sideways, lying over both children. The car was rocking from the impact of the bullets as we passed the line of waiting riflemen. The car collided with the side of the big rig, sending my knees into the dash. Eric's head hit it as well. Even after the car was stopped against the side of the truck, the barrage of bullets continued to make the car bounce and rock and I wondered if they didn't know there were hostages in the car.

As soon as the firing stopped, I told Eric to crouch down low and run from the car when I opened the door. Finally, a chance to get away from all this madness! I reached across and opened the door. Staying low, hand in hand, we ran over to a group of bystanders, joining the crowd watching Rhodes, Jesse and the old man being taken from the car. Amazingly, it was as if we had been covered by angel's wings and rendered invisible! All the commotion was centred on the rush of policemen encircling the car from the roadside. There had been no one between the crowd and the truck, thus creating an avenue of escape for us. In the safety of the crowd, I squeezed Eric's hand and looked to see if he was OK. His head looked all right except for a small red welt, but it was his shirt that made my heart stop beating. There was blood on it. I quickly lifted the shirt to see if he was injured. But he hadn't a mark on his body. I realized then that it was from when he slipped in the blood of the wounded policeman. He hadn't noticed it until now. Up until this moment he had seemed rigid with fear, but now his face began to crack. The shock that had frozen him into silence was about to give way to hysteria now that he thought he was bleeding, maybe shot. I reassured him, 'You're OK, honey. Don't worry. We'll get you a clean shirt.' I hugged him close to me.

Rhodes was taken to a waiting ambulance with a gun-shot wound in the leg. The old man was led away from the Cadillac that sat crumpled against the truck and riddled with holes, large pieces of metal jutting out at odd angles. It was hard to believe that anyone could have survived in that shattered vehicle. Jesse was dragged over to a group of policemen, who proceeded to disarm and handcuff him. They assumed he was the shooter because he had a gun stuck in the waistband of his trousers. It was the one Rhodes had handed him during the getaway in the police cruiser.

I began walking along with the rest of the crowd to get a better look. I saw another policeman running towards Jesse with his gun raised over his head ready to crash the butt end into Jesse's skull. In mute and helpless horror, I watched Jesse crumple to the ground as the gun came down on his left temple with a sickening thud. Handing the baby to Eric, as the cop raised his rifle again I ran to Jesse and threw myself over him. Miraculously, the butt of the gun never came down. Jesse whispered something to me. 'What?' I asked frantically. 'You better get away from me. They're going to kill me.' My eyes lingered over his face, waiting for more words to come out.

I was lifted by someone from behind. I looked up into the barrel of a rifle. 'Are you with them?' the officer said, pointing his rifle at my chest. The look on his face, the barely contained urge to kill, took my breath away. Eric had come over to me with the baby. I pulled him to me and took the baby from him, saying, 'Don't shoot! We had to—' I was given no chance to finish what I was trying to say.

They pushed me into a police car with the children. I looked at the children's faces. They were so wide-eyed, so pale, so filled with fear. I took a deep breath. I needed to stay calm for the children. But it didn't appear that we were being rescued any more. Maybe once we got somewhere where sanity prevailed we would get this nightmare sorted out.

The children and I were taken to a substation and put in a small room to wait. There was a desk and a couple of chairs but I could not sit. People in uniforms came by to look in at us. They stood in the doorway, scowling, then left without a word. I clutched the children to me, seeking comfort in the feeling of their bodies next to mine. I had to find someone who would let me make a phone call. I needed to call my parents. As we stood there huddled together, two people in plain clothes came into the room along with more police, men and women. They said they were from social services and they were going to take the children away.

'No! Please don't take them away. I'll get this all straightened out soon! Please!'

But they said it was necessary. My becoming upset was making the kids upset too. It was a hopeless battle. I could see it tearing my children apart.

'Go with these people, Eric. Don't worry, Mommy will straighten it all out soon, OK? I love you. Take care of your sister.'

Eric was looking at me so frightened, so sad, so brave. 'OK, Mommy, I will, but I don't want to leave you.'

'It will be OK. Go on now.'

I tried to smile and he returned the effort. I gave him a kiss and a hug, and kissed and stroked the baby's head. The woman took Eric's hand. He stiffened for a moment but at a reassuring nod of my head he let himself be led away. The man took Tina. She tried to crawl away over his shoulder, resisting his grasp. My throat closed up and tears filled my eyes as my breasts began to ache at the sound of her distress. I had been nursing her since shortly after her birth. She was just ten months old now and I realized that she would be separated from her food.

'Oh, wait!' I said as the door closed behind them. 'I have to feed her. She can't use a bottle. She's nursing!'

'Just sit down and relax. They'll be fine.'

Where were they being taken? Where was Jesse? God only knew what they were doing to him. When would I be able to make a phone call? What would happen to us now?

I was taken from the room through a hallway and out of a door to a waiting squad car. I could see them putting Jesse into another car. We were being moved again. Where were they taking us this time? How would I find the children? Didn't anyone care that we were victims? They were all acting like we were guilty, tried and convicted. They didn't even know what had happened! Didn't it matter that we had just been through two shootings and almost been killed ourselves? Why weren't we being comforted, given some help to deal with this?

During the ride, the two officers in the front seat talked about how two good men had been killed and began to argue about whether or not to bring us in or just take us the back way, 'by the railroad track', and shoot us, saying we had tried to escape. It was true that those two men at the rest stop were dead! The thought was quickly overridden by the fear of what was about to happen now. The driver of the car I was in signalled to the others to pull over to the side of the road. They all got out of the cars and began a heated debate over whether or not to kill us.

One man, a detective by the way he was dressed, seemed to be the voice of reason. He said maybe they shouldn't kill us. They finished their discussion and I elected to continue the ride with 'the voice of reason', the one who had suggested they try to talk to us first. On the way, he asked me what had happened. I told him I really did not know. I had not seen the actual shooting. He asked if I could have done it. I asked if he thought someone could possibly have done a thing like that and not know it.

We were taken to another substation to be processed and interrogated. It was much the same as the previous one. I considered myself lucky to have got there alive. I wished I had my glasses, lost in the Camaro. So, besides being scared and tired, I was also blind and disoriented. Everything was a blur, faces, places, the clocks on the wall. I could not focus well enough to know what time of day it was or how long I had been there. How long had it been since I last saw Jesse? Where were the children?

A team of detectives had been trying for hours to get me to make a recorded statement of what had actually happened. Again, I told them I couldn't because I didn't really know, I hadn't actually seen what happened because I was shielding the children. When would they let me make my phone call? I knew I was entitled to a phone call. Everyone knew that. I asked one of the officers when I could have it. The big detective who smelled like sweat said that they didn't really have to let me make a phone call. He said they could hold me for seventy-two hours before they had to let me make a call and they might just lose me in the basement for a few days. It was obvious they could do anything they wanted. He said 'that phone call stuff' was just something you saw on TV, but if I would make the tape recording of how the killings happened I could make my call that day. So the battle of wills began. I had to get a call through to my parents so they could come and get the kids. Once I knew the kids were safe I could then deal with the situation at hand. I tried telling them that I didn't know anybody involved with the crime. I was just a hitchhiker who had been picked up by those guys in their police car. They didn't go for that. It was a pitiful lie. I had no clue – it was their ballpark and their rules.

The detective who had driven me there came in to escort me to another room where he gave me over to another group of detectives, who began their own interrogation. I was taken to an 'interrogation room', bare walls with a file cabinet and metal desk. I was given a chair to sit on while they paced around me. It was so primal, being captured and surrounded by a bunch of armed and threatening men who look like they want to kill you.

Two other men came into the room. They seemed different from the others, more calm and better dressed, in suits. They spoke to me quietly and didn't make all those angry contorted faces at me like the others did. They wanted to know about the guns. I told them they were all legal. It was Jesse's way of making an honest living. We bought them from the local gun shops and often directly from the Smith & Wesson man who came by at regular intervals. Jesse couldn't purchase them himself because of his record but I could. They seemed satisfied and left the room.

Another officer came in to escort me to another interrogation room where another team was waiting for me. It had been hours since we were taken into custody and I was tired and dirty and hungry. No one asked if I needed anything. No one offered me a drink or anything to eat. Two of the detectives continued trying to get me to make a tape-recorded statement. They read me my rights and began asking me questions, all the while running the tape recorder. When they didn't like my answers they tried to intimidate me and started all over again, reading me my rights and asking me questions. I told them over and over again that I didn't really know what had happened. I began to cry. The continuing interrogation and the cumulative pressure of resisting their repeated attempts to force me to say what they wanted to hear were overwhelming. I just couldn't take being yelled at any more. We repeated the litany one more time on the tape recorder.

'Did you shoot anybody?'

'No.'

'Did you see who shot the policemen?'

'No.'

'Who shot the two officers?'

'I don't know. Please, you know you're making me do this! I just want to make my phone call.'

I was sobbing. The session was over. They left the room. One of them returned to tell me I was finally going to be allowed to make my phone call. It was approximately 5.30 in the evening. A detective dialled for me. I needed my parents to come for the children, to contact an attorney. But they weren't home. I left a message for them. 'Where are we?'

'The main jail, Broward Sheriff's Office.'

I repeated the name into the phone. At least they would know where I was.

'Could I have something to eat? I've been here all day without any food.'

He said he'd find something for me and left. A matron came and took me to wait in a holding cell in another part of the building, where there were individual cells. She opened the door.

'Step inside the cell.'

'Do you know where they took my children?'

'Social Services has them. Now, step inside please.' I stepped in as ordered. When she closed the door behind me I felt a tight panicky feeling in my chest.

'When can I use the bathroom?' I asked through the barred opening. 'I have to use the toilet.'

'They have to do some tests on you and then we'll see.'

'But I have to use the toilet now. I haven't been to the toilet all day.'

She took me out of the cell and down the hall to a cell with a toilet and sink in it. She was going to stay while I peed. OK. I lined the seat with paper and sat down. It took some concentration to get the flow started because she was watching me. The paper was rough and looked as if it had rolled on the floor. I tore off the first layer, using the cleaner part underneath. I was about to wash my hands but she said I couldn't because they had to test my hands for chemicals. We were almost in front of the holding cell when I heard Eric's voice.

'Mommy!' It was coming from right down the hall. I took off running towards the sound of his cry, which echoed in the air, and in my mind. I saw him, sitting on a bench in an alcove off the hallway on the right.

'Eric! I'm here!' I ran up to him with the matron in hot pursuit. I got in one hug before she caught up and pulled me away. 'Eric, Mommy loves you. Tell them you want to call your grandma and grandpa. You don't have to talk to these people. Tell them you want a lawyer. I love you, Eric.'

'I love you too, Mommy.'

She was pulling me away. He was crying.

'Don't forget what I told you.'

'Let's go. You shouldn't have done that.'

'That's my son! You told me the children were taken away by Social Services. What's he still doing here? Are they interrogating him? That's illegal! He's just a kid! They said the children would be safe. I need to make another phone call.'

We were at the door to the holding cell again. She opened it and guided me in by the arm, shutting it behind me with a bang. That feeling again, intensified by what was happening to my son.

'I need to make another call!' She left. I broke down in tears.

They came to take me for the tests. Barium antimony tests for gunpowder on my hands. I was somewhat distracted from my misery by the tests. Jesse and I both tested negative. So did Eric and the baby. The only one whose test came out positive for having fired a gun was Rhodes. The testing was finished and the matron showed up again to take me back to the holding cell. A dog run was bigger than that holding cell.

'Can I wash my hands now?'

'There is some cream there for cleaning your hands.'

'I want to wash them too. I need to wash my hands

57

and face. And what about another phone call?'

'You'll have to ask one of the detectives about that.'

I had no idea if it was night or day. I was cold. I was so tired. I felt like I was tripping on some bizarre chemical – adrenaline, of course. But it felt like the adrenaline was running out. Someone was coming. I was off the bunk and at the barred opening in the door, straining to see.

'There's someone here to see you.'

My parents? Could they have got here already? Another interrogation? More tests? Someone to tell me about the children?

I was escorted to a room in another part of the building. It was a bit nicer. My escort stopped and indicated that I was to enter an office where a man in casual clothes sat waiting. What trick was this?

'You can leave us alone now, officer, thank you,' the man said firmly. The escort left. This was a good sign.

'Hello, Sonia. My name is Bill Moran. Please, sit down. You must be exhausted after all this. I have been trying to find you since early this afternoon when your brother and your friend John called me. The story's been all over the news.'

'Oh, I see. So you are a friend of my brother and John?'

'I am, shall we say, the family attorney. No one knew where you were. I had my assistant, a private investigator, on it but I had to physically come down here to make them produce you. They said you weren't booked in yet. I'll bet you've been through the mill today.'

'Yes, I have. Do my parents know what's happening

yet? I'll feel better once I know they have the children. How long do I have to stay here? Can I leave with you tonight?'

'I don't think that will be possible. You're to be charged with murder or accessory to murder and you'll have to go to a hearing first. We'll try to expedite matters. Meanwhile, now that they know you have representation things should go better for you. Just sit tight and we'll see what we can do tomorrow. I already have a few calls in. I don't like being treated this way either. What they're doing is illegal. You can't just "lose" somebody and not give their attorney access to them. They're way off base.'

He promised to come back in the morning. I didn't want him to leave, nor did I want to go back to that holding cell. He promised to find out about the kids and told the officers to take good care of me as he left. They didn't take me back to the holding cell right away. After what seemed like half an hour, one of the uniformed cops came in with a sandwich.

'They said you wanted something to eat.'

I took it from his hand, unwrapping the cellophane. 'It's ham. I don't eat ham. I'm Jewish and I'm a vegetarian.'

'That's what they've got,' he answered as he walked out the door. I folded the wrapper over the sandwich and pushed it aside. I would have cried but I was too tired.

4

I FINALLY GOT BOOKED and taken to the cellblock. The booking process was yet another series of humiliations and indignities – stand here, turn to the left, to the right, place your fingers on the ink pad and roll out your prints on the paper one by one, follow the matron into a cell and strip while she 'gloves up' for the pat down, checking between your legs and under your breasts, open your mouth wide and show your tongue, squat and cough, boot over and spread your butt cheeks so she can look up your anus. Then comes the shower and the Quell, a nasty-smelling disinfectant with which I am to bathe while she watches to be sure I lather up the hair of my head and my pubic hair as well.

Dressed in some clothes that had obviously seen much misery, I carried the blanket and sanitary items I had been given as I followed the matron down a corridor to the cellblock area. We passed two large cells before arriving at our destination. She took a big key from her belt and opened the door.

'Go on in. The one on the end.'

The door closed behind me and my breath caught in my lungs. Dropping my bundle of pyjamas, towel, toilet articles and blanket, I grabbed hold of the bars and called for the matron to come back. 'Wait a minute! What about my children! I need to make a phone call!' Her footsteps continued to fade into the distance. I closed my eyes against the tears and rested my head against the bars. Finally, picking up the toothbrush and the old ratty blanket that smelled of sweat and vomit, I turned to confront what hell must be like.

Cellblock 3 was a long rectangular cage for approximately a dozen people. There were bars at the front separating it from the hallway and there were bars along the back separating it from four smaller cells along the back wall. In the centre of the rectangle were four long tables with benches attached, an ice chest and a television suspended from the ceiling. At the far end stood an open shower and a toilet. There were single metal bunks around the entire perimeter of the room.

Someone snored loudly. Someone else coughed. Another farted. Moans came from what appeared to be a pile of dirty clothes on a metal shelf. It smelled of urine and sweat, and fear. I felt I would be contaminated if I touched anything. Someone cursed, 'Shut the fuck up! Stupid bitch!'

Dimly lit by the fluorescent lights in the hallway because it was late at night, perhaps 2 or 3 a.m., my surroundings seemed surreal. I couldn't see their faces but I knew the bunks were full of sinister, dangerous women. Mould and slime were growing beyond the shower walls. My bunk was right next to the combination sink and open toilet at the far end. Walking slowly down the centre of the

61

room, hoping not to make even a breeze, I kept as far as I could from the shadowy forms that lined the walls. I approached the bunk. It was a narrow piece of metal attached to the wall and covered with a thin, filthy mattress. I was sure it had bugs in it. I sat, huddled on the metal bunk, clutching my blanket, trying to slow the images and emotions in my mind. How could anyone sleep in this filth, surrounded by a bunch of strangers who looked like they would kill you for your new toothbrush? I wrapped my arms around myself but couldn't find any warmth. No choice but to fold myself in the thin square of torn and sorrow-saturated wool and take comfort in it.

There was a woman in the bunk to my left. I couldn't see her head because it was covered by her blanket but I could see her feet sticking out right by my bunk. If I lay down with my head that way, I got those feet sticking in my face – dirty, crusty feet, with long, ragged toenails. I lay down the other way. My face was right next to the toilet and sink. I watched as a big, tousled woman with wild, matted hair stood up and approached the sink holding a toothbrush and toothpaste in her hand. She seemed to be staring right in my face. Why did she seem so hostile? Maybe she was a mental case? A maniac? I stayed very still and kept my eyes almost closed. She put her things down on the sink, turned to pull down her pants and sat on the toilet. Her thigh was so close that it almost touched me. I could feel the heat of her body and smell the stench of unwashed genitals. I squeezed my eyes shut and tried not to breathe. She stood up and proceeded to brush her teeth, holding the metal button in with one hand as she brushed and spat and rinsed her brush. I opened my eyes just as she took her brush and shook off the excess water, raining a spray of spittle on to me. I jumped up in my bunk in shock and indignation to see her smiling, letting me know that she had done it on purpose.

Where was Jesse? And what had they done with my children? My breasts hurt. They were swollen with milk for my infant daughter. My son's screams still echoed in my ears. Where had they taken him? Had my parents come yet?

Finally everyone was asleep. I had to do something with the milk in my breasts. They felt like they were about to explode! I needed something to put the milk in. I wasn't sure what to do with it but I knew I had to get it out! I spotted a pink plastic bowl near the sink. I got up and washed the bowl as best I could with the stuff they called soap. Turning towards the wall, I exposed one swollen breast and took the nipple between my fingers, holding the solid weight of it in my palm while with the other hand I held the pink plastic bowl. Closing my eyes, I imagined my child, my ten-month-old daughter, in my arms, looking up at me the way she did when I gave her my breast. And the milk began to flow as my fingers gently squeezed the nipple just as her little mouth and tongue would have done. It is a very sensual act, the feeding of your child with the breast and the food that your own body has created. I felt the tug of it all the way down to my groin, as if there were a direct line from the one to the other. And the tears began to fall from my eyes. When the bowl was almost full and my breasts felt relieved, I sat there with it in my hands wondering what to do with it. It was sacred, the food my body had made for my child. I couldn't just throw it away in the sink or in that horrible toilet. It was my child's food! How would she eat? I agonized over the thought for a few moments, then raised the bowl to my own lips. I would drink it myself, and that way when this was over I would still have milk for her. I drank and I was comforted, knowing I had done this thing for my child. Someone began to scream, 'Let me out of here! I want to call my lawyer!' From beyond the barred hallway the reply came, 'Shut up and go to sleep! No phone calls till morning!'

When I sat back down on the bunk, the tears welled up and spilled into the pink bowl. As I closed my eyes, the events of the day began to seep back into my semi-consciousness in that twilight place between waking and sleeping. What madness had invaded my small, peaceful life and shattered it? It was amazing that we were still alive. I slept.

A toilet flushed. My brain lurched into wakefulness, body sat up stiffly, eyes surveyed the room. The bundle of clothing on the bench to my left began to stir and rearrange itself into the shape of a human being. I had to urinate. I watched to see how the others did it. Wash face. Brush teeth. Take a leak. Just another bodily function. There was no place for modesty here. I wondered how you got to be in one of the smaller cells along the back wall. At least there was some privacy. I had better use the toilet now.

The shirt I was wearing draped in front of me, giving

me some relief. I averted my eyes, staring at the floor. I tore off the first sheets of toilet paper and discarded them, using an untouched portion. I had my period. I would need sanitary pads. And I would have to change my pad in front of all these people. For now I'd use some folded toilet paper. Standing and pulling my pants up in one quick motion, I looked to see if anyone had been watching me. Everyone seemed to be busy with her own morning routine. I pushed the button to flush the toilet and returned to my bed.

I felt filthy. There was only one shower. There were at least thirty women, but I was sure some of them never bathed. I would wait until the rest of them were finished.

I had to find out what had happened to the children. And what had they done with Jesse? How did you get to a phone?

The matron was coming down the hall. The slow measured cadence of her step set off a counterpoint of frenzied activity in the cellblock. The women gathered close to the bars, stretching their necks in an effort to see down the hall. I had an image of the ducks that used to wait at the door of the Ranch, that idyllic house in Miami where I had lived with John so long ago. The matron told them that breakfast would be here soon. Everyone was shouting at once. She left and returned with the supply cart. She handed out toilet paper, soap, toothpaste. I walked into the crowd, making my way to the front.

'I need sanitary pads please.'

'You get one at a time.' She handed me a single sanitary pad and an elastic belt.

'But I have my period. I'll need more than this.'

'You can only have one at a time. Those are the rules. No exceptions.'

'I need to make a phone call.'

'The phones get brought to the cell later on.'

'Can I have a pencil and paper?'

She dug out a nub and a sheet of jail stationery and handed it to me with the admonition that paper was only given out once a day.

The knot of women began to disperse. Someone climbed up on a table to turn on the overhead TV. As she climbed down, she turned to me and said, 'We heard about you on the news. Showed your picture. They say you killed some cops.' I turned and walked back to my bunk.

Breakfast came. I didn't want to interact with these people. I waited on my bunk with the cup I was issued the night before. As the crowd thinned out, I approached the bars. There was coffee and oatmeal and milk. I took some of each. One of the women seemed to be in charge of the sugar. I was thankful that I did not use it. I sat at the table under the TV because most of the others were crowded together at the other tables so they could watch the news. John had heard about it on the news. Jesse's mother must know too. I'd try to call her. She could find out what had happened to Jesse and the children.

Morning coffee here produced the same reaction as it did anywhere and all the toilet stools were in use. There was someone sitting on the toilet near my bed and someone else waiting on my bed! The news came on. Inevitably, my name was mentioned and I was sure they were seeing a picture of me as well.

'Hey, you. The girl they say killed those cops. They're showing your picture up there.'

I had to create a barrier between myself and these people. I set my jaw and hardened my eyes and turned towards the voice. There was silence. I gathered my cup and my bowl, swung my legs out from under the table and walked towards my bunk. It was empty now.

The guard told the other women that there would be no sugar delivery to our cell unless they made sure that I did not get any. The newspaper was delivered with a large hole cut in the front page where news about Jesse and me had been.

I had as little interaction as possible with the guards. On one occasion, when I needed supplies, the guard told me that I was going to 'fry'. She said it had already been decided and all that remained were the formalities.

Some of the women tried to be friendly, but I trusted no one. One of the girls said that when people asked her what she was in for she told them that she had bitten off the nose of someone who asked too many questions. I thought maybe I could use that answer too, if anyone asked. But everyone knew who I was.

At first, I struggled with the physical surroundings. But as I saw others arrive and watched their anxiety, I realized that I had become part of the place. I had found a niche in the horror and filth from which I became an observer. And although the fear and stench with which I was engulfed was very real, it was overridden by the unreality of being plucked out of familiar space and time and deposited in this primal place. Actually, at this point, I didn't even believe that I would have to go to trial. I thought, the truth will set me free. I hadn't killed anyone. Anyone who knew me for five minutes would know that I wouldn't kill anyone. I was disgusted by the whole process. I didn't understand why they were treating me like I was in some way responsible for what had happened. I could not yet see the full picture. That would take a long time to become clear to me – to even become relevant to me. It was a day-to-day, hour-to-hour struggle just to get my basic needs met. And, for a time, that struggle took over my life.

Then, after what seemed an eternity but was only about a week, I had a visitor. I was taken from the cell-block in handcuffs and shackles to an area made up of individual cubicles. There was a chair and telephone receiver inside. On the other side of the glass window there was a similar set-up for the visitor. I sat on the chair and waited for a face to appear.

It was Kay Tafero, Jesse's mom. Her face was drawn but still bright and full of her characteristic sparkle – with a delicacy and elegance that came through even under this terrible strain. She had seen Jesse and he was OK. He was concerned about me and had sent her. For privacy, she wrote little notes and held them up to the glass, which was close enough for me to read them. She had been in touch with my parents. They were trying to get custody of the children. Tina was being cared for by a foster family. Eric was being held in the juvenile detention centre. But my parents expected to have both of the children soon. I wasn't to worry.

Kay left some money in an account for me so that I could purchase snacks from the canteen. I felt much better after seeing her but I was disturbed about the children. I had thought my parents would have had them by now. What were they feeding Tina? And what was Eric doing in the juvenile detention centre?

I wasn't to find out for a long time afterwards but Eric was being grilled repeatedly at secret hearings. His hands were cuffed behind his back and he was taken at night, without representation, to be questioned.

'What is your mommy's name?'

'I don't know. I just call her Mommy.'

'Where do you live?'

'I don't know.'

'Who are those men?'

'I don't know. My mommy said I don't have to talk to you. I want to call my grandma and grandpa.'

They thought he was a smart-ass and treated him accordingly.

He was only nine years old, just a little boy. How could they treat a nine-year-old this way? They had to separate him from the other children for his own pro-tection. He remained in isolation until my parents were able to get custody two months later. By then he had developed a mental block, forgetting how to read and do maths, the things we did together. He had also developed a habit of stuttering, which he carried into his adult life.

My parents came to visit me when they made the trip to pick up Tina. They had to go to court and appear before a judge. They told me that she would be fine. I asked what she had been eating. She hadn't used a bottle since I had taken her home from the hospital.

My mom said they would teach her how to use a bottle. I knew once the children were with my parents that they would be safe and well cared for, maybe even better than they were with me. My mom looked sad and my father looked tired. They assured me that they would get custody of Eric soon. They had been to visit him and had been allowed to give him a comb and a comic book. They had brought a new pair of glasses for me, which would be a great help. I thanked them. We blew kisses through the glass, and placed our palms against it fitting the outlines together, embracing with our eyes. I could see the struggle in their faces, but we ended our visit with smiles and assurances.

I cried my eyes out afterwards. It broke my heart to think of what my children were going through and the look on my parents' faces. No one in my family had ever been in jail, except Grandpa Harry for playing cards. I was heartsick to see what this humiliation was doing to them but I couldn't even help myself. The guard took me back to the cellblock.

My parents returned home with Tina. They went to court for Eric many times until a judge, an Italian with a family of his own, became disgusted with the process and said that unless the state could come up with a good reason for keeping this child he was to be released into the custody of his grandparents. Eric had been kept in solitary confinement as if he had committed a crime. At one time he had even been treated as a suspect, so that now my poor child, who had been so sensitive and outgoing, was extremely nervous and withdrawn. It had taken two months to secure his release.

With the children safe, I was able to focus on my own situation. Now that I had some money I could purchase candy and cigarettes, which I used in exchange for services. In this way I could avoid having contact with other inmates by bartering for food and other supplies. The women would crowd around the front of the cell in order to get their share, and I tried to avoid mingling so that no one could say they had spoken with me or made friends with me in order to claim later on that I had in some way confided in them. People did that in order to make deals with the police in their own case. I'd seen that on the television. I was determined not to let it happen to me.

I heard about the beating through the grapevine. You could never be sure about the things you heard, but I sensed there was some truth in it somewhere. I was frantic. I put in a call to my lawyer and left a message. I finally got through to Kay. She said she would come to visit soon and tell me about it. Jesse had been to see a doctor and would be OK. I was to watch myself carefully because I could be next.

Jesse had been badly beaten. They said he had fallen down the stairs while being escorted back from court in shackles with his hands cuffed behind his back. The way he told it, he had just returned from the last of a series of hearings. He described how, instead of returning him to the cell, the guards had handcuffed him to the bars, tied a

T-shirt around his mouth, and used their fists to give him a beating. They were not aware that Jesse's parents were scheduled to visit in the chief's office later that day.

His face was bruised and discoloured. One eye was swollen shut. His lips were puffed up and cracked, still bloody from the blows that had been administered only hours before. His father was old and sick and the sight of his son's battered face was almost too much. His mother, ever the strong one, demanded an explanation, running to her son and embracing him protectively. The chief assured them that an investigation would follow.

Being accused of the murders of two policemen made me a target as well, but also acted as insulation. I guess they thought I must be really mean or really crazy. As I was later told, when the guards encouraged some of the women to jump on me, they were reluctant to do it.

Some who had been there for a long time were allowed to work in the jail and were called trusties. One of them lived in our cellblock. Her name was Dottie Marie. She was a sweet girl and sympathetic towards me. She occupied one of the four-person cells around the perimeter of the bullpen. One of her bunkmates, referred to as 'bunkies', left and she arranged for me to move in. It was a relief to get out of the bullpen and the constant fluorescent lighting after almost two months. And at least now I only had to go to the bathroom in front of three other people. Mine was the bottom bunk on the right. Brinks slept above me, Dottie Marie across from me, and Susan slept above her. The toilet was on the back wall between the bunks. It seemed I always had my head next to the toilet bowl. But this was a much better set-up and I felt more comfortable.

The cells were racially divided with four girls in each. Cells one and three were black, and cells two and four were white. In cell one were Ace, a tall light-skinned girl, and Finn, a large dark-skinned woman with a good sense of humour who was friendly with the white girls. Finn was the peace-maker in our cellblock. I liked her. I was in cell two with Dottie Marie, Susan and Brinks. When Susan left, Champ moved in. There was a regular turnover. Keesha, a small-boned black girl from cell three, used to come and visit Brinks sometimes. Brinks was the friendly sort and wasn't intimidated by the colour lines that were invisibly but palpably drawn. She got her name from her crime, which was the robbery of a Brinks truck.

Brinks was a great scavenger and she got along with almost everyone. She helped me collect peanut butter sandwiches. No provision was made for my vegetarian preference. Breakfasts weren't too bad, but lunch invariably consisted of baloney sandwiches and peanut butter sandwiches. I basically lived on peanut butter sandwiches, trading for the baloney, which was more popular.

5

My Dearest Sunny,
Something terrible is almost happening . . .

As we got closer to my court date, they began feeding me better. I was given what they called the diabetic diet, which consisted basically of cottage cheese. It was definitely a welcome change but it felt like I was being fattened up for the kill.

I had met with the public defender whose office, at first, was handling all three cases – Jesse's, Rhodes's and mine. He advised me, among other things, not to talk to anyone else. Shortly thereafter the public defender was removed from my case. I was brought to an office where the judge assigned to my case, Judge Futch, told me that he would be selecting a replacement attorney for me. This did not fill me with confidence. I had already heard that the judge had been a state trooper before he came to the bench. I could not imagine that he could remain neutral and unbiased. Later on we would file a motion for him to step down but he would not. He made some calls from an

74

adjacent office, and returned to say that he had found an attorney to take my case.

My second lawyer was an attorney in private practice with whom Judge Futch had a personal relationship. An attorney in private practice is called a special public defender when he or she accepts a case such as mine. I met with this man a couple of times. The first time we met he suggested that I put Eric on the stand. He had, after all, been there when it happened and could testify for me. But so much damage had already been done, he was so fragile, I swore I wouldn't ever let them get their hands on my son again. I told him I'd rather go to the electric chair than see Eric hurt any more.

In one of the little notes that Jesse managed to send me he said he did not trust this new lawyer and that I should test him in some way. So I made up some fantastic details, which I told to him. I said that Rhodes was gay and that his lover, Frenchie, a man dressed as a woman, had been in the car with us. The story came back to me as the latest police theory. I dismissed the attorney.

The next time Kay visited me I told her what had happened. She said she would ask around the courthouse for a recommendation of a good attorney who might be willing to take the case.

Ray Sandstrom was an old war-horse who had been around for many years and had the reputation of a fighter. At the time he sounded like the right man. He was willing to take my case as a special public defender without pay except for what the state would give him. I didn't have any money of my own and my parents said they believed in the system, in that it provided you with adequate representation. We learned, too late, that you had better put your best efforts into the trial, because the appeals process takes many years and you lose the presumption of innocence. But in reality, it is my experience that there is no presumption of innocence. It is all well and good in theory but, in fact, at trial everybody believes that you must have done something wrong if you are up there in the defendant's chair.

Jesse got a special public defender too. His name was Bob. Jesse and I were desperate to see each other. We pushed from both ends and finally our attorneys were able to arrange a meeting.

We met in the jailhouse library, Jesse and his attorney, me and mine. We had not seen each other for many weeks. There was a guard outside the library door. Jesse and I went behind the bookcases. We embraced and kissed deeply.

'I love you, baby . . .'

'I love you too, Jesse.'

He said we might not get another chance to be together like this, not for a long time. And Jesse was right. We never touched each other again.

Jesse's trial came first, in May 1976. He had a record from when he was a juvenile, so he was an easy target. His trial lasted four days. The prosecutor brought in his 'expert witnesses' and even used dummies to show how things could have happened based on Rhodes's testimony. Apparently these dramatics had the intended effect on the jury. This, coupled with his attorney's total inadequacy and a complete lack of any presentation of defence, meant Jesse was convicted and sentenced to death in short order. He was taken to death row, in a men's maximum security prison in the northern part of the state.

Jesse had a juvenile record and had been in prison before. But I was a mother, a hippie and a vegetarian. I had been in trouble before but never for anything violent. Surely they couldn't believe that I would kill anyone? We would go to court and I would tell them and it would be OK. My trial began in early July, two months after Jesse's. I was still in the cell with Dottie Marie, Brinks and Susan. We were sort of an extended family, brought together by need and common circumstances. We had little in common other than the fact that we were locked up together. But for the moment, we were sisters.

The children were with my parents now, and I knew they were safe and well cared for, so my concerns centred mainly on Jesse. They brought him back for my trial, in July 1976.

The local press reported that Jesse and Rhodes would both be brought in as witnesses. Rhodes was to be the state's key witness. And I was to be the first woman in Broward County to face the death penalty since the US Supreme Court upheld the new version of the death penalty in Florida earlier that same year.

Each day I walked into the courtroom, shackled and chained, hand and foot, and turned to look into the faces of the twelve people who would decide my fate. The courtroom was overflowing with spectators and media. I carried my pad and pen with me so I could write down my questions to ask the lawyer later. He said it wasn't good to disrupt the proceedings with questions. I always had a lot of questions. The trial had an atmosphere of unreality, like they weren't really talking about me. Even the language they used was foreign. As we stood, I recognized one of the detectives who had interrogated me that first day. I thought he was the one who had brought me the ham sandwich.

I tried to appear 'normal', smiling at people every once in a while. I was sure the jury would not believe the testimony against me. My attorney said the prosecution had no case, so there was no need to subject myself to the gruelling cross-examination they would put me through if I testified. You had the right to remain silent. But didn't that make people think you had something to hide?

My parents came to court only once. They brought the children. My brother came too. It was terrible. It was hard for them to hear the things that were being said. It was so hurtful. At the end of the hearing my mother rushed up the centre aisle holding the baby in one hand and Eric in the other. She was screaming, 'Please, you have to let her see her children!' She was crying hysterically. Two of the bailiffs grabbed her by the arms. My father tried to get to her but he was restrained as well. I couldn't stand to see their pain. After that I asked them not to come any more. Instead, my uncle Joe came down from New Jersey to be in court for me.

My Sweet Jesse,

I had a dream last night. In my dream you and your teacher were in the middle of a bare floor, you were standing next to me and – we bowed . . . then you took my hand . . .

I woke up so happy. I was all smiles – they couldn't imagine how I could possibly have been grinning like that before court. I went to court today very calm inside and we presented motions, about 15 of them, most were denied . . . I told Ray if he didn't keep his word about my seeing you, that next time we came to court I would sit down in the middle of the floor, right in front of the judge and would not get up until I saw you in front of me. So, I am pretty sure I'll see you today . . . I love you so very, very much. You are my whole world . . .

All my love, always,
Sunny

I never did get to see Jesse, except when he was brought in to testify. I thought I was prepared, having gone over what it would be like again and again in my mind, but the sight of him took my breath away. I saw him first. He was looking around for me, and when ours eyes locked in on each other it was as if something large had fallen back into place. He was led in by the bailiffs, shackled and chained, from the side door to the witness box where he sat not twelve feet away. It was difficult to listen to what was being said because all my senses were tuned to him. He was sent back to prison immediately afterwards. They were paranoid about his presence in court and took extreme security precautions. Seeing Jesse was the highlight of my life at the time. The next best day was when I got to go outside for the first time in more than five months in order to revisit the 'scene of the crime'.

July 23, 1976

Jesse my love my heart,

I just got back from a trip to the rest area on 95. The air smelled so good and there were crickets – I love crickets chirping, and a sparrow landed on a tree branch above my head and sang to me. The sun was shining down through the trees and – guess what – a butterfly – my butterfly, a yellow and black one, was there for me! It fluttered around and flew in front of the car as we left, all the way up the exit. There were two dozen reporters there before we even arrived. The jury came in a bus. I had no cuffs or shackles because the jury is not allowed to see me like that – but they had enough plain clothes deputies with guns just in case – they were just waiting for me to do something. They probably would have loved to cut me down right at that spot . . .

We will make it! Just be strong and keep yourself okay. I love you Jess – I'm going to come out of this and then I'm going to see to it you get off that row and after that I'm going to get you back with me and the kids – you'll see! You don't belong in a cell. Just keep your head together. Many people will

be on our side soon. The prosecutor fucked himself
with his stupid lies – believe me. The people are not
that stupid.

Show 'em that full-faced smile Daddy!
All My Love, Your Woman Forever
Sunny

The press reported that I looked pale as I held my face to
the sun, 'surrounded by two bailiffs, one lawyer and a
battalion of reporters and cameramen'. It felt so good that,
for a few seconds, I lost the sense of being scrutinized and
guarded. I was chatting happily with the reporters and
even laughing, enjoying the pleasure of the moment,
while the jurors were being acquainted with the crime
scene, trying to reconcile the diagrams they had seen in
court with the reality of the place itself. I too needed the
opportunity to organize my own mind around the
physical reality of the place since the whole event
happened in a matter of minutes on a foggy morning and
had been very emotional and traumatic.

The press also reported that some of the jurors
seemed to be having trouble coordinating the site with the
inconsistencies in testimony as to the distances between
the witnesses and the murders.

Walter Rhodes had been given his plea bargain based
on the so-called results of his polygraph test, a synopsis of
which the prosecutor presented in the form of a report
that was not made public. He agreed to accept three life
sentences to avoid the electric chair in exchange for
his testimony in court against Jesse and me. I was

sure that the jurors would know immediately who the guilty party was because who else would consider three life sentences a bargain? But they didn't because the rules of engagement in a criminal trial did not allow the jurors to know about his plea bargain. How could they make a fair determination if they didn't know all the facts? Rhodes's testimony took two days with all the objections and cross-examination. I tried to tell Ray to object a few times when Rhodes was lying but Ray said to write it down on my yellow legal pad for later. He said it would be bad for me to disrupt the courtroom. I wanted to call Rhodes a liar right there! But instead I wrote furiously, stopping to glare at Rhodes occasionally. He said Jesse and I did it. My attorney put up no defence to this allegation, nor to the charges against me. He said we didn't need to and that it would give him the advantage when it came to who went first and last in the final arguments.

And then there was Brenda Isham. It was in the second week of trial. Up until then I figured they were all just doing their job. I didn't think it was anything personal. Then the prosecution announced the existence of another witness, one who had been in the jail cell with me. I had no idea who she was. Ray was going to be allowed to take her deposition before she testified. That night I went back to the cell to ask the girls if anyone knew who this Brenda Isham was. It turned out that my three cellmates had talked with her briefly the one night she spent in our cellblock in order to find out who she was and what her charges were. The usual interrogation. Prisoners had their ways too. It turned out she was a college dropout who had got caught trying to do a prescription scam on a drug store with her boyfriend. They liked some sort of downers. She had been sitting on the bunk in my cell one night when I returned from court. I remembered the incident because I was pissed off that they had someone in the cell when I got there. I always came back tired from court, drained and running on the dregs of the adrenaline that had kept me going all day.

The girls were asking her a bunch of questions about herself. I came in and sat on my bunk, clutching my legal pad tightly to my chest, waiting for them to get rid of her. My pad was a powerful protection that had held up against the rigours of the courtroom as well as the reporters outside. When she had gone I asked what she was in for and then got down to telling them about the day's events in court. I gave a general rundown nightly to my three cellmates. It was my way of unwinding and processing it all back in my head.

I told Ray the next day that I had never spoken a word to Brenda Isham. She was claiming that we had spoken and that I had told her that I did it and I was glad and would do it again. I told Ray that she was a total liar. There was an evidentiary hearing in which she took the stand and basically said the same as she had said in her deposition. Ray cross-examined and called my three cellmates as witnesses that Brenda and I had never uttered one word to each other. The judge ruled that Brenda's testimony would be allowed. They had to have known she was lying! I wouldn't even talk to the lawyer they had appointed for me so why would I have talked to some overnight drug addict? Now I understood that this was not just people doing their jobs. This was a great game in which I was the prize. My trial lasted two weeks. Jesse's had lasted only four days. But I, like Jesse, had no expert witnesses to challenge the prosecution's experts. I had no money for that. And so, with all the resources available to the state, the prosecutor was able to construct his own version of events.

The jury deliberated for nine hours before reaching their verdict. They had requested two pieces of hard evidence during that time. One was the moulding of the police car that had a bullet hole in it. The other was a rereading of the rules on accomplices.

We were called back into the courtroom to hear the jury's verdict. I watched their faces carefully, each one, as they filed slowly back into the jury box. It's true what they say. No one looked at me.

After the foreman of the jury had read the verdict, Ray asked the judge to poll the jurors. One by one they stood and affirmed their decision. 'Guilty.' 'Guilty.' 'Guilty.' Twelve of them. Guilty, on two counts of murder and one of kidnapping. Twenty years later I was to share a meal and a conversation with one of those jurors, who came to apologize.

Ray said, 'Don't worry. We'll win on appeal.'

The bailiff came to fingerprint me at the front of the room. They did it after every verdict, he explained, to leave no doubt the real defendant was present. Ray signalled that he would be waiting for me near the door to the hall-way where I must once again run the gauntlet of reporters waiting to smell my blood. I felt like a wounded animal being pursued until I dropped. I made myself strong and solid while the matron put the handcuffs and leg chains on me for the return trip to the cell to await sentencing. Between trial and sentencing I had sent a written communication to the press, stating: 'I am innocent, and one day – no matter how long it takes – it will be proven – far beyond any doubt.'

They came for me early on the day I was to be sentenced. I had no idea what they would do with me. Neither did my attorney. He was waiting for me when the guards brought me into the attorney-client conference room next to the judge's chambers. It was the first time Ray Sandstrom wasn't late.

'How ya doin', kid?' He clapped me briefly on the shoulder, with a watery smile.

I didn't reply. He handed me an envelope. 'To Sunny, With Love.' It was from Jesse! I opened it quickly but carefully.

Sunny,
I love you with all my heart and soul. Keep your strength and spirit my precious woman, I love you more each day. I'm with you as always. Forever you and me.
    Love and kisses, Jesse

There was a Polaroid photograph of Jesse inside with 'I Love You' written across the white part at the bottom. He had his right hand raised in a fist with the thumbs-up sign. He was smiling, sending me strength with his eyes. I inhaled it, absorbing it.

Leaning on the edge of the table in the middle of the room, Ray assured me, 'Don't worry about a thing. It's better to get a death sentence. You get a better review on appeal, ya know what I mean?'

'Thanks for the picture,' I managed to say steadily, although it felt like my insides were roiling. 'We better go in now.'

The jury recommended life. I turned to see Ray's reaction, but his face was blank. The judge still had the final say. Once again, the bailiff called my name and I rose . . .

I stood before the judge's bench, which seemed to rise up before me like a wooden pillar, atop of which the judge's face sat, disembodied. I was determined not to give the judge the satisfaction of seeing me as anything but strong and defiant. In my right hand I held the picture of Jesse that my lawyer had given me. It would protect me. As the judge's deep voice began to fill the room with swirling sounds, I pressed the photograph to my chest.

'. . . and you shall be sentenced to die in the electric chair by having a current of 2,200 volts pass through your body until you shall be determined to be dead.'

And then he asked if I had anything to say. I met his eyes as he looked up from the paper in front of him, peering over the top of his glasses. I didn't have anything to say. How could you say anything to that?

I wanted to leave the courtroom right away, but I had to be fingerprinted once again. I suppose it was proof that I was the one who was there and not someone else. But it was someone else. I had no idea what they would do with me. Neither did my lawyer. He told me not to worry. He would be in touch as soon as he found out where they would be taking me.

I was led out of the courtroom in chains, a guard on each side holding on to my upper arms. We made our way through the gauntlet of press and media. They seemed excited by the news of my impending death. 'Why didn't you ask for mercy?' one of them wanted to know.

'I didn't ask for mercy. I asked for justice and I didn't get it. Why should I ask for mercy? . . . Life or death – one way or the other – it doesn't matter . . . Only the verdict mattered.'

I became the only woman on Florida's death row and only the second woman condemned in the state's history. I had issued a number of statements to the press proclaiming my innocence.

I was taken back to the cellblock to await the trip to death row. To my astonishment, the prisoners treated me like some sort of celebrity. The women in the cellblock said they were sorry I got the death sentence but they kept a distance from me after that, as if I was the carrier of some exotic and virulent form of bad luck that could be contagious. Well, maybe I was. My cellmates tried to be encouraging. They were sure, as I was, that it couldn't take too long for the Florida Supreme Court to see that a grave injustice had been done and straighten things out. And some of the guards seemed a bit softer, asking if I needed anything.

Jesse had been sentenced a month earlier, and was now on death row 700 miles away at FSP, Florida State Prison for men, in a place called Starke – a fitting name. One of the older jailers, a sour-faced woman, seemed pleased to tell me about FSP and its infamous death row. It was the oldest prison in the state, built in the 1890s. The death house was separated from the main prison. There were three tiers of cells that faced each other with a walkway all the way around. The chair, named 'old Sparkey' by the inmates who built it in 1945, was located on the first level at the front of the building. Later Jesse would tell me that when they had an execution, you could smell the body burning for three days.

August 20, 1976

Dear Jess,

I know that by the time you receive this letter you'll have heard the news . . . I spoke to my Mom and Dad and brother today and to Eric too. I am packed and ready because at this point I could leave anytime. I sent down all my excess clothing this evening. I'll be leaving with about $56 so I'm okay there. Don't be worried about me. I couldn't have gotten a nicer birthday present than the picture and note you sent me. Thank you – it was just what I needed and it was right on time!

I hope your new pants fit you. I have a pair just like them. You're always in my thoughts, Jess. Take care, keep busy, try not to worry—

All my love (and kisses too),
Sonia

I would be Sonia now, no longer Sunny. Anyone who knew me from this time forward would call me Sonia, as if Sunny had been obliterated. They even had the power to do that. It was the beginning of the process of death by sentence.

6

My MOTHER TOLD ME the story of my birth many times. It was a difficult delivery. She was small and I was her first child and I was supposed to have been a boy. They had to use forceps, which left long gashes on the sides of my face, and my head came to a point because the birth canal was too narrow. My nose was pressed flat and I didn't have much hair. And, worst of all, I was a girl. When they brought me in for my mother to see, she screamed and cried and told them to take me away because I was so ugly she said they must have made a mistake and mixed me up with someone else's baby. Everyone had told her she was going to have a boy. In those days they judged by the size and shape of the abdomen. After being convinced that I was truly hers, she was further traumatized because I would scrunch up my face and people thought I was a Japanese war orphan that she had adopted.

I was born by the sea in Rockaway Beach, New York, just after my dad came home from World War II. Newly married, my parents, Herbert and Bella Jacobs, were too poor to have their own place so we lived in the basement of the building where my dad's parents lived. I remember sitting outside as a two-year-old sharing my ice cream with a big Dalmatian named Caesar. And I remember the sea, and the sand, and the sound of the waves. I have always loved the sea. In time we moved to an apartment on Riverside Drive in an area of New York City called Washington Heights. I tried to be the boy my parents wanted. I wouldn't wear dresses. I didn't ask for dolls. I didn't ask for anything. My favourite things were the ones Mom and I made out of old Quaker oatmeal containers – cars, trains and trucks with a pull-string attached. I had one doll, a special gift from the neighbour's daughter – a grown woman who was dying. She'd had the doll all her life and wanted to give it to me so I would love it and take care of it after she was gone. My mother said I should accept. The doll had a porcelain face with full, red, tiny lips, real human hair that was drawn back into a bun, and a heart-shaped charm bracelet on her right wrist. Her clothing was elegant – long, green layered dress, white petticoats and pantaloons, neat white socks and black patent leather shoes. I kept her in the box she came in and played with her ever so carefully. I had that doll until I left her behind along with the life I had known in order to go on a journey into a different life with Jesse.

I was a solitary child. I played by myself on a swing put up in the doorway between the living room and the hallway. And there was an empty wood and mesh radiator cover, which served alternately as my clubhouse and my cage while I was pretending to be a tiger. There were tea parties with the porcelain doll and my little tea set, and confrontations with the demons, which lived under the bed and behind the door and under the stairs and in the darkness outside my window at night. During the day there was the TV and there were books, there were puzzles – wooden ones and then the larger ones with hundreds of small pieces. I loved to find the shapes and patterns that distinguished the pieces and determined their placement in the whole. My dad worked every day and my mom stayed home with me. She was the only one in the family who'd had a college education, and during the war she had worked for a colonel. She had a teaching degree but her major interest was in geology. I think my mom would have been happier if she had continued working. She did crossword puzzles nightly and it seemed she had inherited her own mother's legendary temperament. When my mom got upset, it was as if the ghost of Grandma Sonia would invade her body and my usually gentle, kind mother would fly into screaming rages, which I found horrifying.

I never knew my grandma Sonia, for whom I was named. She died before I was born. But I think I would have liked her, and seen her temper as high spirits.

Grandpa 'Bushzy' Poppy's apartment was just upstairs and across the hall. He was my favourite person in the whole world. Grandpa would sit me on his lap and let me play the piano, accompanying my original tunes with his deep baritone that soothed, and rumbled from his chest into mine. And I would lean back and look up into his face with the brushy moustache under the round nose and he would tickle me with it, saying, 'Bushzy, bushzy, bushzy . . .' And I would laugh! He spoke seven languages: French, Russian, Polish, German, Yiddish, Hebrew and

English, and he sang in Italian. It was all part of the music that surrounded him. His love and protection and attention were the most important things in my life. I was his little princess and he was the most wonderful person in the world. I never wanted to disappoint my grandpa. Grandpa Bushzy Poppy didn't believe in spanking. He didn't need to. If he looked at me with disappointment in those sad, liquid blue eyes I would cry.

Grandpa Bushzy Poppy told me stories about Russia when he was a boy. He told me how his mother bathed him in warm sheep's blood to save him from the polio epidemic. Despite her efforts he contracted the disease, but it was a mild case. His left leg was shorter as a result, causing him to walk with a pronounced limp. Often, he would tell me the story of how they escaped across the ocean in the steerage section of a crowded boat with no sanitary facilities, and Grandma was sick all the time. Visas weren't available to come directly to the US so they came in through Canada, settling in New York City where they thought they could have a better life. It was my favourite story.

So my grandpa Bushzy Poppy, with his beautiful baritone voice and quick graceful hands, became a watch-maker and an optician. He opened the small watch-repair shop on Amsterdam Avenue, where I got to play with all the mechanisms of time – hands and springs and watch faces with numbers on them from one to twelve – trying to put them together again. And Grandpa spent his days at his workbench fixing all those broken pieces of time. I suppose he had a strange relationship with time too.

But he still sang and played and told me the stories.

Education was the most important thing in our family, as it is with many new immigrants. So I learned to read and write early, before I started school. But I still loved listening to the stories of those strong, ingenious people from whom I had come, finding them far more intriguing than the ones I read about in books.

Grandma Sonia died before the war ended. Grandpa's second wife, Grandma Betty, was a large, quiet woman with long red hair that she wore up in a loose knot towards the top of her head. I thought of her as my real grandma. She was always in the kitchen. I watched how she helped exercise my grandpa's polio leg and I would help him get up afterwards. And she would help him in the store. And so did I. He would give me boxes of springs and watch parts to 'fix' for him. I liked the way things fitted together. He said I was very good at fixing things. He made me feel proud of myself.

When I was three and a half my mother became pregnant. She and my dad were having problems and needed some time to themselves, so they found a camp run by Columbia University in a converted farmhouse in the mountains. They sent me there for the summer of my fourth year. They said the country air would give me an appetite. But to me it seemed they were finally going to have the boy they had always wanted and they were sending me away.

On the first day of camp I stepped into a huge cow pie. I had to miss the remainder of the orientation. I got punished regularly for not finishing my food, having to sit there until everyone else had finished and not getting dessert. The attic where the young ones slept had bats that would fly around at night, scaring the piss out of me, literally. And we were supposed to send postcards home saying we were having a good time, to which I refused to affix my childish scrawl. But I loved helping to feed the chickens and the pigs, riding into town on the back of the flatbed truck, and going to the lake, although we younger children weren't allowed to swim.

About halfway through the summer it was visiting day, when all the families came to see their children at the camp. I watched the road all day, waiting for my family to come. When my dad finally arrived, he was by himself. He had bandages on his head and his wrist. They had been in a terrible car accident on the way up and he was the only one who wasn't still in the hospital. My mother, Grandma Betty, Grandpa Bushzy and Uncle Joe, who still lived at home with Grandma and Grandpa, had broken legs and broken ankles and, as children will do, I thought that if they hadn't been coming to visit me, they wouldn't have got hurt. My father told me not to be afraid.

When I came home from camp, my mother was in a cast from toe to hip. I wanted to embrace her, run to her and comfort her, but I was afraid of her cast. I wanted to take her pain away. I opened my heart to her but my arms stayed at my sides. She asked if I'd had a good time at camp. 'Yes, ma'am,' I replied, as I had been taught in camp. She got upset. I stood stiffly, listening to them talk about how I was not an affectionate child.

* * *

When I was four years old, my parents moved to Far Rockaway. I didn't get to see my beloved Grandpa Bushzy very much any more. He retired and sold the store, but he kept my baby teeth and a few chains and watches, and some small diamonds that were part of the original stake that he had brought with him from the Old Country. He and Grandma Betty moved to Coney Island, where they lived in a bungalow behind her parents' house. I loved to go there because I was his princess and from the moment I stepped in the door I was transformed into 'the loved one'.

My two grandpas were so different from each other. My dad's father, Grandpa Harry, had a huge belly, which was great for playing Santa at Christmas for the family party. They ate bacon and ham and pork roast, which was my dad's favourite. My mom's family celebrated Hanukkah and the High Holy Days of Passover and the New Year and she wouldn't allow my dad to have a Christmas tree in the house. We would have a menorah and Hanukkah candles and no lights decorating the outside of the house, unlike many of our neighbours. The two families were so different – it was like living in the midst of a constant paradox. I went to Sunday school and got the basic concept of a God out there somewhere but each side of the family seemed to have its own interpretation of how things were supposed to be.

Grandma Reinie was a short, solid woman with a good sense of humour but she was very strict. And Grandpa Harry was funny – but sometimes he scared me.

He would take out his false teeth and chase me around the house with them, trying to 'bite' me. I would scream and Grandma Reinie would scold me for screaming. I would complain and say he was crazy and she would wash out my mouth with soap. I ate a lot of soap at their house.

My memories of Far Rockaway are of my parents being very involved with my younger brother, who was sick most of the year we lived there. I also remember going to the beach and playing with a friend who had a stump for an arm. She had been a thalidomide baby and no one wanted to hold her stump when we played circle games. I wasn't afraid of her stump.

When we moved to Long Island I had two close friends. There was Sherry who lived around the block and Michelle, nicknamed Micki, who lived on the corner. Micki got me to join the basketball team. While she liked to be the team captain, I liked to play defensive positions. I wasn't very fast but I was extremely agile and tenacious. My dad was teaching me to walk up a rope with my toes and to juggle three balls at once. He said I could join the circus when I got older. Sherry was not athletic but she and I took piano lessons together and spent a lot of time at my house. She liked to sit on my dad's lap. Sherry and I were like sisters, not much alike but in the same family and special to each other as intimate friends. When Micki came along, she and I struck up a separate friendship, complete with our own private world. We played out the fantasies of childhood, shared our dreams, and discovered life together as kindred spirits. Our friendship was her refuge and my security. We were best friends until Micki's parents moved to Florida in the summer of my twelfth birthday. I was bereft.

We moved again, this time to New Rochelle, New York, an affluent suburban community. The house wasn't ready yet so we stayed with friends of my parents whom I called my aunt and uncle. My parents and my younger brother Alan slept downstairs in the den and I slept on a pallet on the floor in an upstairs bedroom. I was lying on my pallet one night when my 'uncle' came upstairs to take his shower. He squatted down next to me. I was immobilized, like a moth or a deer. He asked if I liked looking at him. He asked me to touch him. I don't really remember if I actually touched him or not or if it went further. It doesn't matter because the violation, guilt and shame were just as penetrating.

I kept quiet about what had happened until after we left their house. When I told my mom she said I should never say such a thing again – especially to my father. I felt as if I had been thrown to the wolves. 'Uncle's' behaviour continued in one form or another until the guilt and the anger became too much and I got old enough to say, 'No more.' I would later understand that my mom's denial to herself about the situation was not an unusual response. In her generation, people did not talk or even think about such things. It was shameful.

I was always a good student. In high school I met a handsome young man named Kenny and we started dating. He was older than I was by three years. Dating consisted of going out to a drive-in movie, or the luncheonette for a soda, but most often it meant parking in the cul-de-sac at the end of my street and 'making out' in the car. It was my favourite thing to do. I was exploring the forbidden with a curiosity that had been stimulated earlier by Uncle Fondler. That's what I had come to call him privately and to my friend Sherry, in whom I had confided.

I was bored with high school. I had maintained good grades and a full programme and I wanted to go to college and to work. After completing senior English in summer school, I got my diploma without ceremony, went to work for my dad and signed up for night school at NYU downtown campus. Every day I would ride the trains and subways with my dad to his factory on Eleventh Street in the city, and after work I would walk the few blocks to the NYU campus where I was taking a course in history. I felt very grown-up and mature. These people were serious about their studies, not like the silly glue-sniffers in high school. Anyone who worked all day and then went to school at night had to be serious. It was a good summer for me. I was to begin college full-time in the fall.

My parents felt that the University of Bridgeport was far enough away yet close enough if anything went wrong. They wanted me to be away from Kenny so I would meet new people, get my degree and become a teacher. My mother had told me I was supposed to become a teacher from the time I was a child. So, of course, that was the last thing I wanted to be. After a while, Kenny convinced his parents to send him to Bridgeport too. But for the first year I was there as a single girl. And as an added incentive, I was given the use of an old car, my beloved rattletrap.

My roommate, Rozzy, was from Malden, Massachusetts, and she was Jewish like me. She was also visually impaired, but to a greater degree. I had terrible vision. I am not sure when it started but I discovered at the age of fourteen in junior high school that I couldn't read the board. Even from the front row, it looked all furry to me. And when I offered to clean the board after school the teacher sent home a note saying I should see an eye doctor. It turned out that without corrective lenses I was legally blind.

Rozzy was born in 1946, just after the war. Her mom may have had German measles when she was pregnant, as Rozzy was born with congenital cataracts. For all intents and purposes, she was blind. She could see shadows, but in those days they didn't have the technological miracles of today so she spent her childhood without vision. Later on, after many operations, she was able to read through one eye if she held the paper an inch away. She used a white cane and a Braille writer and had books on tape sent in to her. We tried to take the same classes so I could read her the assignments. And sometimes we would sit in the dark while she read to me from her Braille books. We spent hours listening to Alexander Scourby, who read books on tape. I learned a lot from Rozzy about how to keep things organized, which is the only way a visually impaired person is able to function independently.

On death row I would remember Rozzy saying that God didn't give you anything you couldn't handle. She was an inspiration to me. She never pitied herself, and went on to become a teacher at the school she had attended as a girl, and where Helen Keller went as well. So, if God thought I could handle this then I would!

At the University of Bridgeport, you could sign out on weekends. I would sign out for home but I would head for my old friend Sherry's. We would drive around in my old rattletrap of a car, sometimes to see Kenny, sometimes to party. I wasn't sure what I wanted any more. At one point I wanted to quit school and go to Israel and live on a kibbutz. There was a fire burning in me to achieve something, to do something of value. I wanted to distinguish myself as someone my mother and father would be proud to talk about to their friends. In the end, I suppose, I wanted to be a good person.

My two grandpas came to visit me at U of B. Both of my grandpas loved to sing. Grandpa Harry had learned to sing as a waiter in Coney Island when he was a boy. They serenaded me with duets, singing their tenor and baritone renditions of popular songs from the Mills Brothers, and 'When Irish Eyes Are Smiling' and 'Oh My Papa'. It was great. They clowned around together, making me laugh all day. It was the last time I saw Grandpa Bushzy that way.

Towards the end of the school year Grandpa Bushzy became too ill to be cared for at home. I wanted to postpone going back to college to take care of him. But they said that I wouldn't be able to handle the responsibility. So he was put in a home and I went back to the University of Bridgeport. I have always felt that I let my grandpa down. He didn't live long after that. I came home to go to his funeral. I helped shovel the earth on to his coffin and put some of it in a little box, which I kept for a long time.

When Kenny joined me at U of B, we would sign out of the dormitories on weekends and get a motel room. There was one night I remember, when it felt like I was having an out-of-body experience, hovering over myself, watching us on the bed, and afterwards I felt sure that was when I became pregnant.

'Be the first one on your block to have a baby!' Who knew how to look after a baby? I had never even held one. When they brought him to me in the hospital I was afraid to hold him for fear I would hurt or drop him. My friend Sherry came up to New Rochelle to give me moral support during the first weeks, and my mom taught me how to change diapers and all the rest.

We lived with my parents for the first few months but it was so difficult. Kenny and I wanted to make our own decisions, his parents wanted their way and my parents wanted theirs. Within a year, I was in Juarez, Mexico, getting one of those quickie divorces. It was the last year you could get a Mexican divorce. It was an experience! First you went down to Mexico by plane and the tour group leader met you at the airport. There was a busload of us, all there to get unhitched. We were taken as a group to see the attorney who had drawn up the papers and then to the Hall of Records to go before a judge and then the divorce was final. Each person decided what they would do with their rings and other symbolic objects and then we all went shopping at the bus driver's cousin's store and then to lunch. I felt pretty grown-up about it except that, in the language of the garment centre, in my own mind I became 'damaged goods'.

I went home determined to raise my child and take on the responsibilities of being a mother. My son became the focal point of my life. That meant that my days of school and friends and exploration were over. My parents handled this in the way that all things embarrassing or painful were handled – in a microcosm, where only those aspects that appeared to make life run smoothly were addressed. I was sheltered, looked after, but not given the tools with which to grow. Eric was not only my child but my constant companion and best friend. I took him everywhere with me. I had no peers, no social skills. My job, according to my parents, was to stay home and take care of my baby. They wouldn't babysit for me. I had wanted it; I could take care of it, they would say. It was, I suppose, their way of keeping me safe. I know now that they were doing their best for me.

When Eric was two, my parents sent me to live in Florida. They rented a vacation home in which I would live year round and they would come down as often as possible. I don't remember exactly what precipitated that move, except that it seemed like they wanted their life back, not to have to deal with me and my child on a daily basis.

I'm sure I wanted my freedom as much as my parents wanted theirs. And I know they meant well. But I wasn't prepared. I had no knowledge of how to maintain a household on my own, and the only job I'd ever had was working for my father when I was sixteen. I had no skills to enable me to be financially independent, although I did get a job selling magazines. Every day I went to the boiler room they called an office and made my calls, set up my appointments for the day and then went out in my car to close the deals. The car needed repairs that I couldn't afford, so I had to carry a screwdriver with me to get it going again just about every time I stopped. And then I would pick Eric up from day care and we would go home together to make dinner. My parents paid part of the rent and used the place for vacations when they could.

I missed them. I was completely on my own. I had no friends and had difficulty striking up a conversation with people I didn't know because I felt I had nothing in common with anyone. Before long I had hooked up with a beach bum. I became dependent on him. The combination of his savvy and my ignorance was a recipe for disaster which, when my parents got a whiff of it, convinced them to move to Florida and have me move back in with them. They bought a nice house with a separate room and bath off the kitchen. At first I chose to live in the separate section. But after a while I think loneliness got the better of my wanting to be independent and I asked to move into the main house. But they told me I couldn't. They said I had chosen to live in the separate portion and that was where I would stay. It was as if they were telling me that they didn't deem me worthy to share their home either. And that's where I was living when I met Irish John.

Irish John was a friend of my brother. He fancied

himself to be D'Artagnan, the suave musketeer. One night the 'pit crew', as I had come to call my brother's little cadre of friends who came over to work on their cars in our driveway, decided to go out somewhere. I, of course, would be staying home to take care of my child. As the others got up to leave, Irish John said, 'I think I'll stay here and keep your sister company.' He put his arm around my shoulders with this big grin on his face and a sparkle in his eyes and looked at my brother. Big Al, as Alan liked to be called in those days, looked at us for a moment and then said, 'OK. See ya later. Have a good time.' I thought it was so brave and considerate of John, to defy convention and my brother to stay with me, the older sister and with a child too. After all, he was only eighteen and I was twenty. We were together from then on. I was easy to please.

7

T HEY WERE WAITING. I took a breath and turned towards the open door to my cell and stepped in—
CLANG!

Solid metal door slamming shut behind me. The closing of the door has sucked all the air out of the cell. Throat dry, unable to swallow; tearless eyes, seeing nothing. I am drying up! Does it happen this way? You start to dry up and die here? The whitewashed cement-block walls closing in, enfolding me. Prepared especially for this purpose. This is death row.

Day 1 – Death Row
August 20, 1976

I begin to focus on the steel sink and toilet unit directly in front of me.

Where is the toilet paper?

I move my eyes, slowly, from side to side, seeking the comfort of something familiar. To my left is a bed – sort of a bed – a rusted metal skeleton bolted to the wall, covered by a thin, striped mattress. I can reach out and touch both walls by rocking slightly to each side. They have a cold, relentless feel to them.

Everything about this place feels dead. This is death row.

The door was behind me. I could not look at it. Turning to my left I noticed a window in the wall above the bed. I had to kneel on the bed to look through it.

A cruel joke – the window looks out on to another wall.

At just the right angle though, through a window a few yards down the hall to the left, I can see a small slice of the compound and the fence beyond. I feel some relief from this. Still, I cannot confront the door.

I close my eyes, sitting back down on the mattress that gives me as much comfort as its thin substance can provide.

There is no one here to see me, and so I give in to the tears. As they fall, I taste the stream running down my cheek to see if they are truly bitter.

A wailing begins to fill the space. My body starts to rock forward and back and the sound builds into a moan that cannot be contained. It obliterates all form and matter. And I sit at its centre, feeling myself falling away into oblivion.

It is like the cold fingers of an old nightmare that has come out from under the bed to find me again, but this time I cannot wake up from it because it is inside me, hanging on to my guts, squeezing, turning my insides to water. I curl up with my knees drawn in to my chest, arms wrapped tightly around them. I am a child, and I am alone.

How much time had passed I did not know. Footsteps. I stood quickly, wiping the tears and mucus from my face. They mustn't see that I had been crying. This seemed very important to me. Why were they coming? I heard more than one pair of feet. Maybe they were going to let me out! Maybe I was getting a neighbour?

Standing on my toes, I pressed my face up against the white-painted steel, canted in such a way that I could see down the hall through the small window made of security glass with wire mesh embedded in it. Three people – a tall, slim middle-aged man in casual clothes, a big, beefy ruddy-faced male guard wearing a western-style hat and a tight uniform, and the female guard from the office – were approaching my cell door. As they got closer, their forms blocked out the sliver of light that was all I could see of the hall window. Strangely backlit, they appeared as spectres.

They never made it the rest of the way to my cell. The matron pointed in my direction. The man in casual dress seemed to be asking some questions. The big guard did nothing. They turned and retreated down the corridor. My existence had not been acknowledged. It was as I had begun to suspect. I no longer existed in the outside world.

This feeling of overwhelming aloneness has connected with its counterpart from my past. I am amazed at how vivid it is and how small I feel. I have always needed lots of space around me.

Taking small steps, placing one foot directly in front of the other, I paced off the length of the concrete floor. Six steps. It was six steps from the door to the toilet, which had no lid and gaped at me, mocking me with its rude presence. I turned back towards the door again. Six steps.

I could walk these six steps as much as I liked and there was nothing to stop me. Back and forth – to the door, to the toilet – I began to pace, hands balled up into fists, sparks flying from my eyes.

My children! When will I see them? How long will it take for the court to find out they made a mistake?

The children are safe now, with my parents. But Tina needs my milk. Eric and I have never been separated before. We are best friends. He is such a sensitive child and he has been through so much already! Handcuffed and taken before a magistrate in the middle of the night without even a lawyer. Kept in isolation in juvenile hall for two months before my parents could secure his release. And poor Tina never drank from a bottle before. She didn't even know how!

My babies! Oh God! Please let them be OK! Please let me go to them soon! Oh God, how could you let this happen to us? And even if I was stupid and made wrong decisions, my children and my parents are innocent! Why make them suffer? Please help me, God. Please keep them safe. And Jesse. Please don't let them hurt him. They hate him so much. Please help us, God!

Part prayer, part accusation. I can only cling to the hope that there is something out there. Because, if there is not, then I am truly lost.

I sob with my face in my hands. My head feels like lead and my heart like broken glass. It is only my spirit that flutters around trying to keep the rest of me intact. I must be strong for the children!

I smelt breakfast. I must have slept, finally. They were coming down the hall! I sprang up to wait in front of the door. A face appeared in the window frame. The tray came through the slot midway up the door along with a cup of coffee. At least there was that much.

'May I have some more coffee after this?'

'Well, I guess I could keep some back for you. Yeah, I guess so.'

'Thank you. And I have to make a phone call today, and speak to the superintendent. He was supposed to see me yesterday.'

'I'll find out about that.'

'Thanks.' I took my tray and my coffee. She looked like she had worked here for a long time. It was nice of her to say she would keep the coffee for me. I got a headache if I didn't have coffee. I could do without the cigarettes but if I didn't have the coffee I suffered. I should have just given it up but these were the only small pleasures I could look forward to on death row. I wondered if she would get hold of the superintendent. He should have been here yesterday. They lied to me. They lied about the smoking and what I could have in my cell, and they lied about the superintendent coming to explain things to me. They just wanted to get me in this cell.

I ate one piece of toast and the oatmeal, saving the second piece of toast for later. I wrapped it carefully in the napkin and put it on the edge of my sink so they couldn't say I was trying to hide it. I finished the coffee, hoping the guard would keep her word about more. I had always loved coffee. I drank a lot of herb tea at home but I still liked to have my coffee. I'd really got bad about it since I was in the jail. My mom loved her coffee too. She said I had a coffee-coloured birthmark on my arm because she drank so much coffee while she was pregnant with me.

I heard the guard coming for the tray. 'May I have more coffee now?'

'I'll bring you some next time I come back here.'

'Thank you. And the superintendent?'

'I'll call up there after nine. He don't come in till then.'

'Thank you.'

The guard was coming again! More coffee so soon? Maybe it was a call from my lawyer! Maybe they had realized their mistake. Maybe they had decided to move me somewhere else. She had my uniform with her. I was to get dressed because the superintendent was coming to see me. Finally, some answers! I had made notes on the rules they had given me. Not being able to smoke in the cell, for instance, was stupid. What could burn? I surely wouldn't burn up my bed since I wouldn't have anything to sleep on if I did that. And why only two showers a week? That was ridiculous, especially since it was so hot in here and the shower was right down the hall. The guard handed me a dress. She called it my uniform and told me to signal when I was ready. It looked like a light blue sack made of cotton. It had obviously had previous incarnations and owners. It had a white tag with my name and personal number sewn over the right breast. I shed the pjs and slipped into the dress, trying to slow down enough to get the buttons done right. It was tight under the arms but too large everywhere else.

'I'm ready!' I announced, grabbing my copy of the rules on which I had noted my questions and complaints.

Where was she? I was getting a crick in my neck pressing my cheek against the door to look sideways down the hall. She was coming. And someone else was with her. I stepped back from the door. Didn't want to appear too anxious or undignified.

When the door opened, its frame was filled with the guard and a tall, thin man wearing casual clothes; typical Floridian short-sleeved knit shirt and lightweight slacks. He had an air of confidence and ease about him, unlike any other member of the system with whom I'd had contact thus far. The guard told me that the superintendent, Mr Booth, had arranged for us to talk outside. We filed down the hall in silence, at a processional pace. I hoped I didn't sweat circles under the armpits in this dress.

There were two chairs set up outside the front door to the building so we would face each other. He offered me the one on the right and sat down across from me. I sat with the rules in my lap, planting my feet firmly in front of me, knees together, back very straight. He asked how things were for me. That was my cue and I began to read from the rules and the questions I had prepared.

He unfolded his arm towards the papers. I placed them in his open hand. I was mesmerized by the languid movement, following it with my eyes, fixing on his face as he read over the notes I had made.

'I'll take these under consideration.' He stood up, handing me the papers, and as if on cue the guard came for me.

The next two days are the same as the first – the daily routine – but without the visit from the superintendent or the extra coffee. Breakfast at some ungodly hour – footsteps, tray slides in through slot in door. Footsteps. Tray is taken away. Lunch and dinner come and go in the same way and then the long period that I call night. Nothing changes to delineate day from night. There is just the routine. And I pace. And I cry. And I beg and argue and rationalize with the God I am not sure exists. The walls get closer together and threaten to smother me in my own fear and anger.

Happy birthday to me. It is 24 August and I am twenty-nine years old.

They came every hour to check on me, and would write down what I was doing in a logbook. Sometimes when I heard them coming I would quickly lie down on my bed and pretend I was asleep just so they wouldn't have anything to write. Why were they writing it down anyway? It was an invasion of what little privacy I had left and I resented it. It felt good to cheat them out of that much anyway. No one spoke to me. Still, it was a reminder that I was alive, I suppose.

🐌 *Death row journal, Florida Correctional Institution The sound of the door slamming behind me in jail*

was different than the sound of the door on my
death row cell. In jail, it was a shutting in. Death
row is a shutting out.

All I did for those first days and weeks was pace the six steps from the solid metal door to the sink/toilet contraption. Back and forth. Back and forth I walked, burning a path through the despair that filled the space out of which I could not find my way. It pushed me further and further inside myself.

       They think they have taken my life
from me already! But I am alive!

I had been given a Bible and a pencil and paper. So I paced, and I read, and I wrote and I waited for a bird to land on the bit of fence I could see if I angled myself right at the small window. I felt the need to make contact with another living thing that didn't hate me.

I had never been hated before. It is a terrible thing. I understood why they hated me – because of what they thought I did. But somehow I thought they should know, just from being around me, that I wasn't a person who would do something like that. I couldn't relate to their hatred. I felt I should have been angry at them for what was being done to me and to my family. But they only knew what they had been told. To them, I was a convicted cop killer. I tried, by my behaviour, to show them that I wasn't like that. But I think now that those attempts only served to make things worse.

They say the place is haunted by the blue lady. She walks the halls at night, and sometimes you can hear her scream.

For a short while, they gave me a neighbour. I had been alone for about a week when they brought a woman down and locked her in a cell on the opposite side of the building from me. They said the regular lock-up cells were all full so they had to bring her down here with me. She tried to ask me questions about myself. I didn't answer. I didn't trust her, but I listened. She broadcast to me by standing at her door and yelling. She told me her name was Harrington. Her mother and grandmother had done time in prison, and at one point they were all there together. Three generations. And she told me her mother was the only other woman who had been on death row in Florida. Her mother had been kept in the men's prison in a hospital ward. She told me about the Blue Lady who died in her cell and haunted the corridors at night, and about how four women took a hostage and escaped, only to be caught and locked in this dungeon for a whole year. They moved Harrington out after a few days but she left me the gift of her stories.

I stayed up late, waiting, looking out the small window towards the top of the door. I wished I could see this Blue Lady. We could be friends. I would be glad to have the companionship of this ghost. After all, I was becoming disembodied myself.

During those first months, living in a cage, being fed through a slot in the door, without human contact or any of the trappings of the civilized world, my survival instincts took me to the required level of being. I began to feel like Robinson Crusoe, without Friday. I tried to make do in my new environment, making use of the limited resources I could scavenge without completely losing my sense of being a civilized person. It was animal instinct that enabled me to survive. Being human had nothing to do with it. It was something I practised so I would remember how to do it when it became relevant again.

My hair began to come out when I combed it. I saved it and put it in a piece of paper. Maybe I could have a wig made of it later on. Crazy thing to think about – vanity. But in some cases it is good because it keeps your mind focused on your pride in living and on the future. That can be crucial in a situation where they say you have none.

> *There is no sense of time here. No day; no night. There are no clocks, no calendars, no windows, no sky. It tends to get cooler at night.*

Two showers a week was not enough. And it was like an oven during the day. I washed at the sink as best I could, pressing the button with one hand, but bird baths were not adequate and you couldn't possibly wash your hair that way. The state soap they gave me was made of lye. The prisoners made it at one of the other prisons. It was harsh.

This day is shower day. I am ready! I've got 30 minutes for the whole thing – shower, eight minutes; with shampoo ten minutes; then, dry off and dress. The rest of the 30 minutes is yard time. I go out in the small fenced-in grassy area at the side of the building with a guard. He or she sits while I basically wander around in a circle. I can see a part of the main prison area, dormitories and walkways but there aren't many people out at that time of day and they are forbidden to make any gesture toward me. Last week I picked some tiny grass flowers but I was not allowed to take them in with me. The office guard shook down my cell while I was out on my yard time. And I was patted down when I came in so I couldn't bring anything in with me. This is also the only time I can smoke. I smoke one after the other, getting dizzy as hell but puffing away madly, lighting one cigarette off the other until they say it's time to go in again. I know it's stupid while I am doing it but it's stimulation and I crave that more than anything, except my freedom.

When the yard time is over I am taken back inside by the male guard and given over to the female guard in the office. He speaks to her but has nothing to say to me. She gets out the set of large keys, puts my cigarettes back in the drawer, and searches me as soon as we get inside the barred door. Then back to the cell until next time. It was good to be outside. The small yard reminds me of the house my family lived in when we moved to Elmont, Long Island.

The houses all had a small square of a front lawn and a similar square in the back. We had a tiny swimming pool in our backyard. It was the only one on the block and I was very popular in the summer time. My girlfriend Sherry and I spent most of our time indoors. Micki and I spent most of our time in the garage, inventing things. We made a Spooky House one Hallowe'en, complete with a bowl of spaghetti guts to stick people's hands in and all the attendant sound effects. We used to sell lemonade in the summer. Micki wanted to give it away. I didn't sell lemonade any more after Micki moved to Florida, but Sherry and I had a couple of pool parties. My parents let me bring the record player out to the pool deck but the boys ended up throwing the records into the pool.

I am beginning to lose my sense of self. There are no mirrors, and no one to define myself around. I don't know what I look like anymore. I don't know what I have become or who I am anymore. It is the most frightening part of being here.

The superintendent came to see me. The officer handed me my clothes and told me to get dressed right away. I followed her down the hallway, through the large barred door, past the office, to the usual fresh air seating arrangement for official visits, two folding chairs placed opposite one another just outside the doorway. The superintendent was already seated.

In what became our regular weekly pattern, we talked. Well, I talked, really. He listened. He always listened, or seemed to listen. It was a huge effort to keep myself from appearing to be hysterical, from bursting with all I had to say. I had made notes all over the rules they had given me, objecting to this and that. But I knew that an emotional outburst would have no impact on that cool exterior so I determined to keep control of myself and present a rational picture to this man whose whims could make my life more or less of a hell. I told him it was cruel to keep a woman locked up without a mirror. He smiled. It was not a sarcastic smile. It was in his eyes as well. He looked at his watch and said he had a meeting to go to.

As we rose from the chairs the guard appeared in the doorway to escort me back to my cell and take back the clothes I wore only when someone would be seeing me. It reminded me of the façades they had in some of the concentration camps in Europe, where they would make it look humane but really it was a hell. Stripped of my civilized trappings once again, I put on the white-out pyjamas, neutralizing my identity one step further.

The most important thing, besides finding physical nourishment among the meagre offerings on the food trays that come through the slot in the door, is to find ways to keep from being totally overwhelmed by my helplessness. There has to be some relief from it! Pacing helps dissipate the energy to a degree but it doesn't get me anywhere. Reading the Bible and the law books that I am now allowed one at a time helps to get me out of my own head for a while, but it too is inadequate. I am being suffocated by my own emotions. Today I am out of tears. Sometimes I still find my milk soothing. I sit on my shelf with my back to the door and my eyes closed so I can imagine my child. As I rock gently, hum softly, the milk still flows and I drink it afterwards. I am still a mother.

A rabbi came to see me once while I was in the Flattop building. I had been asking to see one. He didn't stay long and never came back. (I found out years later that he had moved back to New York, but at the time I figured he didn't return because of my circumstances.) But the rabbi brought me a Hebrew calendar so I would know when the holidays were and could keep track of the phases of the moon, the Hebrew calendar being a lunar-based system predating the Roman one. Our brief meeting took place in a room beyond my cell at the end of the hallway. When he left, I asked about the strange object in the middle of the room. The guard explained that it was named the Creech tank after its inventor. The Creech tank was a device made of sheet metal in the shape of a bathysphere in which prisoners were once imprisoned as a form of further punishment. A set of rungs on the side led to a hatch at the top. It had a lock on it like in a submarine. It was through that opening that you were fed and hosed down. You could be hosed down for sanitary or punitive purposes. They kept a fire hose hooked up which they could turn on you at varying degrees of pressure. She said it wasn't used any more because of those 'bleedin' heart liberals' who thought it was cruel. But they didn't get rid of it. Some day, she said, people would see how we had to use things like the Creech tank on some incorrigibles who just couldn't learn any other way. I would have died in the Creech tank. Entombed without air next to your own faeces, no one could survive for long without going insane.

And so I paced, back and forth, those six steps from the toilet to the door. Six steps, back and forth . . .

    Underneath it all, I am, indeed, an animal. What burns behind my eyes and in my heart is a primal, DNA encoded connection to the primitive ancestral rootstock of genus and species. The heat of my anger obliterates all else. Nothing can exist in this atmosphere. It will be incinerated or turned to dust.

I have a wash cloth. Sometimes after I have been crying a lot I wet the cloth and place it over my eyes. My hair is still falling out. I collect it from the floor each day. Like my milk, I feel a compulsion to preserve these little bits of myself so as not to be lost or wasted. So I collect them, these fragile strands . . . holding on to them for dear life.

    This anger keeps me prisoner in ways far more destructive to me than the steel and concrete and barbed wire. If I continue this way, I will become a burnt out husk of a person with

nothing left inside to give to my kids or to anyone
else. I won't let them do that to me! They might be
able to keep me here, take my time and
circumscribe my space, but they can't have my
mind or my heart or my spirit. Those are mine and
no one can take them away from me.

I have been using the Bible like you would a deck of tarot cards. Open it up to any page and see what it has to say. It always says something to me that I need to know that day.

I can't tell you the chapter and verse but one day the overwhelming thought came to me that 'they' don't say when I die. No man says when I die. That would be for some higher power to decide. Now, maybe there was and maybe there wasn't this higher power. But for me, it cost nothing more to choose to believe, thereby giving myself hope – since I was still mad at the Universal Power for letting this happen to us in the first place. The other choice was hopelessness and that just didn't appeal to me. I will die when it is my time to die. Until then, within these walls, it is up to me what kind of world this will be – a joyous one, or a sad one, filled with peace and calm, or misery and fear. They can keep me here but what goes on within the confines of these walls is mine to create. They cannot imprison my soul!

It is just the three of us then – me, my life, and my own death whose presence has become my constant companion in our little six foot by nine foot world. We are inseparable. And we will learn to get along with each other, as parts of a whole that is greater than any one of us.

There is a moment, a moment in time when, through adversity, we are forever changed. It is a moment in which we surrender our self and are both filled and empty. It is a moment in which everything becomes crystal clear. It is a Snap, Flash, Pop, Bang, a glowing silence in which one's personal reality is disintegrated by Truth. It happens in the face of death. We have to see it smile and beckon to us before we can make the leap. That is when it happens, while we are suspended in mid air. And when we land again, we find an added dimension in the world. So it was for me.

I begin to do meditation. I sit – legs folded in strictest lotus position, hands resting lightly on top of my crossed feet forming a circle with the left held in the right, thumbs touching. Using breath control, I slow my bodily functions, centring myself and focusing my energy before expanding outward, searching the cosmic plasma for signs of life. Then quietly I sit waiting to hear or feel or be given what it was the Universe determined that I should be given.

I never did see or hear the Blue Lady. But I found myself, which was much more significant, and it gave me much more than the company of the occasional ghost. I found a sense of myself as larger than just my physical form, and I was never alone. I was joined by this expanded self to all other things in the Universe. I could go to my children at night and comfort my parents. I could send my energy out

123

into the cosmos and be with Jesse. I could sense his mother Kay too. It was a miracle! My world was forever changed. I was a soul on my journey through this world and I was finally aware of it.

I was no longer just a prisoner. I was a monk in a cave, there to do the inner work necessary to grow and to become the best person I could be. The only way in which I was restricted was bodily. Except for that, I was as free, or more free, than I had ever been.

I practised yoga as a part of my daily routine. You didn't need much room to do yoga. It helped me to create an atmosphere of peace and tranquillity in the midst of the hatred and pain that had seeped into the cement blocks of the building. And it cleared away the inner turmoil so that I could function. It was also a connection to who I used to be. I started doing yoga when I was twenty years old, having seen Lilias Folan's hatha yoga on television. I knew immediately that it was for me. But now I had the opportunity to truly grow in my practice. It almost seemed like my whole life had been preparing me for this moment.

It was as if they had given me a whole universe to create – to fill and to make into whatever I wanted it to be.

They say even our cells have memories. What would the ancient people have done, before they had all the resources we have today? I wonder if the cell I am in will have memories of what I do here to mix with the misery?

I had some newspaper given to me by a kind-hearted guard and from it I began to tear strips, weaving them into a mat. What would I do with it? I covered the gaping maw of the toilet that had dominated my space like a black hole that sucked everything up except me and the bunk. I surveyed my handiwork, standing in the centre of my universe. And it was good.

Smiling, I wove another mat, this time to sit on. And, in my mind, I began to divide the space. I will eat sitting on my mat in front of the door. I will store the mat under the mattress. I will read sitting on the covered toilet. I will exercise in the middle of the floor on my blanket, being careful not to get caught misusing it. Doing everything while sitting on my bed was making me feel like I was sick. Not any more.

Lunch will be here soon. My stomach is my clock. It tells me that it is lunchtime. I could hear some activity from the office. They must be getting ready to deliver my tray. I arrange myself in front of the slot. Processional footsteps and a vague aroma of food activate my senses, put on alert status by my stomach. I can't tell what is on the tray yet. The smell is too indistinct. Something mushy and half-warm, as always. Maybe more mystery meat? Ground pork sauce to ruin the rice? I could always rinse it off. I felt like a raccoon. I'd taken to washing everything off before eating it. But it was that or not eat since almost everything was cooked in or with some sort of meat grease. I washed the beans, greens, carrots, noodles and the rice as well. I had asked them to leave off the sauces and gravies but it always came the same way – cold and greasy.

The face appears in the square of window. It is like a small TV screen. The tray comes through the slot, as in the cafeteria my mom used to take me to when I was a child in New York City. I used to like getting the food from the compartment that would open up when she put in the money. The memory tastes good, no matter what the food is like.

'Thank you,' I practise, not expecting a reply, as I accept the tray and look out at the face in the glass square, trying to make eye contact. I always try to make eye contact in order to maintain my identity, lest they forget there is a real live human being in this cell.

She leaves. I feel like a toyland creature that becomes animated only when no one is looking. I get out my food scenery – the delectable picture of a platter of cooked egg-plant and tomato and onion set on a wooden counter in a wood-panelled kitchen decorated with wooden spoons. It is warm and appetizing. I paste it upon the wall with toothpaste where it won't be seen if the door is opened. Decorating is against the rules. I got the picture from the magazine section of the newspaper that I used to make the mats.

I pull my sitting mat out from under the mattress and place it reverently in front of the photograph. This is a ritual when I'm preparing to eat. It is not an indulgence, it is as essential as the food itself. The meal is not just to nourish the physical body. It must also nourish the spirit, even the soul. It is a simple ritual, but very effective.

Placing the tray before me as I kneel on the mat facing

the photograph, I settle on to my haunches, oriental-style, and remove the cover from the tray in front of me. The first thing that strikes me is that there is a napkin, folded and placed with obvious care over the utensil slot on the left side of the tray. My heart swells too large for my chest, throat too full to speak the emotions that well up and spill out of my eyes. Someone has sent me a message. Like a person stranded on an island who finds a bottled message sent from civilization, I see the message in that napkin. Someone cares; someone wanted to affirm my existence as an individual and my dignity as a human being. Someone had lovingly folded and placed the napkin there to give me strength, to nourish my soul. Truly, a gift of the soul. I am truly blessed this day. I have been given the gift of love in a napkin on a plastic tray of chopped mystery meat. Life's mysteries are for those eyes that have learned to see them. I'll have to wash off the rice and the green beans but that's OK. I will keep this napkin. It will be as an icon in my store of small treasures.

'Thank you, dear friend, whoever you are. Thank you for this gift and for renewing my faith.'

The guard escorts two workmen to my cell. They have a polished metal mirror with them, which they hang over the sink. It hasn't been a week since my request. It is the only thing I will ever get without filing a lawsuit. I am well pleased. I write a thank you note to the superintendent. Not a bad guy after all.

8

THE PRECIOUS FIRST LETTER from my beloved Jesse since he was sent to death row has arrived! It has taken four months to get through the bureaucratic red tape, to get approved, since he was sentenced in May. I hold it to my heart and cry with the sheer relief of having it in my hands. Savouring the writing on the envelope, noting the date cancelled over the stamp, I draw the letter out of the envelope where it has been cut open for inspection by the mail room officers. He painted the paper before he wrote on it so everything about it would be pleasing and special. Jesse has a sense of things like that, an elegance of personal style that sets everything he does apart from the norm. It is the Zen influence, I think – the attention to detail that you find in Japanese culture, where the wrapping of a present and the presentation of it is as important and meticulously done as the gift itself. His maternal grandfather, a Welsh coal miner who emigrated to Pennsylvania with his young family, initiated Jesse into the Kiai-Shu branch of Zen Buddhism as a child. But he didn't really practise, except briefly when he was with the sensei in prison. With me, he did his practice in order to teach me here and there when the mood came over him but life didn't demand it from him fully, until now. His circumstances would bring out the best and the worst in him.

Sept. 21, 1976

My Dearest Sunny,

I love you. As you can see I finally can write to you. I've been worried about you. Boy, I love you Mama; I'm just sitting here on my bunk smiling, thinking about you. We're some pair. It's you and me forever honey. I write Eric and Christina every week.

I presume you're in a one-man cell like me, can you see outside? I hear you can't smoke, what's the story? Do you send smoke signals? How many times and for how long do you go to the yard? We go to the yard once a week for a couple of hours, about 6 of us at a time; then once a week we go to the 'tables' for 2 hours which consists of a hall the length of the wing, barred, with 2 tables in it. I'm up on the third floor. There are 17 men on our floor. I can see outside. I'm facing north. Right out my window is the death row yard, a fenced-in area about 90 ft by 40 ft wide. Then about 50 ft from that are our main fences with the dogs in between them. Bow wow. That's outside. Inside, my cell's about 8' by 6' and 8' high. On the right, looking in, is my bunk, and on the back wall (left) is my combination stainless-steel sink and toilet. So there's about 3' x 6' to run around in. All the guys on the row have TVs in the cells up on a platform on the back wall two feet up at the foot of the bed. We are also allowed AM/FM radios. I just got the Sony Matrix so I can do what we call 'Juke-in,' short for 'Juke boxing,' I hope you can have one. Let me know and I'll get you one. Music makes a difference. If you have any kind of problems, you make sure to let me know. You are my main concern. Put your family and mom on your visiting list, no one else, understand? I'll explain at another time. I'll be in close touch. I'll be writing probably every day. You do the same.

You're my woman forever. Know in your heart that we are going to make it out alright. I love you with all my heart, Sunny, my beautiful wife. I'll close for tonight with thoughts of you.

Jesse

The words on the painted page washed over me. I answered immediately, words spilling over the page in tidal waves of questions and answers. It was like finding Friday's footsteps on the barren beach. I wasn't alone any more!

At first I responded in broad strokes. Later, I would pick through the tide pools of words and nuances for the details, stipplings and shades of grey in between the lines. The portrait and landscape Jesse painted were far different from the colourless shadow world in which I lived.

I was filled with a new energy. I would have feedback now. I wrote a request for visits, and another enquiring about walks and TV and other similar privileges to those of the men. This was discrimination, I wrote, either because I was a woman or because I was Jewish – the two characteristics that made me unique among death row denizens. But I knew that it was really just a matter of convenience, although they may have enjoyed being able to make me suffer more.

The face disappears. My attention is focused on the tray. I perform the ritual of getting out the eating mat and picture, placing the food on the mat while I glue the picture up with toothpaste. Picking up the tray, I sit cross-legged on the mat in front of the picture. Placing the tray in my lap, I open the lid to reveal the contents. Beets! I like beets. Beets remind me of borscht, the traditional Russian peasant food; and of iron, which is found in dark red foods; and of stains which beet juice makes on anything it touches, even your fingers; and of primitive painting and the process by which the Indians used to make colours. I could do that! I eat rather more quickly than usual, anxious to try out my new idea.

I reserve the beet juice in my cup, take down the food picture and place it and the mat under my mattress again. They only give me a few sheets of paper at a time so I have to use it sparingly. Often, I make notes on napkins or scraps of newspaper when I can get it. My dad did that, using the first thing at hand on which to scribble his notes. It is a thought that has a smile attached to it. Now, what am I going to use for a brush? Improvise. It has become a satisfying challenge to improvise. Somehow, there is always something that can fit the need. It is a talent I never knew I had. What are brushes usually made of? Hair. Of course! My hair is long now. It was long before but it hasn't been trimmed in almost a year and drapes over my shoulder in a thin fall. I twirl the ends together into a point and see if it is going to be long enough for me to paint with while still attached. My heartbeat proudly signals my triumph to the rest of my body as the exhilaration travels to every nerve and cell, filling me with pleasure. I am going to paint, just like my ancestors did.

Setting myself up on the floor with the paper in front of me, I sit on my heels, contemplating, waiting for the painting to suggest itself. Bending over the paper, I dip the point of hair into the red beet juice, and make the first stroke. It is the bird on the fence. I can see it on the paper even before I lay down the strokes. Jesse will like this. I will send it to him in my letter tonight. I can't get in trouble. I only used what they gave me. I could put a red kiss on the page too if I smear some of this juice on my lips! I do it, carefully pressing my lips to the paper. 'Not bad!' I say to myself. Not bad at all. This has been a good day.

Sept. 26, 1976

My Dearest Sunny,

My heart just overflows with love for you. It's just a matter of time and of politics until we eventually regain our freedom. I'll reinforce and stimulate you as much as I can to make our lives more complete and satisfactory until we're together once again. I'm going to work on a potent routine for us, which will deal with growth, and set aside times in which our energies may be focused toward a common goal. I love you with all my heart.

Jess

A Poem to Jesse

You are the Sun
I am the Moon
I have no light but that
which is reflected from you

Sept. 30, 1976

My Dearest Sunny,

I love you. They turn out the light at 11 p.m. I'm reading a couple of Shakespeare's classics, *Macbeth* and *Hamlet*. I'm studying too much law lately and need to give my head some relaxing reading too. I received your beautiful letter. What beautiful kids we have! We're so lucky. My sweet wife, I love you so much. I laugh thinking about the courage you have, as most 'guys' would be vomiting. You're my woman, as close as my breath. You're the strongest female I've ever even heard of, and *all* woman. We're like hand and glove. Never be lonesome, we're only separated by miles.

It seems we do have more going here than you, because for one thing there's strength in numbers, plus death row had been established here since

133

the state first started murdering people.

Anyway honey, I sure would like to speak to you alone, let's say for a few hours, in my place or yours. I love you Mama. And don't worry, I'm on the case, lover.

Jess

I was lifted up by Jesse's confidence in me and the fact that he said I was strong. It gave me something to think about. I began to reassess the events of my life in the light of this new perspective. And this time it wasn't a new dimension with all the sparkle and wonder. It was something far more grave and complex.

I began to reconstruct myself. Just as I had been doing with my new world, I had been given the chance to create a new self. Maybe my parents had been seeing this potential of mine too. Maybe they just wanted me to be more than I was because they knew I could be. Now I was beginning to think maybe they really loved me – a me they saw differently.

The picking up and delivering of my laundry was an event, as was the delivery of library books. I never could figure out how the selections were made. There didn't seem to be any sense to it. One time I received a book called *The Titanic*. It contained maps and blueprints of the ship, each deck and the placement of lifeboats. It told the whole tragic story of how the boat sank and people died. Why would anyone send me that particular book?

Once a week I received visits from a guidance counsellor. And occasionally I was visited by religious counsellors. The guidance counsellor used to bring me hard candy to eat while we walked around the yard and talked. Jesse knew him from prison before and said he was OK. It was an extra half an hour a week outside my cell. I accepted visits from a religious couple, the Woodhalls, but they kept trying to get me to sign a commitment to make Jesus my saviour, beating me over the head with the Bible, so to speak, until I had to terminate the contact. Later on, I found a way to embrace Jesus and his teachings without causing a conflict with my Judaism. I think sometimes people came to see me out of some morbid curiosity. But whatever their reasons, they became food for my starving senses. I devoured everything that didn't make me choke.

November 17, 1976

My Dearest Jesse,
I love you! I've been so busy the past two days. I had to have a copy of the official form for filing my civil suit. So I wrote and wrote all night and made up another copy of the form by hand. My love, I needed to have this work to do. It was like a cerebral field day. My brain has been in a coma. I guess, like the Caterpillar, I wove a cocoon, and now I have emerged . . . A Butterfly! And I am full of life!

In a series of letters, Jesse helped me compose a civil lawsuit asking for equal privileges. There were seventy-six other people on death row in Florida at the time – all of them men. He said I would need a lawyer to present the

135

case to the federal court. If you didn't have a lawyer they would simply set the case aside. They received thousands of complaints per year from inmates, many of them frivolous.

There was a bright young attorney in Jacksonville who had a reputation for going after the state on prisoners' rights issues. His name was Bill Shepherd. Kay, Jesse's mom, contacted him and he came to see me. He looked like Abraham Lincoln, except his beard was bigger and he was handsome. But his most striking feature was his voice – big, booming, basso profundo. He was impressed with the work I had done and agreed to take the case. It was the beginning of a working relationship and friendship that would continue long past the resolution of my civil lawsuit.

I created a routine for myself. It helped to overcome the feeling of being detached, of free-floating in the absence of a time structure. I would sleep until the smell and sounds of breakfast alerted my senses. Bursting awake, I would quickly wash my face and smooth my hair and wait by the door with my face pressed sideways to the 5″ x 5″ square of safety glass criss-crossed with wire, waiting for the first sighting of the breakfast cart and the guard. Sometimes they would let it sit there in the office for a long time, perhaps talking with whoever brought the food down to the Flattop, so it was cold and congealed before it came to me. I usually kept a piece of toast for later, hiding it in my washcloth in case they decided to search. I wasn't allowed to keep any food in my cell. Since it was already cold it didn't matter if I didn't eat it right away, so I would set it aside and meditate.

I would do things that made me feel strong, not weak and helpless like they wanted me to feel. I did sit-ups and push-ups and squats and the karate horse stance that Jesse had shown me. Then I would run in place on my blanket folded in quarters.

After exercise, I would eat and then go back to sleep. Yoga filled the next part of my day. Before and after yoga I would pray and meditate. Lunch was another marker in the passage of timelessness. Then I would write or draw or do maths problems in my head or think about my children, Jesse, my family and cry. I still expressed my milk every day and drank it, with closed eyes and a heart swollen with longing. I tried to familiarize myself with the language of the law books but I couldn't really concentrate on what they were saying. I would have to close the book before my brain began to boil.

Where is Ray Sandstrom? What's taking so long? When will I receive some news?

Dinner came cold like breakfast. The removal of the dinner tray marked the beginning of the sensory fasting period during which I made every effort to fill the void with activity until I fell asleep again.

137

9

O<small>N OCCASION THERE WAS</small> an incident, some major disturbance, that required the use of the empty cells on my side of the building. It was only during those times that I had company. I never saw anyone. But I could hear them, and talk to them. I wouldn't answer them at first. I wanted to know something about who they were. And for that all you had to do was listen. You found out everything because they shouted back and forth to each other, not seeming to care that everyone else could hear their most intimate secrets. There couldn't be any secrets in this place where everyone lived in such close proximity. Lunch came, meaning the guards wheeled the cart down the hall, distributing the trays, sliding one into each food slot. Being in the last cell on the end, I never saw anyone pass by. The only people I ever saw were the guards. Most of them didn't talk to me.

The women got quiet as the trays were passed out. I heard one woman ask if she could have another towel, and another said she needed more writing paper.

My tray, or what will be my tray for this meal, appears in the food slot. I look up to see the face of the guard who

138

brought the tray. If they look mean I hesitate to eat the food. This one looks OK. I will eat.

It gets quiet during mealtimes, except for the bartering that takes place. It is an interesting example of resourcefulness and cooperation.

'Can I have your bread?' 'Sure. Send something over and I'll wrap it up for you.' 'OK. Here it comes.' Everyone in between the two cells stands up at their door and slips an arm through the food slot. The person who wants the piece of bread takes off her pyjama top to use as a conveyor. She slips it out through the food slot and starts it swinging, building up to a larger and larger arc until the person in the next cell can grab hold of it and repeat the process of swinging it into an arc to reach the hand of the next person, and so on until it arrives at the cell of the one with the bread. She ties the bread into the sleeve of the pyjama and begins the process over again, swinging it back towards the person who wants the bread.

Occasionally someone would drop the pyjama shirt into the hallway. When that happened, it was a bust! And you could be Maced for it. Mace was a wicked thing, a chemical spray used for behaviour control, which burned your eyes. After the first time we were busted, I would never use my shirt in that way. I would rather not have the extra morsel. I didn't want to give anyone the opportunity to use Mace on me.

I don't know what Sam was in for, what her crime was. She was in lockup for thirty days for verbal disrespect, meaning she had mouthed off at one of the staff. Sam was still a girl really, very young and rebellious and outspoken.

139

I hoped they would never break her beautiful spirit. But she really needed to learn how to chill out. She had a terrible temper. She would yell and curse and piss them off. And they would come in with the Mace. Three of them, the female guard on duty and two males. They sprayed it in through the food slot and then blocked up the slot and the air vent at the bottom of the door so as to obtain the full effect for the longest period of time. Then the guards would hurry back down the hallway to the office, away from the fumes.

'My eyes! My eyes are burning! Oh my God! My eyes!'

'Take off your pyjama top and dip it in the toilet. Get it wet and then cover your eyes with it. It'll help!' one of the old-timers who had been locked up as a result of the same disturbance as Sam shouted from a cell midway down the row. Sam was hysterical. She just kept on screaming. A guard opened the solid metal door between the office and the corridor, shouting, 'You better not talk to her. You'll get it too if you do!' In counterpoint to Sam's shrieking and wailing was the silence filled with the fear of being next.

'I can't! I can't see!' Sam's suffering wound its way around the guardian of good sense that was telling me to keep quiet, to the place in my brain that blurted out the words, 'Do what she says, Sam!'

'Do you want to get it too, Jacobs?'

I swallowed the words I was about to speak. They formed a hard lump, sticking like phlegm. I felt ashamed. Sam's wailing tapered off into a whimper. Impotent rage filled the silence.

Some weeks later the guards escorted me up from the Flattop to the administration building where Bill Shepherd, my civil attorney, was waiting for me. A man from Tallahassee was there too. He turned out to be the lawyer for the superintendent, Mr Booth. Bill explained, in private, that he had sent a motion to the court to have me be present at the federal court hearing we were attempting to get concerning my rights. But the judge said that since there was a conflict about whether the federal or the state authorities would bring me, and he didn't want to set precedent with a death row inmate, he had decided my testimony could be by deposition, so I would not have to be there in person to testify. I didn't like it.

The other lawyer did not disagree that I was being discriminated against. His questions at the end were brief. He asked about the lack of fruit and juice, about the legal mail being opened or taken from me open, about the girl who got a disciplinary report for speaking to me and the girl who got Maced and what I had said to her and to the guards. I don't know why he made an issue of that particularly. I had encouraged her to put a wet rag on her face because she had called for help. I had said nothing to or about the guards. He also asked me what I was convicted of and my sentence. Then Shepherd asked me to elaborate a little on each point on the complaint. He said the hearing would be the following Friday. I made it known on the deposition that I strongly objected to my exclusion from the proceedings.

The guards tried to make us stop working on my

deposition at 5 p.m. but the lawyers said they needed more time. They didn't like being ordered out. They had 'rights'. I told Mr Bremer, the other attorney, that he had just had a small sample of how it was to be in prison. The case would stand on its own merits, I felt sure. Bill Shepherd was an odd one, I thought, but he loved the law and he loved to win unique cases. But it would be a year before we would get the lawsuit into a courtroom. In the meantime, the institution would grant none of my requests except for visits from my immediate family.

October 1976

My Dearest Jesse

I'm grateful for this pen and paper puny way of telling you over and over again how I feel, but I want to crumble it up and run and tell you I love you. The children feel it too. Tina is still little and is all surrounded with love but Eric is older and has to deal with the hardest parts now when we're not there. I am desperate to be with him. He feels totally different from everyone else. I think my family will be able to visit soon!

I love you.

Sunny

It had been months since I had seen the children, and the visits at the county jail had been wholly inadequate – looking at each other from behind a glass partition and speaking through a handset like a telephone. I knew they were safe and well cared for with my parents but my heart was like a knot in my chest whenever I thought about them, my babies. I prayed and sent them my love and my energy every morning and every night. Sometimes I dreamed of them, of being with them again. But it was so painful. I tried to concentrate on adapting to my new environment for as long as it might take until the authorities figured out they had made a terrible mistake.

10

For three long days and longer nights
I lay awake and dreamed
eternally, or so it seemed
to see those dear and precious sights
to taste and smell and see and feel

I lay awake at night and dreamed
eternally, or so it seemed
of Saturday when they'd be here
to kiss and hug and hold them near

Just three more days, just two, just one
til into my mother's arms I'll run
one touch enough to melt the sun

November 1976

I WAS DRESSED AND READY to receive my first visit. I hoped
they wouldn't get lost. It had been so long since I'd seen
my children, held them, fed them, talked to them and
heard their voices. I missed my parents, even though we
argued every time we were together. They were my lifeline,
not a smooth one perhaps but a strong one on which I

knew I could rely. I hoped my parents had all the papers they needed. The place ran on paperwork. I was told to tell them to bring their ID. I was starting to sweat. That had become a part of my ID lately, circles under the armpits.

They're here! I hear the guard coming! The usual chamber music in my chest has turned into a brass band, big bass drum booming. Breathe, calm down, slow down; feet, touch the ground.

The guard opened my door. I floated down the hall, struggling to stay behind her.

'Will we be able to get refreshments? Mr Booth said he would arrange something for us.'

'I'll call and find out. They haven't told me anything yet.'

I couldn't hear them. I wondered where we'd be sitting. As the guard opened the big barred door leading to the office, I could see through the windows, but there were no chairs on the porch where I usually sat with Mr Booth. As we walked out the door I saw them. They were in the yard, sitting at the small picnic table! They were waving and Eric was trying to come to me. I looked to the guard standing next to me.

'Go ahead.'

As I thanked her, I ran from the porch through the gate into the fenced yard, laughing and crying and calling their names. 'Oh, I'm so happy! I was worried that you had a problem getting here . . .'

Eric threw himself into my arms, wrapping his strong little body around me. I lifted him up and my parents came and surrounded us in one great embrace. I kissed

Tina's little face and then both of my parents. I felt as if I had been given back my true form, having been disembodied until now. Holding Tina on one side and Eric on the other, I walked with my parents to the picnic table. That was when I first noticed the guard who would supervise our visit. He was sitting in a chair a few feet from where we would be sitting.

'How was the trip? Did you have trouble finding this place?'

'The trip was fine. But they couldn't find the paperwork for the visit when we got here, and they said we needed Eric's birth certificate. They didn't tell us that when we called. Who would think to bring the child's ID?'

'I knew it! I asked them about the paperwork. I tried to make sure it would be there for you.'

'Sit down, dear. Don't worry about it. We're here and that's all that matters now.'

We sat at the picnic table, leaning in towards each other holding hands, faces close together. Eric leaned his head on my shoulder and Tina sat in my lap.

We were all smiling and wiping our eyes, even my dad. They told me all about what was going on at home. Everyone knew what had happened and Eric was having a hard time in school. Even the sympathy of the neighbours was painful for my family. They were thinking of moving to California. My mom told me she thought of me whenever she went shopping. My dad told me how his textile business was going and we talked about the possible uses of different materials for hat bands. He was always looking for new ways to use bindings and trimmings, the staples of the family business.

'They let us bring in pencil and paper to keep the children busy,' my mom said, pulling the things out of her purse. 'We had a hard time with the diapers and baby food.'

'How is she eating now? Is she using the bottle still?' Turning to Eric, 'And you look like you've grown since I saw you.'

'When are you coming home, Mommy?'

'I don't know exactly but soon, baby, I'll come home soon.'

'In a week?'

'Before your next birthday, for sure. Oh Mom, I asked them about refreshments for us. The guard said she would find out. I wonder if she's called yet.'

My dad pulled out a clean white hanky. He wiped the sweat from his face and handed it to my mom, who did the same. She started to hand it to me and I automatically looked in the direction of the guard.

'Is it OK to give you anything? Will you get in trouble?'

'I think it's OK for me to use the hanky.' I hesitated a beat and when the guard didn't seem to care, I took the hanky and wiped my own face and then wiped Eric's neck.

It was brutally hot. There was no shelter, no shade, no relief from the burning sun for the entire six hours. We were able to get some cans of soda and little packets of crackers, which helped a little. I was glad my mom had thought to bring something for the children to do.

I took a little walk around the yard with each of them

separately. Eric was getting in fights at school because the kids were saying his mommy was in prison. Tina wouldn't eat at first, but was doing fine now. She had become the apple of my dad's eye. My parents had talked with Ray Sandstrom and he had assured them he was working on the appeal. They said they had confidence that everything would work out OK. We told one another, each one, that we would be fine.

My mom had been looking beyond the fence, watching the other prisoners go by during lunchtime. All of a sudden she turned to me, looking shocked. 'I thought this was an all-girls institution!'

'It is, Mom.'

'Then what are those men doing up there?' She pointed to the rise where the dormitories were.

I watched the women go by in their blue short-sleeved work shirts and jeans, and turned to my mother, saying, 'Those are women, Mom.'

'But they look like men.'

'They're women, Mom. There are no men here, except the guards.'

Eric wanted to see inside the building where I lived. We strolled over to where he could look through one of the windows. We were on the opposite side of the building so he couldn't see my cell but the general picture was the same. It looked like a dungeon inside, dark and lifeless.

'Let's go play, Eric.' He had the same look on his face as my mother had had earlier. 'Come on, let's see who can run faster!'

We chased around and rolled in the grass near the table. Eric ran over to his sister and kissed her. He was always a good boy.

My mom and dad told me all the news about my brother and his family and brought me up-to-date on the local doings. And then it was time to leave. I didn't think I could do it. I didn't think I could see them leave. The guard told us to start getting ready. It was no use trying not to cry. I kept my voice steady but the tears flowed as we said our I love yous. Eric wrapped his arms around my legs and held on for dear life. 'Mommy, I won't leave you.'

'You go home with Grandma and Grandpa now, Eric. Help take care of your sister.'

'I want to stay with you.'

'I'm sorry but you can't. You have to go home and go to school.'

'Then I'll take you with me.'

'They won't let me go, sweetheart.'

'I'll put you in a big suitcase so they won't see, and I'll carry you out with me.'

'Thank you, Eric. I love you. Please be a good boy and go home with Grandma and Grandpa now. Everything will be OK soon and I'll come home. And then we'll have a big party. OK?'

And then the guards took me one way and them another. My guard escorted me back to my cell and waited outside while I changed out of my dress and back into my pyjamas. I handed her the dress, for once thankful that she didn't want to talk.

An alchemy of every possible emotion had drained

me of the very last bit of energy. I prayed them home safely, even after I fell asleep.

I woke up later that evening, miserable. I needed to wash the sweat from my body, which was burning from having been so many hours in the sun. I stripped and washed at the sink, wondering if they were as burned as I was. We should have had some shelter, an umbrella or something. I didn't see why they didn't let us sit on the porch under the overhang. I would peel for two weeks afterwards, but the memory of that visit burned far deeper than the sun.

11

I DID NOT LIKE HAVING to let someone else do my wash. I did not like the thought of my clothes being washed with other people's clothes. But I couldn't bear to wash them in the toilet like some people did. You put your foot in the bowl to block the hole and then you just kept on flushing it and flushing it and flushing it until the clothes were clean. So I would send my clothes out and they would come back later that day clean, pressed and folded nicely in a warm pile.

February 1977

My Dearest Jesse,

I got your sweet letter, my love. You make me so happy. Really, I could get 10 letters but none would make me happy like yours do! I curled up with your letter, under my sheet, and went to sleep with it. I always sleep under my sheet, all covered over my head now. In jail I slept very lightly, but here I had to get used to sleeping through the hour checks. So, since I don't like the thought of someone staring at me when I sleep, I cover myself completely.

There's been a little four-month-old Doberman

running around the compound lately – with floppy ears. Maybe it will be around on Monday when I go out. They also keep a dog here across the street that is used in customs and Post Offices to sniff out stuff, but I've never seen it.

For me, the occasional neighbours were a mixed blessing – I craved the company, but the noise became a disruption and sometimes I found myself wishing for silence. There had been no Christmas or New Year for us that year, only another day of sadness and frustration, the same as every other day. The only respite came from within yourself. Occasionally there was some relief from outside, but it wasn't always pleasant.

I got a letter from a lady who told me she wrote to two other women prisoners, one on death row in Georgia. I was sad to learn that another state had a woman on death row – I wondered if she had children. I thought about getting in touch with her, but I never did.

    What irks me lately is this total dependence – I either can't or am too mistrustful to do anything myself. I have to depend on someone else for everything, and when this is over I'll be totally dependent – I don't like the feeling of being like this.

I had my second visit in March 1977. My parents drove with the children from North Carolina so it was a big trip and a difficult one emotionally. They would all have problems afterwards, finding themselves unable to concentrate. And no one seemed to understand or know how to help. There was no prisoner family support group. Our story was too embarrassing to reveal, especially with me being on death row. Afterwards my parents would move the family to Los Angeles.

Dear Eric,

I had a great time when you were here – I love you! We had fun. Christina is a good girl – do try to make sure she is safe and doesn't get hurt. That will make me feel very good. You must remember to be very careful on your bike and stuff. You kids are the most precious thing in the whole world to me! Dad told me he had a real nice visit too and he said he gave you lots of kisses and hugs – that's very nice! And he said you played cards and Tina drank her bottle and made a nice poo poo for him! I'm glad you like your [new] school and your teacher. And glad we had such a good talk when you were here. Dad said he had a good talk with you too. We've got a lot of love, all of us! I miss you a lot. I love you sweetheart! Kisses for you and Tina too –

Love and kisses, Mommy

The institution began a series of attempts at pacification, in an effort to get me to drop my lawsuit. They began to allow me limited canteen privileges. I could purchase coffee, creamer and sugar with money deposited in an account for me from outside, and the items would be

153

delivered to me some time later. And I was given permission to receive two plastic containers in which to keep my toilet articles, two scarves, shampoo and conditioner.

Why did I have to file a lawsuit? This set a pattern that would continue for a long time.

My Dearest Jesse,

I found out that tomorrow is the day when everyone is allowed a special visit for Thanksgiving. I'm trying to get your mom cleared. I hope they don't just wait me out – you know, not come to see me until Monday after it's too late.

My counselor came and I ate a couple of lifesavers and then I ordered my canteen and for the third week in a row they were out of everything including stamps – but they will try to get me some from the outside like last week also I just got word that Mr Booth disapproved mom's visits for Saturday.

Now, back to your dynamite letter. That is such a neat setup – the writ room.* We need that here. I'm glad you are able to use it fairly regularly – you stay there a long time too – three hours. I have complete confidence in you honey – keep on truckin' my methodical man. I know you're methodical – very methodical – in the shower, in the car, in the woods, on the rug, from the towel rack, in a

*The writ room is a place reserved for prisoners in which they do legal work, writing writs, etc.

154

swimming pool, through the bars – we manage to be methodical! You are more together than I am. I know that. I feel disoriented and very defensive. I guess it's because I'm not a part of anything – of any society.

Write to Eric even if you wait on the others. He needs contact from us, reassurances and lots of love. I've got my spirits up honey. I can't stay in a down mood for long because when I get your letters each night I'm happy again. I love you with all my heart and soul. I am doing well with your help and love. Don't worry, okay. I tell you every little thought and sometimes I guess I must sound very down but it passes quickly really. For the most part I'm so 'up' that people ask me how I do it! I love you my Jesse, I love you. Until we can be free and together again I'm always with you in your heart.

Love and kisses, Sunny

I found myself struggling to live in my newfound spiritual strength. It was a process in which that 'instant' was just the first step. And it was not a uniform growth process. Some parts of me lagged behind. That wonderful stubbornness that got me through sometimes kept me from moving forward. And yet, just as I had found my own spiritual journey, I had come to realize that we are all souls here on our journey – guards, judges, everyone.

It was a typical morning for me. Alone in the building except for the guard at the other end, lingering in that

155

fuzzy, part-meditative, part-hallucinogenic state between worlds, I brushed my teeth and washed my face holding the cold water button in with the thumb of my right hand, cupping the water to my face with my left. Performing the next part of the ritual, I went to the window. Kneeling on the bed, pressing my face to the glass, I aligned my vision with the window down the hall so I could see the small section of fence out on the south-western perimeter. Today there was more than a bird. Something was going on! There was someone out there, going back and forth through what looked like a hole in the fence! A hole in the fence? That wasn't possible. I held my breath and squinted my eyes. It was definitely a hole! I could see two people, one in uniform and one in a suit. The one in the suit was ducking back and forth through the opening, as if by doing it repeatedly his body would grasp what his mind could not seem to get a grip on. It was a violation of the reality matrix upon which everything else was super-imposed – the inviolability of the fence. But it was definitely real! I laughed out loud. 'Well, I'll be damned! Somebody must have escaped!' I exclaimed to myself. This was not your average escape, which didn't happen often either, where someone jumped the eight-foot, barbed-wire-topped fence or burrowed under it, and got caught hitchhiking down the road. This was a spectacular escape. Somebody had cut the fence.

I couldn't wait for breakfast to arrive, hungry for the morsels of information that would come with the meal. When the guards came down the hall with the cart, I was up and waiting at the door. They were late, but that was to be expected after an escape. It was the nice guard who saved the extra coffee for me. She was talking to the male guard who was with her. I knew she was talking for my sake, so I could hear what was going on. I was always happy to see her.

'So, Officer Jones, any clues where Madelena and her husband went off to?'

'Nope. They say he must have cased the place for the past couple of nights to get the gun truck routine down, and then he went and cut the durn fence, somewhere between 2 and 3 a.m.'

'Didn't he escape from Starke about a week ago?' she added, drawing out his response.

'He's got a lot of balls showin' up here. If they'd of thought for one minute that he would have come for her they could have set up a trap. He must have had some wire cutters.'

There was a kind of admiration in the way they spoke about it, not only because of the guy's ingenuity but because he hadn't just run off and forgotten about his wife.

They were both serving life sentences for murder, but neither had actually killed anybody. They had been in the process of committing an armed robbery when the police came. There was shooting, and a stray bullet hit and killed an innocent bystander. The bullet, it was later determined, had come from one of the police weapons. But, under what is called the felony murder rule, Madelena and her husband were guilty of murder because if they hadn't been committing an armed robbery the shooting would not have happened. Since that was the law in Florida, they were found guilty and sentenced accordingly. It was, as it was told to me, another case where the woman went along with her man and ended up involved in something she would have avoided on her own. She had made her choice. Still, it was sad. How could I judge her harshly when I could see the clear parallel with my own life?

The escape, on the other hand, was delicious! I ate my breakfast with unusual relish that morning. And I wrote all about it to Jesse. I knew if he ever got out he would try to rescue me.

It was something I would both cherish and dread – the thought of being rescued, going on the run, and hiding out in the mountains somewhere. But I wouldn't ever be able to see my children again, or my parents, or my friends.

I put my tray back on the small shelf for the guards to collect when they returned for their hourly check. I wondered how long it would be before Madelena and her husband were caught, or if they would make it out of the country, maybe to Colombia, where Madelena was from. Maybe she shouldn't have gone. Maybe the law would change some day. But her case was different from mine. The truth would set me free one day, I knew it would. It was just taking a lot longer than I had thought. The guard was coming for the tray. As the footsteps faded down the corridor I lay down on my bunk with my thoughts. If Jesse came for me, would I go? That was how this whole thing had started for me in the first place.

My mom's letters kept me part of everything the family

was doing. They were so news-filled. And sometimes I would laugh out loud at her descriptions.

Darling Sonia,

I just came from the dentist. Uncle Joe watched Tina for me in the office while the dentist worked. She was really good. So I'm sitting here like a 'nummy' because I had two shots. I'm okay now, so not to worry. Joe took the kids to Universal and to Disney and last night, Uncle Joe's birthday, we went to Grandma's house and made a birthday party. It was nice. Tina is toilet training very well. She asks to go 'pot' and is dry now when I put her on the seat. Eric does his homework without assistance now. Of course I bribe him with TV shows. I have to leave shortly to be home in time for dinner, so I will send this nutty note.

With love, Mom

12

J ESSE AND I DECIDED to request permission to get married. We had already made our request to the prison officials, who had turned us down. They said our children would get new parents and new names anyway after we died. Now we were asking again.

There were many reasons – some we shared and some were individual. The truth is that Jesse was pushing the idea but I always wanted us to be joined for ever so it suited me as well. He felt it would give us privileges we wouldn't have without legal married status. He wanted more than anything to make Tina legally his and for her to have his name, having been afraid to use his real name on her birth certificate. This fear of using his real name on any document was also the reason we hadn't married. He had wanted to be untraceable. But now there was no reason not to make it official. We had originally asked to be married while on remand in Broward County jail.

It was a difficult time for my family. Once our request became public, it brought back the life-shrivelling notoriety that had so disrupted their lives when Jesse and I were arrested. Now we were further scandalizing everyone by calling attention to the fact that we weren't married, which meant that the children would be stigmatized as illegitimate. My parents had moved to California to get away from the stigma, and now it was raising its ugly head again to taint their new lives. It hadn't occurred to me that our request to marry would affect them adversely.

Dearest Sunny,

Well, you and Jesse made it coast to coast yesterday in all the media. I heard it on radio and it was in most papers (CA, New York, New Jersey). I wish you had let us know what was happening in advance – because to us the whole thing was a total surprise. I don't know what it will accomplish, but Dad had to explain a bit further to Eric so he would know how to reply, if questioned by anyone. Of course our gut feeling is very negative about how all this affects Ray's work on appeal – the psychological effect of the close ties you two have exhibited is not in your best interest. But if this is what you want (and it's all accomplished as far as publicity is concerned) then so be it! Whatever you do, we wish you the best in the world. Just don't jeopardize the appeal – use your common sense and good judgment. Only 'you' are for 'you' because if not 'you' then 'who'? I have said this before so take care, and don't be hasty – think ahead to all possibilities involved and how they affect 'you' and the children – they are mightily concerned and we all want our girl home again.

Love and kisses, Mom

And there was more going on. My dad didn't write to me as often as my mom but he wrote regularly. He didn't give the day-to-day news so much as the overall view and the highlights. He was so hurt by my situation. Sons are expected to get into all sorts of trouble but daughters are supposed to be less notorious. I had always felt more kinship with my dad although I interacted more with my mom. When necessary, my dad wrote about the hard things.

Dear Sonia,

My mother went into the California Villas today. It's really not an old age home. It's very pleasant and it's a pay by the month and it is unusual. Anyway, Grandma Reinie is on her own at 86! And she seems to be enjoying it. She has a nice roommate, and I'm convinced she is actually happier than she has been for the past five years. Yesterday morning Mom heard a news report about you and Jess wanting to get married. Too bad we have to hear things this way. I think it would have been nicer for you to have let us know about it from you. It seems to me that at this time the only thing that can be accomplished is visitation rights and of course this is probably a big plus for you guys, on the other hand the publicity doesn't do any good for the children. I'm so glad that they didn't mention Eric. If you haven't discussed this matter with your lawyer, I'm sure it would be wise [to do so] because it may have considerable bearing on your case. That's about it for now.

Love, Dad

My parents had worked so hard to get the children stabilized and back into the mainstream after their traumatic experiences in Florida. Eric had to be sent to a special school. Tina needed extra attention and nurturing. Mom and Dad were trying so hard to provide a normal life for everyone and now I had brought more notoriety on them. It was as if their identity had been stripped down to that of being the family of the man and woman on death row. It was another old nightmare coming out from under the bed to torment me – being responsible for bringing pain on my family.

February 4, 1977 Friday

Darling Sunny,

There's something new happening every day lately. We now know that Mr. Wainwright* turned thumbs down on the matrimonial ceremony. Let them use proxies by phone, if expense is the excuse and security. The marriage is your legal right if you so desire.

Whatever you do or say to anyone please see that Eric's name is never mentioned, or our exact whereabouts – this would defeat any progress he has made, and certainly make everything more difficult. I know you have little control over this but try.

We received your beautifully written invitation

---

* Mr Wainwright was head of the Department of Corrections, in charge of all the prisons in Florida.

and letter and then had to stop planning when the news came over the air and in local papers as to the refusal by the state. Then we spoke to Kay.

Thanks for all your coupons and clippings. I used the coffee ones already. There are some articles I'd like to send you, but I want to Xerox them first. As for the reporters, when I see something good for a change, then maybe I'll have faith and trust in them. Right now just broken promises and B.S.!! So be diplomatic and cooperative to the degree you see fit – no one has contacted us – hooray – because I will refuse any interview at all. That first one just proved out what my instincts told me. But just maybe it did some good because some people realize how unfair just one side of the picture is and will really start searching for the truth. Remember again you are our one and only concern despite your other loyalties – and you cannot blame us for that. We want you with your babies, where you belong. Don't complicate everything unnecessarily, if possible. We understand your heart – I hope you can use your head. Oh yes, by the way, how come only you and Jesse are the only ones ever mentioned. Whatever happened to Rhodes? It's like no one even remembers – very odd, very odd! And don't let unhappy (rotten hate) mail get you upset. People can only respond to what's fed to them, so really, they can't be blamed. Anyway you can never reason with ignorance. Just keep pitchin' and prayin' and remember some people with reason and faith do exist.

If you need more money write immediately and tell us. One other thing, I am going to try and get permission for Jesse's mom, because I need help with Tina when I visit alone. It will be very rough alone. Maybe Mr. Shepherd in Jacksonville can help out with that. I know we are asking a great deal of him and I love him sight unseen. Take care.

Love and kisses and hugs, Mom

Although the institution had initially turned down our request, the fight had just begun and the issue was now in the court of public opinion, where it was being hotly debated. I was filled with admiration and surprise at my parents' support, especially my mom's. It was dawning on me that she really was on my side! It meant so much to me. I knew it went against what they would have wanted, yet they were with me. And I was surprised at the support we got from some politicians. Maybe I was changing too.

Other people, however, showed a strange attitude towards us. I saved the following article and the coupon attached because I thought no one would believe it. At least they didn't turn it into a weekly game show but at the time it was the equivalent in absurdity.

DEATH ROW WEDDING

The Ledger Opinion, Friday, February 25, 1977 – Earlier this month, Secretary of State Bruce Smathers came out with a strong

165

statement defending the requests of two condemned cop killers for a death row wedding. Jesse Tafero and Sonia Jacobs want to get married to legitimatize the birth of their two year old daughter. 'The marriage,' said Smathers, 'would afford the child a measure of Mercy . . . The state should allow [it], if an hour's ride between Ocala and Raiford can relieve that child of even an ounce of the burden she will carry through life.'

Wainwright's weak rejoinder: if the couple had really been concerned about the legitimacy, they could have married anytime during the 18 months between the conception of the child and their arrest for the murders.

We hope Wainwright changes his mind shortly. But if he doesn't, there's one man who can change his mind for him.

Wainwright reports directly to Gov. Rubin Askew. If Wainwright is to persist in his opposition to the death row wedding, the governor should move to permit the wedding. And may Wainwright be forever branded anti-marriage or worse anti-children.

We invite you to share your opinion with your fellow Polk Countians by using the coupon below. We will compile and report results and print some of the comments, preferably limited to 50 words or less so we might print those of more readers.

( ) I think the death row couple should be allowed to marry.

( ) I am opposed to allowing them to marry.

COMMENT:_____

Signed: _____

Mail to: The Editor, The Ledger, P. O. Box 408, Lakeland, Florida 33802

We were not allowed to marry. After that, Jesse wanted to change the baby's last name to Tafero, but I refused. Having a different last name insulated her from the media. I was determined at this point to at least protect the children.

On 25 March 1977, a month after our marriage request was turned down, I was transported by prison van, in full custodial regalia of shackles and chains, to the federal court in Jacksonville where my civil rights case would be heard. I was so overwhelmed by being outside, in the world again! I found the courthouse intimidating but Bill was there and that made me feel more secure. I would testify for myself this time, as Bill had told me I should. I understood the way things were now. You must always speak up for yourself, even if it is just a few words. I took the stand to testify as to the conditions under which I was being held. I told them I was grateful that they had plugged up the snake holes in Flattop before I arrived, but that my conditions were more restrictive than those of the men. The disparity was obvious. Convenience was not an acceptable reason for not meeting the standard already established on death row.

Bill Shepherd had enlisted the expertise of Natalio Chudnovsky, an eminent psychiatrist.

Dr Chudnovsky said, 'Numerous studies have shown the detrimental effects of sensory deprivation. The clinical symptoms are: anxiety, agitation, insomnia, restlessness, and depression. There have been cases reported in which psychotic symptoms developed as the result of solitary confinement.

'From the information made available about plaintiff's particular conditions of confinement, it seems that solitary confinement is putting this individual in a stressful situation that might lead to severe psychotic damage.

'. . . the almost total lack of human interaction with persons other than her guardians is increasing the risk of psychotic damage.'

Bill Shepherd, with his riveting voice, incisive language and indisputable logic, was brilliant. We won the case, and I was awarded punitive damages of twenty-five dollars for each day of substandard conditions. Bill insisted that a Special Master be appointed to oversee my case because we were aware of a new women's prison being built in South Florida and the possibility of my being transferred. A transfer would remove me from the authority of this court but a Special Master could follow the progress of the case, even after my transfer, to ensure compliance.

I won everything I asked for. But they were slow in giving it to me and then it was done with resentment. I was to remain in Flattop for another three months.

* * *

Whenever I went outside I always thought it was a nice day. But some days were nicer than others.

    This afternoon the superintendent came down to review people in Flattop and I got to stay outside in the yard the whole time. I smoked and walked around and felt more relaxed than usual because I knew I had plenty of time for more than just smoking three cigarettes. And the guard wasn't standing over me constantly so I could get down and smell the clover and stuff without feeling odd. I sat down and did a couple of quick sketches and then the shift changed and dinner came and I thought I might have to go in. But instead, I ate outside! I had my own little picnic out on the grass. I could have eaten at the table but I preferred to sit in the clovers. I had my shoes off and I ate my vegetable and drank ice tea and even had time for a cigarette after my meal – how nice it was!

13

ORF AND HYSMITH. Two prisoners who felt they couldn't just keep quiet after Rhodes confessed to them. They said, in their sworn statements as reported in the media, that Rhodes said he shot the policemen and had to save himself by lying. They quoted Mr Orf as saying that Rhodes told him, 'Hey, man, I had to, no way in the world I thought they would get the chair. If I had of [thought that], I would not have done it, but I had to keep from getting the chair myself.'

Thank you, Great Spirit! Thank you, Universe! I am going home to my children! Jesse and I will be together again soon! I heard it on the news and I received a copy of an article about it too. I am meditating and trying to centre myself before I fly apart in all directions.

In that same month of May 1977, one year after his trial, Jesse received a letter from Walter Rhodes about a copy of a deposition he had given and had sent to Jesse. He said he knew it might not be much consolation but he was sorry. 'It hasn't been entirely my fault. I guess you can understand that from the deposition.' He was ready to go to court to testify and the deposition explained why he had lied previously 'against you (Jesse) and Sonia'. There was a tape that a reporter had, he further explained, detailing the complexities of the situation. He said he wanted Jesse to understand his position, 'now and from the beginning'. He said he wasn't our enemy and there was more to say at a later time, and 'Have Faith,' he concluded provocatively.

Orf and Hysmith were not the only ones who heard Rhodes's statement that day. An investigating officer took the statements of a number of other inmates and guards. A guard named Jowers said that he heard Rhodes bragging about how he killed the policemen. But Officer Jowers's statement was not revealed until years later.

The two inmates did not immediately report what they had heard. They were afraid. They went to another inmate for advice. Jack Murphy, better known as Murph the Surf, was the chaplain's clerk, a born-again ex-jewel thief who had done a lot of time and was well respected as a 'standup' guy. He advised them to do the right thing. They went to the authorities.

Our letters were full of planning and dreaming and believing. Our families were overjoyed. A hearing would surely follow and we would be released.

But no hearing took place. The prosecutor in our case, Michael Satz, was now district attorney. He sent his assistant from the trial, Walter LaGraves, and Rhodes's former defence attorney, Ralph Ray, who was now a prosecutor working for Satz, to talk to Rhodes. Walter Rhodes took back his confession, saying he 'didn't really mean it'. It was a devastating disappointment.

* * *

I was struggling with the length of time that had gone by and the despair of losing touch with my children and my life – the life I had before and the life I wanted to think of as mine, the life I still dreamed of returning to one day. Even with my newly honed spiritual tools I needed more of an outlet for the overgrowth of emotions and frustration and the sense of unfairness that threatened to choke out the 'peace and love' flowers with which I had filled my soul's garden.

> *I have decided to let my milk go. She doesn't need me anymore in that way. I guess it's best. At least she still knows I am her mother.*

My parents wanted to adopt the children. They said they worried about something happening to them. I wouldn't hear of it, but I did send them a letter giving them permission to take them to a hospital or do whatever was necessary in an emergency. I was coming home one day and I was still going to be their mother. I didn't want to give up on the last remnants of my identity from outside.

> *There is only this moment of me, and as I spin in place part of me spins off into the past and part of me spins off into the future.*

Two things were happening to me. I was expanding but I was also shrinking. Jesse and I were still living in a bubble world together, within a construct of our own design, a world that I would sustain for us well beyond the time when I would need it. And it also felt like I had been pushed back to another time when I was just beginning to emerge and I met myself there, waiting.

As a young girl I had decided to paint, like my father. I borrowed paints and brushes and a canvas from him and worked secretly until my painting was completed. She was done all in shades of blue. Head swathed in cloth, you couldn't really distinguish if it was a boy or a girl. The only feature that stood out was the eyes, and if you looked into them you would find me there. I remember feeling so accomplished, so strong and happy after having conceived and completed the painting. I could hardly wait to show it to my dad. When my parents looked at it they both said it was a nice first try. And then my dad said perhaps I could reuse the canvas if I covered it with gesso. He was just being practical, but all I heard was rejection. I was too tentative within myself to withstand the matter-of-factness with which my self-revelation was received. So I never tried to paint again. I would draw cartoons instead. They would like me better as a funny cartoon. The serious little blue child would have to wait – a long time – before I would be ready to reveal her again.

I requested paints and brushes, pastel chalk, art paper and canvas.

I think the need to create is basic to our nature. I no longer have procreation as my outlet and I need a way to express what is inside me – some form of self-expression that feels good to me.

*It's been a long time since the little blue child went
away. And now she is back!*

Weeks went by without any of the changes that the court
had ordered. I continued my own routine of push-ups and
sit-ups and running in place on my blanket. And I
immersed myself in my yoga practice, breathing my way
deeper into the core of my being and letting it tell me
what subtle shifts and changes to make until I could feel
the rush, like an opening and gushing forth all through
my being. Tears would come with the sensation of cracking open, and both spilling out and being filled up. It
made me feel alive!

And then I would meditate. And I would pray – for
Jesse and for our parents and for the children, and sometimes I prayed for the families of the men I only saw in my
mind as dead bodies. I couldn't think of them too much
because it would bring me back to the still maddening
question of 'why?'

The disappointment of the Orf and Hysmith incident
was a huge reality check. So much for my dreams of
getting out any time soon! If the truth could be right there
in front of them, shouting at them, staring them in the
face and they still wouldn't acknowledge it, then on what
could we depend?

I had been trying to understand the legal process that
had been used to put us here. Besides studying the law
books, I had requested a copy of the PSI report that
Sandstrom said the court used for sentencing purposes.
Normally one did not see a Pre-Sentencing Investigation,

even though it is part of the public record. Among other information, it contained letters my friends had sent in about who I was and how I would never have killed anyone. And there were opinions from other people whom I had never met. Most significantly, I found a paper stamped CONFIDENTIAL in big red letters, which turned out to be Walter Rhodes's polygraph test report. It had been hidden away. It should have been given to the defence before trial to be used to impeach Walter Rhodes's testimony, which was contradictory to what the report said. At trial he said I either handed a gun to Jesse or fired it and then handed it to Jesse, but in the polygraph report they said he wasn't sure if I had done anything at all! I called Sandstrom, who was still my appeals attorney at the time, and he said he had no knowledge of it. (Later, I realized he should have had knowledge of it since it was known that prosecutors use polygraph tests to justify giving plea bargains.) Sandstrom requested a Brady violation hearing, which is a hearing based on pertinent evidence having been hidden from the defence. But the prosecutor, now DA, made light of it, saying it wouldn't have made any difference to the outcome, and the court agreed. It was another piece of the puzzle that would wait a long time before being given its proper place in the larger picture.

I needed to see the children – to reassure them and myself that we were still a family. But the institution made it so difficult. I had submitted the usual request for a visit but it was taking an interminable time to get an answer. These visits were too important – for all of us. Finally, I received a memo approving a visit with the children and *both* grandmas! Arrangements were quickly made for visits at both prisons.

My Dearest Jesse,

I just came in from my visit with Mom and the kids! Fantastic! From now on the kids will come alternately so each one will have more time with us. This way there's not enough time to do justice to either of them. And when Eric comes here he wants every minute and I can't blame him. He says, 'It may be three or four months until I see you again Mommy. I want you to play with me and talk to me!' He said he wants to set up a trailer in the yard so he can live here with me (he knows he can't come in the cells). He means it too. 'I want to live with you Mommy,' he said. And this time he called after me when I was taken back inside, 'I don't want to leave you Mommy' and his voice was cracking. Christina didn't want to let go of me and began to cry when I handed her to my mom – and both moms were getting misty. It was a difficult moment. I know it was equally as hard for you, Daddy. I'm so glad we had this visit with our children. We all needed it very much. Jesse – our baby called me 'Mama'! I was so overwhelmed! I know you took some great pictures with the kids. Mom said she sent me some. I tried to get some taken here but I was told that the major 'disapproved' my request. I can't imagine why – except for . . . Well you know how it is, right? So there aren't any pictures of us here this time. I'll have to ask the major why he said 'no' next time I see him. I'm going to close for now with all my love.

Love and kisses, Sunny

When I was growing up and we had an emotional outburst in our family my mom would take me shopping. It was her way of making things better. My dad would sit on the couch next to me and put his feet on me – the closest he could come to displaying affection. Even helping me to buy a car was his way of showing love. I wondered if my mom would take the children shopping after the visit. Coping mechanisms passed down from one generation to the other. She told me she couldn't enjoy shopping like she used to because she was always seeing things she wanted to buy for me that I couldn't have now.

I got a memo saying that since they gave me more comfort items in December, I can't have tissues until they consider giving me any further comfort items in June! So I guess I'll have to ask the judge for Kleenex? Really, just for a few tissues. Oh well, it's amusing in a way.

14

THREE MONTHS AFTER the federal court issued its order to transfer me out of the Flattop, the guards came for me and told me to pack my things. It was very exciting. I fluttered and flew around the little space collecting my belongings, which didn't take very long. It felt as if I was going on a great adventure into a world I had not yet seen, like the night before Christmas vacation.

I finally left the Flattop, once again carrying my small box of precious things over the hill, wondering what they would do with me this time. They escorted me up the hill, past all the dormitories, and into the rear entrance of the hospital, a single-storey L-shaped building. Mr Booth was waiting for me just inside the door. He looked at me with a critical eye, as if appraising artwork in a gallery.

'Take her to the beauty shop for a haircut.' I had no idea how I looked from the outside any more. Although I had my mirror of polished metal, I didn't have a sense of the total picture I presented.

The prison beauty shop was a sensory festival. Complete with bright lights, an array of colours and gadgets, wall-to-wall mirrors – and people! As I inhaled this information overload into my nervous system, the officer in charge led me to one of the padded swivel chairs. I told the operator I just wanted a trim. According to the Kiai-Shu of Zen Buddhism, whose tenets Jesse and I tried to live by, the hair was not to be cut except under special circumstances. But I really needed a trim. In those big wall-to-wall mirrors under the bright lights of the beauty shop, I looked feral, like a wild animal that had just come out of its cave after more than a year. For just a moment the full weight of what had happened to me flashed before my mind. But the excitement and momentum carried me forward as I passed from one stage to another, from darkness into light. The hairdresser leaned me back over the sink so she could wash my hair. She massaged my scalp with her fingertips. I had my eyes closed but I opened them then to look into her face. She smiled back at me and said to close my eyes now while she rinsed the soap from my hair. Then she wrapped my head in a white towel and rubbed it dry briskly.

Her hand on my head felt good as she pulled the comb through my wet hair. I watched very carefully so that she did not snip too much. I honoured the little dead ends as they fell in a small pile on my lap. According to the Kiai-Shu the soul extends to the tips of the hair. At this point, even my soul could use a little trimming. And it would grow back stronger and healthier. My whole being cried out for a little care. Our eyes met in the mirror and we exchanged smiles. She unwrapped the tissue paper from my neck and untied the plastic apron, removing the snippets of hair with a soft-bristled brush. I thanked her. She just stood there, hands folded in front of her, twinkling like the haircut fairy. As the guard escorted me out, I turned to wave goodbye. All faces were turned towards me, and they were all smiling. I felt very good. Now I was ready to see my new home. The superintendent was waiting. He turned and proceeded down the hall in front of us. It made me feel regal somehow, like the man in the iron mask. He stopped in front of one of the closed doors, took out a key and opened it.

It was a converted storage closet. It had been divided in half with a heavy mesh grating. The door, made of the same mesh grating, had a large solid lock. He opened the mesh gate, and with a motion of his arm invited me to step in. I took a quick look behind me to make sure that the guard was still following with my box of possessions.

'Thank you,' I said as I stepped past him into what was plainly my cage. It reminded me of the times when I was a little girl and I used to play inside the radiator cover. I used to pretend I was a wild animal, a lion or tiger perhaps, locked in my cage. There was a window on the back wall that looked down on a walkway. I would be able to see people. And there was a desk and a chair – a touch of civilization. This would be nice. The bed, of course, was just another metal shelf. I was used to that by now. The desk and chair were much needed and welcome.

'Is there anything you need?' The superintendent was standing in the doorway with one hand on his hip. It was as close to an attitude as I had ever seen him adopt.

'I don't see any towels. I'll need a couple of towels and a washcloth.'

He nodded in the direction of the guard at the door

to the hallway. It would be taken care of, I knew. I surveyed the room once more, coming around 360 degrees to see the mesh gate closing. Still separated, I would now live in the centre of a world I had only glimpsed until now.

The superintendent stepped out of the light of the doorway, to be replaced by the face of the guard, who pulled the door shut, sealing out the light from the hall. It was then that I noticed that the light in the room could only be controlled by a switch just outside the doorway, beyond my reach. But there was plenty of light coming in through the window. Through it, I could watch the world. I got my paper and pen, and sat at the desk.

> My Dearest Jesse,
> I love you. I am writing to you from my new desk in the hospital confinement section. They moved me this morning . . .

I would get walks on the compound now, and showers every day. They would take me into the next cell, another converted closet, where a shower had been constructed. Showers would no longer be so strictly timed and I would get to dry off in private before coming out.

I discovered I had a neighbour in the cell next door. Her name was Lara. She was in for killing her child, a little girl. Normally, they said, Lara was a pussycat, quiet, easy-going and never a problem to anyone, but every year at the time of the crime she would lose it, going into a full-blown psychotic episode. This time she had freaked out in the dining hall, screaming and throwing herself and her food on the ground. They had carried her down here and locked her up. They said it had taken five men to subdue her.

'Shower time, Jacobs!'

'OK. I'll be ready in a minute.'

The guard waited outside the closet door while I gathered my shower articles and got undressed. I went to the shower in my robe and flipflops, carrying my towel, soap, washcloth, shampoo and conditioner. I had been allowed a partial package-from-home of plastic containers and hygiene items, but the superintendent was still holding out on giving me the regular permit to order things. It was such a pleasure to have decent soap and conditioner. Maybe now my hair would stop falling out so much. The walks would help too.

'I'm ready!'

The guard opened the door. 'Remember not to get too close to Lara. If she gets her hands on you she could easily kill you before we could get her off you.'

The door closed and locked behind me. In front of me was a small, round-faced woman with curly dark hair staring at me through the grating with the saddest dark eyes I had ever seen. She had her fingers wound through the holes in the mesh, and when I waved to her she wiggled them slightly. I held up one finger and put it to my lips. Placing my shower articles on the floor near the wall, I figured out how to turn on the shower so that we could talk behind the sound of it, like a waterfall.

'Hi. My name's Sonia. I live next door now. I'll be

coming in here every day for a shower. I'm not supposed to be talking to you, but we can talk, if you like, while the shower's running and they won't be able to hear us.'

There was no response, just the staring. Maybe she was catatonic? I turned to get in the shower.

'My . . . my name is Lara.'

'Nice to meet you,' I said from around the corner of the shower wall. Well, all right! Someone to talk to – for both of us. The shower was great. It had a better shower-head and stronger pressure so that my skin tingled with pleasure. I took a very long shower.

Now I would be able to receive boxes from home! And they said I would get a special permit for art supplies to come directly from an art store. Jesse told his mom what to get for me. He would give me lessons in our letters and I was glad to have something else we could do together. The paints and brushes and pastel chalks added colour to my world, although I retained a preference for the clean simplicity of black and white, finding Japanese Sumi-e ink paints most satisfying. It was like a Zen practice – mixing the ink stick and water on a stone, all the while meditating on the exact strokes it would take to produce the finished drawing on rice paper. Jesse would tell me about a practice of walking on rice paper while meditating that I would do daily as part of my personal routine. I painted for the children and for Jesse and for myself. I painted for my nephew and did a couple of self-portraits as well. And I painted the things of my world that pleased me – nothing political or dark. The paint represented joy to me. Colour and life!

I started a pastel of the beautiful food page I had used when I ate behind the door in my first cell.

That painting was my first full-sized work with pastels. The picture had given me such pleasure and that went into every stroke. In the end, I could practically smell the food cooking! I sent it out to my parents. They had it framed and hung it in their kitchen. It made me feel like I was with them at mealtimes at least.

Even though my cell had been upgraded from dungeon to broom closet, I was still in solitary confinement. Lara was my neighbour only for a short while – not that it mattered because she was catatonic the whole time. But I was now getting four hourly walks outside each week, although it was during work hours, which meant that most of the inmates were occupied at their jobs.

My Dearest Jesse,
I love you. It's another hot day. This heat has a way of taking one's incentive away – makes you feel lazy. At least here by myself I don't have to suffer the conglomerate scents of 15 or 20 others. I think I'll do some painting today during the daylight hours. I've put in a request to be allowed to go to the horticulture area where they grow all sorts of plants and flowers so I can spend one of my walk hours painting them. They have one of those great sunflowers outside and it's a beauty! I did another pastel last night. I'd like it if I could have someone to work

from – I mean someone to use for a model besides myself – maybe somebody black so I could see how to do different skin tones than my own. I really like your shower night letters. They, to put it plainly, 'turn me on' heavily. If we could be cell partners all this wouldn't be so bad at all.

At my team meeting today it was mentioned that I write books to you every day. It looks like our letters – at least mine, are famous around here. When I think of some of the intimate sexually tinged words of endearment that I have penned to you in these letters – well, I don't care who knows it – Good night my dearest one. I love you with all my heart and soul.

Love and kisses, Sunny

My 'team' was composed of my counsellor and the regular daytime guard and someone from the administration, the assistant superintendent usually. I don't remember much about the team except that they were supposed to evaluate my conditions on a regular basis. It was in the rules. They told me I would have to write shorter letters or fewer ones. Jesse and I devised a coded way of saying special things. We used *The Rubaiyat of Omar Khayyam* as our code book since we both had access to it. And later on we would do our lovemaking in Japanese.

Next Day

My Dearest Jesse,
An officer came down today and when he saw my

paintings on the walls of the cell he said that it's not allowed and I'd probably have to take them down. He said, 'Is Jesse allowed to hang pictures on his walls up there?' I said I think so but that's not why I do it too. Anyway I wasn't sure if you could or not but that has no bearing. I put them up because they please me and no one to date has said I couldn't. I will miss them if I have to take them down but I lived in here with bare walls before.

I love you Jesse, with all my heart and soul.

Love and kisses, Sunny

I tried to keep to my new and healthy routine. I exercised my body and my brain regularly, and I laughed and cried regularly too – emotional exercises to relieve the pressure that built up every day. It didn't get easier, but it did become familiar. At least it meant I was alive inside!

> *So far I have been locked up for one year and two months. It feels like I am living another lifetime, and yet in some ways it feels like just yesterday that I was with Jesse and the kids. I have a watch now – court ordered – but I only use it to time my walks to make sure I get every minute. Other than that it is simply an instrument of torture – self-flagellation with those tiny hands.*

'You have a visitor.'

I was dressed already because in my new cage I was allowed to keep my clothes and was required to be dressed during the day. I ran a brush through my hair quickly and checked to see if anything needed to be put away. The fact that this visitor received a formal announcement was unusual.

The door opened and a man with a Bible walked in without the usual awkwardness with which my visitors would enter the world beyond the closet door.

'Hi! My name is Frank Cosantino. I figure you were expecting me.' He smiled and then turned to the guard. 'Have you got something for me to sit on here?'

The superintendent spoke from the doorway, telling the guard to bring Mr Cosantino a chair. I hadn't noticed him there before. I smiled, to myself first and then to my visitor.

At the time, I had no idea of the difficulty Frank Cosantino had had in getting permission to see me. He had called in a number of favours from people in high places. He told me about how he had done time with Jesse and given his life over to a higher power, 'turned his life around' as he put it. He said he was doing prison ministry with his wife Bunny, who had waited for him. He was respected now on both sides of the fence and that was essential to being able to do the work, he said with some gravity.

I was comfortable with Frank from the first moment. His tough-guy exterior and gravelly voice were charmingly juxtaposed with the sweet sincerity underneath. He told me not to worry about Jesse and he told me of miracles, his included, and assured me that they do happen and could happen for me. 'Faith was the key,' he said.

'I don't want to stay too long . . . don't want to give them an excuse to say no the next time. Keep your chin up, kid. I'll be seein' ya.' He picked up his chair, carrying it with him to the door. At his knock, the door opened. He turned and smiled, then stepped through the doorway. I wondered if they would allow him to leave the Bible he brought for me. What a funny angel he made, not like you would imagine – but God does work in mysterious ways.

I had more than one Bible by now. Religious people always brought Bibles. If you wanted to you could have a stack of them! And they'd all be written differently. I used to compare them. I wanted the one Frank brought in particularly though because it was a gift from a new friend.

March 27, 1977

My Dearest Jesse,

I saw Mr. Cosantino who seems a very nice fellow. He could only stay for about 15 minutes but I think his ministry will be more beneficial than what I've had so far.

Mail came and I got your No. 66 and No. 67 letters. I had to laugh at your play on words – *'They are in for a big shock, not us!'* By the way, the Swedes will be here for the Supreme Court review. The guy really has stirred up good positive feelings for us. No one else has. Jesse, you are in my every thought – I love you. Dream beautiful dreams – dream of us – in a bathtub, on a couch, almost anywhere!

Love and kisses, Sunny

A Swedish reporter had come to see me when I was in the Flattop. Arne Lemberg and his partner, Haase Persson, a photographer, did an extensive interview and wrote a very sympathetic series of articles about me. Arne Lemberg followed the progress of my case and would continue writing articles that I wouldn't know about for many years. It seemed that the only decent press I could get was in another country. He kept his promise and sent me copies of the photographs. I decided not to give any more interviews in the US because they always lied to me about how they would present my side of things. I didn't even have to read an article to know how it would be. All I had to do was look at the picture or the headline – a mugshot-style photo that made me look crazy or mean and a title of 'cop-killer' were enough to warn me that the content of the article wasn't good.

March 28, 1977

My Dearest Jesse,
It's been pretty chilly at night lately. I hope you are warm enough since it's damp down there. I guess it's like here – the ground is right under the floor and with the cold and cement, it does get a bit damp but I guess I'm used to it and I wear my 'flip flops' and a sweatshirt and socks when it's cold. I'm okay – very adaptable. I hope you have hot dreams and I hope I'm what heats them up – and you. Good night with all my love and kisses and hugs and licks and small bites and little noises.
    Love and kisses, Sunny

My family was still struggling to escape from the shame and pain of our notoriety. It was hard on them but they made it work as best they could, although, ultimately, the move to California would prove unsustainable.

March 31, 1977
California

Darling Sunny,

Dad had to go back to NC to train a new salesman. So, look who's running the whole shebang out here – lil' ol' me – oy vey! At least when you come home, we'll have someone capable around – I'll put you right to work as top salesperson! We'll discuss salary when the time comes, okay? I know all this sounds silly now, but I have every hope the day will come.

Tina is so funny. She has to say hi to everyone who calls and gives kiss sounds into the phone and then says 'bye bye.' Eric plays catch with a large ball during recreation in school. His principal has promised to take him to a ballgame one day. He feels Eric will have more rapport with the kids when he is more proficient in athletics. He is a good boy – just needs pushing and encouragement.

Well, back to work. Stay cool and remember you have many friends watching out for your welfare.

Patience and I love you, Mom

Whenever anything came up in the courts or in the news that related to our case, the media latched on to it and the requests for interviews came pouring in. I had already developed what I considered a healthy distrust of the media. But occasionally I would use it as an opportunity to get my own message across – a look and a wave to Jesse, a statement about our innocence and our struggle, along with a comment about whatever the incident was that had brought them to see me in the first place.

April 6, 1977

My Dearest Jesse,

I Love You

I'm in the yard! It's beautiful out and I brought my papers out so I could sit at the table and work. I made a flower out of orange paper and pinned it in my hair so I would feel pleasant – and I do! I wanted to write to you now because I started a miserable letter to you this morning . . .

I just came in from my interview with channel four. It's going to be on tonight and I hope you'll see it. I wore my flower in my hair! I hope it didn't look silly. It's the style now, you know – but made of cloth not paper.

I love you so much Jesse! It's just beyond all comprehension. I thrive on it – we are so completely together that the pureness alone is too great a force for anyone to reckon with. I really like the picture you sent me. You look so good! And my Mr J. is saying hello to me! . . .

One night all the lights went out! They stayed that way

until almost midnight. The gun trucks were practically bumping into each other patrolling in between the fences – going in two directions at once and meeting in the middle with hardly room enough to pass. I could hear metal against metal when they squeezed by each other. They came by every five minutes. I guess it made everyone nervous when the whole compound went dark – and no moon either. It was a nice change – so dark and quiet. It is true that people get quiet in the dark. I found the incident exhilarating. My senses were stretched and sharpened and my imagination took me beyond the walls and fences stealthily into the darkness.

April 11, 1977

My Dearest Jesse,

I am so glad you saw me on TV! I was hoping you would! I had you in mind when I did it! You knew it too – I wore the flower especially for you! I'm happy that I got to groove you from far away! That makes me feel very good!

I love you! My wisdom teeth are taking turns moving around inside my jaw. No big deal. I'll get them pulled when we're on the outside again. I found a yoga position I can't do! I can hardly get out of it once both hands are stuck! I thought I had actually trapped myself once! You're laughing! I did too. It was funny – a human knot! Oh Jesse – I love you. I hope I will get some mail from you tonight.

I think we will be married soon. I have

confidence in your efforts and in human kindness, hidden though it may be at times. We won't be apart long – anyway, we are forever – what's a few months of forever! Good night my love –

Love and kisses, Sunny

But a few months was like for ever – even the hours could become for ever if you didn't do something to stave off the tedium that could steal your will. I still kept to my daily routine – yoga, meditation, callisthenics, reading, studying, trying to understand the language in the law books. And I wrote letters and journals. I wrote like most people use the telephone, when they need someone to talk to, so they won't feel so isolated and alone with their thoughts. Boredom could be deadly in a world of only one. I had promised myself not to let that happen. I wasn't going to become one of those who mutilated themselves just to relieve the sameness of days.

May 29, 1977

My Dearest Eric –

I love you! I can't wait to see you! I was reading the newspaper and I tore out these coupons for you – the M&Ms one is for Tina, the coffee is for Grandma. I know you'll be surprised to see the sausage coupon but I figured that if you could go to the store for my cigarettes (PU) then once in a while I could contribute to your PU too Ha Ha. I sent a coupon for cousin Danny's candy in a separate letter. All the ones in here are yours – I love you sweetheart and I love Tina too.

Love and kisses, Mom

Eric saved all the coupons. They were still in the envelope with the letter years later.

I was determined that we should all remain a part of each other's lives. I was so determined because I was standing solidly on the belief that we would all be together again some day. More than that, I knew that barely one step away lay the abyss of hopelessness and helplessness that could swallow us up one by one. Deep down, I was struggling with the fear that I would be lost. I, me, the one I used to be – the one whose nightmare had come from under the bed to cast a shadow over her entire being – I was going to hold on to any and every shred of connection that I could.

June 1977

Mr. Booth

I would like to speak to you about the few problems I'm having in my new quarters. The main one is that I have no way of calling the guard when I need assistance between checks. They cannot hear me when they are way down at the other end of the hall. I suggest a buzzer of some sort for that purpose.

Also I think that everyone should knock before they peep their head in to see if I'm on the John – not while they knock be looking in already.

I also want to clarify this inmate visitation set up.

Also my sink button. It sticks and runs for 15 or 20 minutes, sometimes longer, and then cuts off. It is very distressing to have to listen to the water running, hoping it won't overflow. I informed my guard about it and he says it's been that way and can't be fixed. I am sure that with all the training the state puts in to its plumbers that a problem like a sticky sink button is not impossible for them.

It's not all bad. I do appreciate the brightness of the cell and being able to smoke, and my desk and chair, and my daily walks around the compound very much. But I'd like to smooth out the problems that do exist as soon as possible to avoid any aggravation in the future.

Thank you,
Sonia Jacobs FO4015

In June 1977 the local press reported that there was to be an execution in Utah of a man named Gary Gilmore. They were ghoulishly speculating whether or not it would hasten my own date with death. To make matters worse, Gilmore had opted to die by refusing to appeal his sentence. The vultures sensed another story and once again I was inundated with requests for interviews – 'Just give a statement!' I don't remember giving any. I didn't think he should just give up; it was like committing suicide. But I could understand his need for dignity as well. Jesse would know a number of men who would commit suicide on the row, usually by saving up medication. I hadn't really thought much about the death penalty in general – only how it related to me and Jesse. But it seemed, as I thought about it now, to be such a useless gesture, pandering to our lowest instincts – and the mentality behind it was so blood-chilling, more so than that of the murderer for passion or even for profit. Those people are not rational. But the death penalty was supposedly carried out by sane and rational men and women who believed in the value of human life above all else. I wondered about Gary Gilmore's family and how they would feel about his giving up, and how it would affect them.

15

I CAN'T REMEMBER HOW I found out Jesse was cheating on
me. Somehow he had found a way to have an affair on
death row. He was so resourceful. Actually, he had a
number of girlfriends while he was on the row, although
not all of them were physical. Most were pen pals and had
a relationship at a distance – some were legitimate friend-
pals but many sent photos of themselves, trying to look
seductive and initiate a sort of fantasy relationship. Two or
three of the really caring ones came to visit him. There was
one, towards the end, who used to come down from New
York regularly and contributed a good sum of money to
his defence fund. But the one I found out about was a real
live fourteen-year-old niece to one of the other men. That
was how they met, in the visiting park.

The death row visiting park for the men at Florida
State Prison had rows of small tables with benches
attached. There was no air conditioning. Fans and guards
were placed strategically around the room. It got un-
bearably hot. There were soda and snack machines along
the walls and visitors were allowed to get up and
mingle on their way to and from the machines, so they all
got to know each other.

The girl was coming in to visit her uncle. He was a friend of Jesse's, the one we referred to as 'the teacher'. They had done time together before, and their families had become friendly as well. She was in the heavy make-up and nail polish stage of her life. She was cute and she was ripe and she thought Jesse was very attractive. And Jesse was Jesse.

My Dearest Jesse,
Someday I will discuss this with you in person but I feel like telling you about it now. I know you love me but that is not enough. I have had a long time to think about myself, about you, about us, about the time I wasted when you were away and the needless pain I went through by cutting myself off from having any sort of meaningful relationships with anyone for fear of upsetting you. You brought disrespect to me and, in doing so, yourself. Having a totally faithful and devoted woman brings you respect. It only brings me respect if it is reciprocated. You must consider at this time, that I have now had an experience which has made me painfully aware of the senselessness of wasting the precious time one has to enjoy living and I could never again allow myself to be in a position where I was wasting myself – in order for someone else to have meaningless, frivolous, unnecessary pleasures at my expense. You had me living through you

198

and that is stifling. I must grow too. I have gone the whole way for you and I cannot accept less from you now, in any way. It would just make it all pointless if it weren't totally reciprocal and I must know if it is.

Just writing this has made me feel a little better. I can only say I will never again be a shadow. I'll probably see you and talk to you before you ever see this letter, if you ever do. I love you more than anything and I need and want you so much it's driving me to my emotional limits – and if I don't get with you soon I'm going to explode!

Although I never sent that letter, I was wrestling with the core issues that had kept me imprisoned inside myself long before death row. And I was taking the first painful, tentative steps across the chasm that separated me from who I had been and who I was becoming.

I fell into a deep depression. It became difficult to focus on anything. I was shaken to a level that couldn't be expressed in words or accessed intellectually. I wanted to actually be a good person and not just be called a good person. I wanted to believe in something. I was filled with passion and wanted it to count for something. And here I was, on death row, beginning to realize that I had wasted everything. It was my own mortality, the best teacher of all, confronting me with having wasted so much of my life on a dream. It is fine to have dreams, even essential perhaps, but you cannot live in your dreams. Reality is all we really have in our day-to-day existence. It was funny that I had come to see that you couldn't count on Man or Man's law, yet in my personal life I still hadn't put the pieces together. I was still puzzling over my dependence on Jesse. I guess I was still living for the dream. But reality was pressing in on me from all sides and my survival instinct was beginning to take over.

They say that justice is blind. They say that love is blind. They say that we must have blind faith. The blind being led by the blind. For me, it is time to open up my eyes.

This letter I did send.

My Dearest Jesse,

I love you. I got your Thursday letter and was pleased to hear you had a good visit. I'm not going to write much right now because my pen would surely burn holes in the paper! Besides that, I'd hoped for pictures of you but perhaps there were only enough for your adolescent friend. You have been my only haven of peace, the only thing in the whole world that I didn't have to wonder about. You have taken that away, damn it! It cannot be possible that I am the only one who stands firm with no exception. Jesse – tell me the problem is no longer. It's different in here than it was out there – you above all people should know that. I can't

200

handle that sort of thing here. If you only knew what this has done . . . You, this whole unnecessary problem, have turned my cell truly into a cell – a miserable, hopeless place where people sit and watch their insides shrivel up. Not this person though – not me. Perhaps under different circumstances what you are doing would seem trivial. But it is not trivial now when I am helpless. I want to cry. But I have my own inner strength and can stand alone as well. Right now I'm sad – sadder than I've been since I got here. I can't say more.

I love you as I always have from the inside out.

Love and kisses, Sunny

Jesse's response was defensive. He tried to make me think I was being short-sighted and petty, losing sight of what was most important – us. I wanted to believe it but, once again, my survival instinct wouldn't let me any more. Body and mind were deferring to spirit these days. I was finding my own personal path, the one that had burned within me when I was a teenager, before I thought anything else was more important. The struggle to be loved was coming into serious question now.

Family visits in the new cage were better than they had been in the Flattop. We were allowed the use of the regular visiting park. Of course my visits had to be during the week so as not to interfere with the regularly scheduled visiting hours for the general population, which were on weekends. The visiting park was a large room full of tables and chairs and there were soda and candy and snack machines. There was also an outside fenced-in area to walk around in with your visitors, and swings for the children.

My whole family came to visit – my parents and children, my brother and my uncle Joe, and Jesse's mom too. It was really too much for me. I stayed on overload for a week or two after a visit. I felt really full afterwards, although I didn't feel I had spent enough time with any one of them.

Uncle Joe had flown in from New Jersey and was staying with my parents and the children. Kay would spend the evening with them and go on to visit Jesse the next day. My brother, Al, would meet up with some of his old friends, one of whom was a pilot. After the second day of visiting, my brother and his friends buzzed the prison in a small plane. They swooped down so close to the top of my building that the windows rattled. The entire place went on general alert, guards running everywhere. I suppose they thought it was some sort of escape plan. I laughed to myself, knowing it was just Al's way of giving me a thrill. My incarceration was hard for him. Fortunately they didn't hang around for a second pass and I didn't get in any trouble.

I was allowed a daily pilgrimage now. My first stop was the library and I finally got to meet the library clerk who had been sending me the books. She was so happy to meet me and asked if I'd liked the books she had chosen. And I got to ask how she made her selections.

'Oh, well, you see, I knew you could only have two books a week so I picked the biggest, thickest books I could find.'

I said I appreciated them very much.

We promenaded around the circular walkway, my escort and I, smiling and waving at people, until it was time to go in. The rule was that no one was allowed to speak or gesture to me, but sometimes the guard made an exception. And so I began meeting people on my walks. I was able to put faces to the voices and the stories I had heard from beyond the door. It turned out that Judy, one of the more infamous prisoners, who once escaped briefly, was doing my laundry. And Louise, her girlfriend, was doing the ironing and folding and delivering to Flattop. Judy was a handsome, strong young woman with short dark hair and beautiful white skin. Louise was small-boned with pointy features, like a mouse.

I spent only two or three months in the new cage, not long enough for it to get old. I was receiving the mandated four hours a week of walks and visits with my peers, which meant other inmates from population. The institution chose a couple of women to visit with me at my cell. This was done to match the four hours of 'tables' that the men got – a time spent out of their cells playing cards or chess. One of my visitors was teaching me how to crochet. The men were allowed to crochet Afghans that they could keep on their beds or sell through the visiting park. I was making a puppet.

I kept the same hours as I had in the Flattop. I stayed up late writing, reading, thinking. One night about 10 the door opened and the superintendent walked in, wearing a casual shirt and a pair of shorts.

'Get it all, Jacobs. You're being transported tonight.'

'Now?'

'Now. The paperwork just came in. I'll help you pack.'

'Now?' It seemed to be all I could say.

So at ten at night the superintendent and I packed my belongings into boxes. Everything that belonged to the state would remain behind except the dress I would be wearing for the trip. He held up my hairbrush in disgust. 'I can tell this is yours. You ought to clean the hairs out of it.' My hair was still coming out. Even though I was getting more fresh air and sunshine I had taken to wearing a scarf so that people wouldn't see how thin my hair was. It would become my trademark for the rest of my time on death row.

When we had finished packing, the superintendent called the guard in to carry the boxes to a car that was waiting outside to take me to my new home. It was called Broward Correctional Institution for Women although it was originally built for men, complete with urinals. I was being moved so as to better comply with the federal court order concerning my conditions. We were escorted through each county by the local sheriff's car, sometimes two or three cars. Like on the ride to FCI from jail, they didn't let speed limits slow them down. They said the ride would take approximately seven hours, but we made it in six.

16

August 1977

*B*ROWARD CORRECTIONAL INSTITUTION, *BCI, is located at the edge of the Everglades swampland. There are no street-lights. It sits there glowing like a UFO in the vast, black emptiness. An eerie glow from the grid of greenish crime lights shining through the web of thick, wet swamp-fog created a globe effect which extended out into the darkness all around to complete the extraterrestrial image. This other-worldly image seems to surround prisons – and it is really quite appropriate because you are entering another world.*

It was approximately 4.30 a.m. We pulled up to the front doors. I was taken from the car in my shackles and chains and escorted into the lobby in silence. There was a long stairway going up to the right and a glass-enclosed control room like a fishbowl where the UFO pilots sat to regulate the opening between the dimensions. As we approached the control room, I tried to ascertain a re-action on the faces of the controllers. There was none, except for some button pushing and what must have been an announcement of my arrival on the microphone. The officers with me placed their paperwork and their weapons in a metal drawer that slid out under the observation window. The welcoming committee showed up almost immediately. They came from somewhere within the building on the other side of a set of sliding steel and glass doors controlled from inside the fishbowl. There was a sergeant in a uniform so tight it looked painted on, and another male officer.

'Can we remove the shackles now?' I asked in a quiet voice. They looked at each other for a moment and the female officer got out her handcuff key and told me to sit in one of the stuffed chairs. I preferred to enter this phase of my journey without the chains.

With the chains off now, we approached the sliding door. The sergeant appeared framed in the window on the other side, like some sort of military portrait. There was a loud, teeth-gritting buzz and the sliding door on the lobby side began to open.

'Step into the sallyport.' I was herded into the space between the doors. I wondered why they called it the sally-port but stored the question for later. The door slid shut behind us. I was in survival mode. It was a state of mind that seemed to emerge of its own accord. I lost the sense of my body. I was a huge multi-sensory organ, like an energy-amoeba. Observe, evaluate and respond. The door on the facing side slid open and I entered the inner dimension beyond. The sergeant introduced himself to my escort and told them to bring me along. Non-person FO4015.

There was an elevator directly behind the sergeant. He pushed the button and shortly the door opened and we stepped in as a group. It climbed slowly but I could feel the time-lag effect in my stomach. It was a long time since

I had been in an elevator. It almost made me smile. The door opened on to what was obviously the medical department.

It was a waiting area of some sort. We turned the corner and began walking down a long fluorescent-lit hallway. The walls were white. The floor was white. Even the ceiling was white – walking down the tunnel of white light felt like a near-death experience. Casting a sideward glance at my escort, I wondered if they thought of it like that, but I supposed not. They didn't show any signs of whatever they might have been thinking. Blank faces, like the walls. But I could sense their feelings in a general way. The sergeant was hostile. The one with him seemed more curious. The ones who had come with me were ready to leave. I thought they were coming along just to see what the new death row section looked like. We passed what appeared to be a hospital ward but it was empty. I got a sense of emptiness about this whole place.

We reached the end of the corridor of light. On the right a double doorway was chained and padlocked shut. The sergeant lifted the big round brass ring from his waistband and selected the proper key. We entered an alcove about six feet square with two doors on each side and a closet and sink facing us. The sergeant walked ahead to the second door on the left, selected another key, and opened the lock. Holding the door open, he looked at me. I looked to my left and then to my right at the two officers who had come with me thus far.

This is where we part. They say nothing. OK. Let's see what my new room looks like.

I stepped over the threshold. The two officers who had accompanied me filled the doorway behind me. They took a look and then without a word they left. I turned towards the sergeant. I was all his now. He took a breath that swelled his chest and said they hadn't been expecting me so I'd have to make do as I was till morning. They hadn't got any comfort items – no pyjamas, no robe, not even a change of underwear. There was no towel with which to shower; no toothbrush. I would have to sleep in the clothes I came in, with the dirt from the trip still clinging to my body. There wasn't even any bedding. OK, so I didn't have to wonder about how I was going to be treated here.

'Could I have one of those paper cups the nurses use for medication? At least I can use it to drink from until this gets straightened out.'

The sergeant in the painted-on uniform with the steel-grey military haircut looked at me with undisguised disgust. He was definitely going to be a problem. He told me I'd get what I needed in the morning. I was not in a position to argue. The entire building seemed to be deserted except for me. It gave me the creeps being so isolated. I wondered if they had some new version of the Creech tank hidden nearby. He left and I turned my attention to my new surroundings.

The room was far larger than the other two cells I had occupied in my life on death row. And I had my own washing facilities – a toilet and a shower in a separate bathroom! This was good. The sink was in the far right-hand corner of the room with a very skinny window next to it. There was a hospital-style bed on the right as you came in the door. I was in Room 2. There were four rooms in this section of the building but the others were empty. Above the head of the bed was a bright fluorescent light in a casing, with the switch on the wall next to the door. That was good. At least I could control the lights. The two windows were very narrow and appeared to be the type you opened with a crank, except there was no crank. The walls were the usual white. The door was a heavy metal affair, like the one in my first cell in the Flattop, but this one didn't have a slot in it for the food tray. I guessed they would have to open the cage to feed the lions here. I wondered when they served breakfast. I was getting a little hungry now that I thought about it.

The bed was nice! It even had a bit of bounce – more than a metal shelf would. It was a definite improvement and so was the size of the room and the private bath. I'd just have to find a way to deal with the sergeant. Meanwhile, I might as well enjoy the bed and take a rest until someone came in the morning.

At about 6.30 my door was opened and I got my first glimpse of the superintendent of this place. His name was Sorensen. He was a big, heavy-set man with white hair and a gentle face. How interesting. He asked me how I was doing. How was the trip down here? Did I need anything? I told him about them not being ready for me and a dark cloud passed over the warm open face of a moment ago.

'Who told you that?'

I told him about the sergeant and how they didn't have anything for me. He said he would take care of it

209

personally, sending the nurse who was with him scurrying off to find me some sheets and pjs and a robe and some soap and stuff. He really seemed upset and I thought he might be an OK guy. That would be lucky, so I decided I couldn't count on it. I thanked him and he said he would be back later, and would try to come by to see me every day.

'Is there anything else you need?'

'A phone call. I'd like to call my family to let them know I am here and give them the address and telephone number. And I'd like to call my lawyer too.'

'We'll arrange for you to use the phone.'

I thanked him again. The nurse came back in with a stack of the requested items. I was starting to think this might be all right. A pleasant surprise. I sorted out the items she left on my bed. First thing was the toothbrush and toothpaste. It was Colgate – the official toothpaste of the Florida Correctional System. First, a good tooth brushing, and then I would take a nice hot shower. I thought I was going to like this place a whole lot better. I was certainly moving up in the underworld. My own shower, a decent superintendent and a real bed!

❧ *Broward Correctional Institution*

I am settling in to a routine in my new surroundings. They haven't started giving me my walks on a regular basis yet but I have been to the law library a couple of times. It is an unbelievable resource. I don't know how to use it yet but Judy, the girl from FCI who used to do my laundry, is the law clerk here and she has promised to teach me.

Meanwhile, I am able to select three books at a time from the regular part of the library and I can order books from the outside library too. My meals are still taken in my room but here they open the door to give me the tray. It is solid metal – no more slot to pass through. A nurse and two guards are present for the process. I must have been very important to have an honour guard for every meal.

But the food is still cold – some things never change.

Mr Sorensen visits me daily. He is a genuinely nice man – a gentleman. I cannot imagine how he is able to work within the system. He told me he started as a counsellor. He never was part of the security staff. That partly explains it. He is going to set up calls between Jesse and me, once a month. That will be great!

I haven't heard Jesse's voice since court in August of 1976. I miss him terribly. I wish we could take a shower together. That used to be one of our favourite things.

I continue my old routine of staying up until 2 a.m. and sleeping late in the morning. I still get counted every hour but since that is done 'on the hour' it is easy to anticipate and I paint the proper portrait at the proper time.

I like to take my shower after the 2 a.m. count. The bathroom is a really nice little space. I turn off the light, put my washcloth over the drain

and run the water until it is like a shallow soaking
pool. I bring a book in there, something to drink,
and just kick back and enjoy the peacefulness.

I had been alone for a little over a year when I arrived at BCI. As before, I would have the occasional neighbour but for the most part I lived alone in the locked area of BCI hospital confinement. My only regular companions were the ants. They came in through the crack under the window. Though the window itself was meant to stay closed, you could open it with a toenail clipper in an emergency. But ants are so persistent. We could all take a lesson from them. I enjoyed watching their industry. The only problem with having ants for pets is that they get in everything.

I watched how they worked, how they would scout out an area and then retrace their steps back to the group to share the information. They would gather round in a circle to touch antennae. And when they found a crumb or the body of another ant or anything they could use, they would carry it off, no matter how much larger or heavier it was than they were. I noticed they would avoid water. Rather than treat them as pests, I decided there had to be a way to share the space harmoniously. I got a glass of water and poured it in a circle around the portion of the floor I had designated for the ants. It allowed them access to their path in and out of the window crack but kept them from coming into the rest of the room. It worked perfectly because they only used one route, like a safari. It reminded me of what I could see of the prison compound from my window. When the announcement to 'return to your assigned area for count' came over the loudspeakers, slowly and deliberately everyone would head for the walkways, like lines of ants, branching off at their respective dormitories.

I had been an observer for a long time, ever since I came to death row. I wasn't part of the general population of the prison; neither was I a member of the staff. I was an observer. I had no affiliations with either group. I stayed in my tower and accepted visits from staff and inmates alike. They were all welcome to me. As I was alone, any company was good company.

17

O N MY PRIVATE DEATH ROW, the only neighbours I had would be the ones who tried to commit suicide or had become violent in some way, with the occasional pregnancy or drug dealer thrown in from time to time. They almost invariably came up kicking and screaming. It's true I didn't appreciate the screamers, but they could be interesting. I noticed that there seemed to be a pattern to their behaviour. I used to study how long a person could scream before they ran out of energy; before they'd give up. Twenty minutes is the answer. Twenty minutes. They all, without exception, started off cursing the guards; then they called for the Lord to help them; then they cursed the Lord; then they called for their mother, even if their mother had been dead since they were a child. And then they just lay down and cried and gave up. Twenty minutes, from start to finish. These are the things you get to observe, over and over and over again, until you start to notice the patterns.

> All life has patterns – leaves growing
on trees, currents in the ocean, winds in the sky,
the order of life, the habits of creatures,

interrelations – all are according to patterns. What
makes a thing or combination of things special or
different, unique, is its variance from the pattern.
Merely having exceptional characteristics is nothing
if one still follows the average, everyday, mundane
patterns – it is a waste!

I continued to do my writing, often just to build myself
up, like a pep talk.

About 8.30 one evening, I heard footsteps in the hall.
It was obviously more than one person. I jumped up, put
on my housecoat and stood at the door, trying to see who
was coming at this time of night.

It was the sergeant who had escorted me in on that
first night. He had two other men with him, both in uniform. I was alone in this section of the building. There
were no other inmates staying in the hospital ward across
the hallway from my locked area. And at night, in those
days, the control room operator was located at the
other end of the building on the first floor, in a separate
enclosure on the other side of the sallyport doors. As they
entered my section, I could see clearly that the two
strangers with the sergeant were uniformed policemen. I
immediately focused on their gun belts to determine
whether or not they were armed. They were here to see
'the cop-killer'.

They could beat me to death and I could scream my
head off and no one would know. I looked quickly around
my cell. They could try to hang me from the fluorescent
light. They could drown me in the bathroom. I decided to

stand close to the bed where, with one leap, I could use it as a barrier, and pillows and blanket could be used for protection as well. They opened my door and stepped inside.

They were not armed, except for the hatred in their eyes that burned the air between us. No words were spoken. They stood there and stared at me – a deer caught in their headlights. Perhaps if I stood very still they would go away. They looked at each other and at the sergeant. Then they all turned their faces to look at me and, as if on some cue, turned around and left. The sound of the door being bolted and the entrance to the hall being chained and padlocked took on a whole new meaning for me. But I could not sleep that night. The next day, when the superintendent came to see me on his daily rounds, I reported the incident to him and how it made me feel. I had weighed the possible consequences of telling or not telling. I knew the sergeant would hate me but he hated me anyway. The most important concern right now was my safety and the need to feel secure, rather than trapped, in my cell. I was never subjected to that type of intrusion again.

It took a while to get the walk schedule straightened out and to find an officer to do it. Often they would assign pregnant women who couldn't do any rough assignments. The walks would do them good too, I supposed. Again, walks were scheduled during working hours but occasionally I would encounter someone and was able to talk with people, even if just for a few moments. But it was best for me to keep moving or the officer would get bored and cut the walk short. It was also important not to walk too fast. I discovered that the officers didn't like running along behind me as I happily trotted down the path. I realized that if I walked slowly, in a sort of processional rhythm, that I got to stay out longer. So, like a wedding train, my officer and I would proceed at a measured pace.

On one of my walk days, a girl who worked in the staff dining area told me that the local Florida Highway Patrol had been asking questions about me. It seemed they were trying to stir up animosity towards me among the prison staff. She said she felt she had to tell me in case anything happened. But she was afraid she would lose her job if they found out. I wrote a letter about it to the super-intendent, Mr Sorensen. He ended the practice of outside law-enforcement personnel eating in the prison staff dining room. One of the guards who worked in the prison had been a personal friend of Officer Black, the highway patrolman who was killed. He had been at Officer Black's funeral and he was on duty during my walks. Apparently, he was asked to take part in a plan to lead me around the back between the buildings, claim that I had tried to escape and give me a beating. As it turned out, he was a decent man, and so the plot to do me harm within the prison lost momentum. Not so on the outside. There were two more plans that I knew of, which probably means there were more.

Some individuals kept up the vendetta in their own small ways. My friend Colleen's boss was one of them. He was the head of the maintenance department and, to my mind, represented an example of the genuine redneck. For

217

a while, he forbade Colleen to see me during working hours, which meant I couldn't see her on my walks. I could only see her during the thirty-minute visits that I got if someone was free to supervise. He gave her a hard time about it but she always seemed to manage. Anyway, he depended on her because she was the best plumber he had.

Colleen was fifteen years old. When she was fourteen, she had been tried as an adult and was doing a life sentence for second-degree murder. Her accomplice, a forty-year-old male friend of her mother's, had told her he'd hurt her mother if she didn't help him. He said because she was a juvenile she couldn't be punished as severely as an adult. In the end, he tried to get off with a lighter sentence by testifying against Colleen. But I think he got life anyway. Colleen was the oldest of six children. She was used to taking care of everyone, including her mother, as her parents were no longer together. During her trial she had faced the possibility of the death penalty, so when I came to BCI, although we had not yet met, she empathized with my situation and requested permission to do my washing.

Colleen had become friends with Judy, the young woman who used to do my laundry at FCI, who was now the law clerk at BCI. Judy had entered the system at the age of seventeen with a life sentence for burning down the house with her stepmother in it. She and Colleen became friends. I put them on my list of inmate visitors. And whenever I got out for a walk I would try to see both of them. There was no set time for my walks, so sometimes I would miss them. But most often the word would get out through the grapevine and we would see each other. As my guard and I walked, my eyes scanned the walkways. Colleen had Swedish blond hair, which she wore tucked behind her ears. It hung to her waist, covering her thin, reedy back. She wore a tool belt of wrenches and hammers and screwdrivers that weighed more than she did. And she walked with a deliberate, serious air.

Colleen was a regular weekly visitor to my cell for the peer group interaction mandated by the Federal Court. The guards would escort her to the locked area in which I was housed and leave her in there with me, monitoring from outside the glass window in the hallway, like at a regular visit, so we could speak without being overheard. It was the best. Not that we had so many secrets, it was just the idea that we could speak freely. When she was coming I would save up food from my tray and prepare a treat. This time it was a canapé of mixed veggies that I had puréed in cream cheese and spread on crackers. I couldn't wait for her to taste it so I could tell her what went into it. I was very proud of my creativity. She wished I wouldn't go into all that detail about it. It made her nervous to think of what I might have saved and how long I had saved it. But she ate some to please me. It did please me. It was a good sharing.

I had been at BCI for about a month and a half. My parents came and brought the children as soon as they could. A table and chairs were set up in the hall between the rooms for our visit, and the guard observed from the hallway. The door to my room was left open so that we could go in and out. We would start out sitting at the table. My mom would take out a picture of me and point from the picture to me, saying, 'Mommy, Mommy.' Tina, who was now about two and a half, was a little shy at first but she caught on pretty quickly, and Eric helped too. I would take the kids into my room and read to them on the bed. It helped a lot to be able to go into the room – it demystified my circumstances for them. Death row is an incomprehensible concept, especially for a child, and especially for a child who has to visit his or her mother there. Later on my dad would go in and take a nap while the kids and I played in the hall. My mom would bring in a newspaper to read. She still loved crossword puzzles. It was comforting to me to see her puzzling over the squares like we used to do together when I was a child. She would also bring crayons and paper for the children so they would have something to do while we grown-ups talked. After this first visit, they would go back to bringing one child at a time so they could each get the one-on-one time that they needed. It was better for me too. For a long time, Tina liked to be held and rocked and sung to: 'Rockabye, Tina, on the tree top. When the wind blows, the cradle will rock . . .' Eric liked to talk, always holding a hand or leaning his head on my shoulder, touching. And he was always very loving to his sister, leaning over and kissing her on the cheek. I would have to put in a request for permission in advance so we could have pictures taken during the visit. They would take us out into the main hallway for this. I suppose it was for security reasons, not to have pictures of my cell area. But it was much nicer in the outside hallway. The walls were a deep rose, which made a nice background. And they would always position us directly underneath the big round clock at the end of the hall – death row photos with time ticking away over our heads. We would take a lot of pictures and share them out between us. I always sent one to Jesse – one of me with the kids and one of me alone. And when time was up, we would hug and kiss and give last-minute instructions, advice and reassurances.

The end of the visit was so painful. It was so hard to watch them go, looking back and waving at me. Sometimes the baby would cry and Eric would cling to me, not wanting to leave. But the alternative would be not to see them at all, and for me that wasn't an option. And then they would leave and I would go back into my cell.

The children would be asleep in the car almost before they left the prison grounds. And they would have behaviour problems for a week or two afterwards, affecting schoolwork and life in general. My parents had to deal with the children's emotions as well as their own. Although I was grateful, I never really appreciated how much my parents went through because at the time I was so needy.

I lived for those visits. I know there are some people in prison and on death row who don't let their families come to see them because they don't want to put them, or themselves, through the indignities and painful goodbyes afterwards. But to me that's bullshit. I was strip-searched before and after every visit and I would have let them do worse to me in order to be able to spend time with my family. And I know my family felt the same way.

I had, as a means of survival, accepted my situation, in so far as this was going to be my life for an indeterminate period of time and I had to live it in prison. I still maintained the bubble in which Jesse and I were going home soon and everything would be just fine. But because of the disappointment of the hearing after Rhodes's confession, and my new knowledge of the hidden evidence of the polygraph report, I had resigned myself to the fact that this was going to take a long time to resolve. And, considering Jesse's infidelity, things might never turn out the way we had planned. There was still a distinct possibility that one or both of us would be executed.

Superintendent Sorensen believed that if you treated a person like a human being they would learn to behave like a human being. He instructed the staff to call the inmates 'ladies' and to address them individually as 'miss'. He didn't approve of cursing or shouting and he encouraged the women to dress nicely. It was the only attempt at rehabilitation that I ever witnessed in all my years in the prison system. I saw the roughest women behaving like ladies, taking pride in themselves.

He had only three rules – you didn't jump the fence, you didn't commit violence and you didn't take drugs. In his humanity, he also kept his promise and arranged monthly phone calls between Jesse and me. They were to be charged to a third party, Jesse's mom, and would be made from the chapel. It was quite a feat coordinating those calls with Jesse's prison but the chaplain made sure Jesse was available at the appointed time. I had the day marked on my calendar and as it approached I would become too restless to sleep; and as the hour approached I would pace out my anxiety, back and forth, waiting for my escort to the chapel. And his voice, that beautiful deep liquid voice, would spill out over the parched landscape of my soul, filling the cracks and crevices, softening the edges, making everything OK again. And we would kiss and say, 'I love you, talk to you soon,' never goodbye. And I would hang up and when I could I would stand and be escorted back to my cell. I did not speak. I did not choose to share it, not one word of it.

The phone calls lasted only a few months until someone, a staff member in the classification department, called the local newspaper. Mr Sorensen caught a lot of flak from it, even though it wasn't true that our calls were being paid for by the state and taxpayers. The calls were terminated, and I think it was the excuse the hardliners needed to terminate Mr Sorensen as well. He was transferred to a work release centre a few months later. And it marked the end of the rehabilitation era at BCI. Through the sixteen years that followed, I watched the 'ladies' turn into 'bitches and whores' among themselves and 'inmates' to the guards. The state of Florida changed the name of the department of rehabilitation to the department of corrections. The attitude towards the inmates changed accordingly.

18

ALTHOUGH I ALWAYS found it stimulating to have a new neighbour, some were more interesting than others. The most poignant and one of the most regular visitors to the hospital confinement area, specifically the strip cell, was Marianna Simmons.

Marianna was a South American girl. A child of five in the body of a woman, shaped like a troll, she had a sweet disposition and a terrible temper. But what made her outstanding were her extraordinary abilities to create rhyme and to handle pain. And she could sing too.

It was freezing cold inside the strip cell. Marianna would stand there, butt naked, with her face in the small window, singing – sometimes in English and sometimes in Spanish. The strip cell was BCI's version of the 'unpadded cell' – it contained a toilet and sink apparatus and a mattress. They put you in naked. Most people tried to roll themselves up in the mattress for warmth, after they finished protesting. Sometimes Marianna came in fighting and cursing, kicking and screaming. They would shoot her up with some zombie juice. But if the right nurse or officer was on duty, Marianna could be handled.

'Now go on in the cell, Marianna, and be a good girl.'

'Thank you, Nurse Stevens. I'm sorry I threw my medicine down. Don't be mad at me.'

'Well now, Marianna, you behave now and I'll go get you some more medicine. If you take the medicine for me then maybe I can get them to give you some clothes and a blanket.'

'I don't care about their stinking asses! You can all kiss my ass. I don't care what you do to me. I hate you!'

'Now, Marianna, you promised to be good. I don't want to hear that kind of language.'

'I'm sorry, Nurse Stevens. I won't do it any more. But tell them to stay away from me. He's a man. He's not supposed to touch me.' To the guard, 'You keep your hands off me or I'll kick you in the nuts . . . !'

'Marianna!'

'OK, Nurse Stevens, really I'm sorry. I just get mad.'

'Take this medicine now. I have a lot of work to do.'

'Will you come back and see me?'

'If you take your medicine so I can get back to my work I'll be able to come and see you before shift change.'

Taking the medicine, 'Thank you, Miss Stevens. Don't forget you promised to come back and see me. I won't cuss at you any more, Mr Jones. You're a nice man. I didn't mean it. OK?'

Marianna had another talent and that was for flooding. The strip cell was boring. When Marianna needed attention, she would wedge her foot into the toilet stool (prison slang for toilet bowl) so the water couldn't go down and then she would begin flushing, over and over again, until it overflowed, filling the cell, spilling out under the door to fill the hallway and the other rooms too. And there she would stand, poised triumphantly, surveying her handiwork.

The first time this happened, I was sitting cross-legged at the desk end of the wooden cabinet that had been provided for me, writing a letter. I had my new headphones on to block out the screaming so I was oblivious to what was going on until I noticed one of my shoes floating by the desk. My mind didn't accept the implications immediately. I remember thinking to myself, I just saw my shoe float by. I had a fleeting vision of the scene from *Alice in Wonderland* where she is dancing round and round in the water while things float by. I traced the source of the water to the crack under my door. I began rescuing my possessions. Then I got a towel and some newspaper and stuffed them into the crack to stop the flow. With that under control, I looked out through the window into the hallway.

'Marianna, what are you doing?'

'I'm making the flood!'

'I know. But couldn't you warn me first? My whole room is flooded.'

'But I can't tell or they'll come before I get a chance to finish. You might tell them.'

'Look, next time you tell me first so I can block up my doorway. I promise I won't call them until after the whole hall is flooded. But I do have to call them, OK? Otherwise I'll get in trouble.'

'OK, Sonia, you can call them now. I made good flood, didn't I?'

'Yes, Marianna, you certainly did – a great flood. But remember, next time you call me and tell me first.'

'OK, Sonia. I made a good flood!' She laughed and laughed while I called for the guard. It was never dull when Marianna was around.

Marianna had received shock treatments when they were in fashion and had been back and forth to the state mental facility many times. Her father had killed her mother and then committed suicide when she was four years old. She was raised in various foster homes after that until her sister got old enough to take over her care. Marianna loved her sister but she just couldn't control her behaviour so she ended up in prison. She was content with incarceration, being cared for, even being told what to do, except sometimes, like a child, she didn't want to listen. And sometimes she would throw a temper tantrum. Marianna was stocky and strong and wouldn't hesitate to bite.

Marianna would spend hours singing to herself, soothing herself with Spanish lullabies, amusing herself with current hits from the radio. She was missing her upper front teeth, which affected her speech. She would call me her friend and tell me she loved me because I would listen to her and sometimes help her with a problem.

One time they carried her in kicking and screaming, threw her in the strip cell and went in after her to take her clothes and give her a shot of Haldol, a psychotropic drug used for behaviour control. She fought them but in the end, at five against one, they prevailed.

That night when they brought dinner I could hear

Marianna trying to smash her tray. She called me to the door. Holding up the shard of plastic so I could see it she told me she was going to put out her eye with it.

'They'll get in a lot of trouble for that, won't they?' And she was smiling like it was just the best joke she had ever thought of playing on them.

'Yes, Marianna, they would get in a lot of trouble. But you only get one pair of eyes. I'll tell you what, why don't you cut up your mattress? That would get them in trouble.'

She thought about it for a moment. 'No, no, I'm gonna put out my eye.'

'Wait! How about cutting your arm. That would be pretty bad. They would get in a lot of trouble if you cut your arm.'

I couldn't believe I was having this conversation. But anything was better than her putting her eye out. She was still standing in the window so I could see her face and the shard she held in her hand. For a moment it looked like she was going to accept my suggestion. I tried to swallow but my throat was too dry.

Her face disappeared from the window. It was taking too long. I strained to hear.

'Marianna? Marianna?'

Her face appeared, a grotesque mask of twisted glee, as she dug repeatedly into her neck with the plastic shard – stabbing and tearing and laughing. It was as if she was feeling no pain. I could see the blood.

'Marianna, I'm going to call for help now. That's enough. They're gonna be in a lot of trouble.'

But she was gone, tripping, caught up in the rhythm inside her head.

'Help! Help! Officer! Somebody help!' Somebody looked in the big hallway window. It was the inmate hospital orderly who cleaned the hall. 'Get some help! We need help quick! Get the nurse. Marianna is bleeding!'

She seemed to understand, dropping her broom and running down the hall. Marianna was still hacking away at her neck in the window where I could see her, still smiling and cackling insanely. I was going to be sick. Footsteps coming fast down the hall. It was the inmate orderly with the nurse and a guard. They quickly unlocked padlock and chain and entered the confinement area.

'In there! She's cutting herself!'

The nurse looked into the window of Marianna's cell and saw what she was doing. 'Open the door! Quickly!'

The guard rushed to the door, fumbling with the key in the lock, unnerved by the urgency in the nurse's voice. They rushed in and brought Marianna out. By now she was bleeding profusely.

'Get a towel!' the nurse screamed at the orderly, who turned and ran, coming back with an armful of white towels. Meanwhile, the nurse had guided Marianna to a chair, removing the piece of plastic from her hand easily. The guard was calling in on his walkie-talkie. The nurse held one of the towels to Marianna's neck. 'Marianna, why did you do this?'

'They're going to really get in trouble now. They were mean to me. They're responsible for me, you know? They're going to get in trouble for this.'

229

I watched the red stain cover the towel, and my stomach felt like a fist inside. Other guards came and they escorted Marianna out.

As she passed my cell she said, 'I did good, didn't I, Sonia?'

One of the guards asked if I was OK. I nodded.

They brought Marianna back all bandaged, still smiling proudly.

I asked her if she really wanted to kill herself. She said she didn't, and that it wasn't so bad here compared to the other places in which she had been incarcerated. She had an especially strong fear of being sent to the state mental hospital, where she had received shock treatments.

'And I have Nurse Stevens here. She's like my mom. She's nice to me. I love Nurse Stevens.' She began shouting, 'I love you, Nurse Stevens!'

I loved Nurse Stevens too. Nurse Stevens was the only one of the staff who really talked to me. She would come by after her rounds just to chat. They weren't supposed to do that. She would come into the confinement area and open my door just a couple of inches so we could talk. Sometimes she would smoke a cigarette. She would get red, and sweat would pour down her face. She would take off her glasses and wipe the sweat away with her sleeve and just keep right on talking without skipping a beat. Later on, they claimed she drank and that you could smell liquor on her breath. But I never did. Nurse Stevens meant a lot to me.

* * *

We had our four resident crazies, the regulars in hospital confinement. There was Rosetta, Mariangela, Annette, and, of course, Marianna. Annette was the more sophisticated psychotic. But Rosetta and Mariangela seemed to be in competition in the schizophrenic department. It seemed that here too there was a pattern. When either one would come in she would talk incessantly, sometimes sing at the top of her lungs, complain of various physical and mental ailments, and take off her clothes so she could be shockingly naked when anyone happened to look into her cell. They each had a personal style of doing this. Rosetta would strut and pose, hand on hip, head held high, regal in all her naked glory. Mariangela was more of the table-dancer type. When she couldn't wait for the guards, she would climb up on her bed to perform for the women locked up in the cells across from hers.

'Hey, Sonia, come to the door a minute, I want to ask you something.' And when I would appear in the window she would shake her breasts and laugh.

'How you like this, Sonia? Aren't they fine?'

I would leave the window and she would continue to call to me. 'What's the matter, Sonia? Don't you like what you see? Are you jealous? You don't like me, do you, Sonia?'

But Mariangela was not dangerous except that she caused a lot of trouble, mostly for herself. Rosetta could be dangerous, and Annette could be deadly. They were all in for murder. I don't remember the details of the others' cases but with Mariangela they said when the telephone engineer came to her apartment to do some work she tried

231

to seduce him but he rebuffed her advances. So she cut him up and put the pieces in her bureau drawers. But the blood dripped out and she was busted. She got life. 'Hey, mister, don't you like what you see?'

Mail always came with the evening shift. It was still a big event of the day.

December 2, 3, 4, 1977

My Dearest Jesse,

I have been sleeping with the letter you wrote me since I got it. I love the part about how you were giving serious thought to my condition as a result of these years of chastity. And you gave me the new title of honorary virgin, ha ha, I like that!

I'm waiting for them to pick up trays – nasty dinner. I told them I wasn't going to eat it but they said to take it anyway. That way they don't have to write anything extra on your sheet – they are the laziest COs' [correctional officers] I've seen. I really preferred the seasoned old ones to the new ones, now that I've seen both types.

I'm glad Mom came Saturday because now I know what I'll be getting you for Christmas! I hope the books come in time – especially the one on Japanese painting from the place in New York.

Sometimes I feel so impatient to be free again, to be with you again – I feel like that now. All the things we should be enjoying. We will too – in that way we are luckier than some because what we have is real and forever – we <u>are</u> what is real and forever. There are so many things I wish that I could talk to you about – it's a terrible thing they've done – it's been years Jesse. I'm sending this certified, in hopes that it will get there sooner.

I love you with all my heart and soul – completely.

I love you.

Love and kisses, Sunny

It was Hanukkah, the festival of lights in the Jewish religion, akin to Christmas. On my walk I went to tell the chaplain that if the news media were going to be involved then I would decline my invitation to celebrate in the chapel with the other Jewish prisoners. He assured me they would not. So I agreed to attend. I was very firm about my right to celebrate my personal religious holidays and keep my traditions.

There was a rabbi who came to see me at BCI, Rabbi Chaim Richter. He came every month and we had got permission for me to attend religious services on holidays in the chapel with my perennial guard and the other Jewish inmates. There were never many. Sometimes there was only one other, a girl named Cory who had been transferred down from Maine. Sometimes there were as many as sixteen. And the rabbi didn't believe in proselytizing or asking people to come who weren't interested in their religious heritage. He would visit my cell before he went to the chapel for his monthly 'Shabbat', Sabbath services.

Actually he came on a Monday but for us whenever he came it was Shabbat.

My Dearest Jesse,

I love you. I'm still waiting for my laundry to be brought up – as usual the four to 12 shift 'couldn't'. The wind has died down so it's not so cold as it was before. It must be cold where you are. I hope you are warm enough. Next winter I will keep you warm with my hot little body! I just know we'll see each other soon. I guess I'll go to bed. Almost 2 a.m. and no laundry – no sheets, towels, etc. It's ready I know, but they won't bring it up. I hope they don't let my dresses get all wrinkled. This shift may bring them up but if they don't come in the next few minutes I'll just wait until morning. Light stuff. I have to get up early tomorrow and get ready for my visit!

We'll be together again soon. They know it too – just like they know we are innocent. I could go on and on about them, their conspiracy, but that's no subject to sleep on – phooey! TL [Time lapse]. The nurse just came with the guard and brought me two sheets so now I guess it's time to go to sleep. My mattress is plastic covered and wouldn't have been very comfortable to sleep on without a sheet, especially on a cold night. I'll say good night now my love. I'll dream of you. I love you. Pleasant dreams.

Love and kisses, Sunny

Sometimes the dream world was simply better than the reality, and I needed some relief. So there were times when I would fall back into the old pattern, taking refuge in the bubble, because the dharma – truth – was just too hard.

↝ *January 13, 1978*

The Strength of Weakness in Fragile Balance

I rarely allow myself to get so sentimental – I've never abandoned myself to years or tears – sometimes I want to cry and cry until I cry myself out and fall asleep. It is not the time for such luxury. I must be strong – but I really want to be weak! Love and frustration well up inside me at times like this. And when they do I wish I could bury my face in your chest and cry until it all comes out. I usually manage to keep a fairly good balance within myself but there are times when my feminine, my yin, my hormone balance get the better of me. I do cry sometimes – but I hide and try to stop quickly so no one will know. I think when I see you, I will cry then. But how can I take up what precious time we'll have with tears! That would be too selfish and would still not be the time and place to be weak. You will be counting on our combined strength and I could not sap you of yours that way. So I will have to wait. One day, when we are free, and together, and all this is only a memory – the loneliness and the hurt and the injustice – then I will lay my head on your chest and yield to my weakness safely in your arms. I have had to be

235

more yang than yin for a long time and long to be
in the perfect harmony that I can have only when I
am with you – at your side, or at your feet, or
under your body as you cover me, or in your arms,
or in your eyes and your voice, your touch and even
in just the sound of your breath and your heartbeat
– that is where I find harmony and peace,
wholeness and perfection.

I love you.

Our conditions were so severe. I didn't want Jesse to worry about me as his situation was much more difficult than mine. If dreams were the only comfort we could share then why spoil it? We both still needed those dreams.

The phone calls Mr Sorensen had allowed us to have helped bring us closer together and mend the hurt of his previous behaviour. Adversity creates camaraderie – we are brothers and sisters in war; we are one in the face of death.

19

My Dearest Sunny,

I love you. This morning they gave me that DR [disciplinary report] – failure to maintain personal hygiene or appearance (hair under my lip), verbal threat, disobeying a verbal order, and verbal disrespect. I go to court at 8.30 but I've got some legal surprises for them, bet on that. If they lock me we can still write so don't worry. But, as always, I plan to win. This may be a rough one – 30 days locked or more. I won my last DR. In fact, I never lose a case and never will, as I'm just too smart for these turkeys to manipulate me. They can lock me, sock me, but I'm going to 'rock' me. I'll cost them money if they make just one mistake and, being emotional, they will. They are not cool enough to deal with me. I'm cool as a body on ice and they are hot headed when I speak words they have to look up in the dictionary and when I lay case law on the table. Enough of my ego-tripping. I'll let my work speak for itself. We are not their scapegoats. Oh well, so much for their trying to discipline me. I'm already disciplined.

I want to know if Eric got my letter. I want to

see the baby. Maybe they'll have to wait a week or two before they come if I'm locked. Your letter smells good tonight. I've been checking it out. Your bulging fantasy was a turn on for me tonight, I love the way you do everything honey. You are my perfect woman in all ways. I just received *Three Pillars of Zen* and *Psychoanalysis* by Suzuki, Eric Fromm, and Richard DeMartino from inter-library loan. First books from our library they gave me in 18 months, right? They'll probably take them tomorrow. Good night honey.

I love you, Jesse

January 26, 1978

My Dearest Sunny,

I love you. I called Mom earlier. They had second thoughts about taking my visits with the kids, but too late, so Mom told me, as they'd canceled their flight here. As you know by now, Dad is in the hospital too on top of all the other aggravation. I received your Monday letter too. It was right on time. It made me feel good. Courts are hard to figure out. But one thing I do know is that all that is keeping us here is the state's lies and as soon as we produce our concrete proof to the contrary, we are home. Rhodes admitting he did it, all over every institution in Florida is great! But unfortunately it's only hearsay evidence, strong evidence, but still hearsay and the probability of a ruling favorably is only 50-50. But the other evidence, well, frankly speaking, there can't be any stronger evidence Sunny.*

Perhaps we never would have even been indicted, period. We were and are victims of this crime and not its perpetrators. This is the last time we are talking about our case at all in letters until they grant us the confidentiality we should have, period. As for filing on Satz and Futch, I'll take care of the filing for us.† They can't scare, intimidate, lock, or block me filing on them ever! Rock and roll, mama san! Your letter got me in a good mood tonight. I love you my sweet, tasty, precious mama. For now I'll close with all my love and will be giving best regards for you tonight for sure!

I love you, Jesse

Jesse's father was dying. He had emphysema and an enlarged heart and was becoming senile. His mom was trying to cope with him at home but she was running herself ragged with working, visiting prisons, and then coming home to take care of her dying husband, who was becoming progressively more difficult to deal with as the

---

*During our trials someone was intimidated by phone calls and decided not to testify in our behalf. Jesse believed that if he had been able to make phone calls this person would have been reassured and come forward. He also believed Eric's testimony would have been invaluable. I did not agree.

†It was Jesse's feeling that the attorneys had to appear before the prosecutor and judge every day in the course of their work and so they could not be expected to file a serious motion of misconduct by the very same judge and prosecutor.

Alzheimer's took over. Occasionally he became delusional, lashing out physically, and she would end up with bruises.

My Dearest Sunny,

I love you. Don't ever worry about changing in any way as even if you do, I couldn't care less. I love you the same as always. Of course being in here is going to have an effect on both of us, a wrinkle or a line here or there, lose a few hairs, so what! It's light stuff honey, we are us! You look lovely, and a real woman honey, and I say that sincerely. And it's you who are my wife forever. You are my complete woman in all ways and I'm your man forever.

My woman, things will be getting better and better for us as each day goes on, and soon we'll be free.

I love you! Jesse

May 4, 1978

I am the wind and the wind is me
its relentless power flows in my veins
and in my mind you'll find the sea
constantly changing, returning as rain.

December 28, 1978

My Dearest Jesse,

I love you! It's Thursday and apparently a zoo tour day – but this zoo has visits by appointment only, so whoever it was they were out of luck. They waited around, tapped on my window, flashed my light – I was waiting for a banana or a piece of raw meat to be proffered. I stayed in the bathroom. I was busy playing with my new toy (my makeup kit) and didn't care to be disturbed. When a person comes to see another person, they introduce themselves. I don't grant an audience to just anyone!

I was supposed to go for a walk this a.m. but that fell through so I'll get back to the books until after lunch. It's fun having all the colors to play with! I can create many different effects. I'll get to work now. I love you. TL. I stopped lawing for a bit to scrub my floor while I had the chance. I also wrote a request to the superintendent about getting more time in the law library for a few weeks. I wish I could find just one person who had a copy of an appeal so I could see how it's done and what was good and bad about it to have some idea of what the judges look at and for. I'm scheduled for a walk and my last hour of library this afternoon.

Gotta go now. I love you.

Your Woman, Sunny

One day they came to my room to measure the window. They returned with a drill and a set of bars that they proceeded to install. What was this all about? What had I done? Later on it was explained to me. They had found bullets hidden inside a cigarette pack in a box sent to someone from the outside. That person blamed Judy for

241

having her framed. Since Judy and I were known associates from the law library, and since a birthday card from me was found in her desk drawer, and since bullets were considered escape paraphernalia, by their particular brand of logic it followed that I should have bars installed on my window.

At the time I was allowed to have one plant in my room. I trained my plant to grow up the bars like a trellis, weaving in and out of the diamond-shaped openings. And it was a trellis just as it was bars. Both were correct and you had your choice how to see it. I chose a trellis.

> *I look at shapes, light and dark,*
> *and let the solution suggest itself to me,*
> *like in Japanese sumi-e painting.*
> *The answer is hidden within the problem,*
> *like the painting is hidden within the paper,*
> *or the sculpture within the rock.*
> *It is a trellis for my plant.*
> *Better Cells and Gardens!*

I never actually found a piece of tomato in my salad. The tomato went to the kitchen workers and their friends. But I did find a seed. I picked it out and saved it in a wet napkin so it would sprout. Then I got one of the good officers to let me bring in a handful of earth in which to plant it. I grew it in a medicine cup that I got from the nurse when they came around with meds one night for the women in the ward. I kept it on the sink near the window so it could get plenty of light. Then I asked if I could take it out and plant it behind the dining hall so I could see it from my window. I watered it whenever a good officer took me for a walk. And I had my friends looking after it for me. It was my baby. I watched it grow. Soon, it had little flowers from which the buds of the fruits appeared. I had the first generation of BCI tomatoes that year. I was a 'mother'! I was so proud. And they were good – more than good, they were delicious!

I saved the seeds from my first generation and started on a second generation. The seedlings grew and I planted them in the same spot. And I got permission to grow and water them this time. In fact, I was allowed to have my mom and dad send me some seed packets. One of the girls in the kitchen saved me some hot pepper seeds. They really grew well in the BCI soil and soon I had a whole row of pepper plants out back. I tried corn and cucumbers and beans too but only the beans grew. The inside grounds workers started watering the plants regularly. They also started harvesting the peppers that proliferated in my little garden. I didn't mind that, but I wished they wouldn't take the green tomatoes. I soon became the proud grandmother of a second generation of tomatoes.

One day, when I went to the window to gaze out upon my garden, I spied Ms Duncan with a shovel and a gallon can. Elizabeth Duncan was one of the few older inmates we had in those days. She had white hair and a sturdy build, was obviously well educated and at one time of the privileged class. She was in for first degree murder. It seems she went to court in a dispute over some land. The judge ruled in the man's favour and at that moment a

243

gun dropped out of her purse and shot the man right between the eyes.

She was poised in front of my tomato patch. She was looking up at my window. Then she proceeded to dig. She was digging up my plants! I yelled. I cursed. I ranted and I raved behind my closed and barred window, but to no avail. She kept on digging, pausing only to glance up at my window every so often as if she could feel me there, watching helplessly as she committed her crime. What a witch she was. She put my three-foot-tall plants into the gallon can, looked up at my window and waved. The nerve of the woman! Then she pointed down at the can and put it against the back wall of the dining hall.

As it turned out, she wanted to plant a garden of her own and mine was the only area authorized for gardening. I hated her then. But I could understand the urge to grow a garden. I actually tried to get the administration to allow gardening out in the field beyond the ball field. It would be good therapy; it would provide meaningful work; it would save money; it could even be profitable. I was not successful. But neither was Ms Duncan. Her garden was sabotaged irreparably by an unknown assailant. It was retribution. We all knew that. I had mixed feelings about it. Ms Duncan really was a mean woman. I gave up on gardening.

There had been a few women, through the years, who were locked in hospital confinement because they were pregnant. Sometimes it was done to apply pressure because the administration wanted to know who the

244

father was since the woman had been in prison for more than nine months. And sometimes it was because the pregnancy was near term. Normally, the woman spent the majority of the ninth month there. When they brought Bridgette in, handcuffed and shackled and nine months pregnant, I thought it was curious. When they left her there handcuffed and shackled all night, I thought it was cruel. If it weren't for the nurse, a nice woman, Ms Perdy, who used to talk to me at night, Bridgette would have remained that way indefinitely. I don't know how they expected her to use the toilet. And what if she fell down – tripped on her shackles – and landed on her baby? It was very dangerous to leave her that way. The nurse immediately went to tell the doctor and he ordered the handcuffs and shackles removed. I saw him speaking heatedly with security, but medical overrides everything. And if she got hurt, security would have been held responsible.

It seems the whole thing started on a trip to the outside doctor – a clinic for pregnant women. You were always handcuffed when being transported – pregnant, comatose, everything but dead. When the officer was loading the girls back into the van he pushed Bridgette, and Bridgette kicked him in his nutsack. Thus, the handcuffs and shackles and harsh treatment.

Bridgette had come to prison pregnant. Terry Moone, however, got pregnant in the warehouse. She was afraid to take vitamins or anything the medical department offered her in case they tried to abort the child. Obviously the father was an employee of the prison and that was a problem in many ways. She wasn't talking and she was

245

determined to have a baby. It was a love child – although the prime suspect was a married correctional officer. I knew of a statute that permitted the mother to keep the baby with her in prison for eighteen months. I had counselled other women about the statute but they didn't believe me. Classification always told them that the statute had been repealed. That was not true – although it would be soon.

I gave Terry a number for the legal aid society. They sent a young woman who had just passed the Bar. This was her first case. And she won! Terry got to keep her baby right there in the cell with her.

So here we were on death row with the newborn baby. Birth row and death row. I would hear the baby crying. I would hear it in a place that made me wonder if I would get milk again in my breasts. And I would bang on the door, calling Terry's name, until she woke up. She took good care of the baby. They had to take her and the baby outside in the fresh air every day.

It was all just too much responsibility for the admin-istration – what if something happened to the baby? Terry's sentence was shortened by the court and she went home with the baby within a month.

Bridgette didn't get to keep her baby but she had made arrangements for her family to keep it. We spent many hours lying on the floor talking through the door crack, thinking of names for the baby. She knew it was going to be a girl. She had seen her on the ultrasound. In the end she named her Melanie.

When Bridgette told me her labour had begun, we

spent the night timing her contractions. We were to call the nurse when they got to three minutes apart. It was amazing to be part of my friend's childbirth experience when I was on death row.

Jan. 1, 1979

My Dearest Sunny,

I love you. It's almost New Years and I've had your pictures, the kids, our family and assorted others to our little party.

TL. Happy New Year! This one will bring us our freedom. I've been celebrating for almost two days as '79 will be a good one for us! Right at the stroke of midnight you and I are for sure synchronized. I felt you honey!

The next 40 days you're going to have to be totally aware of all I must accomplish Sunny, I have so much to do it's staggering – and I'll be going through a million things too, working from the time I open my eyes in the morning until I go to sleep. My letters may be short, they may be long, I don't know, but I need your moral support and understanding right now badly for this law marathon, regardless. I just want you to be aware of all that's happening in case I get cranky or whatever. I have deadlines to meet. Well, you've read the rules. I'm going to be going full blast to keep up. Forty days Sun, they go quickly too! I've been sitting here thinking about it and I can't think anymore. It has to be put all together right now. I love you wildly, completely and constantly! You are in every thought and action of mine. My woman!

I love you, your husband Jesse

He was filing for clemency and he had only forty days in which to do it. Like the biblical forty days – isolation, purification, purging, preparing to enter the Promised Land. His focus was narrowing; mine was coming into a new perspective.

February 16,17, 18, 1979

My Dearest Sunny,

I love you. I got your letter with the heart* and the two sumi-e paintings. Sun, you're beautiful. First let me answer your letter. The moon has had its effects here too, ha ha lunatics for sure. It's really a bummer that you're getting the business down there from them all the time about the walks. Why don't you write Judge Scott a personal certified letter and ask for some help and to look into the case again. Things here are about the same honey, about the same as there – rotten. But like I said, nothing means nothing to me except us and our family. All this petty harassment or whatever they call it will soon pass us by.

Sun, this heart you made is such a groove. I took it and held it up close to me and could feel it. You made it special for me and I dig it totally my

*I had found some soft material and made a heart out of it.

woman. You've always got something to surprise and make me happy. I like the feel of it too and put my face all over it and rubbed it on my chest. It feels nice! I want to rub my chest against yours! TL. I am putting together a motion for an extension of time to file my brief until March 28th as I've got no ruling on the confidential communication motion as yet and my briefing time is almost up. I'll get it right to the Fifth Circuit pronto.

You will be glad to have a visit this week at least and it will break the monotony for you. I feel so lonesome for you Sun, it really aches me, bummer. Soon though you and I will be together free and that I do know. I love you totally!

Your husband, Jesse

For my Jesse   Oct. 17, 1979

Complements

I have seen us as the moon and sun
the reflection and the source
I have seen us as the wind and river
the power and the force.
We are the two that act as one
the reactor and the giver.
We are separate yet together,
birds of a feather.

Yet upon introspection an awareness has come
that the moon must depend on the light of
   the sun,
and the river on the will of the wind, and
that I am the same as the moon and the river –
dark and still without the giver.

Yet the wind and the sun would not be undone
by the lack of a moon or a river.
Still I wonder though they freely exist
to what purpose the wind without rivers to twist
and the sun to constantly burn?

The wind without rivers at its command
would blow uselessly over the land
and the earth would half freeze and half burn
on each turn
if the moon ceased its daily sojourn.

So though to my essence you give life
I give essence to yours –
husband and wife
power and force
reflection and source
complements – of course!

20

December 25, 1979

My Woman,

I love you Sunny!

Merry Christmas! We'll be free for the next one. It won't be long now until we're free and together again. They've put us far away from each other in little cells to murder us for something we didn't do. They mentally harass us constantly and degrade us as their prisoners, but we're strong you and I and we will make it. We are true, you and I. We have honor and we are proud people. They cannot touch us. Don't let little things simple mindless people say upset you. That's all. I love you Sun, you're my woman. Good night.

I Love You, Jesse

Jesse could be so amazing! He had such good stuff in him. He had the strength of the Welsh coal miner, and the wisdom of the Zen monk; he had the quickness and the focus of the martial artist, the charm and humour of his Italian heritage, and the devotion and depth of commitment that he had learned from his mother, who carried them all on her shoulders. Women loved him and men respected him. But he never made the transition from young man to responsible adult. An only child, prison when he was so young, poor role models, twisted thinking learned from older prisoners, lack of opportunity to learn – I don't know what made him that way but, as amazing as he was, he had a gap in his development that he wasn't able to bridge, and I wasn't able to fill it even with all my love.

To My Children Someday   May 26, 1980

I wish I could tell the children what I know now and what I've discovered to be so. I wish I could tell them now at the moment of discovery – so they could feel it even if my wording is inadequate. I've told them we are different. Different is special – and it's good. Sometimes it's hard, being different. There are those who will try to punish and make you suffer because you're different. I didn't suffer a lot though because I never accepted meanness or-negativity into myself. I didn't deny its existence. I just didn't accept it as necessary for me. So I turned it back on its self altered by my own character. I took their hurtful vibes and kept only the energy and not the feeling – then I used it to project my own. If I had become hurtful too, I would have been altered. Of course I didn't know I was doing all that. I was just following my nature. I didn't ever feel compelled to 'belong.' And now I'm so glad! It's the same thing that keeps me from becoming a miserable person living among miserable people. I refuse to accept their miserableness into myself. I take the miserableness they project at me and change it – returning pleasantness instead – maintaining my own atmosphere. I short-circuit their creepiness! After a while they get tired of wasting their nasties on me and some even become sort of nice. You have to be very strong and self-aware – ever watchful. You must always say to yourself – Does this feel right for me? Is there a better way to look at this? How can I make this into something positive so I can feel good rather than bad? I think negative bad things sometimes – but I don't dwell on them – I let them pass. I even laugh at myself for being, for a moment, caught acting like them! You must be capable of defending yourself and those you love. You must be, mentally and physically. Be strong. Be your self. Be positive. You make things the way you think – if you think this will be a lousy day – it will be! If you think this will be a good day – it will be! You will find a way to make it the day you have decided it will be – and let nothing side track you from it.

Saturday Feb. 23, 1980

Darling Sunny,
I called your place yesterday morning and gave all information to your classification officer because the chaplain wasn't coming in until 1 p.m.

Obviously, they took care of everything and made it possible for you to call Grandma Reina – it was a sad call to make, but at least you were able to make your farewells. So at least compassion was shown and your officer said she would pray for Grandma and that 'our God' would watch over Grandma. I told the officer that we all pray to the same God and that there is only one God for us all – which, though it was a revelation to her, made her happy too – We thank all concerned for their heartfelt cooperation.

We leave tomorrow and will see Grandma on Tuesday. She's back in the home again today and seems comfortable and clean – not in pain – for which we're grateful.

I'd better pack now. So stay well and take no sides in any controversies that have arisen! Think of yourself, my love!

I'll try to write from out West and keep you posted!

Love and kisses, Mom

Grandma Reinie didn't last long after that. My parents asked that I not tell her where I was and why I couldn't come to see her. I had to tell her I was travelling and couldn't make it soon enough. I would rather have told her the truth. At least she would know why I couldn't come and I wouldn't have to lie and claim I was just too 'lame' to make it there. She was my only living grandparent. Grandpa Harry, her husband, the jolly fat man with the vicious false teeth, had died many years earlier, as had my beloved Grandpa Bushzy. So now there were none.

My Woman,

I love you. I found this paper as I was going through a box. It's ripped on the corners as a mouse must have chewed it a bit but I wanted to write on this paper as it's a nice color and know you'd like it. I had a good workout on Friday morning. Just me and Kato – drilled me on kicks and combos. I'm learning and it feels good to be learning. Kato told people in the park (the visiting park) yesterday that I was fast and that I'm one of his best students ever, but he doesn't tell me and I hear it second hand from everybody ha ha. Sun, there is nothing more than simply training and I don't care about praise, I just train. Besides, I know when I'm learning and things are coming smooth like an oiled machine, fluid, and I feel it Sun, but I know nothing in substance. Kato is an excellent Sensei and I under-stand much of his technique and perceived him as a super competent teacher and master of the physical aspects of karate, no doubt in that. It's simply hard to relate Kato's expertise, same with 7,* they've forgotten more than they've shown me. The past fifteen months I've worked out under Kato for

*This was a code word Jesse used for his original sensei.

about a hundred and thirty hours and that's one to one, individual, not counting yard time that's just tables time. I mean I'm in as good shape as you've ever seen me. I have good muscle tone all over, thin but wiry. You'll love it. I have some wrinkles at the eyes and lines around the mouth from snarling, losing the little hair I have left and gray in my sideburns but I still look pretty good ha ha!

I love you. Your husband, Jesse

It's an odd phenomenon, this obsession men in prison have with body building. Sort of a throwback to the apes maybe. Women do it differently. Later on, I learned to use the weights and the exercise machines too and realized the benefits of looking tough but that wouldn't save you without the proper mental respect.

As it turned out, Kato just couldn't deal with the humiliation of prison. He was great for Jesse during the short time he was there, saving up his medication until he had accumulated a sufficient quantity on which to overdose. They found him dead in his cell one day. It seemed as if he gave Jesse his life force before he checked out. And Jesse needed it, the way things were going.

There was a lot going on legally at this time. The Confidential Communication motion from way back was denied. So was Jesse's appeal to the Florida Supreme Court. Our co-defendant, Walter Rhodes, had confessed again. This time he had made a written statement witnessed by two of his cellmates but he recanted it as usual after another of those infamous visits from Satz's assistant, LaGraves. Jesse's attorneys were preparing for a hearing on his appeal. And then, at last, there was the hearing on new evidence in my case from the 1977 PSI report.

The hearing was based on my discovery of the memo documenting Walter Rhodes's statements during his polygraph test. Stamped CONFIDENTIAL in red ink, it had never been given over to the defence. In the statements, Rhodes said he wasn't really sure I had done anything. Ray Sandstrom had filed a motion for a hearing based on newly discovered evidence.

The hearing was held in the Broward County courthouse. The original trial judge presided. I think it is done that way to give a judge the chance to correct his own errors. Before we entered the courtroom they took the extraordinary measure of having the area searched by a bomb-sniffing dog. They said it was because Jesse's friends might try to rescue him.

As I waited through the preliminary statements, I could hardly concentrate on what was being said. I knew Jesse was close by. I could feel his presence. My mind was not on the proceedings in the courtroom. To me it was all so completely obvious I couldn't imagine any outcome except a favourable one. Rhodes lied and we had it in black and white in a report generated by the police polygraph expert.

I had not seen Jesse in three years. They brought him through the side door. He was wearing his prison uniform, handcuffed and shackled. I soaked up the sight of him. My Jesse! But he looked so aggravated – not tough-guy aggravated but bone-deep aggravated. I could see that he had been working out by the way his arms and chest filled out his uniform. But his face was drawn and tight. My heart was so full I felt I would cry. But it was my love that I wanted him to see, not my tears. After they got him settled in a chair along the side wall, he smiled and winked at me and our eyes locked. I yearned to touch his face, to feel those arms around me, to hear him say some magical thing. But we weren't allowed to even speak. It was the last time Jesse and I would ever see each other.

Ultimately, the judge said it didn't make any difference that Rhodes said he wasn't really sure I had done anything. I couldn't imagine how it didn't make a difference since it was quite the opposite of his trial testimony. Rhodes had confessed to the murders twice more since the Orf and Hysmith incident. Realizing he had a bargaining tool, he had used it to get a TV and a transfer in 1979 when he confessed again in an interview with a newspaper reporter. Each time, the district attorney's chief investigator, LaGraves, would make the trip to convince Rhodes to return to his original trial testimony, persuading him that he really did 'want to see [us] fry'. Their conversations were recorded on tape, which I would only find out about much later on. So, even though Rhodes had confessed twice and had contradicted his trial testimony during a polygraph interview, the undeniable proof of his guilt, and our innocence, would remain obscured for another fourteen years.

My parents got me a subscription to the local paper after I

won my civil lawsuit. Every time the paper arrived I would pull out the crossword puzzle, and the recipes section, check through the world and local news briefly, roll the paper back up and stash the rest in my bathroom. I had a whole stack of newspapers in there that I intended to read through some time when I got around to it, which I never did. I don't exactly know why I saved those newspapers. Maybe because my parents sent them. Maybe just because I could. I think I insulated myself with newspaper, just like bums used to do when they lay on park benches to sleep, as protection against the assault of the elements.

I saved recipes from those newspapers while I was on death row, for when I got out. I always loved to cook and I loved to learn new ways to prepare food for the family. I loved to feed people. It was a life-affirming act, I suppose, and I found it comforting. I even catalogued them into the various types of meals, desserts, appetizers.

They never took them from me and I still have them somewhere, old and yellowed, in a box along with other memories of those times.

A girl was put in the next cell because she was nine months pregnant. We talked under the door and she told me that this was her fourth baby and that the last one had come within minutes of the onset of labour. She was afraid that no one would be there when she was ready to have the baby.

The only way I had of calling for help was by banging on my door. Shouting rarely did any good. In between hourly checks, you were lucky if someone down the hall heard the banging and cared enough or was curious enough to find out where it was coming from. There had been seizures, diabetic emergencies, a heart attack, a throat slashing, and a girl who hanged herself. They almost didn't make it in time to get her down. She had tied her sheet to the arm of the door mechanism. At first I thought she was faking, the way she was flapping her arms around. But then her face became distorted – eyes bulging, tongue popping out. I screamed and banged on the door with my fists, but no one could hear me. I turned with my back to the door and began horse-kicking it with my heel. Finally, I picked up a shoe and beat on the door until someone came. The blood vessels burst between the back of my knee and my heel, leaving a nasty purple mark.

The pregnant girl had her baby on the way to the hospital, in the driveway of the local fire department because we couldn't summon help soon enough. I sent a note to the superintendent telling him that I would agree to be responsible for calling for help in an emergency but I needed a way to communicate. I hoped no one would have to die before something was done.

Shortly thereafter, the superintendent installed an intercom in my cell. It could have been a solution to the problem. But the captain saw it as an opportunity for harassment – a bug with which to bug me. He had the receiver placed in his office and ordered me to leave the unit on at all times. So instead of being helpful to me the device became the bane of my existence, making me regret ever having suggested it. And the worst part was that during the night, when it was needed most, no one would be in the captain's office to hear it. The joke was on me.

Every morning, the first thing I did was to turn on the local hard rock station on my radio and place it next to the intercom – let the country and western captain have that with his morning coffee since he wanted to hear something. That way I could cough or spit or fart or sing in the shower in private. I couldn't understand why he would want to punish me for helping him do his job. He was ultimately responsible for security – that included the safety and welfare of every inmate as well as making sure we didn't escape. Paper covers rock, rock beats scissors, scissors cut paper, hatred outdoes good sense.

March 13, 14, 15, 1981 Friday Saturday Sunday
My Man,
I love you! It's Friday and a day to remember indeed! I got a memo from the superintendent saying the intention of the device was never to interfere with my privacy and that I could turn off the device until I needed it for emergency. Isn't that great? I'm so happy and relieved. Our superintendent is a man of principle – it's good to know there's someone with the authority who is willing to use it when he sees a wrong being done. I think it took courage for him to go against the system and I wrote him a note to thank him. It feels so good not to have to wonder who could be hearing me every time I make a sound. The measure of how much relief I feel is an indication of just how much I was disturbed by it. I feel terrific!

When I unplugged it I thought about a suitable sign off, but I decided it was sufficient just to unplug it.

I still had a problem with the receiver being in the captain's office but it was a great improvement and the lieutenant on night shift would often station himself there. I used that intercom on many occasions. Just knowing there was a way to summon help was comforting.

❧ *The thing I've thought about most, besides love and death, is morality. Why have we not made strides in that area? Why does so important a thing fall so far behind?*

It's weird – most things are justified because they make money and are considered lawful. I guess it's in part because morality is not agreed-upon to be one universal code of ethics – it is shaded and altered in many ways in order to suit the society's needs and so must be practical. Is that the answer? To make morality and practicality compatible?

Perhaps a different understanding is needed. That's part of what laws should be for. But the law has become too fraught with self-interest . . .

Love, Justice, Faith – the three blind beliefs that we follow and uphold, and for which we will place our life on the line. In order for this relationship between belief and believer to function properly there must be a balance between the intellect and the emotional. I wonder if sentimental

*people and angry people have something in
common.*

We went through a number of superintendents and I had
many different guards assigned to me through my years
on death row. Some came as rookies, some as old-timers
put out to pasture, so to speak. They usually started out
hard, with an attitude, but eventually softened. One or
two even became friends although always professional. In
1981, we finally got a woman superintendent. I thought it
made more sense to have a woman in charge of women.

21

FOOTSTEPS. MORE THAN ONE PERSON . . . one of them is a woman . . . tapping of women's heels. I am up on tippy toes, face pressed to window, turning away to exhale so as not to fog up my view. There they are! It is Mrs V, the superintendent, and two men. One is a guard. The other is wearing a dark business suit. He is definitely official. You can always tell by the suit, dark blue. He must be from Tallahassee, the state capital and main office of the Department of Corrections. Maybe an inspector. Why are they coming to see me? I haven't sent in any complaints lately. Something must be up. Do a quick check over my shoulder around the cell for contraband. They are coming through the outer doors to my area. Take a deep breath and calm my heartbeat, stepping slightly back from the door. They position themselves in front of my cell. It is definitely something to do with me. I am on alert, all senses reaching outward, unaware any longer of my internal processes. What do they want with me? I wonder. Must be important for Mrs V to come herself.

The guard bends towards the door to open the lock. It is a big deadbolt. You can hear how big it is by the sound it makes as it slides in and out of the doorframe. She has papers in her hand. She looks almost emotional. Her face is more blank than usual. Mrs V is OK. She thinks of us as 'her girls'. She is protective of us, and very principled. I feel safer with her in charge here.

'Sonia, there has been some news concerning your appeal.'

My mind has wrapped itself around the possibilities and I don't hear anything she says about the man with her. My case! Something has happened. She is reading from the paper in her hand now. All ears and eyes, my total attention is fixed on the words as I watch them tumble in slow motion from her mouth. They are like bubbles that pop in the air between us.

My sentence had been changed from death to life, but the conviction remained. This meant that I would no longer have to spend the rest of my life in isolation. The sword of impending execution would be removed from over my head but it also meant I would not be going home.

'The state has fourteen days in which to appeal the court's decision to change your sentence,' Mrs Villacorta went on to say. 'Until then, you will remain in your present location. After that, you will be moved to Reception and Orientation.'

'Can I call my lawyer?'

'Of course. Officer, will you please arrange for Sonia to use the phone today to call her attorney.'

'Yes, ma'am.'

'Thanks, Mrs Villacorta.'

'You're welcome, Sonia.'

They leave. I turn on the radio to see if I can find out anything more about it. This is the first time I didn't hear about something important happening in my case on the news before anyone came to tell me. As the voice from the radio drones on, my mind begins to chew on the tasty morsel it has just been given. I wonder what that means, that the state has fourteen days to appeal. Could my sentence change back to death again? I need to see a copy of the court's decision. I need to talk to my lawyer. Where is my lawyer anyway? Why didn't he call? Maybe he tried. I'd better get ready for the phone call. Where is my phone book? Pen and paper? Shoes? OK, I'm ready. Don't want to give them an excuse to say I wasn't ready and leave. Probably have to wait for me since Mrs V ordered it. Well, they can come on now. Come on with that phone call now . . . I'll have to ask the lawyer to call my parents.

The news! They're talking about it now. It's true! Like everyone else, I believe it's true if I hear it on the news. I want to know what's going to happen. I wonder what I can have and what I can't have in population. I'll have to ask the girls when I go out on my walks. I think my rules are pretty much the same as theirs. I won't be able to keep my radio cord, I know that. You have to use batteries in population. Can't use up state electricity. But I figure they allotted me 2200 volts of electricity and I was using just some of it while I could enjoy it. Oh well, I don't mind having to buy batteries. I'm gonna get out of this cell! I'm going to be with my friends! All right!!!

They do come and get me for my phone call. The

lawyers are sure the state will not prevail in their efforts to appeal. The judge who sentenced me to death had no good reason to overrule the jury. My parents are ecstatic. My dad had been at the Florida Supreme Court hearing. He said that the panel of judges was appalled when my attorney, Ray Sandstrom (who remained the attorney of record until after that first appeal had been heard), said he wasn't prepared to address the fact that his client could be facing a death sentence. They wanted to know if he was court-appointed or privately retained in order to ascertain the state's responsibility for such an unacceptable lack of preparation.

So now we could proceed to the next step in the process. Five years to get to the first appeal. Five years of isolation. Five years.

❧ March 1981

Death row has been my home for almost five years. During that time I have had only limited access to the other inmates. I have had a number of neighbors through the years. I have had my four hours of walks or half hour visits on the days I didn't go outside and I have managed to make a few good friends but I really haven't gotten to know that many people under the circumstances.

I must write to Jesse, to share this wonderful moment with him.

It is day twelve since they changed my sentence. Two more days and I can join the living again. I have been looking over my collection of odd things. I seem to have managed to accumulate quite a lot. I will miss my shower and those 2 a.m. soaks. Nostalgia? Is that what I am feeling? Well, it's worth the trade. Privacy is one thing but isolation is another. My dad used to say he wished he could come here for a couple of weeks to get away from it all and have his food brought to him. That would be a lovely getaway. But I told him that it gets cold real quick.

I hear someone coming. It isn't time for the regular check. What now? Some last-minute hassle? They changed their minds! They are going to find an excuse to keep me up here. Shit! Calm down. Don't panic yet. It could be something good. It could be—

The superintendent is standing in front of my door. My heart is beating hard enough for me to feel the pulse in my ears. Breathe! I had stopped breathing. The guard who is with her is opening the door to my cell. He steps back in deference to the superintendent.

'Pack your things. You will be moved to the registration and orientation unit today.'

'Excuse me, but I don't think I need to go to R&O. I am familiar with the rules, basically, and my friends can tell me what I need to do on the compound.'

'That's what I'm afraid of, Sonia. Believe me, you don't think so now, but you will be glad you were sent to R&O first. And you will only be in there ten days rather than the full two weeks.'

'But it isn't time yet. They have one more day before the decision is considered final on changing my sentence.'

'Yes, well, they have decided not to appeal. Get your

things together. How many carts do you think you'll need?'

'Uhhh, I don't know.' I have no idea. And I don't really want her to know how much stuff I have in here.

She gave a quick glance around. 'Let's start with two and work from there.'

'OK. Thank you.'

She smiled. She really smiled. It was small but genuine. She would be glad not to have to deal with my death row situation any more. She was a decent woman and I believe it bothered her. I wondered how it was for someone to have such a difficult time showing emotions like it appeared to be for her. Was she like that at home too?

They leave and I begin the task of gathering my belongings. I wasn't ready for it to be today. This throws me into turmoil. I haven't even decided what to do with the things I am not supposed to have. The packets of seeds I was still holding on to. The dowels I had made for use as chopsticks. I don't think they will strip-search me and surely they won't do a cavity search of someone *leaving* death row. All my magazines and newspapers. The clothing I still have that I won't be allowed to keep. Where to begin? Be orderly. Keep like things with like. My writing stuff. That goes first. Then my pictures, and art supplies and paintings. The chopsticks can remain with my paintbrushes. OK. Good. This is good. And my letters – all those precious letters . . .

I can't believe it! I am actually going to leave this place today. No appeal. Well, there was no basis for an appeal.

269

The judge just wanted me to go to death row. He had no justification for overruling the jury's recommendation of life or he would have written it down. He should have declined to hear my case in the beginning, having been a state trooper himself for seven years prior to becoming a judge. He must have known he would be reversed on appeal. But he also knew I would spend a long time on death row waiting for that to happen. But I don't want to think about that now. This is a time for celebration! I am leaving 'death row according to man's law' behind me now. Today is the day I am born again, out of a womb of concrete and steel into the world of BCI. It is a world unknown to me, even though I have observed it from my tower for four years. I have met some of its inhabitants and caretakers and heard stories about the culture but it may as well be Mars. That's OK. Mars is better than death row. Anyway, my friends will take care of me.

I begin to pack up my belongings. I have a case of terminal smiles. My heart is singing. My brain is humming. I wonder if I can make a phone call from R&O? I will ask when they come back with those carts. Meanwhile, I have a lot to do!

The canvas-sided laundry carts arrive. The guard and I fill them and find we need at least one more to hold the rest of my collection. It is mind-boggling that I have managed to accumulate so much junk. I just hope I won't get in trouble for any of it. The other cart is brought in and I fill it with the remaining piles of newspapers.

'I think that's it. Can we go now?'

'I have to tell the control room that we are ready.'

The guard, a nice man, called in and we were cleared for movement on the compound. I could hear the answer come back on his walkie-talkie.

Here we go! Down the birth canal. Here I come! Wheeeee!

I am pushing one cart and pulling another. The guard has the third cart. The nurses in the hall are looking at us with bemused expressions. I wave.

'Goodbye. Thanks for everything.'

One of them wishes me good luck.

We can only load two carts at a time into the elevator. It's OK. I am pushing the ones with the most important stuff in them. The guard says they will bring the other one down for us. Fine. The elevator door opens and we load ourselves in. Down we go! The door opens on to the lobby area where visitors come through the sallyport doors. There is no one coming through just now. Someone opens the door leading out on to the compound. The opening is sufficient for me to emerge. I am born with a huge grin on my face. I fill my lungs with fresh air. My first breath as a new being in a new world in a new life! Yes! Here I am! It is so bright! So beautiful! What a great day to be born!

There is an inmate standing to one side of the walkway and she has such a sweet smile on her face, head cocked slightly to one side, hands folded in front of her chest.

'Hi!' I say as we pass by with the carts like a procession. ET, the happy alien being, and her interdimensional luggage – laundry carts. The walkway in front of the administration building is clear but where the path turns

271

on to the compound leading to the dormitories it is lined with people. There are women on both sides of the street waving and clapping and everyone looks happy! The procession becomes a parade complete with throngs of cheering well-wishers joining in the celebration of my return to the land of the living! The guard gives me a hand pushing the first cart, freeing my hand to wave back at the smiling faces. 'Hi! Hi, everybody!' I am waving and smiling and laughing out loud. The silence is over. The loneliness is over. I am one happy baby!

The doors close behind me, shutting out the cheering and the welcoming faces. It is quiet and cold in R&O, the main reception area for incoming prisoners, where each one is processed in and prepared for entry into the main population of the prison. (They always keep the air conditioning on freezing in these areas, for behaviour control, I believe.) Reception and Orientation. The guard is sitting in the office as you come in the door, checking people's belongings. The welcome wagon lady, right? It's the big, sweaty one, dreaded because she is so fanatical about everything. She's the one who put her fingers in my ears during a strip search after a walk. She had been with me the entire time. What could I have secreted inside my ears? It was bizarre. A slimy chill of recollection skitters over my skin. She takes her job too seriously, even for the other staff members. She is a 'serious dog'. (Actually, years later, I got to know her better and found she had another side to her, which was very sensitive and soft. She was a watercolour artist. I think she felt she had to assume a hard and impenetrable veneer in order to perform her duty.) Anyway, in my ten-thousand-to-one-shot life, she has to be on duty when I come through R&O with my three laundry carts.

As I stand waiting for them to haul my carts into the office, I try to see the face of the girl they are processing in before me. She doesn't seem to have much stuff. Must have just come in from jail.

I am watching what the serious dog takes from the girl. Pens. She is saying she can only have five pens. I guess I'll lose some of mine. But I have so much stuff, maybe she won't go through everything. She has all night though, and she is very thorough.

'Ms Jacobs, could you wait outside of the office, please?'

'Sorry, I thought you wanted me in here.'

The girl unpacking her stuff looks up to see who the guard was talking to and our eyes meet. In a mixture of recognition, pleasant surprise and unpleasant wariness, I am looking into the face of Joanne Champ, one of my cellmates from jail. It has been five years since I saw her last. She looks as surprised as I do. Good acting? I wonder if this is another Brenda Isham? She really does look happy to see me. I can't help but smile back. I always liked Joanne. She even testified for me at my trial when they brought in Brenda Isham, who lied about my having a conversation with her. Joanne! Amazing.

I made it through the inspection of my possessions without getting in trouble for anything. 'Serious' took a lot of stuff away, but I was happy with what I had left. Actually, she was pretty nice about it.

The R&O building was shaped like a dumbbell. There was a long central hallway that stretched from one side to the other. Each horseshoe-shaped side had two tiers and 25 cells, 12 cells on the bottom tier and 13 on the top tier. There was a stairway on each side going down to the lower level and a stairway leading up to the left and to the right. There were two toilets and one sink and one shower at each end of the horseshoe upper and lower, making 8 toilets, 4 sinks and 4 showers in total for the 25 women on each side of the building. Each cell had its own sink so that wouldn't be a problem. Sharing the toilets could get a bit sticky but I would wait and see how that went. My cell was in the middle of the upper tier on the left. I called it my room. The word cell gives me the creeps.

I am in my new room and the door is never locked. I leave it open. I like the door to be open. No one is allowed over the threshold to your room. It is a violation of the rules. They have given me a set of rules to read. All of our possessions must fit into two boxes which are to be kept under the bed, the towel is to be folded and hung neatly over the rail at the foot of the bed, and beds are to be made at all times except when you are sleeping in them at night. There is nothing much in the cell, just a sink and a bed.

I really don't think I need to be here in R&O. I told them that my friends would take care of me when I got out on the compound. I don't need to be in R&O to learn the rules. They laughed, literally. Oh well. I am glad I will have these ten days to just enjoy being able to do things with people again before I get assigned to a job. I wonder what they will decide to do with me. I wish my room weren't right here in the middle where everyone has to pass it to get to the bathroom. I wonder if I can get into a corner room on the compound.

Joanne came to my room. I was expecting her. I wondered what she would say about her being here at the very time when I got to R&O. If she was a plant it was really obvious and stupid. Didn't they know me at all by now? She said her case was on appeal all this time, five years, and that she had a baby at home. She didn't have much time to serve, probably wouldn't be here a full year, but it was very disrupting for a family with a baby.

I was not sure whether I trusted her but I had always liked Joanne and she was a bubbly person. Well, I didn't intend to talk about my case and she hadn't asked except to enquire how Jesse was doing. Might as well enjoy her company.

Joanne was sitting in my doorway, just over the crack that separated the room from the walkway. She had just finished telling me about her new husband and baby son, and the trouble her younger brother had been getting into. I was also sitting in the doorway, on my side of the line. I decided to show Joanne some of my photos from visits with my kids. Scurrying on hands and knees the few feet to the bed where my boxes were stored, I grabbed a handful of Polaroids and scurried back to show her.

'Sonia, why do you crawl around like that? Why don't you get up and walk?'

'Well, why would I get up and walk when all I am doing is going a few feet and back again? It's such a short distance.'

I realized that I was in the habit of moving around on hands and knees. There had been no one to see me, and it did make sense after all. But it wasn't how people did it out here, and I wasn't going to be scurrying around in a small space by myself any more so I'd better work on breaking that particular habit. I knew there would be things I would need to change. So this would be the first.

'Do you know I can see right through your pyjamas?'

I twisted around to try to see what she meant. It was true. You really could see the pink of my skin through the material. I'd had these pyjamas for a long time. They were my favourites. I always put on a robe when I knew they would be coming around for check time. I tried to think if there was anyone who could have seen before, in front of whom I would now have to be embarrassed. I couldn't think of anyone. Good, but I had to get a different pair of pjs.

Shrugging my shoulders and rolling my eyes, I got up, fully erect, to find where I had put the state robe they give you when you come into R&O.

'I can't believe you were locked up in there all this time. I got married and had a baby who is going on four years old now. It's unbelievable.'

'But we're both here now, for a little while. I know you won't have to do much time. They'll let you go home to your baby. And you'll be able to see him in the visiting park.'

'What's it like in the VP?'

'I don't know. I used to visit outside my room upstairs. I've never visited in the VP. I do know that you have to get strip-searched before you can go in and when you leave as well.'

'Do they strip your visitors too?'

'I don't know. I don't think so.'

'Maybe Gina knows. She's been here a while.'

Joanne gets up to leave, straightening her blouse and brushing off her pants. I must keep it in mind to be aware of how I look to people.

'Thanks for stopping by.'

'Sure. Isn't it amazing to meet here after being in the jailhouse together almost five whole years ago?'

'Yes. It really is.' I smile at the irony. I can only hope that it is amazing-good and not amazing-bad. We shall see.

We are going to eat breakfast in the dining hall, together. This is a monumental occasion for me. I will get to eat with other people, in a dining hall, at a table!

We are lined up in the central hallway by the door, two by two. We are all wearing the brown corduroy state jackets that we were issued upon arrival in R&O. You have to become one of the population – uniformity obfuscating individuality as much as possible. You have to start thinking of yourself as a prisoner and not as an individual. You are part of a group and expected to behave accordingly.

'Straighten up this line or we won't be going anywhere.'

I look around to see if everyone is straight. It is part of learning to take orders, I suppose, but I already know how to do that. I can understand the need to be orderly, but these new girls are still resentful. They don't yet know there is a practical reason for it. Still, you would think they could say it a little more nicely. They used to talk to us nicely in the early days, while Superintendent Sorensen was here.

The line is finally straight enough, according to the guard in charge, and we are told we can start out towards the dining hall. I turn towards my line partner. My face hurts from smiling. The morning air is cool and fresh. There is dew on the grass and the foliage in front of the dorm as we come out the door and down the steps.

'Wait on the walkway there. Stop right there until the rest of the line catches up. Come on, tighten up that line.'

We stand in place, hands in pockets, until the guard gives the signal to go, raising her arm and bringing it forward like you see on a cattle drive. 'Move 'em up, head 'em out.' I am bouncing along. There is no talking in the line. You can get in trouble for talking in the line. I certainly don't want to get in trouble because I am enjoying this too much.

We arrive at the front of the dining hall. I am starving! I didn't realize how hungry I was until I smelled the food. We file in and take seats in the booths, set up in rows like in a huge diner, one behind the other as they come up, no choosing where you will sit. Then the guard tells one table at a time to get up and go get their food.

The girl behind me keeps bumping me in the back with her tray, like tailgating in a car. The constant

278

proximity of people has my skin tingling as it is but this intrusive touching sends me into an adrenaline rush. Stiffening with the next bump, I turn over my shoulder to look at her, glaring hotly.

'Please don't do that.'

She is just standing there, stupid, grinning. Maybe she is retarded. Whatever she is, I hope she keeps her distance. But then when the line stops again she bumps me with her tray. I spin around, freaked, hands out in front of me, knees bent, coiled and ready. Barely able to hiss the words out, 'Don't do that again,' in what sounded to me like a growl from deep inside my chest.

'OK, baby. I didn't mean no harm.'

The officer is looking. Everyone seems to be looking. I nod at the girl and turn back to my tray, moving it along the railing to the next serving station.

Behind a long counter, inmates are placed at intervals in front of large aluminium pans of food. They will serve us as we come down the line. There is a shiny metal railing to guide you. First you take a tray. They are hot, and still wet from the huge dishwashing machine in the back. Then you move down the line, saying yes or no to whatever is being served. Today, it is pancakes. Most people are saying it is their favourite. We return to our table with the full tray of food, having picked up a spoon and a plastic glass on the way.

'Isn't this great? Just like going to the Pancake House!' I am a fool. They look at me with a mixture of indulgence and chagrin. The other women think I am brain-damaged from being on death row, but I am too happy to be deterred. It is just so good to be sitting in a booth with three other women, eating breakfast together in this brightly lit dining hall. I want to share my joy with everyone. Being able to say what size portion you like, the way you like your toast, whether you want syrup on your pancakes or not – all of these are new experiences for me. My tray used to come prepared, like it or not, and always cold. And here there is salt on the table. You can actually salt your own food! I am celebrating, and anyone who wants to celebrate with me is certainly welcome. If not, that's OK too.

These are the best pancakes I ever had! I can't drink my milk on top of all this food. I am used to saving my food to nibble on during the day. I can't possibly eat all this and drink at the same time. But the milk is important. I don't dare try to take it back to the dorm with me. I don't know how it goes yet. Maybe they search you when you get back from the dining hall.

Back in the dorm, people stop by my room all day. Often they want some coffee, creamer, sugar, or all three. I have a large container of each. The women in R&O only get to go to the canteen once a week. I came in with all of my supplies from death row so I was rich in those precious commodities. I don't mind giving, but my supply of goodies is starting to dwindle and I am not sure when we get to go to the canteen. You have to make things last in here.

One of the results of institutionalization was that I was not able to make decisions for myself about such things as entering and leaving an area without official direction. I could go to the dining room because I had been instructed to do so. But leaving my room was not part of the repertoire.

After several days of getting used to the routines of R&O, one of the girls said, 'Hey, Sonia, how come we always come to your room but you never come to ours?'

I don't know the answer to this question. And it hadn't occurred to me until she mentioned it that I didn't go out of my room except when I was given an order, like being called out to meals or to the office for something. Strange. I guess it is one of the things I knew would happen but couldn't prepare for. This requires some self-therapy. Tomorrow night I will make myself stand just outside the doorway to my room for five minutes.

It is time to come out of the room. I am in my new white pyjamas tonight. I put on the state robe that has a dizzying design of flowers printed on it. The rules say you must wear a robe when you come out of your room. Five minutes. I look at my watch to check the time. Stepping over the threshold and to the left, I press my back to the wall, sliding down into a squat, oriental-style, with my arms wrapped around myself. I settle in for the five interminable minutes that make my skin crawl and my teeth clench. It feels foetal. It feels like when the first amphibian crawled out of the sea. It reminds me of a goldfish that has lived its life in a small bowl and suddenly finds itself in a larger tank. It will still behave as if it had the original space around it. You get used to having a certain amount of space around you and anything more or less is a cause for discomfort. Amazing. Goldfish syndrome. I will make myself spend five minutes tomorrow night standing at the railing in front of my room.

People pass by and look. Some acknowledge my presence and some just walk on by without a glance. Is it five minutes yet? I never realized how long five minutes could be.

Third night and I am standing at the rail directly in front of my room. I even put one foot up on the bottom rung. It feels better tonight. I still wish people wouldn't pass quite so close but it seems to be a cultural thing and I will have to get used to it.

'Hey, Sonia. We're having a party for Gina down in the corner room. Got cake and everything. You know she gets special treatment because her uncle is the mayor of some town out here in the Everglades. Wanna come?'

'Yeah. Why not?'

Cured, I follow Champ down the hall to Gina's room for a party. I won't stay long though. It is a big step for me.

The stairs are my greatest physical joy. I love going up and down them. I do it every chance I get. They branch off from the end of the central hallway going up each side. If you stand at the top on one side, it looks like one of those amusement park rides that are shaped like a half-moon. I like to go down the stairs really fast. I hit the hallway going too fast to stop and so I keep going up the stairway directly across. This is so much fun! Exhilarating! Laughing out loud, I turn to repeat the action. Down one side, up the other, faster and faster until the officer on duty stops me with one raised finger. I come to a screeching halt in front of her on the landing. She wags the upheld finger back and forth. 'We don't do that here.'

'OK!' I turn and speed up the stairway to my cell. Inside the doorway, I take a deep breath to neutralize myself. I hope I won't get written up for it. Some of the officers would love to see me go back to confinement. This one seems nice. Her name is Mrs Lynch. I didn't feel any animosity from her. I am so sensitive to what I feel from people. But my own paranoia could be masking things. Well, it was really fun while it lasted. Change is the one thing you can count on in life. That has been one of the main weapons in my arsenal – patience and the know-ledge that, eventually, things will change if you can just manage to hang in long enough. I wish I could have run up and down the stairs for longer though. Such freedom of movement! I must be getting used to greater space around me now. That didn't take long. But I know there will be other adjustments I haven't anticipated. I will be on guard for them. This is going to be fun! I haven't been called down to the office yet so I guess I'm OK. Time to make a cup of coffee. I can go by the office on the way to the card room where the water is and see if Mrs Lynch is writing in my jacket, the file each one of us has so they can keep a record of our behavioural adjustment.

I am having a hot cup of coffee, sitting on my bed, writing a note in my journal. One of the new girls comes to my door to ask for some sugar. This has become a regular habit with some and they are now sending the new girls up to my room as well. Sucker in Room 18,

283

right? Well, I don't mind sharing, but I think this has got out of hand. I will meditate on what to do and come at the problem from the right place. I am feeling a little resentful.

I make an announcement from the catwalk in front of my room. 'OK, everyone who wants cream, sugar or coffee, the line forms to the right of my doorway. Right now. Bring your friend's cup too, if you want. This is it, folks. This is all there is going to be. Last time for everything. So, come and get it!'

They start coming, slowly at first. They must think it is a joke, or that I am just pissed off and talking shit. But when they see the first ones getting stuff, they start coming faster. There is a long line to the right of my door, and there are people coming out of their rooms to see what is going on.

'My friend isn't here now. They took her to medical. Can I get some for her too?'

'Sure. Bring her cup too. This is all there is. I don't care who gets it. But after this, there will be no more. So don't ask later. Get it now. This is it! Come and get it!'

They are lined up all the way to the bathroom. They must think I'm crazy. I'll still share with my friends, like Joanne and Gina, but the rest of them have got to find someone else to drain dry. I want friends, but not people who just want to drink up my coffee. It's OK. I am learning about myself and about how to get along with all these people in this strange new world. The officer is watching from the landing. She is shaking her head but she has a sort of a tight-lipped grin on her face. She is going away.

'There's just a little more creamer left, if anyone wants it.'

Someone comes with an empty container to get the creamer. That is the last of it. I know someone will ask for more later or tomorrow, not believing I mean what I say. Tossing the empty containers into the paper bag under my sink that I am using for trash, I feel a sense of accomplishment. It is certainly a challenge to figure out the culture of this society.

I had a major transition to make. Just having people around me was so overstimulating that I was living in hyperspace. After the first three days in R&O I lost my voice. I wasn't used to talking and my vocal cords had atrophied – apparently a little-known result of being in isolation for the better part of five years. It came back after a few days, but it was never the same. I had a different voice – one that sounded like my mother's voice, deeper and more gravelly.

My ten days in R&O are up before I know it. Although I didn't want to come to R&O at all, I now feel I could have stayed a few days longer. I could have used more time to adjust. But I won't tell them that. I will be just fine. My friends will help me and I will figure it all out as I go along. I have been assigned to H-5. It is the dorm for people who are just getting out of confinement. I guess technically I am coming from confinement, but not because I was a troublemaker. They use H-5 for 'decompression': it's a transitional place for people who can't get along in the regular dorms, break the rules and get locked up. Then, when their time in lockup is done, they are placed in H-5 to see if they are ready yet to rejoin the society of the compound. Coming from hospital confinement, I qualify by the letter of the law but not by the spirit of the law. I get my job assignment today too. I am very anxious to find out what I will be doing. I could work in the law library. I would be good there. I basically taught myself how to use it after being shown around by one of the inmate clerks and could hopefully work as a paralegal. They are called jailhouse lawyers or writ writers in prison. I could help people file their legal work. I could be productive in the law library. That is the only job I requested.

22

THIS IS MY FIRST DAY out of R&O and I have been assigned to work in the kitchen. It will be my first day without an escort, without a guard at my side, since I went to jail in 1976. It will be my first day having a job. I am to report right after count clears at 8 a.m. It is now March 1981.

It is hard to control my breathing. I want to hyperventilate. My feet barely touch the floor. If I am not careful, I feel I will levitate. I would really get in trouble then! My friend and surrogate mother, Colleen, the fifteen-year-old plumber, will meet me right outside the dorm when count clears. She will walk me to work. We weren't really able to talk while I was in R&O. You aren't allowed to communicate with the population because you are supposed to be learning the rules according to the authorities. You get the inmate version of the rules when you get out of R&O. I am ready to go!

Count is interminably long. I never used to pay any attention to it. It had no relevance to my world when I was on death row. But now it is highly significant. I like my new cell, and my roommate too. She is, in prison parlance, a 'stand-up' woman, meaning she is trustworthy and not a snitch. She has a relative on the 'outside' with a reputation for having been 'connected', which is a definite plus. It gives one a certain amount of prestige, imparting a degree of respect from the guards as well as the other convicts. Her name is Sam. She is funny. She doesn't have a lot of time to do and so she is pretty cheerful about it. Most people are not cheerful here. We have been sitting on our beds for forty-five minutes waiting for them to clear the count and I am getting itchy to go. There is no talking during count and you can't leave your bed, even to go to the bathroom. You have to ask. And you can get in trouble for talking during count if you ask, unless you wait for them to come around to count again and catch their attention. I close my eyes, picturing what it will be like in the kitchen.

'Clear count! We have a clear count on the compound. All inmates report to your assigned workstations. Work call! Work call! All inmates report to your assigned stations for work!'

All right! I jump off the bed and race to the stairs, joining the river of women flowing towards the front doors, down the steps and out on to the walkway leading to the various work areas. I am going to meet Colleen by the green door.

Colleen is living in H-4. They are released before H-5. Everyone is released before H-5 because we are the 'bad dorm'. I really want to get out of this dorm and into H-4 with my friend Colleen.

The hall is jammed with women funnelling towards the door, which is open now. I come down the stairs,

Me with my two children,
Eric (*below*) and Tina.

Our family before tragedy struck: me with my brother Alan and our parents, and (*right*) with my beloved Grandpa Bushzy.

Me aged sixteen.

(*Above*) Broward Correctional Institution, and (*below*) me photographed in the visiting area of Florida Correctional Institution for Women.

A pastel painting of the food I dreamed about while on death row.

Jesse as a young boy.

Jesse with baby Tina.

The entrance to Florida State Prison, where Jesse was held.

With his mother during a prison visit.

Family visits to me in prison.

Dec 25, 1980
We Love You Daddy

A snapshot of me and the children that
we sent to Jesse at Christmas.

The cells on death row
at Jesse's prison.

Sun-Sentinel

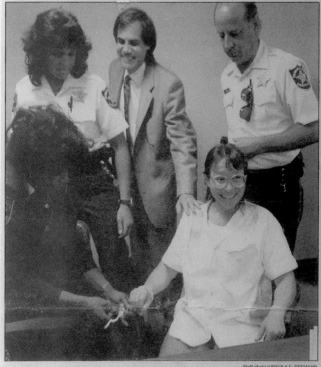

Staff photo/URSULA E. SEEMANN

Sonia Jacobs, at Broward County Courthouse on Friday, reacts to news that she won freedom.

My first swim in the ocean (*left*) after I was released.

(*Below*) Family finally reunited in 1998. From left to right, Eric, granddaughter Claudia, me and Tina.

(*Bottom*) Enjoying my greenhouse at home in the west of Ireland.

joining the flow . . . I am a part of the flow now. It takes a great effort of self-control to remain in the midst of all these arms and legs and torsos touching and jostling me, breathing on me, smelling next to me, giving off heat, and the constant hum of chatter around my head. I feel myself beginning to vibrate. The door is getting closer. I will be outside in a moment. There is the last squeeze through the narrow doorway and I am outside on the steps. I take a big breath.

Now to find Colleen at the green door. I speed on to the path, taking a sharp right away from the dorm and into the horticulture area. I wish I could work in horticulture. I wonder why they decided to assign me to the kitchen. The smell of the moist earth and the lush plantings is like an elixir. I am drinking it up through every pore. There is a magnificent elephant leaf plant growing at the edge of the walkway as I round the turn that forks off towards the kitchen to the left and the green door to the right. It is prehistoric-looking, having grown to a gigantic size in its tropical and protected setting. And it is still heavily laced with the dew that settles over everything during the sweet Florida nights before the sun sears it away into the clouds each day. It is there for me today as a gift from the Universe. Welcome to my garden, it says. I honour that gift. Stooping quickly over the broad, dark green leaf, I scoop the dew from it with my hand, bringing it to my face. It feels cool and clean on my skin. I taste it and am lost in the moment, until I hear Colleen's voice.

'Over here, sweetie. We can't take much time. We only have five minutes to get to work.'

She is sitting in front of the green door. It is the entrance to the hothouse where they work on special projects for horticulture class. I take the moment with me as I head towards my friend. I wonder if floating is illegal. My contact with the ground is very tentative. Colleen notices.

'Sit down here and get yourself together. You have to be serious and pay attention when you go to the kitchen.'

Colleen is my guide and my mentor and a very careful person.

'You OK?' she says with a concerned look on her face.

'Yeah.' I grin. I am seeing the world through the wide-open windows that used to be my eyes. 'I'm OK.'

'We'd better go now. Don't worry. You'll be fine. Just do whatever they tell you and don't let anyone get you upset.'

'Do you have any gum?'

She laughs at my request, digging in her shirt pocket and fishing out a stick for me. 'Here, baby. Now go on.'

I take the gum, unwrapping it as quickly as possible to stave off the major case of dry mouth that threatens to overwhelm me.

'Well, here I go!'

'See you later, sweetie. Gotta go now. You go that way.'

I turn towards the pathway that Colleen had designated. It leads through the horticulture area on to a sidewalk that curves around to the right. As the path opens up on to the compound again I can see the others in their white uniforms heading up the path towards the building where the kitchen is located. It looks like it had been a garage. The other side of the building is the warehouse and clothing room.

The kitchen entrance is locked. Only the small entrance door to the right of the large garage-type door opens, and only when someone lets you in. I knock. An inmate eating an orange lets me in. She must be on break. I look for an officer to tell me what to do next. I see the kitchen boss sitting in her office. She is a free person, not a guard. She is wearing a pants outfit with an overblouse. She is slightly on the heavy side, about fifty years old, and tired-looking. I hear she is nice. I go over to her door and knock. She is busy with two inmates and a guard. It looks like they have been arguing. The inmates have on long, used-to-be-white aprons and the guard, a short, round white woman with messy hair, has a large pot of something on the desk in front of her. They all look towards the door to see who is knocking. I wave and smile. The kitchen boss is telling the guard something. Now the guard is coming to the door. Good! Maybe I can find out what I am supposed to be doing. I wanted so much to work when I was on death row but they wouldn't allow it, not even wrapping bandages or something equally benign that I could have done in hospital confinement. I've been looking forward to this for a long time.

'What do you want?'

'This is my first day. I was assigned to the kitchen.'

'You Sonia Jacobs?'

'Yes,' I say, feeling a bit unsettled at the question, looking at the pocket of my blue work shirt where my name is clearly printed on a white label.

'You have to go to the clothing room and get your whites. That connecting door over there will take you there. Tell them to give you three pairs of whites and a pair of work boots. You will be a floor girl. And make sure you get socks too.'

'OK. Thank you.'

'You'll need a pass. You'll need a pass whenever you go anywhere except when we roll over to the dining hall. Go to the office by the door where you came in. Ask Officer Mala for a pass.' She turns to see the two inmates coming out of the office. She follows them, dismissing me without any further instructions.

The other office she spoke of is right there where you come in the side door. I didn't notice it at first. It is a small, crowded space with a storage room next to it. The officer at the desk appears to be middle-aged and has a head full of thick black wavy hair. Another inmate is at the door in front of me. I wait behind her. I am glad for the pause in which to observe.

'Mr Mala, I need to go to my dorm. I messed myself.'

'You pull this every other week, Martha.'

'No, sir. I don't ask you for nothin' unless it's serious. It won't take me long. I just have to change, you know. I can't go around all day with these bloody drawers, Mr Mala!'

'All right. Write yourself a pass and I'll sign it but don't be longer than fifteen minutes.'

'Thanks, Mr Mala.'

So that's how it's done. Interesting. I would never have talked to a man about my bloody drawers! But I see now how you get things done here. OK. I'm next. I step into the doorway.

'Excuse me. I was told to come here to get a pass to the clothing room.'

'You're Jacobs? Fill out one of the passes on that pad over there and I'll sign it. You know where the clothing room is?'

'Yes, the other officer told me to go through that connecting door over there.'

He nodded, watching me fill out the pass. I filled in the blanks – inmate name and number, date, time, assigned area, destination, reason for pass. He turned the pad around and read what I had written. Apparently satisfied, he signed his name, tore the pass off the top and handed it to me. As I took hold of it, I could feel his grip tighten momentarily before letting it go. My eyes moved up from the pass to his face to find his eyes staring directly into mine. I would think about the meaning of all this later. He released the pass, saying, 'Report to me when you get back.'

'Yes. I will. Thank you.'

There was so much hustle-bustle in the kitchen! Everyone in their whites, like sailors, scurrying back and forth with pots and pans, knives and spatulas, industrial-size mops and brooms, carts laden with trays of food. It made all the hairs on my skin stand up to feel the energy of so many people and so much movement around me. I smiled, taking a deep breath of it, inhaling a dose of this chaotic, frantic stuff in the air.

It will take some time to get used to this. But now I'm

off to the clothing room and the next part of this adventure!

I return with three sets of whites and a good pair of work boots. They are black and shiny and obviously a much-coveted item among the inmates. I see people admiring them and I clutch them more tightly, smiling weakly, hoping no one will try to take my new boots from me. I have my pass with me, signed by the clothing room officer. It has the time on it so I don't want to wait too long before handing it in to Mr Mala. He is busy on the phone and there is a line waiting to see him. I position myself outside of the office window to be sure he will see me there.

The kitchen smells of onions. There is a chalkboard up on the far wall with the menu for the day printed out on it. Spaghetti sauce. The onions must be for the spaghetti sauce. The huge cauldrons sit atop the long stoves and women stand before them with wooden paddles stirring the steaming contents. 'Hubble, bubble, toil and trouble . . .'

'Jacobs!'

'Uh, I got my uniforms. What should I do with them?'

'What should you do with them? You should go to your dorm and put one on and report back here immediately.'

'Um, do I need a pass?'

'Fill out a pass and I'll sign it.'

'Thank you.' I enter the office, squeezing past the other women who are still waiting in the doorway. 'Excuse me. Thank you.' No one responds.

Pass in hand, I hotfoot it to the dorm and back. I am ready to begin my first day at work in the kitchen. Hi-ho! Hi-ho! It's off to work I go . . . ! I wonder what I will be assigned to do.

Mr Mala tells me to ask one of the kitchen girls what she needs done for lunch. I bounce over to where she is cutting up some celery. The floor is slippery with steam and grease. I have to take care not to fall. One does not want to be injured in this place. The kitchen girl is cutting celery with a rather large knife. Looking around me, I notice others with similarly large and pointy knives and other instruments that could be dangerous. I realize that I am now in the middle of the kitchen area, away from the guards and the bosses' office, and there are criminals running around me with weapons. My back stiffens and all of a sudden my senses are on red alert. No one is going to get behind me with a knife, like I have seen in the prison movies, like the stories Jesse has told me about what can happen if someone doesn't like you. The kitchen girl looks up at me with a bored expression.

'Mr Mala said to ask you what you need done.'

After a few moments' hesitation, she replies, 'You can cut up the carrots.'

I look around the table for something to cut carrots but there isn't anything.

'You have to get a knife from the office. Just go and tell them you need a knife to cut carrots.'

I'm not sure if I am really supposed to go to the office and ask for a knife. She may be playing a trick on me. But I will give it a try. I know they won't give me a knife though. Maybe there is something else I can help her with. Just a few days ago, I was too dangerous to walk around by myself. I know they aren't just going to hand me a knife to cut with today.

'I need a knife,' I tell the female officer whom I have seen coming out of the bosses' office earlier.

She opens a cabinet filled with knives and cleavers, every shape and size. 'Which one do you want?'

'I need it to cut carrots.'

'Pick the one you want.'

I know this is ridiculous. She is not really going to give me this knife. I'll play along with the joke. I pick out the biggest knife in the cabinet. 'This one?'

She reaches in and gets the knife down for me. She hands me this machete, to cut carrots! I thank her and head for the door of the office. No one calls my name. I walk towards the kitchen girl and the pile of carrots on the table beside her. No one cares that I have this giant knife in my hand. This is a trick. I am going to get in a lot of trouble for having a knife. I should know I am not supposed to have one.

'Start with that pile. When you finish I've got some more.'

'OK. Thanks.'

I begin to cut the carrots. I have to move so that my back is towards the wall. No one seems to be paying me any attention, but you can't be too careful. I sneak a round of carrot into my mouth, trying to chew surreptitiously. The kitchen girl gives me a sidelong glance, snorting through her nose at me. I'll have to try to look more relaxed. But I'll be on my guard. This is prison now. The carrot tastes pretty good. I have another slice. I figure out how to place four carrots side by side and slice them simultaneously. I am enjoying myself. Mustn't whistle though. Not yet anyway. I hum my way through the stack of carrots.

Another good thing about being in the population was that I could make telephone calls! I could call my family, every day! You were allowed one ten-minute call per day. You had to sign the list right after they cleared the evening count. I would call every night to speak to my parents and the children, to tell them about my new and fascinating world. Sometimes I would switch off and call Kay Tafero or my friend Dottie Marie, with whom I had kept in touch ever since jail. And I would call my uncle Joe and keep myself part of the world out there. I wrote to Jesse every night, but I was never allowed to call him.

Every afternoon after work I would meet Colleen on the compound and we would go to the softball field. We were allowed to use the perimeter of the softball field for a track. You weren't allowed to run but you could walk, fast, around and around. Eight turns was a mile. These days I smelled like the kitchen – dirty sink water; stringy mops; onions and grease. You knew who your friends were when you got off work from the kitchen because no one who didn't really love you would be around for long. But Colleen walked me around that softball field every night until recall. As a plumber, she was on her feet all day. She

297

barely weighed more than 100 pounds and didn't need the exercise. But she was very sensitive and aware of my need to burn up excess energy. After a day's work, instead of being tired, I spun around like a dervish, whirring and humming and skipping in a hyperactive frenzy of over-stimulation. There was nothing in the rules, however, against skipping, which I did frequently when going from place to place – whistling as I went.

Just before recall each evening I would spend a quiet moment watching the sunset. Florida has the most beautiful sunsets. I would fill my mind with it, breathe it into my entire body.

'Recall! Recall! All inmates report to your assigned stations for count! Recall!'

I would turn and run to the dorm, up the stairs and into my room, where I would quickly prepare my water-colours to record the sunset for Jesse while they did count. It was a ritual. It helped to be able to share the celebration with him, so every night I would record the sunset for my love and put it in a letter. This way I could fully enjoy the moment. I was using real brushes now, not my hair. I hoped I had put enough life into the painting so that it would become real for Jesse too.

A few nights each week they had activities at the recreation building. I was always torn between the urge to be with my friends and my need for privacy. I had become used to having ample time for reflection and silence. I used the morning, afternoon and evening count times for meditation. I would choose to go to Rec on nights when we could work out, using the free weights, riding the exercycles. I loved the feeling of physical exhaustion, and the camaraderie. Friday nights they had movies. Sometimes Colleen would meet me on movie night but generally she stayed in her room. She had her own way of dealing with things.

Some of the guards had their own ideas about the way I should do my time. It became an almost daily event for me to be pulled into the lieutenant's office for shake-down. There was no way I could avoid the lieutenant's office because I had to pass by on my way to the dorm.

'Jacobs! Come in here!'

'I'll be right back,' I would say to my friends, hoping to make light of the situation. I was afraid no one would dare be seen walking with me. But my friends stuck by me and would sit on the steps waiting for me to come out. Two or three officers would then conduct the strip search. One of them searched my clothing, while the other(s) watched me. They weren't as thorough as the guards in the visiting park – no bending over, squatting and coughing – but then what these guards were looking for couldn't be coughed out. When the humiliation and intimidation were over, I would be released. I tried to remain neutral about it. No reaction. I didn't feed their sickness. This strategy was ultimately successful but not before they took one last shot.

I had begun to accumulate more stuff, especially paper. So I packed up a box of it for approval to be sent out on my next visiting day. They are supposed to inspect in front of you and seal it. But the sergeant in charge said she was too busy and instructed me to leave the box. Later

I was called back in to receive a disciplinary report for contraband. They said I was in possession of a piece of paper that was used for visitors' passes into Florida State Prison, where Jesse was being held. I had no idea what they were talking about. I tried to explain, pointing out that my box had been left open in the office and anyone could have put that paper in it. They told me that I would have an opportunity to tell my side of the story later. DR hearings were held regularly and it was like going to court except there was no jury, only an officer assigned to preside over the proceedings. I was sentenced to fourteen days in lock-up and told to pack the rest of my things.

In those days they used the corner rooms in each dorm as lock-up cells. The doors to the rooms had a slit in them for viewing purposes so they put a piece of wire mesh over the slit on the rooms used for lock-up. They took away all of your personal belongings. You'd be lucky to get it all back when you were released. All you had in the way of personal items were your pjs and robe and rubber flip-flops and a towel and washcloth. It was similar to what I had had in the Flattop. You had a regular bunk in the cell and your sink and toilet. Thankfully, in those days they didn't paint the entire window over with grey paint so you could see outside. Later on, they got meaner. Even worse, by the '90s they were using one building exclusively for disciplinary purposes. I wondered if they had a modern version of the Creech tank in there. I always wondered if there would be a Creech tank – just the sight of it had been traumatizing. Each dorm had two sides, A-side and B-side. I was locked in the corner room of H-2, B-side.

I could do fourteen days standing on my head. What bothered me was not being with my friends and losing all my stuff. H-2 was on the other side of the compound from H-4 and H-5. But Colleen had a friend living in H-2, someone she knew from work named Ginger. So I would be taken care of during the fourteen days.

Every evening after work, girls would gather on the lawn outside my window and read to me, play guitar and sing, fill me in on the day's events. My dinner tray would arrive with special treats, candy bars and potato chips, that my friends persuaded the kitchen workers to bring me. And during the day they would send in a milkshake or a soda with one of the girls who lived in the dorm. As the solid door of my cell had only a small mesh-screen opening, the girls provided a straw through which I could suck up the liquid treats while the person on the other side held the cup. If an officer came, the girl would simply turn around and walk away sipping her drink. The other inmates weren't supposed to talk to the people in lock-up. But it became apparent that this move, having me locked, was not popular even with the staff. It turned the tide and the officers on duty never bothered me. They never checked my tray; they never tried to catch anyone at my door, and after a week I was informed that I would be released three days early for good behaviour. I refused, remaining in lock-up for the entire fourteen days. The damage was already done. I wasn't going to let them clear their consciences that easily. I would rather do the three extra days with dignity.

When I got out of lock-up they agreed to put me in

H-4. I would finally be allowed to move in with Colleen and Cory and Ms J. Now I'd be able to see my friends in the evening when we were locked in for the night. We could sit at each other's door and have coffee and talk.

23

I SPENT ALL OF MY FREE time with Colleen. She introduced
me to some of the others. If Colleen introduced me to
someone, I knew they wouldn't get me in trouble because
I knew how cautious she was. In a way, it was both amazing and ridiculous that I could trust anyone at this point,
except that I was choosing my mentors with a different
emphasis than I had in the past, and not quite as blindly.
The blind triplets, luck, love and justice, had been
replaced by a spirit of survival and a modicum of
common sense.

Ginger, one of the women who had helped take care
of me in lock-up, came in with a two-year sentence
because she wouldn't testify against her husband. I don't
remember what the actual charge was. She got a job in
maintenance and Colleen scooped her for the plumbing
crew. Ginger was odd. She didn't fit in and no matter how
much time she had she never would have fitted in. She
wore high-fashion *Arabian Nights*-type jeans, tight at the
ankle and billowy up the legs. She walked around with her
nose in the air and said, 'Excuse me?' when anyone tried
to talk to her. She was a trip. And she had a husband, a
smuggler by trade, who sent her packages from home

filled with contraband. She didn't receive the packages herself. The packages were sent to an older lady in another dorm. Her name was Ms J – that was how you knew you were getting old in prison, when they called you 'Ms'.

We never knew what 'Ms J' stood for. We could only guess. She was committed under the name of Nellie Tollover. Tollover was the name of the husband she was accused of killing. She was doing a life sentence. I knew about Ms J because she was in my dorm. She was considered to be a mean old lady and we all tried to give her a wide berth as we passed her room to get to the downstairs bathroom. I never had any trouble with her myself but I rarely hung out at the TV downstairs. She was a dorm worker by day, witch by night, and bitch twenty-four seven.

Ginger's husband would do his brilliant camouflage job and send the pregnant package off to Ms J. We would all keep our eye on the daily list for package pick-up and when Ms J's name came up we knew it would be a good day. Ms J didn't want anything for her part in it. She just liked 'getting over', prison parlance for getting away with things. Ms J felt she had been wronged by the authorities all of her life and she always claimed that the local sheriff had framed her for her husband's murder. She had a score to settle and this was her way of accomplishing it. She would keep the stuff in her locker until Cory, Ginger's gofer, came to get something. In the event of a shakedown, Ms J would put that contraband in her bra or carry it in her hand and walk right past the guards and out the door with it.

I didn't have much to do with Ms J directly until after Ginger left. Occasionally I would have my own contraband to stash and secure. When I did, I would ask Ms J if she would hold it for me. She still kept herself well insulated against personal involvement but we had established a rapport through Ginger. Ms J was an interesting character. She started off by giving me advice from time to time, and then it expanded into tales from her past. I would sit in her doorway, for hours sometimes, while she spun out the threads that formed the tapestry of her life.

Ms J was born to an eleven-year-old girl who was still in grade school. Her family were dirt-poor farmers. Ms J was Nellie then. Her father was the son of a wealthy rancher in the area. He never took responsibility publicly, but he did stick by her mother for quite a while – long enough to have five more children. Eventually the mother found someone who said he'd marry her, an Indian chief, Nellie said, but first she had to get rid of all those kids. And so, one by one, she proceeded to give them away. The first to go was the baby. And Nellie loved her baby brother. He was her little doll, you see. She used to carry him around. The mother just gave him away to some couple. Nobody even knew their name. And Nellie was heartbroken. One by one the children left. Some of them went to families for household help. The younger ones were sent to an orphanage. Nellie was shifted off to live with a relative, who promptly put her to work around the house. But that didn't work out for Nellie. So from when she was nine years old until she was eighteen she lived in the state industrial school for girls, a reform school. It was the happiest time of her life. She wasn't beaten. She was allowed to play with kids. Be herself.

As a young woman, she had a job Apache dancing – a kind of dancing where the man throws the woman around. This was during the Second World War and she had decided to enlist in the Army Air Corps so that she could fly around the world entertaining the troops with her Apache dancing. With her last twenty dollars she took a cab from the theatre to catch the train because she had to report to the army the next morning. Just as she got to the station, a report came over the taxi radio that the war was over. Poor Ms J had to go anyway. They didn't have a uniform to fit her because she was very tall and skinny. She didn't last too long in there. She got discharged and went back home to Kansas to the man she had been with ever since she got out of the state school for girls. When he died Ms J drifted, drinking and carousing, until a couple she knew took her in and began to care for her.

They lived in a trailer that Ms J converted into a whorehouse. She became the madam, hiring the girls she met at the local bars to entertain the customers. It was a genteel place, a respectable whorehouse. Ms J was a stickler for good manners. She told me she could put away a bottle of Wild Turkey every night in those days and did so with regularity. She could hold her liquor and she was proud of it.

She did a Lonely Hearts Club scam. She used to answer Lonely Hearts Club letters and get engaged to the guy, receive presents and then leave. Eventually, one guy had her arrested for breach of promise. She had gone a

306

little crazy and written her promise to marry him in a letter. They prosecuted and she went to federal prison for mail fraud.

She came out of prison with thirty-five dollars. What are you going to do with thirty-five dollars? Well, she took a bus to town, got a hotel room and put an ad in the local paper: 'Home nurse for hire'. She needed a place to live. She had no experience as a nurse but she knew how to take care of men.

She got a job with the man she eventually married and was accused of murdering. She became his live-in carer. He was eighty years old and she was about fifty. He was very sick and she became his housekeeper and nurse. According to Ms J, his son had been abusing the old man, beating him up and taking his things. The son didn't want this other person around to interfere or be a witness to the abuse, so he tried to get rid of her, at which point the old man and Ms J decided to marry secretly. That gave her the legal right to remain in the house. When the son wanted her out she said, 'Forget it. I have a legal right to be here because I'm married to him.' Anyway, the old man was found shot dead on his tractor. He had been shot from above. Ms J had a broken foot in a cast at the time and the gun was found in a shoebox in her mailbox at the end of the road.

Some said she was a bad woman. She was a madam. She had a record. She was convicted and sentenced to life.

Through the years, Ms J became my confidante and my buddy; at times like a mother and, later on, like an old person that I took care of. We never knew her actual age. I think she was close to seventy but she looked ten years older. Ms J had bad feet from dancing. And they were *big* feet. She was very self-conscious about their size. She used to get little sneakers to make them look smaller, so her feet were all cramped and she had big purple bunions. The way she'd sit there smoking with her feet dangling over the edge of her bed, I would see them turn purple because of her poor circulation. I always hoped she'd be wearing socks.

Poor Ms J. She was very conscious of her looks, I guess because she had once depended on them so much. She had been a beautiful, big-breasted cowgirl. She was something. Every time I'd go to court she would help me with my make-up and decide which of my two shirts I should wear; if I should tuck it in or blouse it a little. She would help me fix my hair. Every detail. The fingernails. How you should move your hands when you talk. How you should hold your head. 'Very important, because when they take your picture you want to look right', she would say.

When she had her picture taken every year in the yard to send out to her pen pals, Ms J would tape her face, tape the skin back. Then she'd put her hand in front of her neck, 'because the neck gives away the age'. With her face taped, her hair fixed so you couldn't quite see it and one hand in front of her neck, she would turn her body to one side and then put the other hand across her lap – 'it covers the stomach' – and look at the camera, her legs crossed – 'never the front one to the back, always the back one to the front, because it'll make your thigh look large'. She would smile and close her eyes because otherwise you'd see the wrinkling. She would actually draw eyes on the lids, which was so bizarre. She made a number of attempts to find the best way of doing the photos. In later years, a girl in her twenties moved in who was tall and slender like Ms J used to be, and if you made her up right, fixed her hair right, the general description matched. So Ms J started using her pictures instead.

Ms J never had any affairs with women in all the years that she was in prison. One day she said, 'You know, I've never been with a woman in prison.' And we said, 'Really, how come?' And she said, 'Because nobody asked.' Oh, I felt so bad. We almost got this one girl to volunteer but she couldn't. She just couldn't. She said, 'I think of Ms J as my mom, I just can't.' So it never happened. Because nobody asked. No one would think of it. She was very prim and proper. These days they'd call her a hooker. But she wasn't. She was this poor hurt child from Kansas who just wanted to be an elegant lady. She wanted to be treated nicely. In prison she got what she wanted but it wasn't the way she wanted it. I think that happens to a lot of us. Though we don't recognize it as such. She was considered an elegant, prim and proper lady in prison. I don't think Ms J could have lived on the outside.

I was beginning to have a life. It helped take away some of the anxiety I had previously felt about becoming disconnected from the world and from my family in particular. But now, with the frequent phone calls and the abundance of diversions, both good and bad, I wasn't always struggling with the passage of time. Now that I

309

could be a real presence in my family's lives, in the form of a voice on the phone, I was more at ease with their growth away from what had been our life together.

In those early days, my favourite spot to hang out was the lake, which was really a rather large pond at one end of the compound. The fence bounded it and there was a barrier going straight down so you couldn't swim out. We called it the 'beach'. Some bottlebrush trees with long red brushy blooms grew there and a few bushes, even a rather rare sea grape bush. There was also a family of alligators. The guards would patrol regularly to see that no one was engaging in illegal activities.

There is something primordially soothing about looking at water. And so we would go down there after work or on weekends to spend a quiet moment. For us, the 'beach' was a construct built out of imagination and the tenacious ability of the human spirit to make liveable even the harshest environment. We chose it as a place to sit quietly with our thoughts. It was the only form of therapy we had and it was a good thing. Often, people would have little picnics and feed the alligators. Those alligators had it made!

Colleen, Ginger and I had gone down to the 'beach' to lie in the sun. It was our weekend ritual. Of course, you would get in trouble for lying on your blanket. It was mis-use of state property, as was sunburn since you yourself were state property. Check it out – that number on your shirt was your inventory number. We brought cold sodas with us from the machine in my dorm because it had the brand we preferred. Always there was the quest for more choices.

Everything seemed OK until Ginger started to make funny noises, like she was trying to speak but all that came out were garbled throaty sounds that she couldn't quite get her mouth around. When I tried to approach her she shrank back, as if in fear. It turned out that her husband had sent her something to make her 'feel good' and she was having a bad reaction to it. Colleen was able to comfort her – they were closer – but still Ginger acted like she was having some sort of seizure. I began talking to her, reassuring, soothing, bringing her back from wherever it was her mind had gone. Fortunately for us, before the guards spotted her we were able to get her up and walking, with one of us on each side. There was no touching allowed so we just kept brushing hands with her as we walked her down the compound to her dorm. Then we speed-walked back to our dorm in time for count. The next day, at lunch, Ginger told me that it was as if Colleen's face and my voice had pulled her back like a rope from some place in space.

Ginger left shortly after that incident. She gave me her gold pen so we could keep in touch. I had always coveted that pen. Her husband was on the run so she would go to Hawaii to live with her dad. As it turned out, he was dying of cancer and she would nurse him until his death a year or so later. Apparently, she did manage to see her husband at least one more time because they had another child together. So Ginger ended up with two children and a dying father – but Ginger was a very capable and thoughtful girl.

𝒆🐌 *Today I watched them bring in the* 'new meat.'

In prison you know who you are dealing with. You know who they are, what they did to get there and whether or not you want to associate with them. The more notorious ones are familiar faces because we have seen them on the nightly news. There is only one TV per fifty women and, predictably, it is a regular point of contention. But everyone watches the local news, following the trials of women most closely. So, when someone comes in we usually know what they are in for and how much time they have. It was an advantage you don't have out there in the free world. There were no secrets in prison.

When they bring in the 'new meat', they march them, two by two, right down the middle of the compound. Everything stops. Crowded in doorways, noses to windows, lining the walkways, all watch the parade. Some are picking out their next victims – the weak, and the frightened. Others are checking out the possibilities for new girlfriends. The potential studs get the most attention. Those are the heavyset ones, those with a slight swagger to their walk or short hair or some look about them that suggests they may assume the role of the boy. You can tell a lot from looking at a person's shoes – the feminine type or the work boots. Some even give a demonstration of their tongue action, waggling it obscenely in the direction of their chosen one. 'Hey, my nigga!' 'I got somethin' for you, white boy!' It's a strange courting ritual that puts one in mind of the slave auctions in ancient Rome. And, for the most part, one wants to be dominant, and the other dominated.

It is interesting to observe the process, to watch someone taking on characteristics of the male counterpart. Hairstyle changing, swagger becoming exaggerated, the way they wear their clothes, the cologne, the attitude.

Sometimes a real stud comes through. A real stud is experienced with women, not necessarily gay and not necessarily with women on the outside. There were some truly gay women but they, among themselves, were expected to adhere to a certain level of behaviour, as members of a group that was concerned with respectability. The real studs got a lot of play. Even women who haven't been into the social scene before will occasionally make a play for a new stud.

There are women who only like to 'turn out' women who have never been with a woman before. The thrill of the first time, I guess, or the challenge, maybe both. And some are victimizers, having taken on the worst characteristics of the male whom they are trying to imitate. It is easy to spot a victim. They show their fear. Some girls get into it unwittingly. They don't know they are giving off signals of weakness. A player can smell them coming, spot them in a second by the body language, the way they hug themselves with their arms, darting their eyes from side to side, smiling shakily at a wink or a smile, or just cowering. They look like they want someone to protect them, to stand between them and the world. Although there is no violence, the threat is implied. The price for that protection is debasement. It is the sickest of relationships.

313

Usually the victims get passed around until they are used up.

If you let it be known that you want to take your own chances, you are left alone, for the most part. It doesn't matter what size you are. There is always the occasional 'test', but, if you accept help and protection right away, you are considered 'scary', meaning you are easily scared, and then you have to take on a patron, a master, a dominant girlfriend, a player or a user. No one pushes herself on you if you indicate that you don't want to play the game. I got my share of offers, usually from the new ones who didn't know yet that I didn't go out like that. It's sort of flattering though. Sometimes I wish you could have the intimacy without the whole social scene that goes with it. It has been a long time for me. But I have my friends and we are very tight with each other.

    You learn, all the tricks, all the stories, I mean show me something . . . tell me a story I haven't heard before. I would love you to do it.

Each person is given a number upon arrival in R&O. If you already have a number, meaning you are a returnee, then you get a letter in front of your number: A being a two-time loser, B being a three-time loser, and so on. One of the other inmates, called 'Granddad', has an E in front of her number this trip. Granddad is a tall skin-and-bones black woman in her fifties. She's been in and out of prison all her life. They say she comes back for some R&R, rest and relaxation, to fatten up, get healthy and get her teeth

314

fixed. She has bad problems with her teeth. This is a way of life for Granddad. Most of my friends were first-timers. I did tend to look down on people who came back. There were those who would have given anything for the chance to 'make it' out there. So, I resented people who had the chance and blew it, because each time someone got out and committed a new crime it turned public opinion against the rest of us. What I would have given to be with my children again! And it was beginning to look like I might have to consider parole as an option since it was taking so long to get things straightened out on appeal.

We had our own little group and we stuck by each other. We did everything pack-style, at least in twos and often all five of us. It was such a good feeling to be part of a group. We would walk the compound, taking up the width of the walkway – one for all and all for one.

None of us had been criminals in the past – no As or Bs in our group. And, by prison standards, we were all considered to have committed prestigious crimes. What is a prestigious crime? According to the prison mentality, murder, upper-echelon drug smuggler or wife of one, major robbery, something that has substance, not like a shoplifter, a 'check writer' (fraudster), a drug addict or a petty thief. In our group, between the five of us, we have five life sentences and some years.

The only real diversions in prison are the library, recreation, and the occasional real-life drama when somebody loses it and there is a fight. I did a lot of reading. And of course there was the mail, which was our lifeline to the outside world and to our identity beyond the numbers we had been assigned. In those early days in population they delivered the mail to each dormitory and we would swarm around the office doorway waiting for our name to be called at night before dinner. It was like something you would see in a foreign country where people are all gathered around with their hands out to receive some small bit of sustenance. No one wanted to be completely adrift on the alien planet without a lifeline. Those who had no family or whose family didn't keep in touch would connect with the pen pals or religious people who would visit or write or accept phone calls. Some did it for money and stuff but only if the outside person didn't understand the real value of their friendship and the great need to be part of something outside.

I used to paint when I was on death row. And for a while after I got into the population, I painted the sunsets for Jesse and I sketched the things of beauty in my world. But that was such a solitary endeavour. I craved the company of others, not groups but one-on-one. It was a connection; it was personal. My world was expanding while Jesse's was growing ever narrower, although he did have a number of close friends on the row. One of them, Michael Bruno, had also been wrongly sentenced to death but it was complicated because his son had been brought in by the prosecution, as a terrified teenager, to testify. Bruno had full body tattoos, and a daughter just about the same age as our Tina. The children met and became friends in the visiting park. They would come to see their daddies and their 'uncles' – Uncle Jesse and Uncle Bruno.

316

Jesse and Bruno shared their letters, their stories and their dreams along with their frustrations at the legal system. They were exercise buddies too, pumping iron and keeping fit and watching out for each other.

One of my favourite rituals took place on weekends. Saturdays and Sundays were washdays! You ran down to sign the wash list at 6 a.m. when the officer tacked it up on the office door. Then when it was your time, you did your wash and took it out to the clothesline in your bucket. We all got buckets from the maintenance department. They had originally held some sort of chemical. It wasn't an authorized thing but it was accepted by the staff as the only practical way we had of toting our wash from the dorms to the clotheslines. They used to have lines behind each dorm but they did away with them and built new ones over by the side of H-2. If you lived in H-4 or H-5 as I did, you had a long haul down to the other end of the compound. We made this pilgrimage every weekend – a procession of women with bucketfuls of wet washing, two if you were lucky enough to have procured two of the precious buckets. After we finished hanging the clothes we'd fill the buckets with warm soapy water from the nearest dorm. Sitting on one upturned bucket with our feet in the other soaking in the warm water, we would gossip, discuss the events of the week, and talk about our families.

And when our feet were sufficiently softened, we would give each other pedicures. Using a brush, a pumice stone, and sometimes a razor blade carefully pried from a disposable razor, we would smooth and polish the rough edges away. Sometimes we would do our fingernails and give each other facials as well. It was a closeness I will always treasure.

It was a form of intimacy, loving and touching that seems not to exist out here. It seems there is a closeness about being imprisoned together, a bond of common suffering that creates, out of necessity, a deeper intimacy.

I was asked, fairly regularly, by younger inmates how I managed to keep myself together. I told them, if they really wanted to know, to meet me at Rec on Saturday at 2 p.m. and I'd show them. As I went whistling around the corner I'd see the girl waiting for me in front of the Rec building. She'd put out her cigarette as I approached and we'd go in as I explained the routine. First, we stretched – which is yoga – and I showed her how to breathe. Then we warmed up on the stationary bikes. Then we used the free weights – military presses, squats, bench pressing – with or without cigarette breaks; and then we would head for the track, run a mile or so and sit down on the grass for more yoga – stretching and meditation to settle the energy down.

After a while there were two and then three of us until a class sort of spontaneously composed itself. We met every Saturday afternoon unless we had visits. The staff didn't notice the yoga, but they did notice the weight training we were doing and the results. The head of recreation started a weight training contest, with a prize for the winners. The prizes were always food! There was an explosion of interest in weight training and it became difficult to get time on the equipment.

318

I did pretty well in those contests over the years. I still showed people how to train but my class became more focused on the yoga. There were plenty of people who could show you how to work out with the weights. That wasn't my thing – it wasn't what had enabled me to survive. So, I kept up my training but my little group met to do yoga on the off-hours when the lifters weren't there. That meant we had to come in at dinnertime on the weekends or at lunchtime during the week. But it worked for us. And I continued to do my own practice, as always. It may have looked purely physical but it went deeper than that.

24

O N HIS REGULAR MONTHLY visits to Broward
Correctional Institution, Rabbi Chaim held
Shabbat services for the women in a small partitioned
room to the left side of the prison's chapel. At the time
there were sixteen to eighteen women attending the
makeshift services. Everything had to be approved by
memo in advance – a process that could be difficult, time-
consuming, and not always reliable. But the rabbi always
managed to bring us a treat. Almost all the Jewish
holidays have something to do with food. A Bubbe
(grandmotherly figure) officiated over the latkes or the
blintzes sizzling on the warmer set up on a side table, the
'feasteleh', the Oneg Shabbat, which was a welcome
change of fare for the women at the conclusion of the
service. She handed out and collected the song sheets, and
told jokes, Jewish jokes, of course. He would sing and play
his guitar – 'Lecha Dodi', the Shema – telling the stories
and lighting the candles, bringing the feelings, sights and
sounds of our heritage into the space that was, for the
moment, our sanctuary. The women clapped and sang
and cried with emotion. They would read the Torah
portion together and discuss how it might apply to their

daily lives and problems. The rabbi tried to make it as nice and as 'hamishe' as possible for the women. After all, it was only once or twice a month and the feeling had to last until his next visit. We Jewish women were not necessarily friends on a daily basis but we had a special connection to each other and at holiday times we shared and honoured our legacy. We were respected for keeping our religion.

I don't think we really grasped how miraculous it was to have these diminutive older women led by the mild-mannered rabbi bringing in food warmers and latkes and candles. They never complained so we were unaware of the indignities to which they were subjected on the way in and out. There was always some new rule to contend with – no glass, only plastic containers; no bags that weren't see-through; no exchange of personal information. Rules got bent and even broken, and sometimes one of the Bubbes was banned for having been overly compassionate and bringing in something for one of the women – nail polish, hair clips, nothing dangerous but still not allowed. And we were not permitted to take anything back to the dorms with us, meaning no sharing with our friends. That was a hard one and a number of us got in trouble over it. Rabbi Chaim served as our link to the larger Jewish community at a time when we were particularly open to receiving the teachings and in need of the connection to our heritage. For me personally, he was like my guardian angel, reclaiming me from the garbage heap where I had been cast aside to await my death. The prodigal children would not be forgotten wherever Rabbi Chaim Richter could reach them, and none would be forgotten because of age or sickness or infirmity.

The holidays became important to me. I hadn't paid much attention to them outside but when you have to fight for something it takes on new meaning. I had to fight for every candle. I was determined, even writing the memos so that there would be no excuse for things not getting done. I had been doing all my celebrating alone. Being able to celebrate the holidays properly with others was worth the effort. A candle was a major victory that gave off a special light.

There is a story the rabbi told us about the people who went to a special place in the forest to say the special words and light the special fire. In time, they forgot the exact spot in the forest, but they remembered the special words and lit the special fire. Eventually, they forgot the special words, but they still went to the forest and lit the special fire. And it was acceptable because they did it with their whole heart.

I had always felt a strong connection to the Holocaust, even before prison. When I was on death row I used to think to myself, at least they have to feed me. At least they cannot beat me and work me to death in the snow. So, if those people could survive all that, then I can survive this. I felt I was carrying on the traditions for them, all of those who died. A candle where there were no candles.

Darling Sunny,
Happy St Patrick's Day! We will be visiting you the weekend of April 5th, Saturday and 6th, Sunday. We

will be flying down and we were lucky to get reservations. It's tough Easter week. So we'll see you for the end of Passover – maybe this Passover will be the beginning of our freedom from bondage too – God willing!

Love and kisses, Mom

I had been promoted to diet cook. They needed someone who wouldn't kill off the diabetics and the women with high blood pressure. So, because I was a vegetarian, they figured I was the best choice. It was a great job. I got to go into the coolers to get the food I needed for their meals and while I was there I could make myself something too. I would have a bowl of cereal and milk, some fruit, cottage cheese – major delicacies in prison – and to have them whenever I wanted was the tastiest part. The only drawback was that it was freezing in there and I had to wear a jacket. But it was my private domain and I looked forward to going to work each day. Plus, I got to be creative with the meals. Unfortunately, the vegetables were mostly canned, but I ate carrots quite a bit.

One day, as I was preparing the evening meal, a tour group of officials from Tallahassee came through. We all had on our hairnets and plastic gloves – no inspection team or tour group got in without a courtesy call to alert the area. Afterwards, there was a call for me to report to classification. I got a pass and hurried across the compound, still wearing my gloves and hat. I was told that I could no longer work in the kitchen. I was to turn in my uniforms immediately. When I asked why, I was told that someone from Tallahassee had objected to my position as diet cook, but officially the reason was that someone with a life sentence shouldn't be in an area where there were knives available. Well, that was bullshit because many of the women who worked in the kitchen were doing life. Our best baker was a lifer. No one ever said there were any restrictions on working in the kitchen except for women with hepatitis. I argued that there was no one to finish making the evening meal. After placing a call to the kitchen boss, classification gave me permission to return to work. The kitchen boss kept me for a few more days so I could train my replacement. I turned in my kitchen whites and was reassigned as an orderly in the Education building. How silly of me to think I could do anything but clean!

My parents visited regularly during every school holiday with few exceptions. Sometimes they just had to get away and do something besides come to prison for holidays. It was Easter vacation, May 1981, Eric's turn to visit. He was such a young man already. My dad had written about how Eric was becoming very much aware of girls. But he was my little boy, and when he visited we resumed where we had left off, trying to fill the place that remained unfilled inside both of us. (We had agreed a couple of years earlier to stop waiting for me to come home.) He was growing body hair and you could smell his hormones and he towered over me. And I was almost thirty-five years old. Still, when he was there with me, he would lean across and put his head on my shoulder, like he always did as a boy. And I was glad he still wanted to be my little boy in some ways.

A male sergeant was patrolling the VP that day. He started screaming at me about having intimate physical contact in the visiting park and ordered me into the major's office. Eric started to cry. 'I didn't mean to get you in trouble, Mommy! I'm sorry! Please don't take my mom away!'

As I followed the sergeant to the office with Eric's voice and my parents' attempts to calm him down still ringing in my head, the sergeant told me that having Eric's head on my shoulder was against the rules and my visit could be terminated for it. In the office, I explained that Eric was my son, not my boyfriend, and that your child was allowed to touch you. The sergeant said he was too big and it looked like he was my boyfriend to other people. I said it didn't matter what other people thought – he was my son and I was entitled to have his head on my shoulder. The sergeant said if we did it again he would terminate the visit. Although I complained about it later on, he had the last word at that moment.

When I went back to the seats, Eric and my parents looked drained of colour. The fear and self-reproach on Eric's face almost broke my heart. He apologized again and I told him he didn't get me in any trouble but for now it would be best not to lean on each other while the sergeant was around. 'He has a problem. You didn't do anything wrong.' I tried to be comforting but what was done was done.

'Tell your mother how much better you're doing in

school, Eric,' my dad said, encouraging conversation in another direction. And the visit went on with joking and sharing and discussion of future plans as always.

While Eric and my dad were having a talk, my mom told me about some of the problems at home. As I listened, I looked at them and became aware of how much older they were beginning to look. For a long time they had seemed to stay the same. But my mom had been suffering with kidney stones and dental problems over the last couple of years and my dad was looking kind of grey. I brought my attention back to what my mom was saying . . . 'And your son has been keeping his room a little neater but it's still hard to get him to do his homework.' He and my dad were pretending to spar in their seats. 'Don't get too wild with the child!' my mom scolded kindly. I smiled. They were doing such a good job with the kids. So much more patient than when I was growing up. I saw them so differently now – as people, not just parents. I actually liked my parents as people. We were friends now – and I could see the love in all of their actions.

Anyway, the visit was terrific as always, despite the difficulty with the sergeant, and I floated around on the infusion of love and energy it gave me for the better part of the next two weeks.

I enjoyed working in the Ed building. First, I cleaned. I liked mopping the least; perhaps it reminded me of the kitchen. I liked the bathrooms best because I could be creative. I cleaned the toilet and the sinks and then I made origami soap-bar holders out of paper handtowels, folded

326

in the shapes of flowers or animals or birds. And I looped a piece of toilet paper around the seat like they do in a motel to tell you that the toilet has just been cleaned.

Sometimes I left birthday messages for the staff members in the first-floor bathroom of the Ed building, written on paper towels on the sinks. The most amusing part was when I got to polish the boss's desk. They had recently come out with those sanitary pads that have their own sticky on the back. I stuck one to my hand and used it as a polishing pad. It was great. Not only did it work well but it also got a great reaction from my boss, who was the master of the social faux pas. Mr West told ethnic jokes to ethnic minorities, and in general seemed to have a knack of being insulting or offensive. We all knew it was not done to be mean. He was really a nice man, just socially inept. I liked him. As the head of the education department, he would authorize me to go upstairs to help the GED teacher when I finished my cleaning duties each day. He and I talked about religion and philosophy. He told me his sister was a very spiritual person. He provided the most intelligent and stimulating conversation of my day.

GED, or General Education Diploma, was a class set up to teach the subjects needed to get the equivalent of a high school diploma. Most of the women had not graduated from high school. Many of them couldn't even read, except for the basics. I enjoyed helping the GED teacher because I loved to teach and because I liked the teacher, Ms Scott. She was a skinny thing, soft-spoken and shy, with a pleasant face but she always looked sad to me.

She had me helping with fractions. I never could understand maths when I was in school. I couldn't just accept the process of 'taking away' and 'borrowing from' without knowing why. In the fifth grade, my teacher, a tall thin man named Mr Fifick who always had white stuff at the corners of his mouth, took the time to teach me in a way I could understand. He assigned the class some division problems and took me to the back of the room where he brought out a rack of beads. He explained that it was an ancient Chinese counting device called an abacus. By the end of that day I was a whiz at mathematics and I never had trouble with numbers again. I remembered how I had felt when someone had taken the time to help me and not just decided I was too dumb to learn. I liked being able to do that for others. I liked to watch their faces as they struggled and then see the smile emerge as understanding dawned and lit up their eyes. I knew the feeling, and now I knew the feeling the teacher has as well. It was a double shot of pleasure.

The top bunk, June 30th 1982, 2 a.m.
I feel like a cat – prowling the night, at ease in the
quiet and darkness; lithely, smoothly leaping up
from the floor to my perch by using the strength of
my shoulders and arms in unison with the powerful
thrust of my legs. I stretch like a cat to feel the
pleasure of my own muscles working – and I lay
down to let my whole body relax and go limp yet
alert to every sound and every movement. In a
sleep sound yet still light, curled up in my own

warmth, I sleep . . . And dream of being stroked
and petted and held and loved by my Only One.
Like a cat, I can have only one master. I purr in his
arms. With him I would be content to sleep. It is
there that I want to go. Good night my love.

25

W E CELEBRATED my favourite holiday, 4 July, Independence Day, with an outdoor barbecue like we did every year. I didn't care for the chicken but I liked the corn on the cob and other stuff, and the plastic forks were nice since we usually only had large spoons. I should have been feeling invigorated but something unusual was happening to me. My range of vision seemed to have become narrowed into a corridor directly in front of me. I had no peripheral vision except a whitish blur that seemed to be closing in my world as well as my vision. It was getting harder and harder to think, like trying to think through Jell-O. I knew the teacher, Ms Scott, saw it. She must have thought I was on drugs. But she didn't say anything and I was grateful for that. I didn't know what to tell her. I wondered if maybe I was suffering from some pathology of the brain. I couldn't even meditate outside of it.

8 July 1982

My parents were finally going to take a vacation. While I had been on death row they had never dared to go anywhere, but now, with the threat of imminent death removed, they felt comfortable taking a break. They were dropping Tina off to stay with her grandma Kay on their way to Las Vegas and picking her up on the return trip, when they would also visit with me. Kay would bring Tina to see me, and her dad too. They would be leaving in the morning. Eric would be staying with my brother.

I still didn't understand what was happening. The strangeness that had come over me a few days earlier still lingered around the edges of my consciousness but my thoughts now were all on the upcoming visit. It was the night before they would leave for Florida. I went to bed, having made sure my visiting clothes would be washed and ironed ready for the children and Kay to come on Saturday. I did my usual 11 p.m. meditation with Jesse, sending my spirit out to meet him in the ether and say goodnight. Then I went to sleep and had this dream. Flames shot up into the sky, higher than I could see. And a voice said, 'And now your brother will be in charge of everything!' I sat straight up, dripping cold sweat, pyjamas plastered to my body. I waited in bed, counting my breaths, until 6 a.m. when I could run down to the office to sign up for the first slot on the phone list, 7 a.m. But when I called it was too late! My parents had left early to be sure to catch their plane.

9 July 1982

It was late afternoon. I was back in the dorm. I could hardly breathe. It felt as if all of my bodily functions were shutting down. I tried reading one of Jesse's letters and

331

listening to the radio on my headphones, but something on the news caught my attention. I was drawn downstairs to the TV. The news was on and they were talking about a disaster. A plane had crashed. They were showing the wreckage. Seats and luggage everywhere. I couldn't hear anything the commentator was saying. It didn't matter what he was saying. It was the picture that mattered.

I walked up the stairs and into the hallway, looking for someone to ask if I could make a phone call before the phones were turned on. I didn't bother to get a pass. I saw Sergeant Schinelli in front of B1 dining hall. She was a good person. She would help me.

'Sergeant Schinelli, I think I am having an emergency. I have to make a call to find out. Can you ask the lieutenant?'

'What kind of emergency do you think you are having?'

'I need to make a call to find out what flight my parents were on. Please, can you help me? I have to find out what happened to the children.'

'Let me try to find the lieutenant.' She plucked the walkie-talkie from her hip, pressed the talk button, and asked the lieutenant to call her.

'Thank you.'

The lieutenant gave permission for me to use the phone in the visiting park. I would call Kay. I would call Al. I would find out if they had showed up yet.

I called Kay and Al but no one answered. Ms Schinelli had left and I had been trying to reach them for almost an hour. It would be recall any minute. I left and headed back to the dorm. I would have to wait for count to clear to get on the phone again. I would try calling Uncle Joe. Maybe he had heard something. Uncle Joe was so fragile, so dependent on my mom. They talked on the phone every night. But my parents would show up sooner or later. I prayed it wouldn't be a long count.

'Clear count. Clear count on the compound.'

I rushed for the phone list. I signed my name and my roommate's name. She had given me her time in case I needed it. I tried Al again. No answer. I tried Kay. She told me she was trying to find out more information. She thought it might be their plane. Tina was safe with her. She would keep trying to find out more. I called Uncle Joe.

'Oh, my darling, I am so sorry.'

'Uncle Joe, what happened? Was it their plane? Are they OK? Have you heard from them?'

But all he can say is 'I'm so sorry. I'm so sorry.'

'No!'

'Yes, darling, it's true.'

'No! Noooo!' I fall back against the wall behind me.

'I'm so sorry. I'm so sorry, darling.'

I am howling, a prolonged denial, as I slide down the wall, like the bones of my body have turned to water.

'I'm so sorry. I'm so sorry. Please, it's true. I'm so sorry.' He is getting hysterical. He is sobbing. I am cracking open.

I see the officer looking at me from her office. I must not scream again. I hear Uncle Joe falling apart.

'Uncle Joe, it's gonna be OK. Where is Eric? Do you know?'

'Eric is with your brother.'

'Good. That's good. I'll call Kay. We'll take care of each

other. Don't worry, OK?'

'Oh, honey, I'm so sorry. Are you going to be all right there? Is there somebody to help you?'

'I'll be OK, Uncle. Is someone there with you?'

'My girlfriend is coming over.'

'Good. I have to go now, Uncle Joe. Will you be OK tonight?'

'Yes, honey, I'll be OK. I love you. I will take care of you.'

'We will take care of each other. I have to go now. I love you.'

I hang up quickly. I don't have much time. I am dying. My vision is gone. I can only see through a small round hole in the fog and there is a ringing in my ears. They cannot be dead. They will be found alive somewhere. I make it up the stairs to my room. Mary, my roommate, looks up from her book. I throw myself across the bed on to her chest, heaving deep soul-wrenching sobs, unable to hold back any longer. I have burst open. She is frightened and keeps asking me what has happened as she holds me in her arms.

'My parents were in that plane. They're dead. My mommy and daddy.' The sounds coming from my throat are no longer words. There are no words for this. Mary is panicked. She begins to call for the guards, 'Officer! Officer!' My hand reaches out from the depths of despair to grab her by the throat. She can no longer scream. Her eyes are filled with complete terror. I don't mean to do that to Mary but I cannot have her calling the guards. They will lock me up because I am out of control. I have to be able to make phone calls. I have to find out what happened to the kids. I have to find out what happened to my parents. I cannot be locked up now. 'Mary! Be quiet! If you promise not to call the guard, I'll let go.' She nods her head in agreement. I wonder if I can trust her. But her eyes tell me she is too afraid to scream again. I let go. 'I have to let it out, Mary. Just hold me while I let it out and I'll be OK. Please, Mary.'

'Go ahead and let it out, baby. You just let it all out. I won't say anything. I just wanted to help you.'

I lay my head in her lap and cry, crumpling up on the floor at her feet. We begin to gather a crowd but they disperse at a sign from Mary. Someone tells them to leave us alone. They are taking care of me. They go downstairs to watch the news about the crash. I cry until I am exhausted. Mary holds me the whole time.

After a while she gets me a drink of water. I can only manage a sip. We clean me up and I go to find more phone time.

July 9, 1982

My Dearest Jesse,

This is the saddest day of my life – Jesse, they're gone . . . I can't believe they're dead and burnt, and I'll never see them again – both of them! That was kind though – that they be together. There are so many things to be attended to – Al will have to do most of it. He is broken hearted. Your mom went out to Miami airport to find out about survivors. There were none. She'll have to fly Tina back tomor-

335

row. I will try to call you – I need your comfort . . .
And to tell you what will happen now with the kids.
It's late now, almost 3, but I don't want to sleep –
this night I will sleep without my parents on this
earth! All my life they've been here – I must sleep of
course, and it will be good for me, but . . .

I sat from 11 p.m. to 11.30 p.m. to be as near as
possible when Eric and Tina were told what
happened. I'll have to wait till after 12 o'clock count
to try to call.

I had spoken with Al on the phone. I wanted the children
to be together since all they had left was each other. Jesse's
mom brought Tina to North Carolina and Eric held her in
his arms while their uncle Al explained what had
happened.

I don't remember much about the call to the children
except that Tina was angry with Grandma and Grandpa.
God, she said, should have found someone else to help
him in Heaven. And Eric promised that he would take care
of his sister.

The officer spoke with classification and she said, 1
– I would be able to have a special visit with your
mom on Monday; 2 – I would be able to get a call
to you but it would have to be relayed by your
Chaplain and the superintendent here – our words
related back and forth; 3 – the Broward Sheriff's
Office has to okay my going to the funeral; 4 – I can
get a week's lay-in [time off from work]. So that

> sounds pretty good. They've been real nice about
> everything here, honey.

I had been having a problem with the administration about following the Jewish tradition of sitting Shiva, the ritual of mourning as set out by Jewish law, which requires one to spend seven days sitting on a low wooden seat or on the floor, reflecting on the deceased. Mrs Villacorta had consulted with one of her Jewish staff members – the accountant – who said it wasn't a necessary tenet of the religion. On that basis, she denied my request. I explained that it was not a question of whether or not I would sit Shiva – it was only a question of where, in my room or in lock-up. I called my advocates, Bill Shepherd, the attorney, and Rabbi Richter, who would clarify the necessity of sitting Shiva. My kindly little rabbi turned into Chaim of the Maccabees and let them know in absolute terms that I had to be allowed to sit Shiva and that it was a basic tenet of Judaism. Mrs Villacorta didn't intend to be at all disrespectful, I am sure, but she was a by-the-book sort of person – for the officers as well as for the inmates.

> Al's doing a marvellous, wonderful job and they are
> all handling it fantastically and I'm very proud of
> them. I've been on the phone with them, trying to
> counsel each so as not to allow for anyone's feelings
> to be hurt unnecessarily – since everyone's in pain
> and emotionally upset, words can easily be said
> that one would deeply and irrevocably regret ever

after. Shepherd's been great. He's taking care of all legal matters for us, as a friend. The kids, Pan Am, getting the remains back from New Orleans, getting our call, and me to the funeral.

Honey, I'm so glad you were able to get a call to speak with the children. This is so devastating for them. And I know the worst of it is yet to come – I know that. Mary's been super – Colleen has been real good too, and everyone has been sympathetic and understanding. For two days and three nights I've been given all the slack I needed by staff and inmates alike – to use the phone for unlimited time, my meals brought to me at my room; no one bothered me at all. You don't get that sort of grace period in here – it's never been done for anyone in here. It's been amazing how respectful everyone has been. I've written a short thank you note to put up on the bulletin board in the dorm.

I spoke with Al again tonight. He said he'd be calling there to you so there will be another call for the children, and he said he didn't know what to do about the Rabbi and the cemetery. I was able to find the compromise that would work and he was relieved. The Rabbi said he would work with Shepherd to do everything to see that I can be at the funeral. It isn't real – it isn't yet.

There was a problem with the burial arrangements. My dad had purchased 'drawers' in which they were to be laid to rest in a mausoleum – 'so the worms wouldn't eat them'. According to the rabbi, if we followed my dad's last wishes and had them put in the drawers their souls would be trapped. Unless they were buried in the consecrated ground, they would not be able to ascend to Heaven. So, do we obey our father's last wishes and take the chance that their souls might be trapped here, or do we obey what the rabbi said were God's wishes and have them buried in the ground in the Jewish cemetery? I had spoken with the rabbi about it and found out that the hole in which they would be buried was, by state law, lined with concrete so they would not be eaten by worms. Also, the religious requirement was that the bodies remain in the ground for seven years but after that time they could be dug up and placed anywhere we wanted. It was the loophole we needed. We could bury them, be sure their souls would not be held back, and then in seven years, if still so inclined, we could have their bodies exhumed and put in drawers.

> I've been holding up okay. I've been eating and sleeping, and I am now more aware of what's around me – I'd totally lost the peripheral awareness in my vision until today – I've regained my senses. I've been able to think clearly and well on all the crises that have arisen, but I realize I am still in a state of shock. Did I tell you I dreamed of it? Of the fire – flames actually, and that Al would have to handle the details of the funeral and all? That's why I tried to call them that morning.
>
> I miss them so much already – I think there's a

letter from them coming to me – I hope so. It will nearly tear my heart out but I am hoping I will get a letter from them, mailed before they left. It'll be like they're still here talking to me. I can't accept that they're gone Jesse – I do momentarily and then I don't again.

This seems to have brought everyone much closer together and I know my parents would have liked that – I know it makes them happy now. I feel sadness descending over me again – I can't speak of that much yet –

Love and Kisses, your wife Sunny

My parents had stipulated in their will that in the event of their death they wanted the children to go to my father's brother, Uncle Ed. But he said that he would put Eric in military school and I didn't want the children to be separated. I decided that the children would remain with my brother, his wife Meresa and their two children.

There was another legal problem. The state of Florida might challenge the children's legal status and try to have them remanded back to Florida to place them in foster care. My parents had only been given temporary legal custody, and I wouldn't let them adopt the children because I was afraid I might not be able to get them back when I got out. My parents had had the right to put them in school or in the hospital if necessary. It had been enough. Now my brother would have to get legal guardianship.

My Man,

I love you! Ray Sandstrom called but I wasn't able to return his call today. I needed my phone time to communicate about the children. Classification called me in – No call to you, no visit from your mom during the week, forget going to the funeral, and I will not be allowed to sit Shiva after the funeral. To boil it down, I told them I would do what I must regardless. As for the funeral, I feel there is a very strong possibility I'll be there. I didn't bother to even argue it with the classification officer as she was simply relaying the answers to me. And don't worry, I will sit Shiva and they will neither stop me nor punish me. The Rabbi and the lawyers are on it already, even my old dentist and his wife and a congressman and a Senator, and a state representative will be brought in on it if Tallahassee insists on this absurd and unconscionable violation of a sacred right. It's hardly believable that they would even try! Right after classification laid this BS on me, the Rabbi showed up so I was able to get him right on the case.

I got a call back about the legal status of the children. The state can't do shit! We're covered – the kids are covered – It's already taken care of with no loose ends left. My main concern is that no one makes waves now. Trust and faith in our family is essential now. Please listen to me on this and don't tread on tender toes. You know I wouldn't leave the children uncovered. Don't complicate it – I have

341

referred them to Shepherd so he can act as a backup observer team in our interest in relation to Eric and Tina. I have not mentioned this to Al. Honestly, I do trust him to see to the matter of protecting the children adequately . . . And we consult every evening as to the day's events and the problems to be solved for the next day. Al is doing a fine job – I'm proud of him. Give him your support too. Really we haven't any other choice. Meanwhile, both attorneys are keeping check on things.

Tonight I called Bill and told his office that it looks good for things concerning the funeral, and coordinated that effort further. Then I called Al. He had just heard from Pan Am that . . . They were able to identify my father . . . by dental records. Jesse, you must sit with us on the day of the funeral. We will need your strength to get us through – whether I am able to be there or not. It's so hard for me to accept, so awful – and on the other hand, I know they are dead and gone on, and yet still and ever with us, and I know they went as they wished – together and quick; and I know and accept that. That's how the kids are taking it too – swaying between the two states of belief. I'll describe it all more some other time. We feel they'll find my mom soon too – and then they can be shipped home to rest –

I'm laying here letting all today's questions-left-unanswered-and-on-file go through my head again . . . It's late but I don't care – time is suspended except that the funeral and seven days of Shivah will mark the only relevant time period for me right now. Mary's been so supportive. She really cares. And Colleen's been around and concerned too.

Wow! I fell asleep! I have to make out a big envelope for the kids' letters – Alphabits cereal glued to paper saying 'I love you' – love letters! I love you totally My husband

Love and Kisses, Your wife Sunny

Whatever his suggestions were, I didn't want any inter-ference. I was too swallowed up by events to be self-aware as far as my relationship with Jesse was concerned and I didn't have the energy left to placate him or anyone. All that mattered was the children and the funeral. Everything else was irrelevant.

Although I cannot now recall any one instance, most people were so kind to me during this time – friends, staff and officials. But I was inconsolable. And I don't think anyone really knew what to do for me. It was beyond any-one's experience.

July 14, 1982

My Man,

They found my mom! Oh, I am so happy that they'll be able to come home soon – I don't know what's left of their bodies but at least they can be sent home and buried together and we can mourn and pray and begin to recover.

I spoke with Tina and Eric tonight. She sounded better and happy; Eric sounded much calmer and was glad he saw Foxy (his psychologist) today. As for Al – he has been shaken into the reality of his position of serious responsibility and he has clearly seen and taken hold – he could not have fooled the children, and they feel secure and loved by him.

I've been reading your weekend letter from July 9, 10, 11 – heavy. I know how terribly upset you were, how frustrated not to be able to do anything to help or to comfort me or the children.

So now, just as in my dream, it fell to my brother to oversee all the arrangements for the funeral. He had to identify the remains. The process took two weeks, which would give me time to overcome the obstacles to my going to their funeral. The prison was not willing to allow it.

The state took away my being with my mother and father years ago – perhaps that is what is enabling me to cope with their death now. It put a cushion of non-expectancy between me and the thought of physical nearness to them.

Bill Shepherd called with the news that the state of Florida would allow me to go to the funeral. The state of North Carolina had agreed to provide the security, but certain conditions would have to be met. I would have to pay personally for the North Carolina police officers to escort me, and I would have to provide a private jet because they refused to give up their firearms, which meant we could not travel by commercial airline. I agreed immediately.

July 15, 16, 17, 18, 1982

My Man,

I love you! I know you felt my state of mind lately. It's ranged between sad, mad, and berserk! They've kept me so mad for a while I couldn't be sad – and for the past 24 hours I've been in such a state of high anxiety I couldn't be sad or mad. I can't mail my Thursday letter because it's all too personal. My poor honey, I feel badly that you won't get a Thursday letter. I'm okay and all but I can't think about anything but what happened and the funeral and if I'll be there and I try to grasp that it's real but I can't. I can't accept it.

Tina asked if you'd be there too, and if not then when! I explained that only I would be allowed to be there for the funeral and then I would have to go back to the prison. Meresa is going out to buy me a dress today and said Eric asked to go with her because 'I know what my mother likes,' he said. Beautiful, our children.

I love you.

Love and kisses, your wife, Sunny

My parents had arranged to leave their entire estate to their grandchildren, with the exception of $10,000 each for my brother and myself. I figured that money was there for me to use to get to their funeral. I told my brother to rent me a small jet. He rented me a 'baby Lear', a six-seater, stocked with drinks and an expensive seafood platter.

'Al,' I said, 'that's very nice but I'm a vegetarian. I don't eat seafood.'

'Oh, I'm sorry. I forgot. I just wanted it to be nice for you. And I thought if the guards were happy they might cut you some slack – treat you nicely, you know? I'll change it. What would you like? Fruit?'

'Fruit would be nice. Don't change it, Al. You're right. If we feed them well maybe they'll let me spend some time with you and the kids.'

'The plane cost six thousand dollars.'

'It doesn't matter. That's what the money is for, Al.'

❧ *July 17, 1982, 10.30 a.m.*
Dream – placed plastic guards over cheeks, dusted
with red makeup. It was painted onto my eyebrows
and forehead and it was so red and it wouldn't
come off. I understand it though. It is what I
should do now – to remove my guard and wear my
face – but I will still have to carry part of my guard
on me.

Everything was set except for the ride to the airport. The first ten miles would be the hardest. I had arranged permission from two states, transportation, security, and I wasn't going to let the first ten miles stop me. I began asking the guards if one of them would be willing to take me to the airport in their free time but in an official capacity.

A couple of them said they would. But in the end it was the major and his first lieutenant who would drive me from the prison to the private hangar to turn me over to the North Carolina police. Finally, the last piece of the puzzle was in place.

July 18, 1982

My Dearest Jesse,

I love you. I found out just awhile ago – I'm going! They worked out that last problem concerning transport, and I'm going to go! It's great!

Honey I spoke to your mom just before she left for the airport. She's going up there too. She told me she has the copies of the Guardianship proceedings – so we will be able to work together to protect the children from anyone who might want to usurp them. Their physical well-being is secure living with Al as their legal Guardian, and their financial interests and legal interests will be overseen by me and by the executor and that is how it will be. Do not think concerns for us are put aside. They are intertwined. Right at this very instant, the children are in greatest need but long range nothing's changed.

I checked in with Meresa too. All is well – Eric will see his psychologist one more time before the funeral tomorrow morning; Tina is fine and your mom is there tonight. I have a dress waiting for me and I told Meresa to tell the kids if I am able to be there that I'll probably be wearing chains so not to

347

get all shocked and upset if I am. They've never seen me in chains. There will be things to eat although no one remembered that I'm a veggie so I suggested a couple of things. I don't know if I'll even be allowed time for that. It is a miracle that I'm going to be able to be there at all! Like the miracle of Joshua and his Army – all the little people raising their voice until the walls came down.

I slept for awhile earlier this evening. Right now I can't sleep. It's 1 a.m. They could decide to start moving me anytime now. I wish you could be there too, in person – but I'm thankful I'll be there at all.

In case they surprise me in the night I have an envelope all ready for this letter. I need your support Jesse. I wish we could have spoken by phone. What I have heard via messages has been more confusing than comforting really. I don't know who's got your mom all psyched up – there is only one place for the kids now and that is with Al. And all their assets from the Estate, etc. will go into trust for them. I love you completely my Only One. I know you will be strongly present with us at the funeral and your strength will help us through it – I love you.

Love and kisses, Your wife Sunny

I left the prison at 11 a.m. in leg irons, waist chains and handcuffs in the back of a state van driven by the major with his first lieutenant. When we arrived at the airport, the North Carolina police were waiting in the hangar. There were three of them – big, healthy-looking – two males and one female. The lieutenant helped me out of the back of the van. The major joined us, and with one on each side I was led across to the middle of the no-man's-land where we were met by the three burly bears for the exchange. The lieutenant gave them strict instructions about keeping me chained up at all times during the trip. The three bears listened without comment. When the instructions were over, they thanked him, saying they would take care of me now, and led me away towards the hangar. I looked at the three faces of my new escort. They stared straight ahead. Once inside the hangar, after a brief conversation between them, the female officer took me into the ladies' room. She got out her handcuff key and began removing the chains from my waist and my hands. She explained that they felt they could do their jobs perfectly well without chains. As she knelt to undo the leg irons, she told me they would only use the handcuffs if something happened to make them nervous. She instructed me to walk slowly and stay close. At the funeral, I was to remain calm and not allow anyone to approach me too quickly. I agreed, and we headed for the plane.

I sat in the back of the plane. They allowed me that much privacy – after all, where could I go? They were really pretty nice, asking if I wanted any of the seafood platter or the fruit. I didn't want anything but I accepted some grapes, I remember, and settled back into the seat for the ride. There was a storm. I could see the fluorescent ribbons of lightning playing over the wings, but I was not afraid. I wondered why I wasn't afraid. I knew I would be at the funeral . . . and if I didn't make it I would be with my parents, so either way it was OK. But in my heart I knew it was not my time to die. The guards looked nervous, glancing back and forth at each other and at me. The plane bucked like the roller-coaster ride from hell.

Despite the weather, we made good time, taxiing smoothly on to the runway of the private airport near Charlotte in time for me to change into the clothes that were waiting for me. The female guard stayed with me. It was a green dress, stockings, and shoes with heels. The two male guards brought a car around to the front and when I was ready we got in the back and headed for the cemetery, as promised, without handcuffs. They said I was only allowed to attend the cemetery for the burial and then we were to go directly back to the plane for the return trip. There was no point in arguing.

It was an old Jewish cemetery in a rundown section of town. We found the area where my parents' coffins were set up. I was reminded again about the rules of conduct and then we left the car, slowly approaching the metal chairs facing the coffins. There was no one else there yet.

The coffins stood side by side, dark wood on raised platforms. One had a rounded lid and the other was flat. There was no way to tell which one was my mother and which was my father. I walked towards them. What part of them was in those wooden boxes? I touched the smooth wooden casket in front of me, feeling for any sign of the life it contained. Bringing those fingers to my lips, I put a kiss there and did the same to the other casket. '*Shema Y'Isroel Adonai Eloheinu Adonai Echad* . . .' – 'Hear O Israel, the Lord is our God, the Lord is One' – the words that connected one generation to the other. The grip I held on my emotions began to let go . . . until I noticed the microphone secreted underneath the coffins. Fury filled my mind, fire replaced tears. 'Get that microphone out of here! Can't I even speak to God without them listening? Haven't you got any respect?' I ranted and raved at no one in particular. My escort of guards became alarmed, crowding in on me, and then from somewhere came the hand of the rabbi. Rabbi Rocklin placed his hand on my arm and told me not to be upset. He would take care of the problem. He walked over to the microphone, knelt down, picked it up and threw it as far as he could. 'There! Now maybe you'll have some respect for this family. Haven't they suffered enough?'

'Thank you, Rabbi.'

'I am here to help you, my darling child. I'm sorry you had to endure such insensitivity. What can I do for you now?'

'Which one is my mother and which one is my father? I can't tell!'

'The one on the left, with the flat top, is your father. The one on the right, with the round top, is your mother.'

I stood for a moment, taking them in, feeling myself calming down, breathing again, softening. I asked the rabbi if he would pray with me. He reached for my hands. The guards looked concerned.

'Is it OK, officer? I'm Rabbi Rocklin, and I'll be

351

officiating over the funeral of Sonia's lovely parents. They were dear friends of mine and I have known the family for many years.'

The guards backed off and he took my hands. We prayed together for a few moments as people began to arrive and take seats. The guards suggested that I move towards the front row where I would be sitting and wait while people approached me one at a time, warning me again not to let anyone come too fast. I hardly remember the individual faces, only the love with which they surrounded me.

Then my brother brought the children. They would sit with me in the front row. When I saw them I lost control, gasping, unable to speak. We held on to each other, taking comfort in the living warmth. The closeness, the feeling of my children's bodies, the family all wrapped up together in one embrace. The guards told us to take our seats. Eric sat beside me and Tina sat on my lap.

'Mommy, which one is Grandma and which one is Grandpa?'

'The round one is Grandma and the flat one is Grandpa,' I told them, wondering why they didn't put a sign up so people would know.

'That's because Grandma was round and Grandpa wasn't,' Tina informed us with the sensibility of a child. Eric hugged her and I hugged them both.

The funeral began. The rabbi said beautiful and touching things, the mourners responded at the appropriate times. I could hear all this happening somewhere outside myself but for me there was only the warmth of my children's bodies next to mine and the coffins that filled my world.

'I'll take care of you, Mommy,' Tina said, taking the hankie from my hand and wiping the tears from my face. She dabbed at my eyes and then wiped Eric's face for him.

He kissed her hand and turned to me, 'I love you, Mom.'

'I love you too, sweetheart, both of you. Don't worry. Everything will be OK. We will take care of each other.' Tina wiped the tears from my face again with the old white hankie that had been my father's. I would keep that hankie for ever. I would never wash it.

The rabbi concluded his sermon, saying that it was Belle and Herb's wish that their daughter be reunited with her children, not just for this occasion but for ever, and we would all pray for that day to come soon, to fulfil their wish. Then we were allowed to approach the caskets, which were lowered into the ground, and throw a shovelful of dirt into the hole to help cover them. I threw some in and ate some, to somehow keep a part of what would be with them with me. Then we walked to the car. The guards told me I would have five minutes in the car with my family. I got in the back with all the children. My brother and his wife got in the front. They promised to take care of things. I promised to try not to worry. I told them that I loved them, and to be good to each other. We held each other tightly. The children didn't want me to leave, but they knew I had to go.

'Thank you for the dress. It's beautiful, green, my favourite colour.'

'I know, Mommy. I picked it out.'

'I know you did. I love you.' And turning to Tina, 'And thank you for wiping my face for me. I love you too.' I kissed them.

The guard knocked on the window. Five minutes. I hugged them tighter, squeezing my eyes shut.

'Can't you give us another few minutes?' It was my brother, trying to reason a few more moments out of them. But there would be no more.

'I have to go now. I'll call you when I get back. I love you. Everything will be OK. Be good to each other.'

'I don't want you to go, Mommy! I want you to stay here with us!' The children were crying.

We kissed again and I wiped the tears from their faces, to keep them for ever in the beloved hankie. I got out of the car, closing the door securely behind me, and rejoined my guards. The car window rolled down and we waved and blew kisses and said our I-love-yous and then I turned and walked away, towards the unmarked car that would speed me back to the airport. In the hangar, I changed back into my uniform, returning the green dress to the box in which it came. The female guard let me keep the pantyhose. Back on the plane, I ate some of the fruit, knowing my parents would want me to do that. I had promised to take care of myself, to be OK, for the children's sake. The rabbi said it was their wish. I felt somehow relieved. I felt as if my parents flew with me that night, all the way back to Florida. I had left the prison at 11 a.m.; I was back in time for the 11 p.m. count. But I returned a different person from the one who had left that morning.

When I got back from the funeral, the other inmates brought me hard-boiled eggs and oranges, cans of juice, packets of soup. Knowing nothing of the ritual of sitting Shiva but sharing in sorrow and loss, they knew instinctively what to do. The beauty and the power of our traditions is that they speak to and from the heart and soul. Rabbi Richter guided me through the steps. And I began to recover.

July 22, 1982

My man I love you! It's Thursday and has been a better day – each day is a little better now.

Eric said the other night that he'll be glad when his birthday comes so he'll have a little happiness. It's all been so sad. So he'll have a little happiness as needed. It'll be good for everyone.

I showered and am easing down from the pace I run at all evening – I get psyched up talking with my brother and the children and helping think out the problems and hearing about what's going on. At least I can help – I'm grateful for that because it gets me nuts not to be able to be there so at least I can be helpful from here. I spoke with Ginger who is in Hawaii. She's taking care of the birthday presents for us.

Your weekend letter 16, 17, 18 and your Monday 19 came tonight. Don't let these jerks' behavior hassle you honey. I did accomplish what had to be and their attitudes are irrelevant. Your picture is a nice one. So sexy – it's a good picture of you.

I got a letter from a girl I knew as a kid – she's into films now and has been a professor of film and movie stuff for nine years now. She's into the women's rights movement and all – wants to do a film of me – incarcerated mothers – sure! Anyway, it was something different – I haven't seen or heard from her in many years. I've got the opera *Tosca* on now. It's a heavy – she's about to go over the parapet cursing this dude.

I got a brochure back from Andrew Jackson college tonight – did you? I requested that they send you one too. I was just talking to Mary – there are over 80 people in this dorm now – used to be 60 some odd. That's a lot of people locked in one area. It's getting so noisy and we never have enough supplies anymore. We are always running out of toilet paper.

I think I'll call Uncle Joe in the a.m. I must fill in the gap for him, and my brother will too, for the daily calls he'd have with my mom. He's our responsibility now – and I accept with pleasure. I'll keep contact with all of the relatives that my parents did – they would like that. I miss them so – yet I feel them close. They aren't here to depend on anymore and our security is gone. I never had to worry about how things were at home – now I do, but all will be okay. Al and Meresa are working with me. We'll be okay honey. I will keep you up to date and informed and look for your advice as always.

I love you completely. Love and kisses,
Your wife Sunny

I had been receiving many letters and cards from people on the outside. I kept them all in a neat stack, which I eventually tied with a piece of yellow ribbon. I always meant to answer them – every one of them. But I never did. I couldn't. I still have them, all tied up in the yellow ribbon.

July 23, 24, 25, 1982

My Man,

I love you. It's Friday evening – no mail from you tonight honey. It's Saturday now – I've been very busy and involved with the legalities and details of what's happening now. It's been good for me to have all that to think about. I know Al is worn thin now in all ways and I can't relieve him of what he must still do before he can rest. I wish I could. The kids understand and Meresa helps them. I wish I could be there to help too. Tina, by herself without anyone telling her, went and got out a salad bowl and made a salad for supper. I had called to tell the children to pitch in and help and to see that each other had the right foods to eat and already, on their own, they were doing it! Beautiful ones they are!

I haven't played the radio since this all happened till this weekend. No mourning on the Sabbath and that starts on Friday night – tomorrow, after one or two hours, the Shiva period is over. Tomorrow will be the first time I'll have gone out of the dorm among everyone (aside from being called to classification and medical) in over two weeks. I

357

go back to work on Monday. I feel sort of drained still but I have to get myself back in gear. My muscle tone has left me – I feel heavy and weak, without any bounce, and so slow and sluggish. I'll perk back up after a while for sure – and things up in North Carolina will settle down and I'll be able to put my mind more at ease. My eyes are tired – I started reading a book today – a spy novel. It's diversion for me – little by little . . . Soon I'll be able to groove on the Nippon [sexy letter] you sent me. Good night my love, sweet dreams. If you were here you could easily distract me from bummed out thoughts. I love you Jesse – we are one – send me some good vibes my love. Help me to come back up.

I love you. Love and kisses, your wife Sunny

Jesse had written that I needed to be more concerned with his welfare because one day the kids would grow up and leave me, but he and I would be for ever. If I didn't realize this I ran the risk of becoming 'a lonely old woman'. Oh well! I could have done with a more supportive attitude from him and I could have been more annoyed but I just didn't have the energy. And I knew he was upset because his situation was getting narrower. Legally, the pressure was on and he had been informed that he could expect his death warrant to be signed soon.

July 29, 1982

Wailing wall – to cry and willing to be 'a lonely old woman' if necessary.

The pressure of this is breaking me . . . My spirit is so overwrought that I could almost cry – 'Enough! Let me go home now! I can't stand it any longer!' like a person being tortured in some foreign country – but it's here and it's me – and I can't let my spirit be broken.

July 30, 31, August 1, 1982
Friday Saturday Sunday

My Man,

Last night I looked at my parents' picture, for the first time since the crash. I waited till supper and told Mary I didn't want to eat just as she started out the door so she couldn't say she didn't plan to go and stay behind too! She went and I got a few moments to myself. I took another picture today for you. Dottie Marie came. She is three and a half months pregnant now.

Spoke with Meresa. She told me all about what they're doing for Eric's birthday tomorrow. It sounds like he'll have a good day – a fun day. I'm glad. I spoke with all kids yesterday morning. Danny picked the vegetables from Grandpa's garden, Eric is going to work with Al tomorrow, Tina is playing with the puppies. Eric will get lots of presents and they'll be going to putt putt in evening. So it will be a fun evening and a good party.

I've been using stuff for my eyes and they're getting better. It's 11.30 lights out now. I wish we

could pillow together. I love you with all my heart
and I want and need you!

Love and kisses, your woman Sunny

It was Labor Day, 1982. Three months had passed since
the plane crash. I had been trying to reorder my mind,
find a perspective I could live with. I was cleaning up the
pile of pictures and papers by my pillow when I came
across the pictures of the visit from Labor Day last year. It
made me so lonesome! And I was even wearing the same
dress I wore that day for the visit.

      *It is the New Year 5743, according to
the Jewish calendar, and the first year that we will
spend without the physical presence of our
parents/grandparents. I wish my brother would go
with Meresa and the children to temple, to Rabbi
Rocklin. He would help to release them and fortify
them. I wish I could take them with me this
evening and tomorrow to Rabbi Rocklin's temple. I
think that the New Year ends the period of
mourning.*

    Aleinu
    Atonement
    Avenu Malchenu

I have always loved the ancient Jewish New Year tradition
of ending the year with forgiveness so as to start the New
Year clean and fresh – that is, should God grant your
petition for entry into the Book of Life for another year.

One spends ten days forgiving: first, forgiving others all debts uncollected and any hurts of the past year; second, asking forgiveness of others whom you might have owed a debt, or in some way hurt or offended. Finally, after cleaning your spiritual house, so to speak, you may go before God in his temple and ask his forgiveness for any sins you may have accumulated through the course of the year, either by commission or omission. It involves a good deal of soul-searching. For me this time, the ritual marked not only the transition from one year to the next but a total reality shift. I was so glad that I hadn't neglected to say 'I love you' to my parents on that last visit, when I finally saw them as the two wonderful people that they were. Thank God I would not have that regret on my heart as I sat in judgement on myself.

    Before this all happened to us, I didn't see past my own small space. Like an addiction, it was my whole life – this devotion to another person and to a dream life. I gave myself up to it. And the consequences will reverberate to the end of my days and beyond, through its effect on others' lives. It was a terribly tragic mistake – without intention. I cannot imagine how such a thing could have happened to me. I realized only tonight that I must never again give myself up to another human being, but to God alone, the universal conscious-ness. When you give yourself up to someone else you give away your free will – that is a danger, and a sign of danger should someone else accept it.

The fire that I saw in my dream, the flames that devoured my mother and father, became the crucible that burned away the dross of my life. I no longer had the buffer of a generation before me, of parents who could take up the slack of my life. I was an orphan now and the eldest in my family. I had to take up the burden of responsibility for my own actions and well-being, as well as the welfare of the whole family. I would still maintain the bubble, and the love I had and would always have for and with Jesse. But now the decisions would be made with the greater welfare in mind.

I called Kay, Jesse's mom. She was feeling like no one cared about her or how she felt. I told her that I felt that way too, only more so. She tried to tell me that it wasn't so and, in her efforts to comfort me, ended up making herself see how it really wasn't so for her either. Kay was trying to keep up with the legal status of Jesse's case and she made regular calls to his attorneys. She was a rock.

My brother Alan brought the children to see me. But first he brought Tom, the attorney who had helped make out my parents' wills, and my father's lifelong friend and accountant, Mickey Weinstein. This was a business visit. We also discussed the custody of the children and decided that we would file in court for Alan, my brother, to be made their legal guardian. Jesse and I thought we could simply write a letter authorizing it.

> Honey, I had a real good visit with them. We talked through a lot of things and got a lot done. At least now each one knows where the other stands on

362

things. On the kids, we're going to have to go the legal custody route rather than the guardianship. In North Carolina the only way that guardianship can be transferred from natural parents is if the natural parents are dead – which we are not! In North Carolina when someone goes to prison (I asked this question) their children are given over into someone else's care by way of a custody hearing. That's the way we have to go too. It means we are going to be served, by mail or a sheriff, papers saying Al is the plaintiff vs. us, the defendants. I've read a copy of it already. It is saying that Al will be appointed by the court as legal custodian of the kids until I get out. That clause, about 'until I get out' is in there so it is clear that we get our kids back! It says me because you don't have quite the same legal status as I do concerning the kids. It's a formality simply so the children's custody will be legally secure with Alan until we can be out there.

The next day my brother came to see me with his wife and all of the kids. They looked better and everyone seemed to be getting along well together. The kids all hung on me, like puppies, and I filled myself up with the feeling. They visited both days. It was a whirlwind of emotions, tears and laughter that swept away the emptiness and grief that had covered my path, bringing colour and light back into my life. I kept one of the pictures we took – of me surrounded by the children – and it became the talisman of my comfort for a long time afterwards.

26

J ESSE WAS HAVING a hearing concerning his religious
rights, having proclaimed himself the head of the Kiai-
Shu sect of Zen Buddhism. He had twenty or thirty
followers in the prison and he was suing for the right to be
their religious counsellor and to have meditation
cushions, wear beards, and eat vegetarian food. The suit
had merits and was being heard in federal court. His new
attorney, Liz, was helping him with it as well as with his
appeal. Liz wanted some sort of letter from me but she
hadn't gone through Bill Shepherd as I had asked so I had
not yet complied. I knew Jesse was upset about it. But I
was keenly aware of the need to make responsible
decisions now. I did nothing legal without Bill's advice.
Jesse could be mad if he chose to be, but now I had to
think about the impact on the children of everything I did.

September 1982

My Dearest Jesse,
Your attorney, Liz, was supposed to be in touch with
Bill. But I know he was trying by phone and hadn't
been able to reach her and she hadn't returned his
calls. He wouldn't lie about it. One day we will talk

and I will elucidate on this and other things as they come up, but for now I can only hope that you know that I love you no less and am no less loyal, no less with you than ever, and that I would not do anything to lessen our chances for freedom – and if you do feel let down or disappointed, I hope you will love me anyway. If you can no longer love me because I'm no longer perfect, I think I'd like to be loved anyway – as I have always loved – 'anyway.' So, my love, if you are angry or disappointed or whatever, don't fault me for learning well and being true to my nature – as I have never faulted you for that.

I love you Jesse – with all my heart. I think you've done some very serious thinking lately – about all things important, in our case and beyond that too. I've thought about how the children need their parents now more than ever – and you must see how, without harm, I must preserve every avenue of reaching them. I will not diminish their chances. I will wait for your thoughts on this – I have great faith in you. I know your mind and heart and your capacity to understand . . . And to love. I wonder when I will meet Liz?* I wonder a lot . . . But I have faith, in you, in myself, and in the future! The kids have grown so much. It's amazing. I can't wait to be with them again!

*Liz was the attorney who had taken Rhodes's forty-five-page deposition and filed for Jesse's clemency in 1979. She was now Jesse's appeal attorney.

October 3, 1982, 9.39 a.m., Sunday
Today is my mother's birthday. The fifth, Tuesday,
is my father's. There is a full moon and I suppose
that makes me even more sensitive. I dreamed of
my parents – I dreamed I was yelling to someone
about giving it all back if I could have them back
again. But I can't—

The press eventually reported that the national transportation safety board said the crew of the Pan American World Airways flight on 9 July had received warnings of 'possibly dangerous wind changes' prior to takeoff in a heavy storm. The warnings of a general low-level wind-shear alert were included in the information recovered from the cockpit voice and flight data recorders. Wind shear, the papers explained, can cause rapid changes in wind direction and force an aircraft to descend sharply. The tape showed that, after takeoff, the captain said the plane was 'sinking' and spoke of what he might do to correct this.

I wondered if they'd had time to be scared. I wondered if they'd had a chance to hold on to each other and say a prayer. I would think about that for years afterwards. There would be an inquiry into the cause of the crash and reports occasionally in the press. My brother would collect the reports but I chose not to read them. I decided to believe that they had time for a last 'I love you'.

366

October 11, 1982

My Man,

I love you! It's Monday. I do manage to clear my mind sometimes. Just walking out into the sunshine and hearing the birds is enough to totally focus my attention and clear all else away . . . And then I am clear and bright as the sun!

I got a letter from Ginger – she's okay and the baby is too. Also, Sherry was approved to visit – she'll be so happy! She will bring the children to see me!*

TL. It's your birthday now! I sent you intense happy birthday vibes at midnight. I love you completely Jesse – we are one – always. Good night, pleasant dreams, have a happy birthday. I love you. Love and kisses,

Your woman Sunny

P.S. I can feel you writing to me now. I look forward to everything you say to me. You are so wise.

October 12, 1982

My Woman,

I love you. It's Tuesday and it's my birthday. I've been kicking back today and relaxing, thinking na to wa [you and I] and generally hanging out all day. I celebrated last night at midnight with you. I love you my woman. There was no mail for me tonight.

---

* My brother didn't fly again for many years. But Sherry, my childhood friend from Long Island, would arrange with him to bring the children to see me. My brother had more than enough on his plate.

I still didn't get a card from Eric yet so I'm going to wait until tomorrow or so until I write the kids back again. I have all my cards set out so I can look at them and pictures, so I'm grooving with all of us tonight. Today I painted for you. I did a really neat little sea scene. You will really like it honey. I felt like grooving you for my birthday. I'll have to make a big envelope to send it out in as nothing I have will fit it. It's been a pretty decent day honey. Someone sent me a few really good books to check out so I've been into a few chapters all day. The time just zoomed by today. You've been so heavily in my thoughts my love. Next year we'll be celebrating all our birthdays together. I'm going to make this envelope and send you my birthday present to you on my birthday. I love you Sunny you are my woman forever.

I love you, your husband Jesse

I had gone back to work. I was now assigned to the library – as a cleaner. The effects of the stress I'd been under were manifesting in physical ways – I thought I was beginning the change of life. I mentioned it to Kid, one of the younger girls with whom I worked. She was having a rough time that month too. So we decided to make a Hallowe'en sign with pictures on it to decorate the library.

❧ *Hanukkah 1982*
It's Saturday and this morning I made out some of
my Hanukkah cards and spoke to Tina and Eric to

wish them a happy Hanukkah. I got a Christmas
box. We need to take precautions. One thief
already was checking out the room – I sat here and
watched her, very quietly. It scared the shit out of
her when she finally noticed me. She said she
thought someone else lived here – I know that's a
lot of BS but it served to let me know thieves are
definitely eyeing this room and we're being extra
careful for awhile.

I talked to Eric about being mainstreamed
back into all regular classes with the full program
now. He said he likes it except for the part about
getting home an hour later. He won't have much
time for play during the week at all. And he goes to
the dentist tomorrow to get the stitches out. He had
dental surgery and he cut his finger on the cutting
machine at work with my brother Alan.

The children seemed to be settling in and I was trying to
get everyone working together as a tight-knit group rather
than being at odds with one another. My brother and his
wife had their faults and their difficulties, but their
children and mine were like brothers and sister with each
other, and I needed Jesse to accept the situation. They were
doing their best. I reminded Jesse that we could not forget
the debt we owed for the help we'd been given, no matter
how imperfect. It was the best solution I had available.

I began to pick up more hints of problems. Tina was
now eight and Eric was sixteen. Eric was doing poorly in
school. He wasn't keeping his room clean and he didn't

want to shower. All signs of depression to me, but through his own pain and anger my brother saw it as rebellion. I thought it was stress and blamed myself. Sixteen was a difficult age under the best of circumstances.

🐌 *December 1982*

The thought of how my brother, Alan, looked and sounded, especially how he sounds when we get choked up and reaffirm, to our great self sadness, that the folks are really dead and how we need them and miss them . . . it's the little boy that I hear – that boy when we were small, and scared to be left alone. And I know again how very much I love, and have always loved, my brother.

27

🐦 *Jan. 16, 1983*

This is my gold pen – with the new refill it writes
nicely! This is a quote from a poem by Zenrin
Kushu in a book by Alan Watts: 'Trees show the
bodily form of the wind; waves give vital energy to
the moon.'

I am one of the few Jewish women of this and the
younger generation who knows the experience of
prison – when I'm asked, I would like to be able to
have answers as to what can be done! I don't mean
this on a personal level; how I dealt with my time
is too individual. But I think the answer lies in the
realm of responsibility. And we, as Jews, are
responsible, each in our own community and our
own home.

THERE WAS A NEW Jewish girl in my dorm. We met in the water room one evening while waiting for them to open the doors for dinner. 'Hi. What are you in for?' she enquired perkily. It was an offensive way to start a conversation, but because she was Jewish I decided to see if I could find something about her to like.

Heidi was young – only twenty or so. She was in for kidnapping but she only got a year and a day for it because the judge understood that her intention was good. She just went about it in the wrong way. Her neighbours had a baby who was left for hours unattended – dirty, wet, unfed. So Heidi took the baby home with her. The parents didn't even seem to notice. After a few days, Heidi decided to leave for Mexico and took the baby with her. When she got there, she left the baby with a couple in Mexico City and went up into the mountains to look for peyote. When she came down from the mountains, she knew she couldn't keep the baby. So she called her shrink and told him to arrange for her to turn herself in. Her sentence of a year and a day meant that she would have to go to state prison. Under a year and you go to the county jail.

Heidi was the only person I ever befriended just because she was Jewish. She was adopted as a baby by a Jewish couple from Minnesota. She was desperate for love. She was also used to just taking things.

She came to my door to talk one day and later I noticed that my good pen was gone. It was the one Ginger had left for me, gold with designs etched into it. It was a prized possession. No one else had been around. I checked with the neighbours. It had to have been Heidi. Colleen wanted to confront her and make her come up with the pen. But I asked her not to do that. I wanted to give Heidi a chance to give it back herself. I thought she might value the friendship over the pen if she thought about it. I went to her room. She was up on the top bunk, reading. I stood in the doorway and said, 'Heidi, my good gold pen is missing. Now, I don't want to know who took it, or how it got to be missing. I just want it back. It had sentimental value to me. It was given to me by a very good friend. I'm going to go out for a while. When I come back, I want to see my pen back in my room, on the bed where I left it. No questions asked.'

'What are you telling me for?'

'Just so you'll know.'

'OK. Have a nice walk.'

'Thanks. See you later, Heidi.'

I collected Colleen and we went out for a walk on the compound. The pen was on my bed when I got back. It was placed under the pillow. Heidi came around later on to visit.

'I got my pen back,' I said.

'Oh, yeah. That's nice. I'm glad you got it back.'

'Me too. Want a cup of coffee?'

'OK. I'll go get the water.'

Colleen didn't like it, but I became friends with Heidi. We went to services together when the rabbi came. You really couldn't help but like Heidi after a while. She was so funny and so cute and so good-natured and she was smart too. Heidi was only there for a few months, having received time off her year and a day for good behaviour, but we got to be very close.

🐌 *January 18, 1983*

Ah! I was just reading about the diarists of the
Holocaust. They got more unrealistic in what they
perceived their life as becoming as they got closer to
their deaths! Well then, that's who would know
how it is to be on death row. Being in a ghetto or

373

death camp in those days (they equated them and so do I) was the equal of being on death row – or knowing someone on death row.

I was envisioning being home and holding Eric in a comforting embrace – like when he was small. I don't think he'll ever be too big for me to hug. I yearn for the pleasure of holding and comforting my children. And then I thought how it must have hurt my own mother to see me in such unhappy circumstances – to see the children too in such a situation. But her child, her daughter in prison – even on death row! And to have had to leave this world with her child still in these circumstances . . . How awful! I am crying. I wanted to tell my brother – that I know how Mom must have felt – but this will have to wait until we can be together . . . It's too much to open up on him alone.

&❧ *Feb. 7, 1983*

Alan said power without responsibility creates corruption. It's very true – and I told him I was going to write it down. He's grown so much in the past month. I'm very proud of his development. I wish he were more benevolent and forgiving though . . .

&❧ *February 11, 1983*

This is the first Valentine Day when I won't be able to send cards to my mom and dad. I started crying and haven't been able to stop . . . No holiday will

ever be the same again without them here. I know
they are here but not like before . . . But still, they
are here and I hope they know my feelings. I love
you Mom and Dad!

Jesse's father was dying. His mother was trying to care for him at home. I was urging Jesse to write to her more often. I think the thought of his father's dying and his mother being preoccupied was scaring him.

There had been a stabbing on the row and Jesse and some of his friends were getting a hard time over it – shakedowns, harassment, delays in the mail . . .

March 8, 1983

My Woman,

I love you. I'm being harassed every day lately in one way or another. I can hardly sleep with the noise and yelling half the time and even my eyes have dark circles and I had to catch catnaps whenever I can. I don't really mean to be complaining and all . . . Everything is just armpit here continually and it's affected my writing and everything else. I start writing and then I turn angry and focus all my aggressions about everything onto A and M [Alan and Meresa] or anything and everybody except you. I realize it and rip up the letter. It's very frustrating to me. I'm very sensitive emotionally lately Sunny, and I'm so bored too, I'm really going through a trip inside and I never let myself get aggravated . . . I just have no constructive reading, there's no fun, no kicks or excitement and frankly this little cell is getting old. It will pass in a week or two. I haven't written to mom for weeks as I just don't want her to feel all the suffering perhaps, but I'll write. I got to write to the kids too. This is the first and most serious time I've had like this, it's just everything all at once too overloaded a bit. It would do me a world of good to be able to pillow with you.

Don't worry about hassles here, I handle them baby and it's all just part of their punishment program here in the pits; up their nose with a yellow rose. We'll be rockin' soon. I love you.

Your husband, Jesse

Jesse had been insisting that Eric should be called to testify for him. The possibility hung over my son's life like a dark cloud, threatening to engulf his world once again as it had during those first months when he was held in custody by the prosecutor, taken to the hearing in chains, alone and without anyone to help him or protect him from the all-powerful 'authorities' who were posing as the good guys but who became worse than the worst nightmare a little boy could have had. Jesse was so angry – he was seeing evil plots everywhere.

March 11, 12, 13, 1983

My Man,

I've already mentioned writing mom, and the same goes for Tina. If you want to maintain a relationship with her as a person, as her daddy why don't you write to her? You can't be there right now, you can't call, you can't take her places – but you can write! Why should I tell her this or that, daddy this, daddy that. Why don't you tell her yourself? She wonders about these things. Until you can do more, at least do the best you can with what you've got! The children are being fed, clothed, cared for, loved and given a home by A and M. You must take care not to alienate yourself by forcing a choice – the kids must choose survival. You're her daddy – no one could change how she feels about you or that she wants her own mommy and daddy like other children! Now, as to Eric – ever since I released him from any further involvement with you and legal matters concerning that situation he has absolutely blossomed! And you should be glad for him – he had it real rough for a child, and now he's in transition to adulthood at a great disadvantage. Rather than posing a threat to him and his little bit of security, you could be helping him too – even if it's just not to hold it against him that he needs to be free to grow up. You haven't thought about helping anyone else in years – only if it also serves you. Well, I understand . . . Because of the situation . . . But that really isn't an excuse – it's unnecessarily selfish and if you want your relationships to improve, you will have to accomplish the change. You don't make family by use of terrorist methods. To make trouble for A and M is to make it harder for the children because they need them to live with.

Understand, before going any further, that I DO NOT have control – I have been telling you that, but you keep coming back with stuff about my losing control or no longer having control. I never had and I never said I had. I am here in prison, BCI, and all I can do is talk on the phone. These are things you must know, even if you won't like it or might get mad at me, for the sake of your relationships with the rest of the family including your own mother! You aren't abandoned, you have let go. I know how lonely it is – but you can't sit there and pout about it and lash out about it and not do anything positive and then expect people to understand and respond accordingly. I know how the time and space begin to get on one's nerves. I've been there. Without having been there how can anyone have any idea of it?

The Tae Kwan Do lessons for Tina were started as a means for her to take part in things with the others in the family. It is a therapeutic measure* – I still intend to see that she gets her ballet. And she won't be used as a punching bag. My goodness! I told Tina she should speak to me about whatever bothers her especially if it has to do with family things because I love everyone involved – they don't always love each other, but I love them one and all and I know them all, so I can help her understand.

* Jesse's concerns weren't totally paranoid because Tina ended up with a broken arm after one of those home practice sessions.

I've been in a very serious mood lately – trying to
get everyone to see things in a realistic way – even
Uncle Joe. He's been really strung out . . . I told him
I even pray for him. He may have to go into a
psychiatric hospital. He's trying some medication
first. I hope it helps.

In April an execution was carried out in Alabama. They
had to pull the switch three times to kill him. The Florida
media reported on the feelings of the men on the state's
death row and Jesse was on the news and I could see his
feelings on his face. The flood gates, according to
informed sources, had been opened, clearing the way for
other states to begin systematically signing death warrants
and performing executions. I told Jesse that he, personally,
had too much going on legally for them to mess with him.
But, as Jesse pointed out, they would really be able to fuck
with people on the row now by signing death warrants.
Jesse had been told he could expect his warrant to be
signed any time. They wanted him.

     *It is an eating away process, the
process of the creation of the pound of flesh that
must be paid, being on death row.*

Jesse and I were still having problems. And then I met
Carol, the aunt of the teenage girl he had been fooling
around with in the visiting park. She was also the wife of
the sensei who had been Jesse's mentor in the early days.
She was having problems with her 'old man' for not doing

things his way and I was having a similar problem with Jesse. She and I had heard of each other from Jesse and felt we knew each other even before we met. She told me all the stories about Jesse and the sensei. A charge against her of having some illegal pills in her purse would have been dropped if she had agreed to testify against someone else. Instead, she ended up doing time for it. The sensei was very pissed off with her. She was pissed off with her whole life. While we were sharing our photos I came across the one of her niece sitting on Jesse's lap. The Cosmic Humour was at it again. Fate had brought her and her photo album to me.

We became partners in disillusionment – dreamers whose reality had come suddenly and undeniably crashing in on the dreams with which we had fallen in love. We went through that narrow space in our lives linked arm in arm. We were very different people, Carol and I, but for a while we were sisters.

28

• *June 11, 1983, 2.09 p.m.*

Surely it is comforting to know one is not alone –
that there are others who mourn on this day, that
there are others that mourn every day . . . as I do.
Not until now did I realize what prayers were for.
They are to comfort you. We must go on – not to
waste life but to live it correctly, in love and peace.

I was just reading over the unveiling service
that Rabbi Richter sent. I have to go over it today
so I can read it, as they will, tomorrow. To honor
my father and mother.

I WAS STILL WORKING IN THE library, and although it was
not the law library, I had access to the law books and
all the resources in the next room, and so I was happy. I
was supposed to be cleaning but the librarian taught me
to access the books according to the Dewey Decimal
System, and I helped at the checkout desk when we got
busy. Of course, I did manage to slip into the law library
and I began helping people to file simple pleadings like
divorces, and even a 3.850, which is one of the steps in the
state appeals process. I also helped people to file grievances

and civil suits against the institution when the incident was really serious or offensive. Cynthia, a young black woman I knew from the dorm, came to me for help in filing a grievance after one of the more redneck guards spat his tobacco juice on the front of her blouse. We filed the grievance according to institutional procedure and then went on to file a civil lawsuit, which she won. But you had to know that, whatever the outcome, you would ultimately be punished for exercising your rights. That particular sergeant and his cronies 'dogged her out', meaning they picked on her, for a long time afterwards.

There was a woman in my dorm who fancied herself as the queen of BCI, in that she ruled the dorm and her influence extended throughout the compound. There were a couple of older women who wanted to run the place. This one decided she wanted my job – not the cleaning but the librarian's assistant position. She complained to classification because I hadn't gone through the clerical training in the Education Department. I was removed from my library job, to which she immediately got herself assigned. And I got reassigned to Education, but this time to the office and clerical skills class – a job that didn't involve cleaning.

July 15, 16, 17, 1983

My Man,

I love you! It's Friday and has been nice for me. I started the class in Office Occupations – got my chair desk and typewriter assignments and a bunch of workbooks. It's neat! We get a canvas bag to carry

our books in and we get to drink coffee in class
(which is like an elite thing ha ha) I'm an 'Off. Occ.'
Girl now – very high class! It's a trip really.

My brother had given permission for Tina to visit her
grandma Kay so that Kay could bring her to visit us. Kay
had decided it was best not to have Jesse's dad at home
during Tina's visit because his mental condition had
deteriorated badly. He wasn't responsible for his
behaviour any more. Grandma Kay made Italian dinners
and Welsh breakfasts and she and Tina created a
Hanukkah bush, which became a tradition between them
for many years after.

August 12, 13, 14, 1983

My Woman,

I love you. It's the weekend and I had such a great
visit with our daughter. I am ecstatic! It was such a
surprise Sunny, it completely wigged me with
happiness. Tina and I had so much fun together
and I daddy-ed the whole day. Everything is great
between Tina and me Sun, and if there was anything anyone wondered about, I think it's certainly
time to look elsewhere as any problem does not, in
any manner, arise from me. You'll have seen Tina by
the time you'll receive this letter so you know. We
had a ball together and she clung to me all day and
hugged and kissed me and told me her plans for us
and it was super honey. She didn't want to leave!
When it was time to go she put her legs around my

383

waist and her arms around my neck and held on tight and sobbed she wanted to stay with me as we sat there. She's so cute and she loves me so much, it's heavy Sun and I told her how much you and I love her and did it up with our baby girl. We had great talk about you and me, the whole visit was simply terrific Sunny and we took pictures which you'll see soon. She was hugging me and kissing me and brushing my hair and sitting on my lap all day long. She'd look at me and smile and say I love you daddy and give me a kiss. She's such a little doll and smart, wow! I mean sharp! I'm so proud. Everyone came over to me and said what a beauty she is too Sun, strangers and all. I was so pleased ha ha. Then we drew pictures together and she drew flowers and a mountain scene and then I showed her how to draw different kinds of flowers and how to use her 'vision' to draw, and I told her about landscapes and how to always represent heaven, Earth and man in a landscape and then I showed her how to do it, and she did. Then I showed her how to draw a cute monster ha ha, and she copied it. She has a lot of potential as an artist Sun, seriously she has talent and she'd like to take an art course and I think we should send her to an art school. I asked her what painting she liked best at Mom's and guess which one she likes best – Pierre. So I'm giving it to her for her room. So our daughter will have it with her Sunny. When Eric comes down I'll let him pick out one he wants too. We played tic tac toe for awhile and laughed and then I sat with her on the floor and played telephone with her. Sun, we just had a ball together. It was a great visit for both of us. We ate together and she fed me and I fed her too. We split everything up and ate real good. I'm thrilled with the visit. I've been smiling so much my cheeks ache. Our daughter is the perfect blend of the two of us Sun, even down to her mannerisms. She's so lovely, just like Mommy I love you Sunny. When I came in from the visit I fell out. It exhausted me. I slept from about 5 until three in the morning and woke up still smiling to myself. I sat in meditation for a while, then turned on the radio and listened til breakfast. We talk about how much she likes the name Christina. I told her how when we named her that Christina was the prettiest name I could think of for a girl. And she wanted me to hold her so she could go to sleep but she really didn't. She just wanted me to cradle her and whisper and sing little songs to her and I did for about ten minutes, then she jumped up and sat on my lap smiling. Words alone can't describe how good it was. We are her parents, we're her blood, and she is us. With us she's different than anyone else in the world. She's very wise, perceptive, and emotionally attuned to herself and us as her parents, Sun. Her love and attachment to us is beyond all comprehension. We'll be free and together with our children before much longer. I'll definitely be celebrating with you at midnight on 23rd and 24. It's just a matter of substantiating our defense fully now Sun, and we'll be out of these pits. I love you. Have a great visit with our daughter. You are with me each moment of every day and night.

I love you.

Your husband, Jesse

My visit was a good one but I still didn't get any insight into the problems the children were having in North Carolina. I felt so helpless. Like she did with her daddy, all Tina wanted from me was to be babied and cuddled and loved, and so that's what we did.

In August 1983, young Heidi got her GED High School Equivalency diploma. They did the whole cap and gown thing in the chapel and we all attended the ceremonies. I felt *so* proud of her and I wrote her a little note about it. She saved that note and gave it back to me years later when she was working towards her college degree. Heidi was always a very sensitive person. In her quiet way, she was very strong. Later on, she would offer to give me a job if I got out. She grew up but she didn't forget. I think the bonds created in adversity are, of necessity, very strong ones. Not the ones that are based on the needs of the moment but the ones that come from the deeper, more lasting needs of the spirit.

ॐ *October 23, 1983*
We in prison depend on those we have left outside
for our very existence. Without their support and

acknowledgement we cease to exist in the outside
world. We fade before our very eyes – we feel life
slipping away as the people drift farther away from
us. It's like being shipwrecked in a hostile land, the
land of the lost. And, half the time, the people who
supply you with the vital elements of life and hope,
get tired, or too busy, or simply don't care anymore.
So, like the old Eastern adage about the tree falling
(does it make noise if no one hears it?), we cease to
exist.

In rereading Jesse's letters about his visits with the
children I cannot help but think of those children whose
fathers are on death row in states where they are forced to
visit behind a glass partition. They never get to touch their
fathers, even once in their whole life that they can remember, before their fathers are executed. In Florida contact
visits are still permitted for death row inmates. At least our
children would have the memory of how their father felt
and smelled and sounded and how he looked without a
partition between them and him.

Dec. 6, 7, 1983

My Woman,
I love you! I am your husband Sunny and you have
a real, a loyal and totally pure man who loves you
completely. You are numero uno in my life just as I
am in yours. We are really all we have Sun. It's our
future together which is most important in our lives
and it's forever. Our parents can disappear from our

lives in many ways, and eventually our children grow up, leave the nest, but we will always be us – good times or bad – we are constant and sure and we will grow old together my love as I've always said and will live long and laugh together when we're 90 my love. Now let me give you some feedback. First off, if my warrant is ever signed, which is doubtful, with Rhodes's confession and all else, it's you and others I depend on to substantiate and push our position vigorously in all ways. And as we've already discussed we can use Eric's original statement. It's going to come up soon for us Sun. We can and must prove Rhodes did it, or else neither of us will ever get out and you know that as well as I do. We must prove our non-involvement. It's up to us, you and me, to prove our positions to get out together. I've done all humanly possible for us obviously Sun and always have, just as you do for us. We will make it Sun. So just be prepared just as I am and let's do it! That's what I have to say about all this Sunny and I want your feedback to me on it too. I can tell you were upset over Sullivan's execution.*

TL. I just came in from the shower. It's freezing here! I put on four sweatshirts! It went down to 34 degrees last night and the windows are still broken

---

*Sullivan was a giant of a man with the intelligence of a five-year-old. He was retarded and everyone knew it. He saved his dessert from his last meal for when he got back. He couldn't grasp the concept that he wouldn't be coming back. They found it in his cell afterwards.

and open on the wing here, three that are 15 feet from me Brrrr! I want to cuddle up under the covers with you and pillow all night long! It's really like a dungeon in here. I'm going to bed early – too cold to be out.

I love you.

Your husband, Jesse

I loved to move fast. It felt good to me, inside. I guess it was because I had had to live at a dead stop for so many years. One day when I sped into the dorm office to get some sanitary pads I came face to face with a new officer sitting at the desk. She raised her head and our eyes met and there was an instant recognition! We had never seen each other before but we knew we would be friends.

'Hi!'

'Well, hi! What are you doing here?'

'I was assigned to this dormitory for the day. I'm new.'

'I know! My name is Sonia . . .'

'My name is Franny but I think you're supposed to call me Mrs Martino.'

'I need some sanitary pads.'

'Go on and get some from the cabinet.'

'Thanks, Mrs Martino, but you know we're not supposed to go in the cabinet by ourselves.'

'Oh, well, I don't mind. I'm not assigned to any one dorm yet. Just the relief officer for now.'

'Well, when you do get to pick a dorm, tell them you want to work in H-4.'

'Yes, I think I will. I like this dorm. It's quieter than the others.'

'That's because it's the old people's dorm. We don't like it noisy.'

Franny and I talked about everything to do with prison life. She was doing research for her doctorate on aberrant behaviour in women. I wasn't sure what she meant by aberrant and I wasn't sure that you could call it aberrant behaviour when you studied it in an aberrant setting.

December 16, 17, 18, 1983

My Man,

I love you! It's Friday and since there was no class today, I went over to Carol's and hung out awhile and then came back to the dorm and painted my face. I felt like working on Colleen's portrait, but she wasn't available so I did mine instead. I did it in blues and purples with pinks.

I stopped at Mary's for awhile. Poor thing, they really traumatized her with that strip search and all yesterday – she's an older woman! She told them 'if you see anything up there, it's my hemorroids.' That's sad – making her bend over and cough as if she would have anything up there! She'll never get over it. She never tells her family about stuff like that, so I go over there to let her bitch and get it out of her system.

Colleen will be home for Christmas, for sure. That doesn't leave much time. I told her it was time for her portrait . . . And that she'd be gone soon. I'll miss her a lot. It will give us a real good friend out there. That's good. But I'll miss her every day.

Good morning! It's Saturday and you are having a visit – poor mom is so exhausted. I know she needed to cry on your shoulder. She's strong, but she's also a mother, and the wife of a man who is dying rather quickly now. Jesse, my love, my husband, these are the hardest of times for our family. It's starting to age Mom – the strain is so intense and constant. I am going to have to force myself to start sitting [meditating] daily again. I haven't been but if I don't start again very shortly I will not be able to build to the full strength I need – and I'll be affected like Mom.

TL. Colleen and Carol and I decided that today would be our Christmas together. We had a picnic and gave each other cards and I gave Colleen her puzzle. After our picnic Colleen hung my wash for me while Carol went to do something at her dorm and I went in to do something. Then we met back up.

Colleen and I started the puzzle tonight. She needs to keep her mind busy as much as possible these last two or three days. It's heavy. I'm starting to feel so depressed thinking of how different it will be here without anyone to fully trust in daily living. In here you need someone to at least watch your back – and I've never been without Colleen for all the time I've been in population. It will be lonesome. But, for now, we'll enjoy these days and I'll call her every so often when she's out.

I love you, my Man!

Love and kisses, Sunny

I was finally able to arrange for my old friend Sherry to bring both children to see me. My brother was still unable to fly because of what happened to our parents. He was weighted down by responsibilities and by his own grief and anger, which would dominate his life and, in a way, imprison him for many years afterwards. Eric was now sixteen and Tina was eight. It had been almost a year since I had last seen them. They looked good, so grown-up, yet there was something in their faces that spoke of sadness. By the end of the visit, I understood that the situation had become overwhelming for my brother and I needed to find an alternative for the children. Sherry said they could come to live with her. But I couldn't just send them to New York from the visiting park. Legal formalities had to be dealt with before I could assure Sherry that there would be no repercussions. So the children went back to North Carolina to wait and I began the process of getting the custody transfer arranged. I called Rabbi Rocklin for help and he put me in touch with an attorney friend – 'a good man, an honest man' – named Mike Shulimson. Mike became my friend and attorney and was able to intercede for me and be of help in many ways. In the end, Tina went to live with Sherry and her family on Long Island while Eric ended up staying with my brother and his family for another six months and then went off on his own.

Sherry brought Tina to see me pretty regularly for the first year but then, according to the usual pattern of these things, the visits became more sporadic and they began limiting my phone calls, until I didn't have much contact with her. Visits and phone calls made her emotional and interfered with their daily routines, creating problems for Sherry and her husband Bob. But Tina was still in touch with her grandma Kay and her brother so I could cope. Jesse's mom and I remained friends but the relationship was strained. She felt cheated because I hadn't placed Tina with her. But with Jesse's dad in his present condition, Kay's home was no place for a child and Tina would have been visiting prison every weekend. I wanted her to have a more normal life than that. So, even though I knew I wouldn't get to see her as much, I decided that living with Sherry in New York was the best option. My relationship with Sherry was greatly damaged by our new status in relation to one another. I got upset about the situation at times, but I couldn't hold it against her because I knew how it was likely to be when I made the decision to send Tina there. I didn't ask Jesse's opinion. I was doing what I knew was best for the child. Everything else . . . was irrelevant.

Looking back on it now, I wish Tina had been able to spend more time with her grandma Kay and get a sense of herself as a part of her own family. But I still think that, at the time, though it was not ideal, I made the best decision. Nothing was ideal.

Carol had been working as secretary to the manager of the

optical lab that fabricated eyewear for prisoners and state Medicaid programmes. Prison Related Industries and Diversified Enterprises or PRIDE was a new system whereby private enterprise set up businesses within the prison and employed prisoners to do real jobs. Starting pay was 15 cents an hour and you could work your way up to 40 cents an hour take-home pay after deductions for your upkeep and restitution programmes.

The best part was that there were no security staff in the optical lab building. Working there was to be like a real job – and if you didn't behave properly you were simply sacked. Carol arranged for me to take over her job when she left. I had to come in as a filing clerk but within three months I was in the secretary's position and I stayed there for the next eight years. It gave me the opportunity to learn and to grow. Under the circumstances, this was pretty darn good.

Today what we know as the 'Prison Industrial Complex', using inmate labour for pennies per hour, is listed on the stock market. Big bucks are made off prison labour, at least by some. But in those days it felt like the best deal in town. And I felt like a person, not dehumanized like you hear people say today. But maybe that was because of the management of our optical lab. My boss was a great guy. My supervisor, Mrs George, became a good friend – although she never did anything against the rules for me and I never asked. I was doing meaningful work in a pleasant atmosphere with air conditioning, production parties three times a year and Christmas parties, and we got paid too – even if it was 15 cents an hour take-home, which at the time I was happy to get.

One lunchtime I was waiting in line when a strange sound drew everyone's attention skyward. A plane was struggling to stay in the air, sputtering, stalling, turning its nose towards the earth and going into a spin. It went down fast, gaining speed as it spiralled downward. It disappeared behind the warehouse building and we all ran towards the fence as we heard it hit the ground.

I began to recite the Shema, *Shema Y'Isroel Adonai Eloheinu . . .*, as the plane went down. Who was in this small plane I did not know, but I'd send a prayer after them. From the sound of the impact I was sure they must be dead. But later we were told that the two men in the plane were basically unhurt. Somehow the incident served to resolve something for me. Somewhere, on that day when my parents died, someone may have seen their plane and said the Shema for them too.

I had quit smoking after their death. I couldn't stand the thought of inhaling smoke that I knew had choked their last breath in that burning plane. I missed them. I would miss them all my life.

29

IT WAS STILL EARLY and I had things to do outside before we got locked in for the night, so I went out on the compound looking for the Kid. She was the young person I was currently working out with and walking with on the field. We worked together in the optical lab. She was always getting in trouble but she was smart and good-hearted and I thought she could make something of herself with some help.

After a walk with the Kid I went on to do my workout at Rec. Fifteen minutes on the stationary bike, fifteen minutes on the treadmill, then an upper body workout with the free weights.

I had to get back to the dorm before recall and before everyone took showers so there would still be hot water. You have to time your life well or all the little things in life are too difficult.

I got back to the room and out of my clothes in record time, throwing on my robe, grabbing my towel and shower stuff and heading for the shower right by my room. I preferred it to the others because it seemed like it was 'my' shower, and the dorm worker on our side kept it well scrubbed. The water was hot, just the way I liked it.

'Recall!'

Shit! They called it early. I hadn't finished washing the conditioner out of my hair. Have to hurry! Don't panic. You have five minutes. Rinse hair; grab towel; dry off; hussle to the room; get on the bed; ready for count. I'd have to blowdry my hair later. Opening the drawer under the bunk, I got out my writing pad and pen. I picked up Jesse's letter to reread and answer, line by line.

'Clear count! Clear count on the compound.' Time to dry my hair. I was feeling happy. It had been a good day.

Franny had to do a shakedown – it was her first so they sent another officer to help. She was in Colleen's room. We all stood outside the door, watching. Franny picked Colleen's stuff to go through and the other officer did the roommate's stuff. Colleen had a shitload of extra clothes. She needed them for work but she was only issued the usual amount. Her job as plumber could get messy and she needed to be able to change more than once a day.

'Everything's in order here!' Franny announced cheerily. The other officer looked up at her and said she was almost through. We knew Franny had given Colleen a 'pass'. She was OK in our book. She told us later that she didn't want to get anybody in trouble just for having some extra jeans. It would affect your time if you got written up for extra clothing just as much as if you got caught for some serious offence.

Franny Martino left after only eighteen months but she made a difference for us while she worked at BCI, giving us some relief from the more predatory kind of guard or, even worse, the ones who would stalk certain of us in order to make our time worse. Franny went on to become a macrobiotic cook in a health food restaurant, and then married a Norwegian tour guide and moved to Spain where she became a yoga teacher. We're still in touch.

Bert came while Colleen was still at BCI and became her new roommate. We called her Bertie. She looked like a bird – small bones held tightly together, small dark eyes that never seemed to stop moving, and a tightly closed little beak from which came the occasional high-pitched, clipped utterance – almost always in the form of a question. She and her boyfriend had been involved in the gruesome torture and murder of a woman in a motel room. They had tied her up, put cigarettes out on her flesh, violated her with various unpleasant devices and starved her for days until she died. Bertie only got seven years because she was deemed to be certifiably nuts, incompetent and under the influence of her boyfriend, against whom she testified. I thought it was ironic that Bertie as a grown woman had got off with a seven-year sentence while Colleen had been given a life sentence as a child when she had been under the influence of a forty-year-old man. Bertie was way too crazy for Colleen, who got a room change after a couple of months. Colleen would be leaving soon and we figured Bertie was some sort of test that the Universe had devised for her 'short-time nerves' to handle. Bertie's new roommate was a black girl – Bertie was afraid of everything but especially the black women. Colleen convinced her that it would be OK if she was friendly. For days, Bertie did not speak. Her roommate tried to give Bertie her space, knowing she was mentally 'off', and it always seemed to me that the black culture, like the Native American culture, allowed for and had a kinder tolerance for mental illness – at least in prison. One morning, the roommate came boiling out of the room asking for a room change. Bertie was cowering in a corner. Apparently, Bertie had popped out of bed and cheerfully exclaimed, 'Good morning, monkey!' We asked the roommate if it could have been 'Good morning, bunkie,' but she was sure of what she had heard, and refused to spend another day with that nutcase! Bertie must have spent those silent days observing and listening to the friendly banter on the compound in order to select the proper colloquialism for the occasion. The situation resolved itself with Bertie falling back into the safety of silence.

Bertie was a smart girl but I think she was schizophrenic, which interfered with her ability to function. She desperately needed help. But unless you 'acted out' in some violent way you didn't get help. So one day Bertie went down to the lake and lay out on the wooden picnic table and baked all day. I don't know what went through her mind but she gave the appearance of a corpse that had been laid out for burial. By the end of the day she had third-degree burns and had to be taken to medical. Sunburn was a disciplinary offence, especially if you couldn't go to work because of it. So the sunburn got

Bertie a DR but it also got her psychological treatment. She became a patient of the psychiatrist, which meant she would be put on psychotropic medication. As her behaviour improved, she was placed in office occupations for clerical training. You couldn't let Bertie work with chemicals or utensils and she couldn't be trusted outside in the sun, so I guess they figured office work was the answer.

Colleen served seven years on a life sentence. When she was getting ready to be paroled, she was faced with a dilemma. They weren't going to allow her to go back to where her mother lived. They were of the opinion that her mother was in part responsible for her problems. Colleen was devoted to her mom, who was really a benign person, gentle and in some ways seemingly naïve, fragile physically but with a strong spirit. She had had a complete breakdown when her daughter was arrested and sent to prison. Colleen was thinking of refusing her parole, serving more time – until she could be released without those restrictions on her freedom. Eventually she decided it would be better to be out where she could in time persuade the authorities that it was all right for her to be near her mom than to stay in prison where she could do nothing for anyone. She was twenty-one years old when she left on lifetime parole. We would remain in touch and our friendship would endure.

30

*I*T TOOK A WHILE, *but I learned in my years in prison that most of the women weren't really dangerous. In fact, once you've been around them for a while you can always tell when one of the certifiable ones is going to 'go off'. They give out signals for days in advance. In between incidents, they can be endearing in a tragic sort of way. Sooner or later, even the worst child killers were somehow accepted into the fabric of society.*

Prison isn't like a commune. People don't see themselves as a team working together for a common cause. But there is a sense of being a part of the whole. Whatever one does affects the whole community and that's most evident when someone breaks a rule and everyone suffers. That was how we lost most of our 'privileges'. It was almost always a short-timer who screwed it up for all of us. The long-timers were careful not to be too blatant about breaking the rules. The community would shun you if you were the cause of getting a benefit taken away but a short-timer didn't care because they would be leaving soon anyway. The most reliable ones were the murderers. They weren't usually criminals before they came in. For the most part, they had held jobs and been fairly functional in society. Some got involved in a homicide because of a boyfriend or husband. The majority of the women who were in for murder seemed to be there for some crazy, once-in-a-lifetime loss of control or act of self-protection. Then there were the baby killers. They each had their own story.

I preferred not to know what a person was in for, although I tended to stay away from the baby killers because I just couldn't deal with that, although I realized they were suffering terribly at some level and I tried never to add to that suffering. The check writers, 'paper hangers' in prison parlance, were all pathological liars, personable, intelligent, likeable, resourceful, big-hearted bullshitters. I liked a couple of them very much, but you couldn't depend on them. Maybe they were people pleasers and just said what they thought you wanted to hear. I don't know. The druggies had their own group, very insular, always on the scheme. The ones who were in for prostitution seemed to be perpetual victims, with a few exceptions. The ones who had become prostitutes so that they could lure men in to rob them were different. They usually became studs in the prison. It was a strange phenomenon. It wasn't a sexual thing, although I suspect it was a hormonal thing. And although they often ended up being studs in prison, when they got out they would return to men. I believe that everyone is to some degree potentially bisexual, whether they act upon it or not.

On 18 June 1983 the correctional officer on the morning shift wrote a disciplinary report. It went something like this:

While on post at the rear gate, I
observed a group of approximately fifteen
inmates at the lake behaving in an
unruly manner including physical contact
and dancing. It appeared they were performing some sort of ceremony. Inmates
Barbara Waters and Edwina Huff were
holding hands, jumping over the broom
while two other inmates held it. I was
not able to identify the inmates holding
the broom. Inmates Huff and Waters were
observed kissing and embracing and it
appeared that inmate Huff had her hand
on inmate Waters' buttock area.

I called in the violation and
Officer Rollins responded. Officer
Rollins and I then dispersed the crowd.
The broom was confiscated and returned
to H-5 dormitory. They denied having had
any unauthorized physical contact and
called me 'a dried up old blind bitch.'
Inmates Huff and Waters were taken to
confinement charged with Possession of
Contraband and Unauthorized Physical
Contact.

&ed *June 18, 1983*

*Bobbie and Ed were married today! It was so
beautiful! We all went down to the lake and had a
real wedding ceremony. Janet and Dorothy held the*

403

broom and we made a line on each side, like a
corridor for them to run through. Bobbie and Ed
held hands while Granddad said, 'I hereby
pronounce you joined together as one.' It was really
nice, and they looked so happy!

In our dorm we decided that there would be no stealing
this Christmas. An especially difficult time in prison,
Christmas is, for the most part, depressing. The cheery
holiday music began in November so that you couldn't
even use the usual escape route of radio and headphones.
By December, it was everywhere – Hanukkah, Kwanza,
Christmas – no matter how you spell it, depression by any
other name still stinks. By the time the actual holidays
rolled around, we had usually found a way to get into the
spirit of things. Small family-type units formed, token
gifts were prepared and exchanged, bonds of friendship
and emotional support were formed and strengthened.
Adversity had its advantages, bringing out the best in
some people. It also had the opposite effect, making
Christmas the prime time of year for stealing.

Many of us got boxes from home at Christmas. I no
longer got boxes from my parents and children, but
friends who had got out already would send things to Kay
who would then box them up and send them to me. The
permits had been cut down considerably, but you could
still get perfumed lotion, make-up, even jewellery. The
line between the haves and the have-nots grew more pronounced. Resentment wove itself into the blanket of
depression, turning it into a hair shirt whose constant

404

irritation gave licence for antisocial behaviour. It was a yearly phenomenon that had become an accepted part of life.

During the winter months, we were escorted to meals because it got dark so early. You had to wait for guards to come and escort the dorm as a unit, one hundred women two by two, to the dining hall and back again. But you didn't have to go. You could choose to skip dinner and stay in the dorm.

As soon as count cleared, I changed into my free-time clothes and went down to Ms J's to wait for the doors to open. As usual, she had her chair waiting for me in the doorway. I pulled the chair just outside the door, to where it was legal for me to sit.

'Hey, Ms J!'

'Well sit down, dear, and tell me all about your day.'

'Nothing much happened at work. We have to have our bags searched every day now because someone is stealing frames. Of course, we all know who it is but I don't really think the bosses want to get mixed up with security any more than we do. So we all have to suffer because of it.'

'It's starting here in the dorm too.' The doors opened for dinner and everyone began filing out.

'Ms J, how about we stay in the dorm and make a couple of soups? I don't really feel like going out just for that mess they're having tonight.'

'I have a couple of soups in my locker. Let's stay home and chat awhile.'

I checked over my shoulder to make sure it was safe

to reach my arm in and get the soups out of Ms J's locker. Dried noodle soups in styrofoam cups were a staple of our diet. We added various items to them for variety – cheese crackers, hot sauce, tuna, ketchup. 'I'll go get the hot water,' I volunteered, tearing open the paper lids just enough to allow the water in to fill the styrofoam containers. You have to get your water early, before the showers start, or it runs out and you can't get a cup of coffee or soup made until after 10 p.m. when the water heats up again. We used to have a coffee maker in each dorm for hot water but they were taken away as a hazard because of Big Al aka Alice and her girlfriend. (I always thought it funny that I knew two Big Als – one a short white guy and the other an enormous black woman.) They had been arguing for days. Alice's girlfriend came down the hall, unplugged the coffee pot which she had filled and brought to a boil earlier, and carried it to the card room. She walked up behind Alice, lifted it up over her head and began to pour. Alice screamed. Everyone freaked out, pushing away from the table so as not to get splashed with the scalding water as it cascaded down Alice's horror-stricken face and on to the table in front of her. It was a twenty-five-cup coffee pot and Alice's girlfriend was a little slip of a thing. Everyone marvelled that she could carry that heavy pot full of water and lift it over Alice's head. It was the topic of conversation for a long time. Alice had third-degree burns on her scalp, face, neck, shoulders and breasts. They both went to lock-up over the incident. After that we had to make coffee and soups using tap water.

Ms J had the forks and spoons all ready when I got back to her room with the soups. We used a fork to clip the paper lid closed while the soup 'cooked' and then ate the noodles with the fork and the liquid with the spoon. We got the plastic utensils from the 4 July picnic. Ms J was a superb scavenger.

'So, how were things in the dorm today, Ms J? I heard Officer Bentley had to give Pat a DR for fighting with her roommate. What was that all about?'

'It wasn't really what Ma Bentley thinks it was. Pat's roommate is that new girl. She is a dorm worker so I've had the chance to speak with her on several occasions. She's a nice girl. She was a thief on the outside but she is trying to make it in here without stealing. She does people's ironing and shops for a couple of the women. She cleans my room for me and won't even let me pay her. I am helping her to learn how to read and to do nails and cuticles so she can make some extra money and get a better job when she gets out. She says she wants to change her life now and I believe her. I don't think she is stealing. But most people think she is because it started right after she moved in.'

'I never thought it was her, Ms J. I think it's one of the others using her for cover. I'll bet it's either Kendra or Shamika. There's always stealing wherever they are. But I think we can stop it, no matter who's doing it, if we just refuse to put up with it as a group.'

'Well, I'm not afraid of them. If I see anyone stealing I'll tell. I always keep an eye on your room while you are at work.'

The new girl, Ms J's newest adopted daughter, came up to the door.

'Mama J,' she began hesitantly, 'I brought you a milk from the diet cart.'

'Thank you, dear. Just leave it there on the table. Did you have any more trouble with Pat?'

'No, ma'am. But you know I didn't do none of that stealin'.'

'Listen,' I said. 'We have this problem every year. Ms J and I were talking about a way to put a stop to it. Maybe you can help us.'

'Just tell me what you need me to do. Ain't nobody got nothin' much in here to be stealin' from. We all the same in here. And Mama J, she give me some shampoo and hygienes so I don't need to steal.'

'Charlene,' Ms J began, pausing to stifle a cough, placing her long thin fingers across her lips politely, 'find out who needs what among the younger girls. Don't let them know what we are up to, just find out. Mama Annie from the second floor and I will find out what the older ones need.'

'You got it, Mama J.'

'See you later, dear,' Ms J said, smoothly dismissing her young friend. 'I think our soups are ready to eat. You must be hungry after working all day.'

'I'm starving.' We dug into our soups with no additions. It was Wednesday and we wouldn't get to go to the canteen again until we 'got paid' on Thursday. The soup was hot and made our noses run. Ms J handed out the tissues.

'Ms J, if you women who are in the dorm all day will keep an eye out and holler when anyone tries to steal, the officer will have to respond. We will have to let everyone on our side of the dorm know that we will protect anyone who tells on the thieves. It's not like snitching to get someone in trouble or to get brownie points. It's the only way we can have a decent holiday – it's a favour to everyone. So, you dorm workers watch the rooms, and the rest of us will see to it that you are protected.'

'And then we find out what people need and make sure no one goes without. Is that your plan?'

'Exactly, so there will be no need to steal. And we put out the word on the compound that there will be no stealing allowed in H-4 this year, so those who want to steal can go somewhere else.'

Ms J made a pinched face. 'Some people are just nasty. They steal for a living because they like the feeling of taking from others.'

'Well, we can't cure their sickness but we don't have to support it. I won't buy anything off the compound unless I'm sure it's not stolen. I don't support thieves. If they have no one to buy the stuff then it won't pay them to do all that stealing.'

'I can contribute some shampoo and matches. People can always use those things.'

'Thanks. I have some stuff too. I think this can work. It's up to us, you know.'

'Ma Bentley is too nice and the girls take advantage of her sometimes. She's a good officer but I wish she would be more stern with the girls. She's a very religious woman.

409

She doesn't want anyone to have to go to lock-up for Christmas.'

'She knows how hard it is during the holidays, that's why. She's been around a long time. Probably the longest of anybody.'

It was a very successful Christmas! Ms J and the rest of the older ladies watched the dorm during the day and set up a howling any time they caught someone trying to steal. Soon all the thieves moved out and we got a reputation as the old people's dorm. We really didn't care what else you did, just no stealing. So nobody did without and there was no stealing in H-4 that year.

Eight years into my incarceration, three years since I had been released from death row, I was seriously thinking about my sexuality. I was still being approached fairly regularly but that was too complicated. If you could just have a sex partner, without all the social life and relationship stuff that went with it, I might have gone for it a lot sooner. But that wasn't possible. Women are like that. We want to be in a relationship – Nature's way of translating the nesting process to human beings. I thought about it. I was flattered by the offers. I was even attracted to some. But I wasn't up to it. Jesse wouldn't have minded if I'd had an affair with a woman. He had even told me as much.

❧ *May 15, 1984*
I just realized how very symbolic it was yesterday
that the events of mother and bird-child took place

outside my window. The bird mother was battling,
swooping and screeching at the mean people who
were keeping her from her nestling. They did
everything to chase and evade her, to discourage
her, but she kept trying, all the while signaling to
her young. I don't know the outcome of her struggle.
But it was symbolic of the one I am engaged in and
what is happening with me and my young ones at
the very same time in another place.

I had begun working with a brilliant forty-year-old attorney named John Evans and his two young associates, Holly and Richard, in April 1984. Michael Shulimson, a friend of John's, had recommended him to me. John was now handling my appeal. Bill Shepherd, with whom I would remain friends, had achieved such a good reputation that he was now overloaded with work. John Evans already had an established career and was willing to take my case. His assistants did much of the work. They filed all my state appeals, which we considered to be just a formality, although they were important for preserving the issues. We had no expectations of getting any real attention until we reached the federal level, which would take years more.

My new roommate was Linda the plumber. She was put in my room when my previous roommate got locked up for some infraction. Like Colleen, she worked in the maintenance department. Linda was an AFO, a second-time offender, in again for robbery. She should have tried doing something else since she kept getting caught at that. Linda was also a lesbian, one of the few true lesbians in the prison. Linda had just broken up with her current girl-friend and didn't want me to be put off by the problems they were having. I offered to talk to the girl for her.

'No. I respect you too much to get you involved in this shit.'

'Well, thanks, Linda, I have a lot of respect for you too. Want some coffee?'

'I'll get it.'

We were using my jar of coffee this week because the ex-girlfriend had been Linda's source of supply. Linda didn't have anyone to send her money from the outside. She worked on tips she made from people who needed her services as a plumber and general handyman. But Linda was broke now. She was ever the gentleman though.

'You just relax up there and I'll be right back with the water.'

Linda had been a manual labourer before she came to prison, and so she was well muscled for a woman, with ropy forearms and biceps that popped up under her leathery skin. Her hands were large, bony and calloused. She was meticulous about how her clothes and hair looked, always pressed and combed to the extreme. And she always carried a coffee cup. It was her trademark. She walked with a swagger and talked like a hillbilly, 'How do you do, ma'am. I'm here to fix the slop sink for ya,' southern accent, crooked teeth, ready smile and all. It seemed as if she was imitating some man she had known. She was very much the old-fashioned butch type in looks and demeanour, but she had a kind of sweet, shy femininity behind it that made her endearing, and she wore her hair long. Anyway, Linda was well liked and much sought after in the prison.

We had the corner room and the bunks were up against the wall with the window. When I sat up in the top bunk it was as if I were perched in the window that was directly behind the bed. I liked my nest up there. The bottom part of the window was painted over from the outside so you couldn't see in or out of the bottom bunk.

Linda brought in the coffee water and mixed the coffee into it. She took creamer and sugar as well. I took mine black. Two less things for them to take from me.

'Want to play some backgammon?'

'OK. I'll come down.'

Backgammon became our nightly pastime. We played every night, sometimes on the floor and sometimes on the top bunk, up where it was lightest. It was illegal for us both to sit on the same bunk. But we only did it when a good officer was on, meaning one who wouldn't look or wouldn't care.

One night about a week into our new arrangement, Linda said she had something to tell me. Reaching out a hand to brush the hair back from my face, she brought her face closer to mine and pressed her lips to my mouth. I did not resist.

'Was that OK? I didn't mean to offend you but I wanted to do that for a long time.'

'I'm not like that. I'm not looking for a girlfriend. But I appreciate it and I am flattered.'

'I know you want to keep your privacy. I wouldn't put

your business out on front street. I just want to be with you, in any way I can. Is that all right?'

'I don't know, Linda. I have to think about it.'

I lay back on the bunk and pulled the covers up over me. I usually spent count time meditating on Jesse and the kids and whoever I was missing that night, but tonight I was meditating on the heat in my groin and the woman in the bunk beneath me and what it would be like to feel someone's hand besides my own . . .

> 🐦 *It is intoxicating. It is a feast for my starving senses – all of them. It can't last but I will enjoy it while it does. Yes, I will!*

No one knew for sure that we were lovers. Some suspected, but none really knew. We were careful and respectful so we never got busted. It was bad to get busted 'homosexing'. Very embarrassing. She said she would never let me get busted because she respected me too much.

Gentle Warrior

> Come take my hand –
> Walk with me
> Through the sand
> Of time –
>
> My heart can be free
> though my body is bound.
> Hand in hand, I can see
> through time.

Boldly yet gently
pressing onward,
making a way –
But it's tiring me so.

It's hard going alone –
Friend, take my hand.
Help this gentle warrior through time's sand.

Linda and I remained lovers for a long time – over a year,
until she became infatuated with a young girl of fifteen.
But we remained friends until Linda left, meeting under
the overhang of the warehouse after work to talk and just
be easy with each other. I started smoking again – passing
the cigarette back and forth was a sharing.

I never took another lover in prison. I had offers
though and occasionally I was tempted. But I never gave
in to the temptation to use someone in that way again. I
didn't want a relationship. I was still with Jesse. We had
our ups and downs, but he was my man and I was his
woman and nothing short of death could change that.
Even death wouldn't end it.

Linda stayed out for a few years, but I heard she came back
on another robbery charge. She will always do all right in
prison though. She is 'somebody special' in there. Out in
the world someone like Linda is a misfit. To me, she is a
good person.

I was spending quite a bit of time in the law library where

Judy, the woman who did my wash in Flattop, was working. We worked on prisoners' rights and civil law suits for the women. Some needed help with divorces and custody; others had complaints against the institution for brutality or sexual harassment or other human rights violations. There were, through the years, varying institutional philosophies concerning the most effective forms of behaviour control. In the men's prisons, Jesse said they unofficially condoned homosexuality as a means of keeping the men 'happy'. Guys would strut the catwalk in makeshift skirts and make-up and some of the guys had their 'girlfriends' in the regular prison section. Even the guys on death row occasionally got the opportunity when locked in holding cells together. There was also a lot of physical violence, both guard on prisoner and prisoner on prisoner. In the women's prison, drugs were often used for behaviour modification. And they used the locked sections such as hospital confinement and the new segregated units to beat and involuntarily medicate people. In the old days, in Flattop, they could Mace you, take your clothes and blanket, put you on Ps and Cs – peas and carrots – or all of the above. Ps and Cs was a substitute for regular meals. They claimed it contained all of the necessary nutrients in a base of powdered mashed potato mixed with canned peas and diced carrots. You got Ps and Cs three times a day, with water. Then you could curl up on the grey concrete floor to try to sleep your hunger pangs away. Before I got there, they didn't have the metal shelves attached to the wall that served as beds. You were given a mattress to lay on the floor. And if you were bad, they took the mattress away and you slept on the concrete. There is such a thing as concrete poisoning. You get it from sleeping directly on concrete.

Louise got concrete poisoning when they took away her mattress and blanket and put her on Ps and Cs because she had been part of an escape attempt with three other women. They each got another fifteen years and were taken to Flattop where they were put into individual cells, holes in the ground, without light, warmth, beds, blankets or clothing. They were fed Ps and Cs and water. If they cried out or complained, they were Maced. Each one handled it in her own way. Louise developed a rash all over her body from the concrete poisoning. They removed her from the cell wrapped in a blanket so they didn't have to touch her. She was taken to medical in the 'meat wagon' – a wooden device like an old ox cart that was pulled along by two inmates. Judy, also in Flattop for her part in the escape attempt, had found her own way to ensure survival. She peeled strips of skin from the bottoms of her feet, laid them out to dry and then ate them. Her body was starving for protein. They might be able to fool the courts into believing that the Ps and Cs contained all the elements of a balanced diet but her body knew better. It is a picture that will always remain vivid in my mind.

Judy eventually got transferred to a prison in another state. I heard she did very well there and was able to get paroled. She became a physical therapist.

31

❧ November 2, 1984

*It's Friday and has been another of the strangest
days of my life. Last night I was so disrupted I was
in a daze. This morning I cleaned the room
(unheard of) and then proceeded to cry . . . I still
didn't know why. I felt something radically wrong.
Still, I didn't know why. I figured I was personaliz-
ing what they did to that woman in North
Carolina – how I could have been in her place if
some people had their way.* I wasn't even able to
go to work because this sadness was over me.
Finally, by 9.15, I went over to work. By 10, there
was a call from the superintendent. She told the
inmate operator to put Mrs Schwinke on the phone
– she told her to send me to the major's office. I
knew then what it was – even they knew by looking
at me, and they asked, 'What do you think it is?'
And I told them I thought they signed your death
warrant. And then I knew what had been wrong
all morning. The Superintendent was very nice and*

* They had executed a woman in North Carolina.

418

she wrote all the dates and times down for me and
told me she'd already spoken with someone there
and arranged for a call for us! She said it would
probably be Wednesday. She said your attorneys
were there with you and you were okay. I went
back to my room after that.

THE DATE WAS SET for November 29th, less than a month away! I had known this day would eventually come, and I was afraid. I was afraid for him and for myself. I spoke with Mrs George about it. She was my supervisor at work but she had also become my mentor because she knew about energy and the uses of it. I explained my fear that Jesse would somehow take me with him and only the empty husk of a person would be left. I felt that my mortal soul was in peril. I asked her to teach me how to close myself off. She told me it was possible to do that but she couldn't tell me how to do it. Just knowing it was possible should be enough for me to figure out how to accomplish it.

I tried writing to Jesse about it. But he could not devote any energy, not the slightest thought, to the possibility of death. I had to decide how to handle the children if they really did carry out the execution. They would have to be told and given the opportunity to say goodbye if it came to that. And they would have to be insulated against the storm of publicity that rages around the gruesome prospect of an execution. I called Sherry to work out the details. We agreed that if it happened, it would be best for them to take Tina away to a secluded place we knew. She

419

said that she and her husband did not want to deal with a last visit. I argued that it was the child's right to say good-bye to her father and that she would resent them for ever if they denied her that right. We hoped and prayed it would not become necessary. I didn't know where Eric was but I had to assume that he would handle it in his own way if he even knew about it.

November 2, 1984

My Dearest One,

I love you! I know you'll get a stay! You know our minds and hearts are one and our spirits soar together as one, so I am always with you – no matter what.

TL. It's Saturday now. I was laying in bed think-ing about how you would be in a different bed now and how you wouldn't be very comfortable or be able to sleep well either. I had a cup of coffee, wondering if you'd be able to have hot water when-ever you like now. I spoke with John Evans. He said when I speak with you to ask if you still want to see him and he'll be there within a week. He said it is the general opinion in the legal community that Gov. Gruesome did this to you merely to speed up your case, nothing had been done in too long. They feel you've got a good two years worth of further fil-ings and appeals. I liked hearing that. So, in case they decide not to give us our call – you'll still know he's coming. He said to ask you to put him [John Evans] and his two helpers Richard Strafer and

Holly Skolnick on your list. Tonight I'll try Mom again, although I had the feeling she was with you today.

I know that it hurts you not to be able to hold me and tell me how it is Honey – it would be so much better! But be assured I am okay. Everyone's been very compassionate, believe it or not. I started to get sick today. So, I did the family cure and got under lots of covers and sweated it out. It would have been better to have a hot shower then too but our hot water wasn't on. I really do feel better now. I needed to sleep.

You know, I think they did it this way just to bust your balls – they don't usually hand out warrants so far in advance of the time it even becomes effective! It pisses me off – don't they realize that they could give your mom a heart attack, or cause untold effects on others? The Chaplain here said I seem to take these things real well – I said I guess you develop a knack for it. We've suffered so much with all the awful things that have happened. But I hope this will give us the forum we need in order to be heard. I have to go to the phone now.

I love you, my Husband.

TL. I spoke with Sherry's husband, Bob. I told him that things weren't really as bleak as it may have seemed, and Tina and I had a fun talk.

Can you have privacy enough for *shuin* [masturbation]? I feel you tonight in that way – I love you completely. It's Sunday and I'm still trying to get over the worst of this cold. I got upset, that's why it got me like this. I need you to lay with me – then I'd be all right!

Nov. 27, 1984, 7.10 p.m.

I've decided – tomorrow I will fast and Thursday if all goes well I'll have something. If not then, I'll fast into Friday and then start eating tamasic [Ayurvedic] foods to ground me, so I can ease the transition from earth to spirit to earth again. I felt death around me today. It's been building all day until tonight. My pupils were dilated and I've felt like I'm getting off on some chemical all afternoon.

The feeling receded. Jesse received an indefinite stay of execution, only a day before the scheduled date. Death passed over us that time, but not without effect. Like a ship cutting through the water, its passing created both a separation and a coming together. It would not catch me unaware or unprepared again. I had become more whole as an individual being than ever before. I was able to strengthen my bond with Jesse while at the same time separating myself out. It was OK to be an individual outside of the relationship – in fact, it was essential.

For Jesse, the effect of having his death warrant signed, being on death watch and then getting a reprieve, taking that leap in the face of his own mortality began to show in two ways. Creatively he began blossoming outward with his painting but emotionally he began shutting down. 'This is not a drill,' he would tell me, 'Sun, this is the real thing. It's serious. They really want to kill me.'

It was a terrible period in all of our lives. And although Jesse lived through that first warrant, he was never the same – and neither were any of us. There would be a second warrant, and again he would receive a stay at the last minute, putting all of us through the torture again. But we recovered in time and returned to our daily routines because that is what you do in order to get a grip on a reality whose structure gives you continuity and security. Funny, needing security in a prison full of security!

         December 15, 1984

Part of me is going forward and part of me is going backward. Just like time itself – going in two directions simultaneously. There is only this moment of presence. And in the next moment it will be past and it will be future.

Backwards Day

Here we are –
the three Stooges
walking backwards
into tomorrow;
forging onward
looking backward
thinking ahead.

423

December 16, 1984, 1 p.m.

*The celebration is returning to my daily life. I
learned to celebrate life – every day – while I was
alone in my solitary confinement. But there hasn't
been any – the celebration had been gone from my
life for a long time now – in general for at least
two years. It left after their death. And it took the
near-death of Jesse in order to bring it back! After
being so close to death and destruction, very
literally, and yet still being alive and all in one
piece makes for celebration of life! I guess what
Jesse called 'the intensity of feeling good' is what I
call the celebration of life. I want to maintain it –*

*I'm just starting to find out who I am alone.
Not alone physically – that was the finding out of
my mind. This is the finding out of my spirit. My
spirit alone.*

December 17, 1984

My mind is in an uproar. I need to have peace.

I wasn't getting visits any more. Kay spent most of her time
visiting Jesse. Eric was out in the world on his own somewhere after a very difficult time separating from his uncle
Al and aunt Meresa. Sherry had stopped bringing Tina to
visit and no longer accepted my calls (we could only call
collect) because of the upset that it caused them. I had, in
fact, lost contact with the children completely. It was the
most terrible thing of all. I asked the rabbi to find a social
worker who could be discreet (God forbid I should make

trouble!). I asked Mike Shulimson, the civil attorney, to try to locate Eric. And I kept sending money for the phone calls and whatever else Tina needed that my $80 a month could provide. It was the only money I got from my parents' will – $80 a month. I could only hope Tina knew and that they used it for her needs. I wanted her to know that I was there. I tried to keep track of Tina through Kay, who was still allowed to call her. My nights were filled with images of the children – some hopeful and some too frightening to remember. I was crazed, pacing the hall by the phone at night until bedtime.

     Youth is self-centered and short-sighted, idealistic and insular. It is blessed with a congenital blindness to consequence. It is, in a sense, a state of grace. That state of grace is worn away by the cumulative effects of experience, and the corrosive effects of disillusionment. And with it goes the blessed blindness that holds judgement at bay. Shorn of that saving grace, I stand condemned in my own eyes.

I had reached my lowest point. The horror and the helplessness of the situation brought me to a place within myself that made me feel like I was going to die. I still had not managed to completely resolve the lingering sense of guilt I felt about the stupidity of my decisions that had caused so many families so much pain and loss. At least the children of the dead policemen could be proud of their fathers, who died courageously

425

doing their jobs. My children felt ridicule and shame.

This was the secret guilt that I had been attempting to avoid. Now I was wrestling with it. My newly emerging spirit was locked in mortal combat with my own feelings of guilt and self-loathing. Finally, I was confronting my deepest issues.

&❧ *May 25th, 1985*

I now have sight of peace. Tonight I let all my tears
flow freely and with them all my fears and
weaknesses and hurtful pride.

And then Uncle Joe died. We had spoken every week. After my parents died I had tried to call him more often. But I couldn't sustain him like my mom did. I told him we would open a store together when I got out. He had a girl-friend whom he had met at the psychiatrist's office. My dad used to make fun of their relationship because they were both on medication. She was a gentle soul and they cared for each other very much.

&❧ *July 19, 1985*

I think I'll write a note to Uncle Joe's friend, Jean.
He obviously thought a lot of her and I just thought
I'd let her know that meant a lot to me and
wanted her to know it. I got papers about his estate
today. I miss Uncle Joe. Dear, sad Uncle Joe.

My brother was called to identify the body. Poor Al, it seemed always to fall to him to identify the bodies.

*   *   *

Uncle Joe left the bulk of his savings to Jean. The rest was split between my brother and me. Uncle Joe had said he would take care of me. He said it when my parents died. And he kept his word. Uncle Joe was too good for this world, I guess.

I remember a conversation Eric and I had at one of our visits, about waiting. He said he didn't want to change or grow up until I came home. He was waiting for me. I told him that he didn't have to wait, that it wasn't really possible to hold back time like that because the body changed whether we liked it or not, and so did the world. He would only be making things more difficult for himself by trying to stand firmly fixed within the natural flow of time. After all, he was beginning to have tufts of hair, under his arms and other places. I asked if he would just let me see by lifting his shirt a little but he was mortified and refused. My little boy getting hair! It was a bittersweet moment. I think the older we get the more bittersweet life becomes. But, much as we would like to do so, we cannot hold back time. Trying can make it more bitter than sweet.

32

&❧ *August 12, 1985, p.m.*

*I went through a big trip this weekend. I'm starting to
figure out what's been wrong with my way – my short
circuit. I'm waiting for time – like Eric. He's been
doing it too. That is part of it. But even before, my
personal short circuit seems to be that I've been looking for someone to be with me – with me, not just me
with them, and I've substituted being useful for being
needed and wanted. It is a way of being needed and
wanted but there's no security and it is all one sided.*

*There is only one person without whom my
world cannot exist, and that's me!*

I WENT THROUGH months of sometimes painful, sometimes delightful self-examination and reflection,
reviewing and reordering. Parts of myself that had been
obscured were now clarifying and being transformed. It
was an exciting time because I was now conscious
of my own process. And I was forming a new relationship
with myself in which I was able to see where I had been
and where I was going for the purpose of correcting my
course without blame getting in the way.

≈ *October 20, 1985*

I've figured out that my mistake, on a grand scale,
has been to lend my strength to the bad instead of
the good. The problem is that the good are all so
weak and scattered, and most, when they do gain
power, get poisoned by it.

≈ *December 17, 1985*

If you choose to see only the positive you miss half
of what's going on – and it's dangerous!

The way is to see it all, as a whole. And then
choose. This is what practicing Zen does.

Idealism can be deadly.

Another Christmas season passed and another year began
with no change in our situation. I didn't count the days
and months but I did keep track of the years. I was twenty-
seven when this began and I was now thirty-eight years
old. Eric was now twenty and Tina was an eleven-year-old.
I didn't see much of either of them now with my parents
gone and both of them living so far away and so far apart.
Once Eric had left his uncle's house, I really didn't know
where he was for a long time. He was on his journey,
going through his rites of passage, of which I was not a
part. Tina was trying to be cute enough or needy enough
to ensure that she would survive in a world where she had
no one and nowhere to turn if the people with whom she
lived decided they didn't want her any more. Not that they
did, but it was how she felt. After all, she had no parents,
her grandparents died, her other grandma could barely

manage and her brother was trying to grow up himself. And so, each of us did our best to make it, to survive.

Maria got me accepted on the soccer team. But first I had to learn to speak Spanish because the team members were all Spanish-speaking. It was a regular United Nations, with members from all over South and Central America and Cuba. I practised my Spanish at work with my supervisor every day. I practised on the mechanic who came to fix our machines and he taught me some slangy phrases with which to impress the girls. I followed my Spanish-speaking friends around, picking up a word or phrase and then using it all day. *'No hay vida para las pobres!'* – 'No life for the poor!' *'Mi vida esta cagada'* – 'My life is shit.' *'A la esquina!'* – 'In the corner!' When I was ready Maria called a meeting of the team. She basically sponsored me. I knew I was in when my teammates started calling me Sonia Maria. I enjoyed those games very much – it was the first time I had been part of a team. It was like belonging to a close family, a feeling I would always yearn to recreate. *'Yo soy en el tiveri tavera!'* – the Cuban equivalent of 'I'm over the moon!'

1986

I had been at the clothesline all morning. It was my turn to watch the clothes. Maria was off somewhere using her skills as a source of income, charging three dollars for a facial and three more for a manicure. She also gave haircuts, using a razor since scissors were illegal. Cutting hair was illegal too but, done carefully on a windy day, you could get away with it.

430

I was settled into my warm soak when I saw Maria coming from 'the cut' on the side of H-2, where the old ladies were holding court. You had to come early to take possession of the cut. There was a cut-out section on the side of each building where the outside tap was located. A square housing of cement blocks nearby doubled as a seat big enough for two small women to share or for one larger one. The cut made a great place to homosex in the early mornings before the clothesline crowd arrived with the first loads. It was our lovers' lane. If it offended you then you didn't look in that direction. But on this day, the *viejitas* were the early birds. No sex in the cut today. Talking about birds, Maria looked like the cat that ate the canary.

'Hey! Granddad's back!' Maria was plugged into the Hispanic information pipeline. The *viejitas*, the older ladies, hung out in the dormitories, watching and listening to everything that went on.

This time Granddad was totally toothless. She had close-cropped hair and no breasts, which made her look like an old man. Granddad was noteworthy for one reason – she could get anything you wanted from the kitchen, as long as you were willing to pay for it. She'd even extend you some credit if you didn't have the money. But you'd better pay her back or she'd go to the cops on you. She'd tell them you had contraband or make up a story that would get you put under investigation. She could get away with a lot because she was an informant. She'd been out and back three times since I'd been there.

'Oh, no! What is this, her seventh time? That would make her an F.' I was horrified.

'She comes back in to get her teeth and stuff, you know, get her health together. Then she goes out again.' Maria is being uncharacteristically understanding.

'Like visiting a health spa?'

'Yeah, BCI Health Spa. But she's the best thief there is. I'm gonna put in my order as soon as she hits the compound.'

'I'm not going to support her in any way.'

'But if I get some good stuff from her, you'll help me eat it, right?'

I looked sideways at Maria. She had this big shit-eating grin on. Maria was raised a Catholic and was always into the moral issues, although that didn't stop her from doing what she needed to do.

'If it's from her, don't tell me, OK?'

We had a thing in prison about food. I guess it was part of the survival thing. I still hoard food to this day. They would reward the dorm with the best cleanliness record with fast-food meals like we saw on TV. And all our production parties in the optical lab were about 'free-world food'. But the prize for the best procurer of food, without exception, went to Matty Webberly. Matty was pencil-thin and sharpened to a fine point when it came to conniving, which is resourcefulness nearing an art form, and she could obtain the things that made life a bit more tolerable. It was hard when your kids were in trouble or your husband was dying of stomach cancer or your parents were getting old and you were stuck in prison where you couldn't help anyone. People would say that each one should have thought of that before she

432

committed her crime, but that didn't make it any easier. That was the real torture of being in prison. And all of those things happened to Matty over the years.

We were roommates for a while and we both worked in optical. Matty was a trip.

She would figure out a way to get what she wanted. It wasn't that Matty didn't care if she got you in trouble. It was just that she didn't think about it. It was up to you to figure out whether or not you would get in trouble. But we were really like best friends and we shared all our 'scores'. When I got stuff from the Jewish services, I always brought some back for Matty. And when she connected with a staff member who was willing to give her food, she always turned me on to her goodies. One time, she came up with a whole mango. We took it outside on our break and ate it next to the big trash can so we could throw away the evidence. We managed to consume the succulent fruit without getting caught even though those little stringy bits that get stuck between your teeth were a dead giveaway.

One day Matty came in from her break all freaked out. She was breathless, telling me to come with her next door. PRIDE was building a dental lab, expanding. After all, they didn't call it Prison Rehabilitative and Diversified Industries for nothing.

I got a pass and met Matty outside. She told me she had something special to share with me. Matty had been working on this construction guy for a week. She told me he was ready and willing to have sex with us. She told him she had to share with me because we always shared everything and he said OK. I wasn't sure I wanted to get involved. It had been so long, and I had fantasized so much about how beautiful it would be. But this was so meaningless. I did go over and take a look but I decided to pass on it. It was something too valuable to me not to have meaning. I thought about it for a long time afterwards – about why I didn't jump right on it when I had such a perfect chance. I never got another one. The same guy was also doing some breast fondling in the Maintenance Department. He got escorted out about a week later and wasn't allowed back inside the prison. Boys will be boys. But you certainly couldn't blame a woman for going for it – I mean, this wasn't voluntary celibacy we were practising. For me, the next best thing was working out, hard, at the gym in Rec.

Ms Klarke, the head of Rec, got word about a national prison weightlifting competition. It was meant for men's prisons, of course. But there was no rule that said it had to be men. So Ms Klarke sent in an application and we ended up competing on the record with these men's prisons in the different weight classes and age groups. We did OK. Some of our girls were really strong, especially in the legs for squats and dead lifts. I won regularly in my weight class among the women for upper body bench presses. There was a speed bag that was great for taking out frustrations and a heavy bag for resistance. And there was the element of commitment that went with the regular training and exercise that some people got into as their daily after-work activity. Ms Klarke taught us responsibility and gave us choices, made us make choices – with consequences. I didn't like having to miss a meal or my mail in order to go to a class, aerobics or whatever, but I made my choices, and I had accepted the consequences, no mail or no class, beforehand so I was not resentful of them. Sometimes it was annoying but it gave me a necessary skill for getting along in the world. Thank you, Ms Klarke.

Nancy was the butcher. She went to work every morning with her heavy jacket and scarf and stayed in the meat locker, which was almost freezing, all day long. She would probably end up with arthritis. She was one of the older inmates and a charter member of the BCI population. A quiet woman who never got involved in any of the craziness, she never gossiped, just minded her own business, an old-fashioned convict. Day after day she worked alone in her meat locker, hacking and grinding bloody slabs into lunches and dinners for the rest of the population. She would do the special order stuff for the staff too, which made her a good inmate and insulated her from harassment. After all, she prepared their food, did them special favours. It was like that, even in there – politics, backscratching, bartering. Nancy didn't want to make waves or get caught up in anything that could jam her time. She was doing life with twenty-five-mandatory for murder. They said she killed her boyfriend, who, like her, was a 'carny', worked in a carnival. He was cheating on her, so the story went, and she caught him. She killed him in a moment of anger and passion. Cases like that should be second degree but it all depends on what county you come from, and whether or not it's an election year, and how much money you have.

In Florida, if you come from the middle of the state you will be less likely to get a first-degree conviction for a crime of passion and rarely have to contend with someone asking for the death penalty. But if you come from a big city, especially one in South Florida, you have a greater chance of facing life for first degree, or even the death penalty. Each county is different. Some counties are known for trying to get a death sentence, like Broward, where I came from. It's all up to the prosecutor. He gets to pick and choose who faces a death sentence, without having to answer to anyone. He could have been constipated, or had a fight with his girlfriend, or consulted a Ouija board, or just have political aspirations and want to create a hard-on-crime public image. If he decides he wants you, he gets you, and he has the resources and power of the entire system, police, coroner, ballistics and other experts, at his disposal. And if you are without funds or influential friends, you're basically through. I think that's how the plea-bargaining system became so popular. Anyone who's been through the system before knows you haven't got a chance. And if you do choose to exercise your rights to the full panoply – the hearings and the trial by jury – then you'd better be sure you win, because if you lose they will punish you for making them work for a conviction. You will get the maximum penalty, and maybe even more than that. After all, they can do anything they want. And don't just depend on the truth to set you free. Even if you manage to get it straightened out down the line, they know it will take at least a few years, and they won't be held accountable. The sentence will be reversed or lowered, deemed harmless error, and no consequences will be brought to bear on those who abused the system. That's just the way it is. The parole system is similar. Clemency as well. They don't have to answer to anyone and can make a decision without any real guidelines. I had decided that I would never submit myself to that particular system, to have to beg and hold my breath, and ask for clemency for something I didn't do.

They came to me once while I was on death row and said we all had to do a financial disclosure. I, of course, refused to do anything of a legal nature without first consulting with my attorneys. They said if I didn't sign it then I would never be eligible for parole. Can you imagine? I was on death row! How could they think they could persuade me to do anything by threatening me with no parole? Is there a chance of parole from a death sentence? It was so bizarre I laughed out loud.

But it could also be deadly if you had no other choice but to play the parole game. Nancy, our butcher, felt she had no other choice. In fact, it was her only hope and that hope sustained her through the eleven years of hard time she had put in without even one write-up, not even a verbal warning. She was a perfect inmate.

It was during her eleventh year, and my tenth, that we became roommates. She had emphysema, coughing constantly yet refusing to give up smoking. You were allowed to smoke in your cell in those days and the smoke from her cigarette would waft up to the top bunk where I slept, choking me and making my eyes water. But mostly she would leave the room to smoke out on the tier or downstairs in the TV area, or on the toilet. She was a good roommate, clean and considerate and quiet – didn't have a lot of visitors at the door and didn't keep any contraband. I tried to keep a low profile and didn't want any heat either, so we got along great.

She applied for clemency, which was the only way someone with twenty-five-mandatory could get a waiver to go before the parole board short of doing the whole twenty-five years first. There was a provision in the Florida statutes that said you could apply for a waiver of the twenty-five-year minimum after ten years of good behaviour without any disciplinary problems. Well, Nancy certainly fitted those requirements. And she waited and gave them an extra year just to be sure – to show them that she could do even better than they required. She pinned all her hopes on that waiver being granted. And we all knew that if anyone would get it, it would be Nancy. But it was just another illusion, like Truth and Justice and the right to a fair trial and being innocent until proven guilty.

Maybe her faith in the illusions of Man killed her. I watched it happen. When she received official notification that her petition for clemency had been denied – because they felt she needed to do more time – she seemed to die inside. She just gave up. She started to need an oxygen tank to breathe, making frequent emergency trips to medical, until she ended up staying in the medical ward. Before the year was out, her body followed her spirit and she died.

*   *   *

The statute that had given us hope was repealed. It's a funny thing about hope. A person can live on hope and a little food and water. But hope can also stand in the way of the very action that could mean survival. Sometimes it is not until all hope is lost that people take action, fighting and defying the circumstances that threaten to overwhelm them, their spirit, their will to live.

33

I N 1987, JOHN EVANS hired an investigator to devote just one day of his time to trying to find Brenda Isham, the girl who falsely testified that I had spoken to her in jail. He cautioned me against being too optimistic. She had been a drug addict and by now, eleven years later, she was probably dead. But we agreed to a one-day effort. The investigator found her easily. She was alive and well and living in Wyoming. A born-again Christian with a family, she had made a good, clean life for herself and was taking care of her ailing father.

When we first found Brenda, she was so filled with remorse that she was willing to make a taped statement, give a deposition to a court reporter, anything to make up for what she had done and the consequences of it. She hadn't kept up with what had happened and was horrified that I had been on death row and was still in prison after all these years, at least partly because of her false testimony. The only thing she wouldn't do was return to Florida, the prosecutor's jurisdiction, to testify in court. All these years later she was still afraid of the prosecutor – the same man who had prosecuted me and, according to Brenda, coerced and coached her to say what she did at the trial, and who was now the district attorney. He had made a lasting impression. We tried to get the court to accept her taped testimony and to arrange for cross-examination to take place in a similar manner – without her coming to Florida. But the court would not accept any arrangement we put forth, and neither would the prosecutor. We were stuck – until one day we got a call from Brenda.

She had changed her mind. She told my lawyers that some men had shown up at her ailing father's house in Wyoming to tell him that he should convince his daughter not to get involved any further in my case on my behalf. That was what changed her mind. You see, she really was a decent person. Young and scared, in 1976 she had succumbed to the pressures of her situation and the well-crafted, much-practised tactics of manipulation with which she was faced. She felt badly enough about what had happened to me and my family, but now the repercussions were coming home to roost in her own backyard, on the doorstep of her sick father. She said later that she couldn't let what she had done hurt anyone else any longer. She wanted to come to Florida to testify and get the whole thing cleared up once and for all! I was elated to the point of floating.

And then I got news that John Evans had died. He went to bed after a game of tennis and never woke up. He was only in his mid-forties. I was devastated. Richard and Holly, his assistants, promised never to desert me and Richard became lead attorney in my appeal.

So Brenda Isham came to Florida to testify in federal

court. I had all my hopes up, although I knew from past experience that hope was dangerous. Brenda was the needle the state had used to tie up their otherwise loose ends. They had her stitch up the case for them. I hoped their needle would prick a hole in their case at the hearing.

I was seated at a large, polished wooden table towards the front of the courtroom waiting for my attorneys, Richard and Holly. Holly now worked at a different law firm and was no longer as deeply involved in criminal law but she was still working with Richard on my appeal. Bert Peña, a bright young attorney from Richard's law firm, was in the courtroom with me. It was to be his first experience at a federal evidentiary hearing just as it was mine. He was apprenticing with Richard and José Quiñon, the senior partner and trial attorney. I was seeing the mentoring cycle into the next generation.

I watched Bert's hands, held loosely in front of him to give the appearance of calm, the fingers clasping and unclasping to keep the nervous energy in check. And then I noticed a spider! It was hanging from his tie, threading its way upward. I didn't know him well enough to feel comfortable just reaching up to brush it away. And he was so taut with anticipation that I was afraid he would jump if I touched him suddenly.

'Bert!' I whispered. He looked down at me attentively. 'You have a spider on your tie.'

'Where?' His hand shot up in the 'Eek! I saw a mouse' gesture.

'May I get it off for you?' I asked softly.

'Yes!' So I brushed the now suspended spider away.

442

When we looked up again, the prosecutor and his team had entered the room and Richard was on his way over to our table.

'Everything OK?' Richard enquired, sensing what I am sure he interpreted as courtroom nerves. Bert got right down to business, pulling a sheaf of papers from his brief-case. Everyone was seated, waiting for the judge to make his entrance.

After the usual fanfare, the judge called for the witness to be brought into the courtroom. Brenda took the stand and cried the whole time, telling the judge how and why she had lied. She literally shrank back into her chair when the former prosecutor, now DA, approached her. And then, to my horror and everyone's astonishment, she had a heart attack, right there on the witness stand. The judge called for a nurse. The nurse called for an ambulance. The judge called for a recess. The paramedics came and took Brenda away, and the hearing was over. Unless she could recover enough for cross-examination to take place, we would not be able to use her testimony. She had come to do penance, to right a wrong, to make amends, and to protect her family from further stress at the expense of her own reputation and in the face of possible perjury charges. No one in her community had known about Brenda's past.

Brenda spent five days in a local hospital until she could be flown home. Thank God she didn't die! But I felt jinxed . . . it wasn't fair! Ha! Fair is not something one looks for from the universe – only from friends. The universe runs on a different set of principles. When she recovered sufficiently, we asked if she felt she could continue. She was willing to testify but not in Florida. It was too much for her. Ultimately, the court gave us permission to conduct the cross-examination in Wyoming on videotape, with the defence and prosecution teams sending representatives. In the end, Brenda's testimony was deemed harmless error because we couldn't prove that the prosecutor knew she was lying. It was her word against his. There were no other witnesses to the coercion that Brenda claimed who could, or would, corroborate what Brenda said had happened.

ₑ April 19, 1987, 11.30 p.m.

Flow; don't float.

Flowing isn't floating. To be as water is not to float – it is to flow.

ₑ December 8, 1987

Strong people look for someone to control them. Weak people look for someone to control. We really need to simply control ourselves.

The most important thing is to make my own energy each day.

Jesse had begun a study of Vincent Van Gogh's paintings. He was doing a series of Van Gogh reproductions, some exact and some with his own personal touches. He was growing as an artist, pouring his passions into his paintings, just as the original Vincent had done. Kindred spirits, I suppose. He was pouring himself into those paintings and sending them out through the visiting park to his mom, who would send photos of them to me. They would become his legacy.

It was the New Year of the Trees, a Jewish holiday called Tu B'Shevat, and the rabbi had got permission to bring in a baby olive tree for us to plant. Linda came by and took over the operation. She carried the tree over to a clearing between the buildings where it would get lots of sun and I would pass by it on my way to work every day. She dug the hole deep and filled it with water, planting the tree and packing the dirt in around it securely. It was a nice thing, and the tree would stand as a bond between us in the years to come.

When Linda left, the tree would remind me daily that I was loved. And years later, long after I had left prison, my friends told me that there was a terrible storm, the compound was flooded and my tree fell down. They said Linda, who had returned to prison on a new charge, went out in the rain with a rope and pulled the tree back up again by herself – she wouldn't let anyone else help her, and it may have been the rain but they said she was crying.

Occasionally, the administration would carry out a shake-down on the staff in the morning when they came in to work. There would be a long line coming in the front door as they waited to be searched one by one. I believe the staff shakedowns were done randomly and on the spot so they caught everyone by surprise. Everything would have to wait until our bosses got checked in. It was OK because we didn't have to go to work. But one day they locked us all out of the dorms at lunchtime. Nobody knew what was going on, not even the officers. They couldn't possibly do a shakedown on every dormitory during lunchtime, and some of the older inmates had to be able to go back to their rooms. Strands of speculation wound around and through the knots of people gathered along the pathways leading to the dorms, trying to figure out what was going on. Then they brought in the dog.

The major and two lieutenants filed out of the administration building followed by a string-bean-looking female K-9 unit officer leading a flop-eared, drug-sniffing Dobermann. An announcement came over the PA system that we were all to report to work. But what about the people who worked in the dorms? In the end, it was decided that the dorm workers and older inmates would report to the library until further notice. The guards began trying to unwind the knots of people but no one moved until we saw which dorm they were headed for . . . It was H-5! H-4 was probably next, I thought as I turned and headed for the optical lab.

I knew that Ms J would take care of any contraband but no one was sure how sensitive that dog's nose would be. As it turned out, they didn't get to my dorm that day. They hit H-2 next, on the other end of the compound. I guess those were the two dormitories where they expected to make the biggest busts. They knew where the drugs were coming from and who the dealers were. They found a lot of contraband food – the dog was great at finding food, like Snickers and marshmallows. They trashed a bunch of our lockers, and the dog left its hairs on our beds, but it came up empty in the drug department. We knew they would be back.

The next day at lunchtime they came in during count, stood in the doorway and made us file out one by one past the dog. We found out that day that the dog could not smell pot stuffed up inside you. But it could smell the residue behind your light switch, or in the pipes under your sink, or in the shower behind the knobs. They blamed Linda for the bag of pot they found in the shower, and she was locked for investigation because she was the plumber and lived in a room near the shower.

A runner, one of the dorm workers, came to the optical lab to tell me they were in my room taking my sink apart. I thought perhaps some seeds were stuck in the goose-neck pipe underneath. Could they blame that on me? There had been others in that room before me and any one of them could have left seeds in there. The dog lady came back again with the dog to take my light switch apart. And again, to go through my locker.

It was evening – time for the day's excitement to settle down. I had decided I'd go out for some air before they locked us in for the night. I hadn't gone far when one of the girls ran up to me, breathlessly announcing that the dog lady and company were in my room again.

Later on, I found out that it was old Ms Duncan who had set the dog lady on me because she wanted my room. I had one of the corner rooms, which were larger and situated in such a way that passers-by couldn't see inside. The same Ms Duncan who had pulled up my tomato plants years ago now coveted something else of mine and was just as ruthless in going about getting it. She would pay people off in candy bars to say that they saw or smelled or heard something. Old Ms Duncan couldn't stand not getting what she wanted. But this time she was not successful. After a while, the dog lady and company found other rooms to ransack.

Those were the dog days, and it made for a very unpleasant atmosphere for about a month. It wasn't that you couldn't smoke pot, because you could. All you had to do was wait until the dog went into one of the dormitories, and the rest of the compound was then safe. It was just that it felt so uncomfortable. I think it must have hurt business for some, but those people just sat back and waited it out. For some of us, that had become a useful strategy for life in BCI – if you wait long enough, things will change. Change, my old friend, could always be counted on if you could just wait for it.

The dog didn't accomplish much. I don't think it was particularly cost-effective. They began to get a lot of complaints about the dog lying on people's beds and eating their food. And people began sprinkling pepper in their lockers because we were told that would confuse the dog's sense of smell. So that was the end of the dog days.

34

ONE VISITING DAY Eric returned after three years' absence. He brought Debbie, his wife-to-be, to meet me. He was a man now, no longer the boy who came to tell me he was getting hair under his arms. We sat and talked for a long time about how it had been for him since we spoke last. I asked him why he hadn't kept in touch and said how worried I had been, every day and every night. He said he hadn't wanted to bother me with his problems because I was in prison and had enough problems of my own. And I told him that some day when he had kids of his own he would know that it is much better to know what's going on than to have to imagine it. He'd had a $500 car, which he slept in until he got his first paycheque, delivering pizzas. Then he got himself a room at the YMCA for $42.50 a week, which was where he stayed until he saved up some money, met some kids and moved in with them. He met Deb shortly after that at the House of Rock and Soul, a club in Charlotte, North Carolina. She was swinging on a rope swing, hanging from the ceiling . . . 'How are you doing up there?' he enquired. 'Just hanging out,' she replied. They got together that night and had been together ever since.

They were enjoying living together, and obviously very much in love. I had prayed for someone to come along to give him guidance and love and not to lead him astray. I had got my wish. He promised to keep in touch and I told them how happy I was that they had met.

🐌 *Nov. 27, 1988*

I'm going to be a 'Granny'! Eric told me on Thanksgiving. One more miracle, and a blessing to give thanks for. I had always wished I'd be there for this at least, but it will be there for me whenever I do get there. Tina will be an aunt. Eric says he could tell from the sonogram that it looks just like him! Especially the nose. That's so cute!

Eric visited and his family visited whenever they could, but it was hard. They both worked and had very little money. It was a major trip to come from North Carolina to the southern tip of Florida and required taking days off from work. The first time they came, I was amazed to see the man before me. The next time they came, they had the baby with them! They had named her Claudia Sonia, after me. In those days she looked like me too. Eric was the primary carer of their child. His wife preferred work outside the home. When they came again, Claudia was walking and talking. She liked to sit on my lap and wear my glasses. She called me Grandma Sunny. I found a constant in Eric's sweet face and good heart. Like a familiar pattern, or a well-worn routine, it was comforting. And the love that was clearly there between Eric and his wife Debbie was comforting too.

We had a core population of mentally ill women, mostly doing life sentences, who were maintained on psychotropic drugs. You could always tell who they were by the way they walked. We called it the 'Thorazine shuffle'. It took every bit of concentration they had just to put one foot in front of the other. Arms hanging limply at their sides, glassy eyes staring at their feet, they shuffled along. After a few months the medication would begin to have the opposite effect and they would become uncontrollably violent. Of course they would exhibit signs of this for at least a week before 'going off' but no one would ever do anything about it until they flipped out or did something to get in trouble. This was the humane equivalent of the shock treatments they used to administer. Sometimes, in cases like Maria's, they would still send an inmate to the state mental hospital for shock treatments. She would come back 'fried', a pussycat for about three months, and then she would begin to exhibit the old behaviour patterns again. In those days, all of these were updated versions of the lobotomy – electricity replaced scalpel, chemicals replaced electricity, but it was all the same and sad to see.

Rosetta Schiner, Alicia Rosman, Margie Dorset, Bertie, big Barbara Salome, and there were others. One day Rosetta was on the pay phone, talking over her ten minutes. We were still only allowed ten minutes for each phone call. We signed up for our ten-minute slot right

451

after count cleared before dinner. You were responsible for knowing when your ten minutes was up. If you went over, stepping on someone else's time, they would tell you to hang up. That was what happened to Rosetta. She got upset, went to her room and broke a coffee jar. This took a while and by the time Rosetta returned to the phone room the person she was angry at was gone and someone else was using the phone. But by that time Rosetta was on automatic pilot. All she could see was red, blood red. She tapped the girl on the shoulder and when she turned around Rosetta jabbed a glass shard into her face and twisted it. They took the girl to the hospital and Rosetta to confinement. Fortunately I was spared from seeing it because I was at the movies that night.

Rosetta would never ask for help. Unlike the others, Rosetta and Alicia had crossed another line and were beyond reach.

One day there was a big commotion when I came in from work. Ms J was waiting for me. That meant there was some big news.

'They brought in that Kirsty Rawlings woman, the one who killed all those children.'

'The babysitter?' I asked.

'Yes. That's the one. I knew she'd be coming here.' We always knew.

'I'll see you after count!' I said as I beat it up the stairs. You only had five minutes to get from your job assignment to your bunk when they announced recall. Usually I had to pee and that took two minutes (I had timed it exactly). Fortunately, count cleared quickly. We were all curious to know what Kirsty Rawlings was like. It would be two weeks before she was allowed out on the compound. She was very young. They had tried her as an adult. Her victims, at least half a dozen, were all babies that she had been babysitting at the time of their death. They were each pronounced dead of IDS, Infant Death Syndrome. Kirsty was infant death syndrome.

I changed clothes and went down to Ms J's room after count cleared. She was sitting on her bed, waiting, with the chair fixed up in the doorway for me, just like always. Ms J's emphysema was getting to her these days and she spent most of her time on the bed. She kept an eye on my room though. It was directly above hers. 'So, what did she look like?' I asked. She looked weird, Ms J said. She looked weird around the eyes, and very young. Still had baby fat herself. Can you imagine suffocating all those little innocent babies? Ms J really had a problem with child abusers because she had been an abused child herself. We were all horrified by the stories of how Kirsty Rawlings had used the pillow to smother the life out of those children. But there were worse stories. It was just that Kirsty did it so many times. She was our first serial killer. One of the victims was her own niece.

Kirsty got life. No one ever got death for killing a child, especially their own. It was like you got sentenced by the pound weight. Kirsty would get a hard time from the women when she got out of R&O. They would refuse to sit with her, call her names, cut in front of her in line, steal her stuff. Some would make believe they were being her friend and get her to give them her money. Kirsty would be the victim for the rest of her life. No one would ever befriend her.

There were child-killers who eventually gained acceptance. And in time everyone found their place in our society, because there was nowhere else they could go. Kirsty eventually found her place. She worked in the dorm and regularly visited the shrinks and lock-up for protective custody.

Every so often a Christian crusade would come through the prison. Occasionally, my good friend Frank would show up on a crusade. He was a great speaker, although I think the men could relate to his story more than the women could.

This year the crusaders got permission to come into the dorms. Ms J was livid. She had a pet peeve about religious types. Her cruel stepmother was a religious woman who wouldn't allow Ms J to continue her 'chalk talkin' evangelism'. That meant she drew pictures, inspired by the divine hand of course. Many of us were annoyed at the invasion of our privacy. I heard that one of the church ladies was looking for me but I ignored it. I didn't feel like talking to her. But this church lady was determined to find me. She asked around the compound and showed up at my door.

Who the hell was knocking at my door? No one knocked – the guards didn't knock, and the inmates just called your name through the vertical slit.

'Hold on a minute. I'll be right there.' I got down from

my bunk and opened the door to see a bushy-tailed, wide-eyed born-again holding a Bible in one hand and extending the other towards me. I took the proffered hand, finding it a bit sweaty. She took a big breath and began.

'I was trying to find you all morning. My name is Maryanne and I've been absolutely dying to meet you. I told my husband I was going to look for you here today. By the way, could I come in?'

Well! I said I guessed so. The inmate who had brought her left with the rest of the group she was leading. And my church lady proceeded to tell me why she was so hot to see me.

'I was Jesse's girlfriend in junior high school! My family just loved him. He was so polite and so cute! We were all so shocked when we heard what had happened. I'm still in touch with a few of the girls from then and none of us could believe it. Jesse just wasn't that type of person. He wouldn't have done that. I just know you didn't do that either,' she went on, and then she said how hot it was outside and asked if I had any powder she could borrow. I was sure my mouth was hanging open from the bottom of my eyeballs. I got out my powder from the locker – the kind with the big puff on top – and handed it to her. She took out the big puff and, to my utter and complete astonishment, pulled up her skirt and patted it vigorously between her legs, sending up a cloud of white dust. I stared at her through the cloud, as if a perverted genie had just popped out of my powder box, while she finished the job by patting herself under each arm. It was like one animal marking the territory of another. It was so primal that I wondered if she could possibly be aware of what she was doing.

'Well,' she went on to say, 'you certainly are pretty – even prettier than your pictures.' I thanked her and said she was pretty, too. She said to tell Jesse she was here and send her love. I said I would. She said they wouldn't allow her into the death row unit at FSP or she would have visited him too.

Jesse had something about him that women seemed to find irresistible. He didn't have to do anything – they'd just reach across me to touch him. Apparently he was always that way, even in junior high school, and the effects were long-lasting!

When we went in to work one Monday, it was Mrs Shirley Schwinke's sixty-fifth birthday. She was the office supervisor in the optical lab. We had spent a lot of time together and we were friends – she was like one of the girls. She broke the rules for her office girls regularly – but she never did anything bad and no one ever asked her to, because she was so damn good to us. It was just the occasional little thing we needed, but it made life so much nicer. If it was allergy season and you needed those eye drops to wash out your eyes, you could ask Mrs Schwinke and she would get them for you. You couldn't do that through the medical department. Or if you ran out of cigarettes, you could always bum a pack from her until payday. It was like having a mother there. She would listen to your problems, help you out in the small change department, and you could even call her at home in a crisis. She was the best. But she got a hard time from the administration because they knew she was one of those bleedin' hearts who didn't know we were convicts, never to be trusted. We protected Mrs Schwinke – if we heard anyone was trying to get her to do anything we made sure it wasn't bad.

So we had a little party in the back office for her that day. And, later on, I asked her a question that I had often wondered about but had never felt comfortable asking.

'Ms Shirley,' I asked, 'how does it feel to be sixty-five?'

'It feels like I'm eighteen years old, trapped inside this old body.'

She looked at me with an open face so that for a moment I could see the eighteen-year-old behind the eyes, and then she reached for her cigarettes.

It seems like everybody's mental image of themselves stops somewhere in their life – eighteen, twenty-eight, sometimes even younger – and they stay there inside as the rest of their body ages. In some ways, I had stopped when I was arrested. At first, I thought it was time that had stopped. But now I realized it had only stopped inside me because outside it kept right on going, leaving me behind. And now I knew it didn't just happen because someone locked you up in prison.

Whenever we needed medical advice we went to Dr Orla Inamor. She had been a heart specialist on the outside but she got involved in a Medicaid fraud scheme and was convicted of having her partner killed to keep him quiet after he found out about it. So Dr Orla became our primary care consultant. She read the ingredients on everything we had available to us and would prescribe whatever was appropriate since the medical department did little or nothing for us and it took for ever to get to see the doctor. We put vaginal cream on our athlete's feet and gargled with douche mixture for a sore throat. One day, I noticed that the faces of all the Hispanic girls in my yoga group were looking shiny and rosy. Maria told me that Dr Inamor had been teaching them how to do a chemical face peel with aspirin, better known as salicylic acid – the main ingredient in expensive free-world facial peels. We all started doing it. But you had to be careful to stay out of the sun.

Orla had bad arthritis. She was a faithful participant in the yoga group and had helped to bring in many a convert from among those who started out thinking it was some sort of pagan ritual. In those days, I never approached the spiritual aspects of yoga for fear that the women would get the wrong impression and be afraid to participate. It helped a lot when Shanti, a teacher from the local college, started coming in to do classes with us in Rec. And then she brought in the Swami, Sri Naranda a.k.a. Edith Epstein.

> Naranda loves the ocean
> The ocean loves Naranda
> Naranda is the ocean
> The ocean is Naranda

Naranda was eighty years old. She could still stand on her

head. Her back was as straight as a rod and her handshake was firm and strong. She didn't need glasses and her eyes twinkled with elfin delight. She spoke with assurance and pulled no punches. She became my mentor, my first real teacher. In Naranda, I had the proof of what I had always taken for granted – that yoga really works, not just for me as a healthy young woman but in the long run. I loved Naranda.

Shanti was Naranda's most senior student, and she became like a big sister to me. When they came in to conduct yoga retreats, Shanti would help teach, and Naranda would use me as a demonstration model, making subtle corrections in my postures, teaching me to teach as well. And there would always be a vegetarian feast afterwards. It became a monthly event, sanctioned by the prison and facilitated by Ms Klarke, the head of the recreation department, where it was held. Even Ms Klarke participated. Those were good days. Of course, the food brought an expanded interest in joining the yoga retreats and that was OK. My regular yoga group continued meeting at lunchtimes – the food hounds all went to lunch instead.

One of the regulars in our yoga group was a young girl we called Dukie who had come in with her mother. They were one of those mother and daughter teams that sometimes came into population together. This pair weren't allowed to room together because there was some bickering going on between them as to who was responsible for killing the husband/father. Later on, they were reconciled and allowed to share a room. Dukie's mom got released on her appeal but Dukie wasn't able to get out. She was a kid – like Colleen had been – but she had twenty-five-mandatory life. Dukie wouldn't be out in seven years like Colleen, even though it was known that the father had been abusive. Well, who knows . . . I only know that Dukie's life was wasted, like so many wasted lives in prison. She loved her mother dearly – she worked with me in the optical lab so at least she had a little money to help her out. Her mother died shortly after being released. She had cancer, undiagnosed until it was too late.

You don't want to get sick in prison. The only people who could even get a vitamin were those dying of AIDS, and since they knew they were dying – no AZT or any of those fancy new drugs for them – they would often trade their vitamins for a pack of cigarettes or a soup from the canteen. That was the only way for the rest of us to get vitamins. I used to trade for food. I would refuse the substitute for meat they started giving us after the population of Black Muslims increased. The substitute was almost always peanut butter. I took the fried chicken and traded it for a week's worth of veggies, fruits and milks – delivered to my room if I wanted! I ate huge quantities of greens and other veggies. But years later, when I had access to testing I found I had an elevated lead count in my body because it was almost all canned food.

Prison is not set up for people with handicaps or special needs. So when the trans-sexual who hadn't quite completed her surgical changes came into R&O it caused quite a stir. What would they do with him/her? And there was even more speculation about what they would do with her organs! Would they tuck them up inside? The administration decided to keep her in R&O until she finished her surgical alterations and until her hair grew out to acceptable 'girl length'. They had a thing about women with short hair. So they kept him in R&O until he became a she – which meant there was an innie where there used to be an outie – and then Briana, which is what she chose to call herself, was released on to the compound. I was as curious as anyone to see what she was like, not least because she was going to be Ms J's roommate.

Briana turned out all right. She was respectful, clean, courteous, and perfectly willing to explain the miracles of modern surgery. Simply put, they slit the penis lengthwise and stuffed it up inside the body cavity – basically, turning it inside out – and then created the lips and clitoris so that there was an opening that appeared to be a normal vagina. After she finished explaining the procedure, Ms J sent her to get the coffee water.

'She'll show it to you if you ask. She doesn't mind.'

'Have you seen it?' I asked Ms J, forgetting that she had been a madam.

'Oh yes. They've done quite a good job. You really can't tell it's not the real thing.'

'I couldn't ask her, Ms J.'

Briana returned with the hot water, being very feminine about it.

'Briana dear, would you show my friend Sonia the beautiful job they did on your pussy?'

'Oh, Ms J! I love it when you talk dirty to me,' she said and then turning to me, 'Only kidding, dearie. I wouldn't do anything to disrespect Ms J. I'd be happy to show you what I've got. Just keep your eye out for the guard. And I should tell you that I just love women. I don't care for men at all except as friends. I just feel like a girl. Always have. Now, get ready!'

It did look pretty normal. I only took a quick look, although I would have liked to examine the details more closely. She explained that it worked the same as mine did. Except for now she had to insert a dildo-type apparatus to stretch the opening each day until it healed completely.

Briana got along better than anyone thought she would and she was an excellent roommate for Ms J. She treated her like a mother – cleaned the cell, got the hot water, made up the bunk for her on sheet day, and generally pampered her.

35

My Dearest Sunny,

I love you. It's Monday and this is just a quick letter just to fill you in Honey. I've been lawing it frantically since Friday when I saw the lawyer. That case mine was waiting on to be decided was decided – and I'm enclosing an article on it Sun, not good. I hear they'll be re-conferencing my case up there very shortly now so I've been trying to get this CC motion* all together and ready for filing. All the rest doesn't look too hot honey so I want you to send me an updated CC motion affidavit as soon as this letter comes! I have to file within a week and a half – and send that affidavit to me certified mail. This is not a drill! This is it honey. I'm okay, just sort of moving quickly, up all night and all, researching, going through all my papers and sent for some cases tonight too. I received your weekend letter with the 5x7 picture of you. I have it right here with

---

* The confidential communications motion was to enable us to speak privately about certain key issues in our case.

me, on my writing board. I love you with all my heart and soul Sunny. Don't get upset with all of this legal stuff. Feel me with you each and every moment. Keep your spirits up. We are Us!

I love you.

Your husband, Jesse

JESSE WAS RUNNING out of legal avenues through which to bring his evidence to the attention of the courts. I was working on what would be my own last chance in the federal courts – a federal habeas corpus, which is the final appeal after exhausting all other state and federal remedies. My attorneys said it was a 10,000-to-one chance since the courts received thousands of them each year and granted but a handful. The legal situation that concerned me most at the time was Tina's.

Tina's guardians, Sherry and her husband, had decided that she needed to go to a boarding school. I thought at the time that having a teenager in the house must have been too disruptive for them. They sent me a letter saying they were planning to send her away to a school in Maine for problem children. They had heard about it from a psychologist. But they hadn't talked to anyone who had sent their child there or they would have known it had a terrible reputation and had been sued for mistreatment of the children on numerous occasions. It was used primarily for court-committed juvenile offenders and children with drug problems. We wouldn't find this out until Tina was there in late August 1990.

My Dearest Sunny,

I love you. I received your March 27 letter tonight.
That thing about school in Maine really sucks – as
far away as they can get her from us, right? I decided
to go to the yard and take a break from all this legal
stuff. I worked out a little but wasn't into it much.
Got some rays and played some volleyball, so it was a
decent afternoon all in all honey. This is such a trip
right now. Hopefully I'll see the lawyer this week too.
I need to get a copy of that motion you filed to the
judge about all you wanted prior to your trial – that
included your confidential communication claims
too – it's a handwritten one you did Sun, about 'Even
with Right on Our Side It's Hard to Win with a
Stacked Deck Against Us.' I've been going full on
everything. I have to now. This is real serious Sun. It's
nice you went to dance class and hung out with Ms J.
and her roommate and I know you are hearing a lot
of stories from that one ha ha. You've been in my
thoughts and in my heart constantly my wife
Mmmmm I love you with my entire being. I've been
on a real trip the last few days, trying to get all these
things together. I've been up late into the night and
going all day. It's exhausting. I'll be sending Tina a
couple of birthday cards from us this week. Keep your
spirits up Sunny. Things will be okay. It's time to get
all these things together and fight them!

Good night my wife. I love you,
Your husband, Jesse

April 10th, 1990

April 10th, 1990

My Dearest Sunny,

I love you. Nothing on my call to Tina – never even responded to my letter Sun and I think I'll write again now. What a trip. They should bring Tina to see me. I really do need to see our daughter. It's Passover – it starts today and Easter this weekend. I haven't even sent cards out. Happy Easter Sunny! I love you my wife.

Your husband, Jesse

In mid-April 1990, Jesse's death warrant was signed again. His execution was scheduled for 5 May, only three weeks away! The wheels went into motion on all sides – plans for last-minute appeals, plans to safeguard the children. This was Jesse's third death warrant. Third warrants were usually fatal. In fact, no one thus far had survived a third warrant. I was trying to keep my thoughts positive.

The chaplain sent word that we needed to make some arrangements – in case. No one had any experience with this sort of thing and the seminary didn't teach how to shepherd a woman through the deliberate execution of her husband. I was asked if there was anyone official I wanted to have with me when it happened besides the chaplain. I was to be sequestered in the chapel. I called Frank Costantino, the man who had been Jesse's friend and had visited me in FCI. He would understand my loss and my pain because he knew what the loss would be – this amazing, complex, passionate, funny samurai warrior who loved to pick flowers and berries. I knew it was a hard

466

thing for Frank to do. He told me once when he came to BCI on a Christian crusade that it was hard for him to go to the row because so many of the guys there were just like him, like he used to be. And he had done time with some of them, like Jesse. Frank said he would be there with me.

          I believe that one's death is a very private experience that each person is absolutely entitled to orchestrate as he or she desires. In the East, in ancient times, the person wrote his own death poem, setting the mood and tone for the moment that was to come. And sometimes they committed seppuku in a ritual fashion at a precisely chosen time and place with or without witnesses, as they desired. I agree with that premise. It is each person's right to make that decision. I respect Jesse's decision not to address any of the practical issues. I will take care of them in the way I believe to be best without his input. That is how he prefers it, and it is his death.

It had been agreed between the guardians and me that Tina would be taken somewhere where the media could not get to her. Eric was not reachable. He was safe. I could get a message to him through Mike Shulimson. I asked that Tina be brought down to Florida to be with Jesse's mother and hopefully me if they did carry out the execution so that we could grieve together. It would have been the healthiest thing. But Sherry refused. It was wrong, but I knew they thought they were doing the right

467

thing. I was still hoping for a stay, so I didn't want to give too much thought to the 'what if' process.

A week later, Deathwatch stage one moved into Deathwatch stage two. They had taken most of his possessions from him by now. I knew what Jesse needed from me, the last two trial runs had taught me that, and I provided it as fully as I could with my right hand while holding my broken heart together with my left. Sex, even in letters, was life-affirming.

> ❧ *I am trying not to be overwhelmed by this whole thing. I have tried to get as much information as possible about the deathwatch process. It goes in three stages. In Stage One, the condemned prisoner is taken from his regular death row cell and placed in one of six cells located directly behind the death chamber in a separate area in front of the building on the first floor. At this point he is allowed to retain most of his possessions. In Stage Two, his possessions are removed from the deathwatch cell. He is only allowed to retain minimal clothing and writing materials and some books. The time for Stage Three is when there are only three days left until what they call 'Fry-day.'*

I write every night. 'My Man, I Love You. I get so hot just thinking about you and when we will be together again and stroke each other's naked flesh, to feel your heartbeat against my chest.' It is the flesh they want to burn up. It is the heartbeat they want to silence. 'I want to taste you on

468

my lips. I want to feel you inside me . . .' These are hard letters for me to write. I don't feel sexy. I feel sick. I feel a heaviness inside my chest and my brain feels poisoned by the unspeakable horror that I have forced back so it cannot become a fully formed thought.

Jesse's letters are short. I understand. He does not want them to know what he is thinking or feeling. He is keeping his dignity. 'I am fine. Keeping in touch with the attorneys. We're gonna beat this thing, Baby.' His lawyers, a coalition of pro bono attorneys, were filing appeal after appeal. They were all denied.

He was so vital. He was so alive. He was so strong. I could not deal with the thought of what they were doing to him, and what they wanted to do to him ultimately. This was the man I loved. This was the flesh I loved. This was the mind I loved. This was the spirit I soared to meet each night in my meditations and my dreams.

    There is still hope. His attorneys are working on a stay. And I don't feel death as strongly as I did for the past few days. Maybe it will pass us over again, like the last two times. Angel of Death pass over us! We just commemorated the miracle of the biblical Passover last month. I pray for the same miracle to happen again. Deep down I have a dark feeling though.

No stay yet. Time was getting short and beginning to accelerate. I got word back from a good guard. Jesse was

469

holding up well. He said to tell me he loved me and to keep the faith. I wanted to ask if he had a lover there who would be left behind. It was possible. I wanted something to take the edge off my own pain. But my mind and my heart and my spirit were still entwined with his. A part of me would die with him. A part of him would live with me too, but that was of no consolation at that moment. The Pope in Rome had issued a plea for Jesse's life. The bishop in Northern Florida had issued his own plea. The media was hot on the story. There were protesters and revellers. It was a circus.

Jesse's death warrant sparked renewed communication between Sherry and me. I had to fight for Tina to be able to contact her dad. They let me speak with Tina but they monitored the call.

Towards the end the mail between Jesse and me became very slow. We both felt that it was being delayed at his end. I found someone who had a *tomodachi* (friend) working at Jesse's prison who was willing to hand-carry a letter for me. There was nothing secret or illegal in it. I just needed to be sure that Jesse would receive my letter.

April 26, 1990

My Dearest Jesse,

I got your 20, 21, 22 letter today, and the picture of you. You look terrific! If I didn't already know, I wouldn't know that anything was wrong from this picture. You are amazing and I love every amazing inch of you. I guess you assume I knew because you didn't mention anything about it until the end of

470

the letter when you said they only gave you 14 days to work on your response. Well, anyway, I'm glad you're sitting with me at midnight. Now I know why I haven't been able to go to sleep! It takes till about 2 a.m. for me to go to sleep – even if I'm tired. I'll start sitting with you at midnight every night now that I know. Oh Jesse, I'm so glad to get a letter from you! I was beginning to wonder what was up with the mail. I sent you one letter by a *tomodachi* rapid mail. There's a counterpart there too. I don't understand when you say you don't have any attorney working for you on the appeal at this point? I'm happy you have my pictures there with you while you work. I have yours everywhere that I am too – at work and in my room, right in front of me. And now I have this new one. I didn't think you'd be able to take any during visits once they 'signed'. Maybe I'd better send you another picture – a small one like the five by seven I sent, because I seem to recall that they take them away at some point.

I spoke to Tina tonight. She has written you a beautiful letter Jesse – I was so proud of her – it brought tears to my eyes. She loves you so much. You'll get it after the visit. I wish I could visit! I'm glad you're okay – I'm okay too. I feel a lot better now that I've heard from you. Reporters called here today wanting an interview – of course I said no. So I figured maybe something happened today – maybe you filed the Confidential Communications

471

Habeas? That could have been it. Usually that's what it means when they start asking for interviews on a certain day – that something has occurred. I'll call your mom tomorrow night. I love you my husband – with all my heart and mind and body and soul. I am with you every moment. We are strong, we are one, and we are forever – and we will win! We are beyond them!

Love and kisses, your wife, Sunny.

P.S. – all my friends send their love and their prayers.

Jesse was moved to stage three Deathwatch, to the cell just behind the electric chair. In stage three there is a guard stationed outside the cell twenty-four hours a day, leaving the condemned man no privacy at all. They remove all articles from the cell to prevent suicide.

I know he has no toilet paper now. I know there is someone looking at him when he tries to take a shit. I know they have taken his cigarettes away. Everything I do makes me aware of what he cannot. I know it is the same for his friends there. I know he was very close to some of the guys, the Kiai-Shu members, and especially his best buddy, Mike Bruno. He and Bruno have been tight for years. They are workout buddies, and they have shared everything from their food and cigarettes to the feelings at the depths of their hearts, to the pains in their guts. In a way, it is worse for

Bruno than it is for me. He will get no special breaks. He will see the lights flicker when they turn on the juice to kill Jesse. He will have to take his food tray from the same guards who took his best friend away, maybe even participated in the end process.

The attorneys went to a judge and were able to get him a two-day stay. When word came about the stay, Jesse was moved back from stage three to stage two Deathwatch, so at least he could wipe his own arse without asking and he could have his hygiene and writing articles again. There was hope.

36

I WAS CALLED TO the chaplain's office, where I was told that Frank would not be able to be there with me because he had a prior commitment that could not be cancelled. He had been scheduled, months earlier, to speak before an audience of hundreds of people. I said I understood, but I didn't really. The chaplain asked if there was anyone else – the rabbi perhaps? But I chose a stranger to be with me if the execution was carried out. I chose one of the church ladies – someone I had heard was nice, for real, and not a gossip; she respected people's feelings – someone whose face I would never have to look at again, in whose eyes I would never have to see my own pain again. I explained the situation to her, and she agreed to do it.

If it looked like there would not be a last-minute reprieve, Jesse and I were to have a final phone call. The execution was scheduled for 7 a.m.

&❧ *May 3, 1990*

Reality comes crashing in sometimes – Reality isn't always bad, but it can be. This is one of those times. There's no use fighting it – just have to allow

it to come in. I still hope for a stay, but I know it's
not likely. I'm trying not to 'feel' too much right
now – not to connect too much with Jesse's feeling.
A last shower – feeling how alive one feels, each
muscle, each expanse of flesh, for a last time. I felt
those feelings in the shower and I had to stop!
That's not good to do. I'm going to try to rest now
and compose myself for our phone call, if it comes.
It may not. I'll be sad if it doesn't, but I believe it
will. So I'm waiting – it's hard.

May 4, 1990

They came for me at 3 a.m. It was Lieutenant Ritter. I had
known her since the days of Ginger and Colleen – the
good old days – and she had matured into a good officer.
It was a break for me. I was truly happy to see her.

Ms Ritter escorted me to the lieutenant's office. We
would be alone. She sat me down at the desk and
explained how it would go. She would initiate the call;
when Jesse was brought to the phone we would have ten
minutes to talk.

'Ten minutes, Ms Ritter?'

'Sorry, I didn't make the rules. That's the way it was set
up. Are you ready?'

I nodded. She leaned over the desk, turned the phone
towards her and began dialling. No one answered. She
hung up.

'I'll try again, Sonia. Someone is supposed to be there
now. This was the arrangement.'

She dialled again and we waited, listening to the

unanswered ringing. Finally, there was a response.

'Hello? Hello, yes this is Lieutenant Ritter down at Broward Correctional. Who am I speaking to? I have inmate Jacobs here with me now. Are you ready on your end? Yes, I already explained that to her, sir. OK, I'll put her on the line. I'm putting her on the line now.' She handed me the receiver, turned the phone towards me and walked to the doorway, hesitating just long enough to make sure I got through.

I held the receiver to my ear, waiting for permission to start speaking. No one spoke. Finally, after a glance at Ms Ritter, one anxiety overrode the other, and I began . . .

'Is it you?'

'Of course it's me! Who'd you expect?!'

'You sound just like you!'

'I am me, baby.'

'It's you!'

'Yes, baby, it's me.'

'Oh, Jesse, I love you.'

'I love you too, baby. How are you doing?' The sound of his name was strange inside my head. The sound of his voice made me feel dizzy.

'I'm OK . . . How are you doing?'

'Hey, I'm OK, you know. I mean, they want to kill me, and I filed a motion in Judge Futch's court and the district court today and they're not gonna even hear it! Refused to even look at it – they just wanna kill me.'

'But I didn't think they could do that! They have to hear it – I mean, under the circumstances they can't refuse to at least read what you filed!'

'That's what I thought too but they're doing it. Somebody's pushing it – somebody high up. And the state is gonna do what they want to do. So, if they want to kill me – fuck 'em. You know what I mean, Sun?'

'Well, you know, Jesse, you could do what you did once before – I wrote to you about it in that letter I sent in a special way – remember how you once meditated so intensely that you said you could have just left? And it was hard for you to come back that time – well, you could do that again and be out of that body, hovering around laughing, saying, "Suckers! You didn't win after all! I did!" Did you get that letter?'

'I don't know if I got that one . . . I could do that, but I might just stick around to experience it. It's a unique experience – and you know we're all really just energy, and it's energy, so maybe I'll just get into the flow.'

'However it is you want to do it, I know you can.'

'I lived like a samurai warrior and I'll go out like one, and give them a hard time, ya know what I mean? A hard way to go. They're gonna remember me, Sunny. The whole world is gonna remember me, you watch and see. And you remember to take care of things the Kiai-Shu way and look for a high master to pass it on to.'

'I will, Jesse.'

'You know there's an afterlife and I'm going to let you know when I get there – I'll find a way to let you know.'

'I know if anyone can you can. Like Houdini.'

'No, better than Houdini, because he didn't make it back. But I will. I'll be back! Maybe I'll take you with me.'

'I'll always be with you, Jesse. We are a part of

477

each other. No one can change that or take it from us.'

'I know it, baby. You know, I spoke to our daughter tonight.'

'Oh, you did. I'm so glad.'

'Yeah, it was great. She started to cry a little but I calmed her down – she'll be OK. She's strong – she's like us. I would have liked to talk to Eric too. Hey, I should have had him talk to the governor – maybe he could have talked him out of killing me. Well, too late to think of it now.'

'And what about Mom? How is she doing?'

'Oh, she's great. We had a visit, you know, and she cried toward the end – so did I. But that's only natural – after all I'm her only son. But I fixed her up. She'll be OK, Sun. I told her not to be angry at anybody – it's the state doing this. No one could do anything to prevent them from doing what they were going to do. She shouldn't blame anyone or be angry with anyone – except the state.'

'I know, I feel the same way. Did you get my picture, with the garter?'

'Yep! I really like that one.'

'I'm glad.'

'Hey, listen. I don't want you writing to no other guys. I don't want you to be with anyone else – you hear me? No one.'

'Yes, Jesse.'

'You're my woman.'

'I couldn't love anyone else the way I love you, Jesse – it isn't possible. Our love is for ever – no one could be like you are to me. You're special.'

478

'I am, aren't I. And you're special too. My Puerto!'

'That's how I signed that letter – the special delivery one!'

'Oh, yeah! I got that one! I got it!'

'All right! It probably had different handwriting on the envelope. Oh, I'm so glad you got it. That's great. I miss your letters – but I'm glad you got mine.'

'Well, I'm sorry but I just couldn't write, you know?'

'It's all right. I understand.'

'Well, they're giving me the finger across the throat sign here, so I guess that means to hang up. They'll probably shave my head soon. Hey! I'll save you a lock of my hair! Would you like that?'

'Yes, Jesse, but you know it's contraband here so I'll have to have someone keep it for me until I can have it.'

'I'll try to get someone to get it to you.'

'OK. I'd like that.'

'And we're not going to say goodbye.'

'No, we'll just say, "So long. See you later." Right?'

'Right. And I'm gonna do something to make it nicer for you – I'll hang up first, because I know you don't want to.'

'That's nice of you, Jesse, because I don't . . . Couldn't you call me back again? I mean, I just can't deal with that this is the last time I'll hear your voice. It's the first time in so long. Do you think they'd let you?'

'I don't know – I could try to persuade the sarge here.'

'I hope you can . . .' I was beginning to cry. Oh, God help me – that was not what I wanted to leave him with; not how I wanted to spend these last moments.

And then Jesse said, 'Well, we better hang up now. I love you.'

'I love you.'

'I love you so much . . .'

'And I love you.'

'I love you, baby.'

'I love you, Jesse, with all my heart.'

'I love you with all my heart and mind and soul.'

'I love you.' The phone went dead.

'Jesse,' I said, one last time, to the air, to the universe. The buzz of the dial tone. My head fell on to my arms – and the tears spilling from my eyes felt like blood.

Ms Ritter allowed me a moment alone with my grief. Then, gently, she came over and put a hand softly on my shoulder.

'Are you OK, Sonia? Would you like to take another few minutes before we go back to the dorm? I could wait outside.'

'They might let him call back. Do you think they'll let him call back? Could we try to call back?'

She said she didn't think so. I asked to wait just a couple of minutes longer. She promised to come to get me if they called again and I said I was ready to go back to the dorm. We walked down the cold, dark tunnel of the compound, back into the lighted hallway of the dormitory. I went to my cell and wrote down our last conversation, word for word, so that the cataracts of time and the colours of my emotions would not alter them in memory. He was very brave in the end, my Man.

🐌 *A SAMURAI FAREWELL (and the last fuck-you)*

Five days before the scheduled execution, Kay Tafero, Jesse's seventy-two-year-old mother, brought her breaking heart and my fifteen-year-old daughter to see her father for the last time. Hand in hand, they were escorted through the labyrinth of gates and barriers as they passed from the world of the living into the world of those who were about to die – death row special visiting section.

They were seated before a glass partition. Jesse was led in and seated on the other side of the barrier. He was in chains.

'Hello, son. I brought Tina. Isn't she beautiful?'

His voice was thick. 'Thanks for coming, Mom. So, how's my little Koocher? Do you remember I used to call you that when you were little?'

Tina nodded.

'You look so grown-up I hardly recognized you.'

'Grandma, do you have a tissue?'

'Certainly, dear,' Kay said, foraging in her bag. And they watched as Tina removed the make-up she had worn for her father so he could see the child's face that he knew; and then she put the make-up back on again so he could see how she did it.

As the initial discomfort fell away, they began to talk. He reassured her that everything would be all right, no matter what happened, because she came from good stock, and she was smart and talented and beautiful and special. He told her, again, the story of how he named her Christina because it was the most beautiful name he could think of for a girl. They decided he would call her Christina rather than Tina from then on.

Kay begged the guard to give Tina and Jesse a little privacy – to let the child touch her father – just to be able to have a hug and a kiss before they took him away from her. Putting aside her own needs she pleaded, 'Please! For the child's sake! Do you have any children? What if it were your child? Please!'

The guard made a call. After a brief conference on the walkie-talkie, permission was given for Tina to have a few moments on the other side of the barrier with her father. But first she would have to submit to a strip search. She agreed without hesitation and a rubber-gloved female guard took her into a small room off to the side. From there she was led through a door into the enclosure where Jesse was waiting. They had removed his chains. Her father moved towards her slowly, brushed her cheek with the back of his hand, and wrapped his father's arms around her.

'I'm sorry about the strip search, Christina.'

'It's OK, Dad. I don't care. It didn't bother me. I love you, Daddy!'

'I love you, my baby girl.'

They held on to each other as he sat her on his lap and told her all of the special things a father wants his daughter to know. It would be years before Tina would talk about it.

'The last thing my father told me was to be strong.

And I told him that I would. And he told me that he would always love me and be there for me, somehow.'

And the visit was over.

Kay Tafero was allowed a last visit with her son late at night on the eve of the execution. She, like Tina, had to submit to the strip search. With their arms around each other, they talked, and hugged, and kissed. She never spoke about it afterwards, as if it were too precious to be shared. All she could tell me was this: '. . . and I drank his tears. I licked them from his face and took them into myself. He was my son, you know . . . and they were going to kill him. Those tears were precious . . . and he did the same thing with mine. And we never said goodbye . . . you know he didn't ever like to say goodbye, just "see you later".'

I was called to the chapel at 6 a.m. The chaplain was there with the church lady. It was going to be a long hour. Jesse's execution was scheduled for 7 a.m. There could be a last-minute reprieve any time up until that moment. The attorneys had submitted a final appeal to the trial judge, and the governor could still issue a stay. There was still hope.

Some of the women began to gather on the steps in front of the chapel. They were concerned and wanted to be of some help or comfort to me. Cherokee was among them. We went back a long way together. They were upset at the idea of my being isolated at a time when one should be surrounded by friends and loved ones. The chaplain wanted to call for security. I did not want a legacy of violence in my name and I asked permission to go out and speak with my friends to tell them to disperse.

The crowd filed back down the stairs. Cherokee promised to come back as soon as she could. I told her not to do that but I knew that she would anyway. I went back inside the chapel to wait.

The chaplain offered me a comfortable chair and he took his place on the other side of the desk. The church lady sat beside me to my left. He was talking, probably out of nervousness, in an attempt to fill the uncomfortable space and time in which we waited. He meant well but his incessant babbling felt like ants crawling on my skin, and the closer we came to the appointed hour the worse it got, until I asked if we could just hold hands and have a moment of silence. He was so relieved to have found some way to help me he jumped up with enthusiasm! Here was something he knew how to do! We stood up and joined hands.

'Shall we say a short prayer together?'

'Yes. That would be nice.'

I lowered my head and he intoned the words. It didn't matter what words he said. It was soothing and gave me the chance to go within myself to that place of peace which I had so painstakingly created over the years. *Shema Y'Isroel Adonai Eloheinu Adonai Echad* . . . I said in my head. It was a way of centring my thoughts and my energy. It was my way of invoking the universal force that we call God. It was time but I felt nothing. I opened my eyes to look at the clock – it was 7 a.m. We should have heard something by now if there had been a last-minute stay. Why didn't I feel anything? Closing my eyes again, I tried to connect with what was happening to Jesse. We had been too close for too long for me not to feel his death. Something was wrong. We waited. And finally, all of a sudden there was an agonizing wave of despair, like the air rushing out of a balloon. I felt as if I were being pulled inside out. I felt a desperate urge to be alone. The sound of the tears falling from my eyes on to my shoes filled the room. I asked if it would be all right if I went to the ladies' room.

I ran through the chapel down the aisle between the pews to close myself in the bathroom. I shut the door behind me and turned on the water in the sink for privacy. I needed to let out the pressure that had been building in my chest. But, just then, I felt a presence, as if there was someone in the room with me. I looked up to see Jesse's image in the mirror, as if he were standing behind me surrounded by an aura of bright light.

'Jesse . . . is that you?'

The image just smiled back at me, arms folded characteristically across his chest.

'Jesse?' I said again but this time I knew it was him. The aura brightened and I felt the warmth of his presence. He was comforting me, letting me know he was all right.

'Jesse,' I whispered, smiling this time, 'thank you.' The image faded softly, leaving a swirl of energy behind which wrapped itself around me like an embrace. I left the bathroom to return to the chaplain's office and announce that I was ready to go back to the dorm.

The church lady hugged me and I hugged her back. She asked if I was sure I was all right. I said I was. The chaplain picked up the phone to call for an escort, but I asked him not to. Everyone was at work now and I was sure I could get to the dorm without any problems. He let me go.

Cherokee was waiting at the bottom of the stairs in front of the library. She threw her arms around me and asked how I was doing. I told her I was fine but I wanted to go to the dorm. She said she would walk me there. On the way, she told me there had been reports about the execution on the news, and she didn't want me to hear about it unprepared. She wanted to tell me before anyone else did. And so she did – in detail.

Flames two feet high shooting out of the top of his head, smoke coming from his ears, and his heart was still beating and his chest heaved for fifteen minutes after the first of the three jolts that it took to finally cook the life out of his body. They had to pull the switch three times. So that's why I didn't feel anything at first. He gave them a hard way to go.

I could hear the droning of the TV downstairs but I did not try to listen. I already knew everything I needed to know about what happened to Jesse.

I'm so proud of my Jesse. He was so brave – and he gave me strength. He gave each of us what we needed to make it through this – strength and love. That's what we were always about and that is how we will continue to be. He told me so.

I felt him. I felt him come to me and I saw
him, smiling. It was as he promised – he said he'd
let me know. And he sure did 'get into the flow' –
he gave them the last fuck you. He told mom – 'I
gave them a hard way to go from beginning to end.'
He sure did.

Now they can't use his death as a political
stepping stone! Three times with smoke and fire.

You are the Sun
I am the Moon
I have no light but that which
is reflected from you.

I thought you were the one with the Destiny
and I was the one with the Fate.

But it turned out that I was the one with the
Destiny
and you were the one with the Fate.

37

M Y ROOMMATE AND ALL of the women in my dorm were so good to me in those days following the execution. They brought me food and juice and candy and little handmade cards. My classification officer stopped by to see me, and so did many of the old-time officers. Regardless of the uniform we wore, we were all part of a single community. The rabbi came too but I did not sit Shiva this time. I sat in meditation, in the Zen Buddhist Kiai-Shu style, in order to touch the aura that remained behind. As soon as I could, I returned to work – to the comfort of routine, to the security of doing something meaningful, to the strong sensitivity of the people I worked with there.

I thought a lot about our life together before all this happened. Jesse had always been so strong and yet he had a soft side, like a puppy dog belly. Wherever we went there was always time to roll in the wild flowers on the mountainside. He had such a good sense of humour – but there was a darker side as well. I always attributed that darkness to the shadow cast over his life by his experiences in prison and the teachings of his mentor, the sensei. But there was that one summer when we camped out in the

Cherokee National Forest, and then drove all the way up to New York in the converted bread truck we called the Puerto Rican Van. Tina was conceived in that forest.

Not long after Jesse was killed, a reporter who had been in the death chamber viewing section and witnessed the execution said he was still having nightmares about it. The priest who had been with Jesse until the end was unable to talk about it. Sister Helen Prejean, who had stood vigil outside the prison, began her famous walk to Washington DC to give a speech from the pulpit of Martin Luther King about the evils of the death penalty. Jesse's mom spoke to the congregation of the local church that night, as Jesse had asked her to do. She told them how the state of Florida had burned her son at the stake, tortured him repeatedly with killing jolts of electricity for fifteen minutes. His lawyers were sick at heart. And our daughter tried to jump off the balcony of her room in Disney World. That was where her guardians took her to take her mind off the fact that her father had been killed that day. But I wasn't yet aware of that. It would be years before Tina would talk about it. A woman who had been coming to visit Jesse and had put up quite a bit of money for his appeals, his pen pal from New York, had disappeared. Later on, she would write a note to Jesse's mom saying she was sorry she couldn't be there at the end but she just couldn't take it. And his friends on the row smuggled out letters telling how the chair was purposely fixed so that Jesse would suffer. His closest friend, Michael Bruno, said the worst part was that he could smell the burned flesh of his friend for days afterwards.

There was an article in the North Florida newspapers about the use of an artificial sponge instead of a natural sponge in the headset connected to the electric chair. A journalist had spoken with the man who was called in to fix the chair, who said they should have known it would malfunction because the artificial sponge would affect the flow of electricity. There was international outrage at the barbaric use of torture in a state-sanctioned murder. Everyone would know his name. They would not forget Jesse Tafero.

THREE JOLTS USED TO EXECUTE KILLER

Saturday, May 5, 1990 – The execution of Jesse Tafero in the big chair at Florida state prison went awry Friday morning. Flames and smoke rose from his head as the headset conducting the killer current to his body caught fire.

Tafero's execution coincided with the first march of the first national movement against the death penalty, and national pilgrimage for the abolition of the death penalty. Members gathered outside the prison as it lay shrouded in fog early Friday.

'No execution is normal,' said Sister Helen Prejean of New Orleans, who led a march to Atlanta today. Prejean stood in a field opposite the prison with a small group of protesters, holding a vigil as the execution proceeded.

Tafero, his brown eyes piercing and angry, had these last words before the executioners fixed the faulty headset to his skull: 'Well, I'd like to say that the death penalty, as applied in the States, is very arbitrary and capricious. I think it's very unfair. I think it's time that everyone wakes up to see that the same laws that can go against crime can go against you tomorrow.'

He never received my 26 April letter. It was returned to me marked 'DECEASED'.

For a while there were no more executions in Florida, and Jesse's case was cited as an example of cruel and unusual punishment. The law books included graphic descriptions of his ordeal. The newspapers reported he had a last meal of scrambled eggs, fried pepperoni, toasted Italian bread, two tomatoes, steamed broccoli, asparagus tips, strawberry shortcake with whipped cream, whole milk and Lipton tea. One tabloid newspaper even published a picture they had somehow got from the coroner's office or the funeral home showing the damage to Jesse's head. One of the girls told me about it and asked if I wanted to see it. I told her to put it in an envelope, seal it and give it to me. I have never opened it, just like I never opened the coroner's report about my parents.

Jesse's mom had chosen to have his body sent to Pennsylvania for burial in the family plot next to his grandfather Bo, the one who initiated him into the

Kiai-Shu of Zen Buddhism. I had asked to be allowed to go to his funeral but the request was denied. So I stayed home (in my room) that day to sit – to be with them for the funeral. The priest who performed the ceremony told Tina that her father was in heaven now and that he would be her guardian angel and look after her always. As I sat, I sent myself there to wrap myself around them, Tina and Eric and Kay. Jesse's aura was there but it was no longer swirling and bright – now it was quiescent and softly pastel. Jesse's mom had laid her Bible down on the seat next to her. As she was leaving, the priest stopped her to give her the Bible she had left on the seat and the rose that had been laid on top of it. No one could say how the rose had got there. But Kay loved roses and she took the rose as a sign from her son. It had been his way of letting her know that he was OK. At the cemetery, Eric placed the death poem I had written and Jesse's favourite sword in the grave with the casket. The men, Jesse's friends left behind on the row, sent flowers. Kay would receive flowers from them every year. No one who knew him will ever forget him.

  Hope can be taken away by outside forces but faith can endure beyond reason. Love is like Faith. Love is stronger than fear because even if you are afraid of someone – someone else can come along and in a second make you more afraid! Not so with love. No one can come along and in a second make you love them more. Love is stronger than hate too – because hate destroys and therefore

it cannot endure and must come to an end whereas
love builds and goes on.

It was during those days of hope, just before the execution, that I received a letter from my childhood friend Micki – the one who had become a film-maker. She had been teaching film-making at a Boston college for the past fifteen years and had recently moved to Los Angeles. She had produced and directed documentary films, some of them award-winning. She told me of her struggles as the only girl in her film school classes back in the '60s and '70s. I told her about Jesse and the pending execution. At the time when one of the last remaining connections to my past was being severed, it was as if another one was being given back to me – from further back, before my life changed, from a purer place and time, and I grabbed on to it.

Micki's letters began to come regularly. When they came I would not wait, as I usually did, to take them to my room where I could open them and read them properly; rather I would tear them open and read them as I walked, fully absorbed, cutting a path on automatic pilot. Sometimes, a moment that fills the soul is more important than survival itself. Those letters were an open door through which the sights and sounds and emotions of my friend's world came tumbling, swirling around me, and through them I was transported. Turning time inside out, she took me back to a time when we were Indians – sisters called Red Warrior and Running Deer – pouring our passions into other letters, the ones we wrote to our

493

imaginary Indian chief boyfriends. Girls always play Indians. Boys play cowboys and Indians. We saved those letters too. Years later, Micki told me she found one in some things her mother gave her when her father died.

    I feel connected to the world again, in ways I haven't felt since my parents died. My past has come together with my present and I feel the pieces come together inside myself as well. I'll be ok. I can hang on to one thread. And I have that thread now. It is a strong one. It is a thread made of the innocent love of a child's heart, the purest love of all. In its purity lies its strength. It is, after all, in childhood that the strongest parts of us are formed. This is a gift back to me from the Universe. Thank you Universe! I love you!

July 1st, 1990

Dearest Micki,

I've been reading a book I ordered from the state library – it has to be sent back on a certain date and I only have until Monday to finish it. It's really not enough time but I'm using this three-day weekend to plow on through it. The book is by Richard Hofstader. It's about mathematical theory but it extends into art, music, physics, biology – just about everything including parallels to Zen. It's complex and my mind boggles after a while. It is fascinating though. So I've curtailed my normal routine and activities in order to finish the book.

This all started because I found out about 'recursive' math when discussing computers with the guy who is installing our system at work. He recommended the book. My intrepid curiosity took over from there. My curiosity has been both a source of salvation and downfall to me. It has kept me from ever being bored and led me to much valuable knowledge and many fascinating discoveries. It has also led me into my greatest troubles. I should have been afraid of Jesse – instead I was fascinated. And yet, as a result of that fascination I learned and experienced many wonderful things. But at what price! I try daily to make the result equal the price.

We were very close – sometimes weeks would go by where we had no contact with anyone else and spent 24/7 together – me, Jesse, and Eric. Eric and I were always together. The only baby sitters he ever had were my folks, and then only for a few hours. If Eric couldn't go with me I just didn't go. Jesse accepted Eric and spent time with him like a father. They seemed to get along very well. It wasn't until this past year that Eric told me he was afraid of Jesse. I never knew that, and I asked him why he never told me. He said, 'Mom, I was a kid. I didn't know how to tell you that.'

There was a settlement with the airline after the crash, but it wasn't as large as anyone thought because they said my brother is grown and can take care of himself and I am taken care of by the state. Alan wouldn't go to a jury. He said he couldn't handle it. So we split half and half on what they offered. My lawyers got half of what I got right away and I gave them the rest as time went on. I get 85 dollars a month from the will. I use it for my expenses here and used to send the rest to Sherry for expenses until she cut me off. Now I send that money into an account where it will accumulate for Tina and will give it to her when I know she will be able to use it for herself. Sherry has been very ill – she has had at least seven operations and she is still on morphine from the last operation. I am very angry and disappointed with her but I can't hate her or want to strike out at her because she did take Tina at a bad time and had to help bring Tina out of a very deep shell. When Tina got there, she was so withdrawn and they brought her out of it. I can never forget that. She was a good friend. She was there for me when I had Eric and didn't even know how to hold him, and she was willing to take both kids this time too. Maybe one day we will grow past this difficulty.

Now, you must tell me more about how you got to be who you are now. If you have any questions just go ahead and ask.

Love, Sunny

We began talking on the phone. It was the most amazing thing hearing her voice! It was different yet it was the same . . . the way she said my name – Sunny, not Sonia, which was what everyone in prison called me – recalled a part of myself that had lain dormant from what seemed to be at least two lifetimes past. And when I answered, the sound of my voice saying her name, 'Hi, Mick!' shattered the barrier of intervening years so that we were children again while at the same time experiencing each other as adults . . . no longer prisoners of time. We decided on a limit of one call a week, on Saturdays. Between the letters and the calls I began to feel full again.

It was so strange how things had turned out. I remembered when Micki and I were kids and how she was always such a paradox of aggression and shyness. Our relationship had remained undisturbed, pristine, like untrodden snow deep in the forest. I wondered what she was like now. I wondered what she thought of me, being in prison – for murder.

It was 4 July, a celebration of freedom, even in an American prison. We had our yearly cookout and the smell that clung to the thick summer air was hypnotic. Like flies, we hovered around the cooking area waiting for our chance. The lines were incredibly long but they were orderly – this was serious food and even the smallest women would fight you for their place in line – no cutting in front today. We weren't supposed to take the plates of food inside with us, but many did and the officers didn't really care. They'd have a shakedown later anyway so it didn't matter. But I planned to finish my food right after my regular Saturday phone call with Micki.

The call was upbeat and full of news as usual. I had signed for a double spot on the phone but the next person was already standing behind me waiting for her turn.

'Mick, my time's up.' There was a pause. 'Mick?'

'May I ask you a question?'

'Sure.'

'Promise you won't get mad?'

She sounded like a little girl. We had both so recently found that part of ourselves again. I knew this must be something important for her to risk it.

'No. I won't get mad at you . . . now tell me what it is.'

'What the hell happened that day with the policemen? I'm sorry but I just have to know. It's all right, whatever happened I'll still be your friend but I have to know.'

'Mick, I didn't do anything. I was just there. It was out of control. I couldn't stop it.'

'You mean you didn't do it?'

'I didn't kill anyone, Mick.'

'Sunny. Call me back.'

'I can't. I'll call again on Monday night. Is that OK?'

'Yes! Don't forget!'

When we hung up I went back to my room to finish my corn. I was a little put off that she had asked me about it – I mean, if it didn't matter then why was she asking? Micki, she later told me, was hysterical. She had never asked me anything about the crime before. She was just trying to be there for a friend who had suffered a terrible tragedy and loss. But for Micki our renewed friendship filled a big space too. She had just finished one of the biggest projects of her life. It was a documentary and then a short feature about AIDS, the first of its genre. Her days had been filled with people, some of whom did not live to see the completion of the project. Now that it was over she was feeling a bit empty herself.

Later on she would tell me that the first person she talked to about it was Christie, an attorney and good friend. Christie's first reaction was as an attorney: 'That's what they all say, Micki. Don't you know there aren't any guilty people in prison?'

'But Chris, she said she didn't do it and I believe her. I'll have to go and see her, look her in the eye and ask her to tell me how it happened. Then I'll know if she's telling me the truth.'

After that phone call, Micki said she wanted to visit me. She said it might take a while for her to complete the formalities. I told her not to worry because however long it took I'd be here. The first visit didn't take place until November 1990.

'Sonia Jacobs, report to the visiting park!'

I was ready to go. I had been waiting down at Ms J's. I had told Micki it was best to try to get there early so she could be first in line. Visiting didn't start until 9 a.m. but people began lining up as early as 8 a.m. If you got in early you could get the best seats, furthest from where the guards stood, and you could get the best food out of the machines, and with such limited time to see each other I didn't want to lose a minute. As it was, they didn't announce the inmate's name until the visitor had been searched and processed in, and the inmates had to wait in line to be strip-searched before they got into the visiting park.

499

I hurried over to the VP and looked through the glass door to see if I could catch sight of Micki. The guard wasn't paying attention so I knocked on the glass to let her know I was there waiting. Strip me, search me, make me cough. I just wanted to get it over with so I could see my friend. I had told Micki what to do and what not to do so she shouldn't have been subjected to anything too degrading. Later she told me that they had taken the pencil and pad she had brought with her and asked why she was visiting 'that inmate'. There was an armed guard outside in the parking lot who would not let them get out of their cars until just before nine. They weren't supposed to run to the door either, but people were fast-walking to line up. She said the guards were so mean to the visitors that it was intimidating. And once you got in, you then had to empty your purse and pockets and go through the metal detector in between the electronically controlled doors. Many of the women refused to let their families come and be put through the indignities of the process.

Once inside the visiting park, Micki tried to sit where I had told her but a guard ordered her to take a different seat. She got a little indignant and said she would really rather sit where she had chosen. (The guard would later come around to harass us about sitting too close.) So Micki secured the seats I had told her to try to get, sitting on the metal chair with her little see-through plastic purse, looking around at the other visitors as they took their seats to wait for their loved ones.

I had almost finished buttoning my dress in the strip-search room. I couldn't believe my bad luck in getting the guard who looked up your butt with a flashlight. No such thing as 'where the light don't shine' in prison. I was still working on the top button as I came through the door into the brightly lit time warp of the visiting park where worlds meet – where I would find my friend who had come across a continent and three decades to find me.

I scanned the room and saw her immediately. That face! That was my little Micki's face! And the copper-red hair was still the same. She was standing up waving to me. 'Sunny! Over here!' We were as two children wrapping our arms around each other in a moment of pure delight. 'You're not allowed to touch. Only a brief hug and kiss on the way in and on the way out,' I told her as we took our seats.

'Sunny, tell me what to do and not to do. I don't want to get you in trouble. You look the same. It's like no time has passed at all,' she said, taking my hand.

I took my hand back after a short pause. 'Mick, that's touching. It's not allowed.'

'I'm sorry. I would go crazy in here, or be in trouble all the time.'

'You probably would.' We laughed.

The guard approached, as if on cue, to tell us our knees were touching. 'Your visit could be terminated for physical contact. Don't let it happen again.'

'Yes, Ms Cornfield.' I thanked her for telling us and bobbed my head in acquiescence.

When the guard left to disturb other people's visits, Micki said, 'What was that voice you used? It sounded like you were a child, so subservient.'

'Look, it's best to give them respect or they feel they have to prove their authority to you. If you were here you would do it too, if you wanted to have a decent visit. I could mouth off to her and they would put you out. After you've come so far I don't think that would be a good idea.'

'I didn't mean to hurt your feelings. I just don't get it. But, enough of that, tell me how you're doing? I'd really be interested to know what it's been like for you, if you don't mind telling me.' And so I told her. For the next six hours I told her, until she stopped me and asked, 'Don't you want to know about me?'

'Sure,' I said but she hadn't got far when I thought of something else to tell her.

And we ate machine food. Oh yeah! That machine food was a real treat – a change of fare from what we got in a repetitive cycle of preplanned menus year after year. We put my sweater on the chairs and went over to the row of vending machines on the side wall.

'You have to hit the machines right away or the good stuff gets taken,' I told an incredulous Micki, who just stood there feeding quarters into the slot as I pointed to my selections. We weren't allowed to handle the money. We ended up with two armloads of sandwiches, candy bars, chips and sodas.

'Are you really going to eat all this?'

'Yeah! We can't take stuff back in with us. You can't leave the park with anything you didn't bring in with you. They write down everything you have on you and you have to come back out with those things, no more and no less.'

502

'Oh ... well, you better get started,' Micki said, grinning at me with that ten-year-old face sitting atop her now mature body. She didn't eat much. I guess machine food wasn't that big a deal to her, but I was enjoying a different kind of bagel with real cream cheese and some kind of chips I had never had before and there was a frozen Snickers too. And they had different soda selections in the VP from what we could buy in the canteen. Choices! Delicious in themselves and more so when you could eat them too!

The visit was over in a blur of reminiscences and plans, present and future slamming together at high speed. Neither of us could believe it was over. We were both crying. Micki would be back. 'First one on line tomorrow,' she promised me – the little face so serious now. She reached out to touch my cheek, to wipe the tears. I flinched and drew away from her hand. 'Do they beat you here?' She was upset. I explained that they were really serious about physical contact, even wiping away a tear could be interpreted as a violation of the rules, and I wanted to be able to see her again the next day.

'Can we hug now? You said on the way in and on the way out?'

'Yeah, we can do that.' We stood up and hugged, long and hard. Micki gives the best hugs, right up close, nothing held back. I loved her again as I had when we were young. Always the captain of the team; always pushing the limits; always vulnerable, but not letting it stop her.

'I love you, Mick. Thanks for coming.'

'I'll be back.'

The guard came by to remind us that it was time to say goodbye, and the hug was supposed to be brief. I didn't reply, but instead looked at Micki and we both started to laugh.

'Please try not to use that voice. I hate that you have to do that.'

'OK. But don't bug me about it. I don't need you to rub it in.'

'This is how you say "I love you" in sign language,' she said, folding in her two middle fingers with her thumb leaving the pointer and pinky standing. I formed the same symbol with mine. 'See you tomorrow.'

We separated, drifting towards our respective exits. I would have to take a seat at the door to wait for my turn in the shakedown room. We were the last ones to leave the visiting area. I volunteered to help clean up around the seats so I could watch Micki go through the sallyport and give her the 'I love you' sign in answer to hers. I was so hyper I couldn't sit anyway. It was like a dream! I felt the parts of me click, like the pieces of a puzzle, coming seamlessly together inside me. A piece was taken and a piece was given back. A little karmic relief on the wheel of ups and downs. I felt the life swelling my soul up like a balloon – *mustn't float; it's against the rules!*

Back in the dorm, I had a lot to think about. Micki had filled me in on the past thirty years of her life. We had seen each other once during that time, when we were twenty. She was in college and I was taking care of my two-year-old son. Before that we hadn't seen each other since we were twelve, back in Elmont, Long Island. I had looked her up by locating her parents who I remembered were living in Hallandale, Florida. I was living in Miami at the time in the rented house that my parents used for holidays. As a divorcee with a young child, I was trying to look acceptable in my pumps and stockings and nice little summer dress. Micki was still in her hippie days complete with headband and posters of Bob Dylan and Janis Joplin. We had nothing in common and the meeting was a big disappointment for both of us. When we talked about it later, we marvelled that she hadn't been the one to get in trouble. Her parents, over the years, would say they wished she were more like me – before they heard about my trouble, that is. They were the ones who first told Micki what had happened. She had tried to contact me then but had never received an answer to her letter. I explained that the jail held my mail and I never received it. She said she had tried writing again in 1982 and then figured I didn't want to be in touch. Micki and I just seemed to intersect at times of major change. This time, though, we clicked! I fell asleep that night feeling full and fine.

I have been very loved in my life. You might not envy my position, but I have been blessed. John, Irish John who thought he was D'Artagnan, always felt responsible for my troubles. He told my brother that if he hadn't messed up we would still be together. My parents loved me – more than I ever realized, until I was in prison and had little chance to reciprocate. But we shared our feelings openly at every visit towards the end, so I didn't have to regret not having told them I loved them. And

Jesse had loved me – in his imperfect, totally sincere way, he loved me with his whole being. And there had been Linda, too – also imperfectly but sweetly. And the children – against every hardship the love of mother and child had prevailed and would continue to prevail. Friends and family who had remained supportive of me through it all. And now, a return to the heart of innocence.

I had changed Micki's name when we were kids at camp. The other kids were teasing her and I told them her name wasn't Michelle Dickoff – her name, I told them, was Micki. And so she became Micki. Her dad used to send us salamis in care packages that we kept hidden until we had to wipe the green off them to eat them. Micki showered in her underwear and I never went out of the bunkhouse without my cap because they made me get a haircut. We defended each other to the end. We were indomitable together. We vowed to be best friends for ever. At home we spent most of our time at my house because her house wasn't as much fun. Micki reminded me about how we used to sell lemonade in the summertime. She wanted to give it away. She was already big-hearted and impractical. Micki talked a lot about her memories of my folks. It was painful and joyful at the same time. She told me about her family too. Her sister was an elementary school teacher and rock and roll aficionado. I told her that my brother was teaching Tae Kwan Do and running a furniture store. She also asked if she could talk to my attorneys. I gave her the number. We would talk more about the legal stuff. And I fell asleep dreaming of tomorrow.

Micki spent four days visiting that first time. The second two days were special visits because they were on weekdays and the visitor had come from a great distance. There were no other visitors in the park.

Of course, the guardians were ever-present but on special visiting days they weren't so uptight. I think that was because they didn't have a room full of people to contend with and, besides, I was never one to overdo breaking the rules. Our special visiting days were spent at a table in the middle of an empty visiting park with the guard spending most of his or her time in the major's office. The more relaxed and comfortable setting made it easier to talk and to show emotion without feeling like we were on display.

Micki would finally get around to asking me about the legal issues and I told her to get in touch with the attorneys. I would tell them to let her see whatever she wanted. The visits were for happier things, a diversion, to be enjoyed.

38

Dearest Ginger,

I tried to call during the hours you said, but I get the machine. I'll keep trying. Meanwhile will have to keep writing.

My son, Eric, and his wife, Debbie, are trying to arrange for a lawyer to help us get visitation with my daughter, Tina. I haven't seen her in two years and even when Eric goes to New York to see her they won't let him be with her alone to talk. They refuse my calls so I can't even talk to her. When Eric is able he'll come down here so we can all meet and talk. Then I'll see Claudia! She's nineteen months old now. It's amazing that my little boy is a father now. Tina is 15. We can't go to the lake anymore – they built another building and the lake is off limits. I miss the serenity. I go to rec and work out most evenings, so I stay fit. And I just got my own computer at work in the optical lab office.

I'm entering the eleventh circuit court federal now. The brief should be in around Oct. Then we'll see. There are so many things I want to do!

Keep in touch and take care –
Love as always, Sonia

T INA WAS HAVING TROUBLE dealing with her emotions after her father's execution and Sherry and her family were struggling with the notoriety. One morning, Kay Tafero got a call from her granddaughter that sent her on a frantic search.

'Tina called this morning,' she said, which shocked the heck out of me because that was unusual in itself.

'She said they were taking her to a place in Maine, to live at a school there. She called me from a bathroom in a restaurant somewhere on the way. She said she couldn't stay on long because she wasn't supposed to be telling anyone where they were taking her.' Kay was near hysteria.

'Mom,' I said, wanting her to get a grip on herself, 'what was the name of the place they were taking her to?'

'I don't know. That's all she could tell me. I don't think she knew it herself. I can't stand it.'

'Listen, Mom, don't worry. We'll find her. I'll call Sherry, and if she won't take my call I'll have Mike, my attorney friend in North Carolina, call. You just calm down. We don't need another tragedy in the family, OK? You have to be strong for your granddaughter now.'

Poor Kay. She was always having to be strong for someone else.

When I hung up with Kay, I was almost out of control myself. The anger I felt coming from the pit of my gut threatened my ability to think rationally at a time when it was essential. Breathe! God help me, breathe and push the

509

anger down and out. It would have its time and place and usefulness, but not now! As soon as I could, I placed a call to Sherry, who accepted my call. She said that her husband Bob had written me a letter about it. She said that they were doing what they felt would be best for Tina. They would miss her. They loved her too. True, they would be the only ones allowed to communicate with her for the first few months – it was the school's rules. If she merited it later on, they would decide about communication. Meanwhile, Sherry said she and her husband would keep me informed by letter of Tina's progress.

'Not even Eric? He's her brother! They've never been out of touch with each other. He's been her only constant thread, through it all.'

It was unacceptable. A young girl locked away somewhere without any means of communication was a set-up for abuse. Until that time, I had been willing to let things be, as long as the guardians still allowed contact between Tina and her brother and grandmother. It was intolerable for me to think of my daughter in a situation where she was cut off from her support group, as odd and unusual as they were, at a time when she needed all the assurance and sense of belonging that she could get. And I needed it too. I couldn't deal with another loss just yet. Still holding anger at bay, I waited for the letter to arrive.

When it came, with its brief description of a school in Maine, I went to see my friend Cory who was a transfer from Maine. I remembered that she had once told us about having gone to school there. I asked her if she had ever heard of the school.

510

'If your daughter's in that place, you better get her out of there as soon as you can. I've never told anyone about it because it is too painful for me to remember. They broke my arm there – I got pushed down a flight of stairs. And they chained me to a tree outside for trying to escape, in the snow. Is your daughter tough? I hope she is because they put boxing gloves on the kids and make them fight until one of them can't fight any more. You really need to find out if that's where she is and if it is, get her out before they fuck her up like they did me. I thought that place was closed down years ago. They had a number of lawsuits against them for physical abuses. Some of the kids there were pretty violent too – court committed instead of sending them to jail.'

I was devastated. Cory gave me the address and I passed all the information I had to Kay.

Tina was indeed at that school, and she was being openly rebellious, acting up and taking lessons from the other teenagers, most of whom had been sent there for behaviour problems and, as Cory had warned, some had been sentenced to go there by the court. It was not a positive peer group for an emotionally mixed up, hormonally active fifteen-year-old girl looking for love and feeling abandoned. My oldest child had suffered so much emotionally and been deprived of a normal life, and now my youngest child was suffering too. I felt the full weight of it on my soul. It was my fault – all of it, somehow. It was my stupidity that had led us all to this place. Fatherless children – mine and the dead policemen's; widows; mothers whose sons died violently before

511

their time; so many lives disrupted and ruined; my parents' agony and my own losses. All of those evil things sat on my chest, on my heart, on my head, suffocating my very soul with guilt. Filled with anger, as much with myself as with the situation, I began my quest to find my child and rescue her.

September 30, 1990

Dear Ginger,

I've been using all my call to deal with the situation with my daughter. Hopefully, I'll have a handle on it this week and will be able to call you next week.

You mentioned knowing something about habeas corpus in federal court – I'm interested! But that will wait for a phone call. Getting out of here would solve all the major problems. For now, I've put all else aside to find out what's happening to my daughter. I can't sleep at night not knowing what's being done to her.

So, I'll call when I can. Meanwhile let's keep writing. It's good to know you're still there!

Keep in touch.

Love as always, Sonia

When Micki returned from her trip to Los Angeles, we talked about how we might reach Tina. In my desperation I suggested hiring a skywriting plane to fly over the school, sending out a message that we knew where she was and we loved her. Smoke signals! Like Indians! Micki explained very patiently that the idea was impractical. Maybe she could go up there to Maine with Eric and his family, she suggested, and find out what the situation was. A show of support for Tina would make the school more careful of how they treated her. That became our plan.

With all that was going on, daily life in prison remained the same. It could be frustrating but there were times when it was comforting to be carried along by the humdrum routine.

The next time Micki visited, it was the week of 3 November 1990. There had been no more news from or about Tina. Micki spent the days between visits talking to my attorneys and to Kay. The attorneys were more than happy to let her read the transcripts and appellate briefs that had been filed thus far. We were fast approaching the time to submit my federal habeas corpus. It was, for all practical purposes, my last chance. If we did not prevail on it I would most likely spend the rest of my life in prison.

Habeas corpus is only for the purpose of arguing the legal issues – the process, not the facts. It is not permitted to present new evidence in a habeas corpus. You couldn't even argue innocence based on new facts any more because technically the time for that had passed. To me, it seems like it should never be too late for the truth. I was trying to explain to Micki how the recantations of Walter Rhodes and the confession of perjury by Brenda Isham could be deemed harmless error. She was determined to find a way to help. I trusted her, not just because she was my childhood friend, and not just because I knew she was sincere. I trusted Micki because when I looked in her eyes I saw truth there. And I could feel the strength of this woman who sat across from me day after day. At first it was a shy thing, a child peeking out from behind its mother's skirt. But as the days passed, it grew bolder and more confident, standing out in front to explore and expand. And so, as I explained the legal process that up until then had failed me so badly, Micki got more and more upset.

'I'm an intelligent person. At least, I have always considered myself to be intelligent but I don't understand this at all,' Micki ranted. 'How could they ignore that woman's testimony? How could it be harmless error? Harmless to who?'

She was almost screaming and I had to remind her not to call attention to us by getting too emotional. I explained that unless you could prove that the prosecutor knew and actually participated in the coercion, then even if you could prove the person lied at trial, it didn't count. It only counted if you could prove the prosecutor was in on it. So they called it harmless error.

'That's how it's done,' I said. 'We'll win on the federal habeas corpus. They can't ignore everything.'

'Well, I think the public should know about this. I think people would be outraged if they knew. I have a lot more reading to do. There are thousands of pages to read through. And I've asked my friend Christie to help. She's a California lawyer and she's smart and she can help me figure out the legal stuff. Is that OK with you?'

'Sure. I can use all the help I can get.'

Micki stayed in her sister's apartment in Florida, sleeping on the guest couch, until just before Christmas. She

514

visited every weekend, spending every day when she wasn't visiting reading and talking to the attorneys. Before she left, she had come up with a brilliant visual way to present the facts, all the facts, concerning the independent eyewitness testimony of two truck drivers, one of whose statements had not been brought out at trial, explaining the discrepancies in their testimony, making it clear that neither Jesse nor I could have done the shooting. The brilliance of Micki's solution was that the presentation of new facts was so inextricably intertwined in the legal arguments that it couldn't be rejected as untimely new evidence. She told me she was going to consult with a graphic artist in Los Angeles. Graphics had never been used in a federal habeas corpus before but we could try. Richard Strafer had said that the chances of winning were 10,000 to one. With that, Micki went off to do battle with the system – for Truth, for Justice, and for me.

39

Micki had gone back to LA and I, feeling a bit let down – poor Cinderella again, no longer busy and special – involved myself in the preparations for the holidays. I had been talked into doing a Christmas skit with Matty Webberly for the annual dorm competition. She was to be Maid Marion and I would play Robin Hood. We, the heroes, had stolen the purse of the Sheriff of Nottingham and distributed its contents to the poor for Christmas. Typical point of view for convicts to take. This was serious business because the first prize was – you got it – food!

The rabbi came and with him came the Bubbes – arms loaded with latkes and a warmer, apple sauce and sour cream. We each got a care package of candles and a menorah made of gold foil to take back to the dorm with us. People would stop by to look and I would get to tell the story of the Lights. Matty and I would compare customs and knowledge. Matty and her group of friends asked for matzoth in April when we had Passover, with which they would re-create the Last Supper. It was a sweet blending of traditions, based, of course, on food!

Our dorm was the winner that year. Fried chicken was

the prize! For a piece of fried chicken I could get a week's worth of veggies and milk and fruit. But for a piece of free-world fried chicken, I could get . . . whatever I wanted.

I called Eric to see if the presents had arrived. And I called Micki to see if she had been able to determine whether my daughter had got the gifts we had sent to the school in Maine. Tina was still not allowed any communication with me but we hoped that Christmas presents would be considered an exception. Micki had helped me with the shopping.

She had moved to Florida and taken a tiny apartment, put her life on hold and begun a campaign to right the wrongs that had kept me in prison for so long. She had read thousands of pages of legal transcripts, met with my attorneys, and become involved with the *20/20* news team, trying to convince them to do a feature about my situation.

Micki had become a familiar face in the super-intendent's office. She had sent a copy of two of her films to Mrs Villacorta and had got permission to do an AIDS workshop in which she would get to show her AIDS films to the inmates.

It was a Wednesday afternoon. I was at the optical lab, working. Mrs Villacorta was escorting Micki down the compound to the Recreation bay to show *Too Little, Too Late*, her Emmy award-winning documentary about mothers of people with AIDS. Ms J was waiting on the path. As they approached, she moved to intercept them as they went by. She explained that she knew Micki would want me to see the movie, but I wouldn't be able to come because I was at work. Good old Ms J, looking out for her buddy! Micki explained that it was really important to her for me to see her work so I would have some idea of what it was she did. We had recently experienced our first AIDS-related death in the prison – a girl named Nadine had been sick for many months and no one really knew what one could or could not do. We were still debating whether you could catch AIDS from kissing or even from touching doorknobs. Nadine had died alone in the hospital ward, with only one or two of her closest friends daring to go up and see her.

In those days we didn't even have hospice care-workers coming into the prison. None of our population had ever been so sick before. Heroin addicts and even the cocaine addicts who came in would eventually regain their health if they stayed clean. But the crack addicts were often irredeemably damaged, and the prostitutes and addicts who shot up their drugs were developing the first signs of HIV. And there were those who were just plain getting old in there, like Ms J. It had been unheard of before, for a woman to do so much time that she grew old. Now women were beginning to die in prison, not just from the occasional heart attack, and we needed to be educated about long-term care.

Mrs Villacorta agreed to let me attend the film show. I must say I felt great! I tried not to think I was special but Micki's presence in my life had given me such an infusion of hope that I couldn't help but be somewhat overcome. I floated out of the optical lab trying to look cool. It was heady stuff, that hope. And it was so uplifting to have someone care about you that much. Micki had gone to a lot of trouble on my behalf.

There was a full house waiting for the movie to start. I was surprised at the interest. I saw Cynthia waving at us from the front row. For years, Cynthia had been my protector and dear friend. She had saved us two seats. 'Had to take care of my baby,' she said as I walked over and sat down. Ms J took the seat on my other side. Micki looked my way and smiled just before the lights went dim and the film began. She had made me promise not to say anything until it was over. The titles came up, 'written and directed by Micki Dickoff'. I felt like I was going to cry – my little friend Micki was showing me her baby, the creation that had grown inside her and come from her labours. She had never married or had any children. She was devoted to her work and the kids she had taught for fifteen years. After a while you could hear sniffling from the audience. The other women were as deeply affected by the film as I was. Ms J handed out the tissues she always carried in her uniform pocket. When the lights went on again, the audience was still applauding. It was an amazing film and I was so proud of my friend. Mrs Villacorta had promised a question-and-answer session. She escorted Micki to the front of the room and called for quiet, and Micki pointed at one girl who was standing up waving her hand, tears still running down her cheeks.

'My name is Mary Dalih. My friend Nadine just died of AIDS last week . . . and nobody even held her hand!' Mary went on, an avalanche of anger and guilt and resentment, burying us under the weight of her words, accusing, condemning. 'And I'm gonna give Micki a hug and I don't care if it is against the rules. We should have hugged Nadine too!' Mary began making her way up the centre aisle towards where Micki was standing. Others began to applaud and follow Mary to the front, forming a circle around Micki. Cynthia, Ms J and I joined the circle. I wasn't sure if this was going to be OK and I wanted to protect my friend should it get out of hand. But this was an outpouring of love and gratitude and relief. In a way, it was as miraculous as the film had been. That it had provoked such an emotional response was astounding. That Mrs V let it happen was equally astounding.

Recall was announced. It didn't look like the women were going to leave. They were still gathered around Micki, making no attempt to get to their assigned stations before count. I told Ms J she'd better start out now because she couldn't go very fast. But even she insisted on staying to tell Micki how she felt. I hustled her up front, through the crowd, so she could say what she had to say and I could give Micki a hug.

That film was the talk of the compound afterwards and the inmates began their own little hospice care group. In the end, it would be the volunteer inmates who would tend to the dying. No one would ever again die alone without a hand to hold, like Nadine.

Micki came back to show *Mother, Mother*, the dramatic adaptation of *Too Little, Too Late*, which she also co-wrote and directed. Then she went back to Los Angeles for a while. In February 1991, *Our Sons*, a TV movie based on *Too Little, Too Late* that Micki co-produced, aired on national television. I had put up a sign on the television a week in advance claiming that two-hour spot, and my friends had all added their names in support. Micki always took on the big challenges – Aids, homelessness, hunger, the prison system, the justice system – but her work was really always about love and reconciliation. I knew how hard Micki had struggled in order to maintain the integrity of the story. She was a fascinating person – so full of self-doubt and yet so courageous and determined.

Later that month, Micki went to Boston where she met with Eric, his wife Debbie and baby Claudia, who had just turned three. They drove up to Maine together to see Tina.

It was the end of February, and the snow was still thick on the ground. When they arrived at the school, they were met by a contingent of counsellors and administrators. Eric, Debbie and the baby would be allowed to visit with Tina. Micki, however, would not. In fact, she was not to be allowed on the school grounds. The guardians had given explicit instructions that if Micki tried to enter, the school would call the police and have her arrested for trespassing. Why, we can only speculate. She reasoned, argued, cajoled and threatened, to no avail. The answer was a final no – she was not allowed on the school grounds. She waited in the car for the next three hours while Eric and his family were escorted in to see Tina and one of the other students, whom Tina had selected to come with her. Apparently, it was the school policy never to let the students be alone with their visitors. Later, Eric told me that Tina said she was not being mistreated. But I did not feel she had been truly free to speak. It was some comfort at least to hear that she had received the Christmas gifts. And although Micki was not allowed in to see Tina, she did receive a letter thanking her for the gifts. At least now Tina knew that we, her family, cared about her.

I had collected as much information as possible about the school. They had been shut down on more than one occasion for physical abuse of students. They had no college preparatory courses nor did they offer SAT testing. It was run like a drug rehabilitation programme, with meetings and groups throughout the day. Actual school classes were only held in the evenings between 6 and 9 p.m. Upon entering the school, each student was required to write a letter of apology to their parents (in Tina's case, to her guardians) before being able to graduate to the next level. Tina resisted this step for many months and they said that until she fulfilled it she could not communicate with us or anyone else. In order to reach the final level, the child had to become a Capo – one who tells on others who might try to escape. They were training military spies! Nothing she would learn in that school would get her into college or prepare her to make a living or have a healthy relationship. In my heart I was proud of her resistance, although I knew the price one paid for that.

When Micki returned to Florida, we talked about the possibility of finding an attorney to help extract my daughter from the school. I asked if her friend Christie knew anyone in the north-east who could help. Christie said that the ultimate question would be 'the best interests of the child'. She recommended an attorney in New York named Susan Bloom, who would take the case for a reduced rate. It took all I had left and Susan still ended up doing much of it pro bono. She filed a motion with the court and the judge appointed a special child advocate for Tina. She would go to the school to talk with the child and determine if Tina really wanted to leave. If she did, she could be placed in a proper boarding school. As it turned out, she was afraid to show her true feelings and so she remained with the devil she knew. I didn't want her to suffer or to have her spirit broken but there was nothing more I could do, and I felt defeated.

We were eventually successful in getting the court to order the school to provide me with monthly telephone reports as to how Tina was doing. Tina's school counsellor would accept my collect calls at prearranged times. By the time we got all this arranged it was May 1992. Meanwhile, Richard, Holly, Bert and Christie were working without pay on the habeas corpus for the federal courts, including the colour graphics that Micki had created. The brief had been submitted on 1 April 1991. It would be my final chance, 10,000 to one.

My friend Mike Shulimson was helping me handle all money-related matters. He was also acting as an adviser, like a Dutch uncle, to Eric. He played devil's advocate for me, trying to make sure I examined things from all sides before I jumped into anything – like hiring a lawyer or terminating Tina's guardianship. He visited on occasion, whenever he was in South Florida for business. He dressed nicely and smelled good and always brought me a new pen and candy to eat while we talked. He was such a kind man, but always so formal and proper. He always unwrapped the candy for me. He had nice hands, soft, and manicured like my dad's used to be. At the end of the visit he would shake my hand and give me a hug. I could smell his scent on my hand for a long time afterwards.

In August 1991 Micki's letters were filled with excitement and anxiety as the court date for the oral argument drew near. She told me how much our friendship meant to her and expressed her confidence in the persuasive and compelling new way in which the facts were to be presented for my appeal. She had done a huge amount of good work. She also praised Eric for being such a loving son to me, and expressed her concern for Tina and her wish to visit her at the school in Maine. She assured me that she would be willing to come to Florida to be with me on the spur of the moment, and prophetically added that she had a feeling she would be coming to Florida sooner than I thought.

In the event, Micki was back before the month was over. August was a busy month. They had the oral argument on my habeas corpus, which I did not get to attend personally but Micki did, of course. Also, the producer of the *20/20* show came down to meet with us. Micki laboured many hours convincing the producers of the show that this was not 'just another innocent person in prison' thing. The producers said that had already been done. She had to interest them in another angle, which was our childhood friendship and how we had been reunited thirty years later for her to rescue me and take on the system.

Micki returned again in October to do the interview with the *20/20* film crew. Micki had fought for them to talk with Brenda Isham, which they finally did. Brenda did an interview in which she not only courageously confessed to lying but also asked for my forgiveness. Brenda was determined to make amends fully and publicly. On national television, tears streaming down her cheeks, she confessed her youthful transgressions to the world. 'If they won't correct their own mistakes then I guess I'll have to tell my story.' No one in Wyoming had known about her past before. Brenda had become one courageous lady. I never got back in touch with her because the attorneys said it could be misconstrued. But I forgave her, admired her and thanked her in my heart many times over. The *20/20* team also did a re-creation of Micki's graphic representation of what really happened – even hiring trucks and going to the scene. Micki had agonized over whether to involve *20/20* because they could either champion your cause or destroy you overnight. But ultimately the decision as well as the consequences would be mine.

I was intimidated at first, by the equipment and by the man in front of me and his questions. And although I didn't know what the rest of it would be like since they had also interviewed the prosecutor and some of the detectives, I was still anxious to see it air before my case was decided. We hoped it would influence the outcome favourably, or at least make the public aware of what was going on. But as it turned out, the show was not broadcast until after my case was decided.

40

IN FEBRUARY 1992, with only one dissenting vote, the federal appeals court overturned my case. This time, both the sentence and my convictions were quashed. This was it! We had won! I was a free woman again!

But not exactly. You see, the state had the right to appeal. And they did. Meaning Mr Satz did. Although the federal court decision threw out almost everything the state had relied on previously except for Walter Rhodes's testimony. Even though it had been deemed worthless in the first appeal, they weren't about to concede. Their appeal would serve to keep me in prison a while longer. I could do another few months standing on my head – but short time is always harder. The short-timers lived a schizophrenic existence, bodily here but mentally there. I couldn't be too sure of anything but I knew I mustn't get too happy yet.

Feb. 7, 1992

Dear Franny [my friend the guard now living in Spain]

Today the 11th circuit court of appeals overturned my case and ordered a new trial! I won my appeal –

and I am so very happy! The state has 21 days in which to ask for a re-hearing – and then the decision will be final. After that, they have 90 days to either retry me or free me. My attorney has never won a federal appeal before so we don't know what to do next!

My son and his wife and the baby were here visiting so I got to share the news with them in person.

The state lost their appeal to reinstate my sentence and conviction. But they still had the right to take me back to trial again, even though there was hardly any basis left on which to do so. It had been more than sixteen years since the incident. After so much time it would be difficult to locate witnesses, and difficult for either side to present their case properly. To me it felt like they wanted to keep me in as long as they could. From a political perspective, they could not and would not concede that a mistake had been made. If that were the case, I would be entitled to sue the state of Florida for compensation. Politics and money against love and public opinion, with truth and justice standing helplessly, almost irrelevantly, in the middle, and with me on the sideline.

'76 MURDER CASE HAUNTS
STATE ATTORNEY

Miami Herald, Thursday, February 20, 1992 –
In 1976, prosecutor Michael Satz scored

first-degree murder verdicts in a sensational cop killing case, helping him win his first election to Broward state attorney a few months later.

Now, after 16 years, the case is back to haunt him – with allegations that the state concealed evidence and relied on questionable testimony to put Sonia Jacobs in prison and her lover Jesse Tafero in the electric chair.

'If this had come out before Jesse was executed, it would have made a difference,' Attorney Bruce Rogow said. 'I am delighted for Sonia and of course distressed for Jesse. But the law is not a science, it does not always add up.'

Satz last week angrily denied doing anything improper, pointing to a series of lower court rulings supporting his handling of the case. He said politics never played a role in his prosecutions. 'No one likes to have their integrity challenged,' said Satz, now running for a fifth term.

In a Feb. 6th opinion, the eleventh U.S. Circuit Court of Appeals overturned Jacobs' conviction. The court found that the state unknowingly used perjured testimony and didn't tell defense lawyers about a damning document (to the state's case against Sonia Jacobs) – a polygraph examiner's report supporting Jacobs' contention that she never shot police officers. Defense lawyers claim Satz won the celebrated case by concealing the report and plea bargaining with the man they believe pulled the trigger: Walter Rhodes.

'The state was so obsessed that it hurriedly – and tragically – made a plea bargain with the wrong man.'

Satz said he didn't think it was important. 'If I thought it was going to be an appellate point, obviously I would have given it to them,' he said. 'I don't think it would matter one bit.'

After the trials, Rhodes gave a sworn statement saying he lied, that he was the one who shot the officers. Then another prosecution witness said she also lied at Jacobs' trial and claimed she was threatened by Satz and Fort Lauderdale police.

Satz denies any threats and said he didn't think Isham was lying. 'She never told me it was gossip,' he said. The state appeals court found that the state didn't know Isham's testimony was perjured.

The court cast doubt about the credibility of Rhodes, and it would make another court hesitate to rely on Rhodes's word to convict Jesse, said Rogow, Tafero's attorney.

Despite the ruling, Satz says he's ready to try the case again. The state Attorney General's office is planning to challenge the

appellate opinion. If that effort fails, Satz will
be forced to recreate what happened 16 years
ago today.

Satz declined to say how he'll proceed.
'I'm not going to comment on what's going to
happen,' he said.

20/20 aired the segment about me shortly after the court
hearing. Although too late to influence the decision, it did
elicit a strong reaction concerning the fact that the state
had made a deal with the real killer. According to Richard,
this question was raised most strongly by the family of the
state trooper who had been killed. The word in the legal
community was that the family was very upset with the
prosecutor's office. I felt that that family and I were allied
in some way by a sense of betrayal. We had both been
betrayed by the system on which we had been taught to
rely. I felt badly for that family, having to suffer one hurt
upon another, but I also felt I was the last person in the
world that they would want to hear it from. When you
have hated someone for so long, believing with your
whole heart that they did something vile and evil and
unforgivable to you, even if later on you find out that it
wasn't so, the feeling has somehow embedded itself into
the fabric of your being, like a stain – like blood. They
were supposed to have gained satisfaction from Jesse's
execution. Now it was apparent that the state had executed
the wrong man, they would have to take back their satisfaction at his death. Can healing ever be achieved through
hatred?

The federal bond hearing was held in Miami in the federal district courthouse in April 1992. Micki made the calls and did all the necessary footwork. This time, I wasn't alone. This time, I had someone to watch over me and do what I could not. She asked everyone on my list of supporters, and then some, to be in the courtroom that day. She enlisted Mike Shulimson's aid in getting Eric ready – haircut, new suit, plane ticket. I was not allowed to go to court, but Micki told me it was filled to overflowing with an overwhelming array of supporters and the ever-present media. The rabbi was there with a bevy of Bubbes; friends from all across the state, former convicts and former schoolmates; even Micki's parents and her sister Karen were there. I didn't have much faith in the outcome of this hearing. It would not be a politically popular move to let me out on bond and, federal court or not, I didn't think it would happen. But we had to try. I had warned Eric that success was unlikely but I knew that the big brass band of his long-awaited dream come true had drowned out the voice of reason.

The judge, 'after due consideration', came to the conclusion that the federal court did not have jurisdiction over the matter of bond in this case. We would have to seek relief in the state court. That meant another bond hearing would have to be set, and that everyone had come there for nothing. Micki told me about it on the phone that night. She said that she and Christie were going back to Los Angeles for a while since it would take many months to get another bond hearing scheduled. We would talk more when she came to see me.

Micki sat across from me, patiently explaining everything that had happened at the bond hearing. She had got
permission for a special visit since she was now a designated part of the defence team, like a paralegal. She told
me how hurt and angry Eric was, and how sad. I could
picture his face as clearly as if I had been there.

As usual, the table was stacked with chips and sandwiches and sodas and chocolate milk with the addition of
my lunch tray, which had been delivered from the kitchen.
If you had a special weekday visit, they brought your
lunch tray to the VP. Today's main course for the BCI
inmates happened to be fish, a breaded square with white
flesh inside. I asked Micki if she would taste it to tell me if
that was really what fish tasted like. She looked so sad and
promised to feed me when I got out.

That night in my cell, I lay awake in the dark wondering if public opinion had changed enough to give me a
chance to get out on bond. I wasn't looking forward to
having to go through a new trial. I thought they should
just let me go after all the time I had done for something
they knew I didn't do. Richard's partner, José Quiñon, had
agreed to be my trial attorney. I heard he was awesome in
court. I felt confident that José wouldn't have let them do
what they did in the first trial, although we fully expected
them to be as dirty or worse, since their careers and lives
were in the balance now too. But I really just wanted to go
home, wherever that was. I wondered how it would be to
be free. And then I got kidnapped.

We had requested and obtained a court order that I was

not to be removed from the prison unless I was being taken directly to court for a hearing. Previously, when my sentence was changed to life, I had been told by a guard that there had been an aborted plot to kill me while I was being transported. There was still a lingering animosity among some of the law enforcement community partly because they used my case as a teaching tool in the Police Academy. This time, however, the plot was a bit more slick. The police showed up with what appeared to be a legitimate transport order. I had not yet received my copy of the federal court holding order but I told the dorm officer that I wasn't supposed to go anywhere. I had her call the superintendent's office to tell them about the court holding order. But they had no knowledge of it yet. And so they shipped me out, handcuffed and shackled in the back of a state van. I was taken to an out-of-the-way substation and placed in a cell with a plexiglass enclosure in the front. They could see everything – even when I used the toilet. I asked why I was there but no one knew. Later that evening, the sergeant, a man with bright red curly hair and a clipboard, came around. I asked him why I had been brought there and why I was being kept in this glass cage. He said, 'I don't know. Maybe somebody wants to get you. Maybe it's me.' OK, so now I knew I was there to be harassed and intimidated, at the very least. I asked to call my lawyer. He made a note of it, but said it would have to wait until the morning. I didn't sleep that night.

What no one knew, including me, was that Ms J had sent word to the optical lab about my abduction and someone there had made a call to my attorneys, who had been looking for me ever since. As it turned out, the judge who had been persuaded to issue the transport order was not aware of the federal holding order, and the judge who had issued the holding order was out of town that weekend. José Quiñon called on a judge who was a friend to issue an order to transport me back to BCI. So, even though it was the weekend, I was able to get back to the safety of the prison that had been my home and my community for almost seventeen years. I was sure I owed my life to Ms J and the person in optical who made the call. The state made one more attempt to take me out of the prison but they used an outdated transport order, which was noticed by the officer on duty at the back gate. Obviously, this was still a dirty fight.

The second bond hearing was held in July. Would I be celebrating my own freedom this time? I was allowed to be present at this one. All of the letters that people had written on my behalf had been submitted to the court – Rozzy, my former college roommate, had written one, and Mike Shulimson, and Eric, and Kay Tafero, and many others. It was like being privy to your own eulogy and I felt I hadn't really appreciated my friends enough before now. And many of those people showed up for the hearing – Dottie Marie, Colleen, Heidi, the rabbi from North Carolina and Rabbi Richter, Larry Achler (my former classification officer); and I had letters from former officers, and from friends all over the country. This time we were allowed to present witnesses to testify as to why I should be granted bond. Both rabbis took the stand; so

did Larry Achler. The judge had read all the letters we submitted and was struck by the one Heidi wrote. In it she
had stated that even though she was pregnant she would
be glad to trade places with me if they would let me out.
He asked for the person who had written that letter to
stand up so he could see who it was. Heidi, in full bloom
and the mystical majesty of pregnancy, slowly rose and
told the judge that she meant every word of what she had
said in her letter. He seemed impressed. I felt so full at the
gesture she was making for me, and so proud of my young
friend who had become a woman. There was more testimony. And then Micki took the stand. I watched with tears
in my eyes as she told the judge that she would be willing
to put up her house in Boston as collateral for my bond,
and that she would provide a place for me to live and be
responsible for me. Then the prosecutor challenged her.
Rather than attack me and my character, which would
have been an acceptable and expected assault tactic, he
attacked Micki, questioning her motives. I'm not sure
what her motives had to do with her reliability or the
safety of granting me bond, but, true to form, they were
going for the shot below the belt. He pointed out that she
was a film-maker and accused her of just wanting to make
a movie. Micki stood up in the witness box and answered
him from a place inside that reverberated with primal
force. 'Yes, I am a film-maker. But if you will let Sonia
Jacobs go today, I will give up any plans of ever making a
movie. That's how much it means to me to see her free.' I
was so struck by the passion of her words and the power
with which she faced down the prosecutor that I could no

longer control my tears. I knew how intimidating it was to be up there on the witness stand being attacked. But my little Micki wasn't letting them intimidate her. She was Joan of Arc! I stood in awe of my friend.

The courtroom was silent in the wake of Micki's powerful retort. Then they applauded! It was magnificent. The judge called for order. Micki was told she could step down from the stand. We smiled at each other as she took her seat in the gallery. I felt such love for this wonderful woman, for all of these wonderful people who were my friends. The judge denied bond but it almost didn't matter. I think I smiled all the way back to BCI.

After the hearing, on 10 July 1992, the media reported that 'about fifty' of my family and friends, including my son, had crowded into the courtroom to try to persuade District Judge Edward Davis to release me on bail. They quoted Eric as saying, 'My mother has been locked up for sixteen years and now they say they are finally going to give her a fair trial. Great!'

41

In August another petition for bail went before Judge Zeidwig, who would preside over the hearings to follow. He said he wanted to study the 1976 trial transcript before making his decision. At this point, I had been in prison for more than sixteen and a half years. The media reported that 'witnesses who implicated Jacobs have recanted their testimony' and Walter Rhodes had, as the press so aptly put it, 'spent the past decade recanting his recantations'. José Quiñon, who would lead the defence team should there be a new trial, openly accused Michael Satz, now Broward state attorney, of 'blatant conflict of interest'. Satz's chief assistant, Ralph Ray, had been Rhodes's defence attorney in 1976. Satz was the prosecutor. José pointed out that the link involving Satz, Ray and Rhodes was unethical. We filed a motion asking Judge Zeidwig to recuse Satz's office and appoint outside prosecutors. Bail was ultimately denied.

The recusal hearings, asking for the prosecutor and his office to be removed from my case and replaced by an uninvolved team from another county, were set to begin on Thursday, 1 October. The prosecutor should have recused himself because it had become so personal. So should the judge in my trial. I felt if I could get an honest prosecutor, like Janet Reno, who was the state's attorney in Dade County, I would have no fear of going to a new trial. But under the circumstances, it was sure to be another dirty deal. We had already heard that a 'professional' witness had been contacted and her payment was being negotiated. Word was that she had got a new white couch for her living room the last time she testified for the prosecution.

Micki began to get calls from people – well-wishers and supporters – with information about the prosecutor. Apparently, the public defender's office had noticed a pattern in the use of 'jailhouse informants' and plea bargaining in capital cases handled by Mr Satz. This set Micki on a course which would ultimately prove to be the prosecutor's undoing. She began questioning everything. Richard, Holly and José were preparing for a new trial while Micki was plugging away at every bit of information we already had, convinced that there was more than what we had already seen. She and Christie went over every piece of paper and made a list of things that were mentioned but not given over to the defence in the discovery proceedings prior to this point. Formal demands for complete discovery and disclosure were filed. Boxes and boxes of previously unknown material began to arrive. Micki, with Christie's help, went through every one of them.

José had been happy with Micki's help thus far. But they had a terrible falling out over Micki's insistence that they get hold of a true copy of the original polygraph test.

She told me what happened. They were in José's office arguing. Micki's point was that the initial plea bargain with Walter Rhodes was made on the basis of his passing the polygraph test administered by an examiner named Carl Lord, who worked for Satz at the time. We had seen the report saying Rhodes passed but no one had ever seen the actual test. 'How can we believe it when they say he passed the polygraph test when we know they lied about other things?' Micki kept insisting. She was becoming overemotional and José responded by telling her it was his case and I was his client and he was in charge. It was his decision to save the entire issue of the polygraph test for trial. He explained that trial strategy was very important and this was just a preliminary hearing. But Micki couldn't understand why we wouldn't want to use it to show that Satz should be recused. Then we could get a fair prosecutor and simply present the evidence of wrongdoing. She insisted that they at least get hold of the test and look at it. José absolutely refused to be dictated to by this woman who questioned his expertise. He ordered her to leave. In her zeal, she threatened to jump out of the window in his office. He finally gave in. They would get hold of the actual test. I wished I had been there! Poor Micki. She was an emotional wreck by this time. Having taken on the responsibility for making sure everything that needed to be done would be done, the proximity of the conclusion to all her efforts kept her in a constant state of near panic.

José hired an ex-police officer by the name of George Slattery, who was known nationally for his expertise in interpreting polygraph results. José and Holly went to his office. Later that night they called Micki to tell her that she was right. The results of the test were skewed – where the polygraph indicated yes, Rhodes had said no, and vice versa. In describing the test, Slattery used the words 'Mickey Mouse' and said that at best it was inconclusive. Certainly no one could say the man had passed the test from those results. Shortly afterwards, José took a deposition from Carl Lord, the original polygraph examiner, and during it Lord was served with a subpoena to appear at the hearing.

The recusal hearings began with Walter Rhodes taking the stand. He was chained to his chair, and we were glad of it when at one point in the questioning he became agitated. He said that the *20/20* show had upset his parents and that it was all Micki's fault. 'There she is!' he shrieked, spittle spewing from his mouth. Trying to rise out of his seat, pointing a finger at Micki, who was seated in the gallery, he went on, 'Sonia's knight in shining panties!' There was an audible intake of breath, like a wave receding from shore, and all eyes turned to the judge, whose own eyes were wide in astonishment. Micki's parents, who were in the gallery that day, were sure he was going to kill their daughter.

José spent the next two days taking Mr Rhodes apart. He was truly a psychopath and the years in prison had stripped him of all pretence otherwise. José asked Rhodes if he ever told the truth and Rhodes replied that he only told the truth under oath and then only during a certain two-year period.

During these hearings, in open court, the judge had said he had known Satz for twenty years and knew him to be honest. They had gone to parties together and he had helped with Satz's campaign, including giving financial contributions. His wife had made the food for campaign meetings.

José and Micki discussed asking the judge to recuse himself, too. It was my call to make because, of course, I would be the one to bear the brunt of the consequences. I was no longer so naïve as to think that the consequences wouldn't have a spillover effect. I had been a bit shocked at the judge's admission. But I found myself admiring him for having been so honest. I decided that I would rather have an honest man, even if he did have his prejudices. If he was willing to be honest then he would have to go with the evidence, and that evidence was overwhelmingly in favour of granting the recusal of Satz. I would keep the judge.

I was chained to my chair every day in court. I told Micki it was because they had been losing a lot of chairs lately. It was a Friday night and they were short of bailiffs to escort Rhodes and me, so we ended up being escorted from the courtroom together. We were taken to a stairwell and I wondered if he was thinking of trying to throw me down the stairs, or if he was afraid I would do something to him. We were both in handcuffs and he had his prosthetic leg but still he was a lot bigger than I was. Rhodes was led down the stairs first. I guess our escorts felt the same way I did.

It was strange being so close to him. In a way, he was as

542

*responsible as Satz for Jesse's execution. Now everyone would
know Jesse didn't do it but it was too late for him – and for his
mother, and for his child. And for me . . .*

The hearings reconvened on Monday, 5 October,
my father's birthday. Funny how I didn't remember my
parents' birthdays when they were alive but now I never
missed one. I felt like they were there with me in court.
The judge came in and the day's contest began with the
introduction of the polygraph material and Michael Satz,
the prosecutor, taking the stand. The polygraph as the
basis for the Rhodes plea bargain was discussed and José
did a brilliant job of conducting the examination. The
next day, Tuesday, José introduced what came to be
the coup de grâce – the previously undisclosed statement
of a guard who had heard Walter Rhodes's confession to
having done the murders. It had been buried for ten years,
and had, only recently, been delivered up in a box of
papers. Micki had found it. If Jesse's attorneys had been
made aware of the guard's statement they could have used
it to save his life because, having been made by an official,
it would have been considered credible. Jesse was killed
because someone had hidden that evidence. Tampering
with evidence in a capital case is a serious felony – and
when it ends in death isn't that murder? Mr Satz denied
any prior knowledge of the guard's statement. But since he
was ultimately responsible for his staff and could be held
accountable for their actions, he was livid. He asked for a
recess and it was granted.

We were sitting in the courtroom waiting for the hearing to resume when one of the prosecutor's staff came to

speak with my attorney. José gave us a look and a hand gesture, letting us know he was as puzzled as we were, and followed the emissary out into the hall.

Twenty minutes later, José came back looking like a balloon, about to burst with news. He strode quickly over to the table. 'This is the first time in my career that something like this has happened. OK, here's the deal. He wants you to say that Rhodes didn't do anything. That's the deal. You say that Rhodes didn't do anything and you can be eating a steak dinner tonight. You would leave right from the courthouse and not have to go back to the prison at all. Free. Tonight. Right now. What do you say?'

We were all stunned into a momentary silence. Micki was the first to recover but José put up a hand to silence her. 'This has to be Sunny's decision.' I looked from one face to the other. There was no need for words because the answers were in their eyes. Micki broke in with an acerbic 'I can't believe he had the nerve to ask her to do that!'

'Listen to me,' José interjected, softly but with deep conviction. 'I am the Minister of War. People do not hire me to make deals. If they want to make a deal, I send them somewhere else. I do not make deals. I make war. This is known to my colleagues as well. So it is a shock to me to receive this kind of message. But it is something to consider. They may not make another offer, and a new trial could take a long time.' He paused. 'You know how dirty they can be. And you never know how a jury will react . . . but, as I said, I am not a deal-maker. I prefer going to court.' He drew in a long breath. 'This has to be your call, Sonia. What do you say?'

I held a brief conference between me, myself and, of course, Death, who had become my constant companion and my connection to those who could no longer speak for themselves. I knew I would not do what they had asked.

'I won't lie for them. If I say Rhodes didn't do it, that's like saying Jesse did. They took his life and now they want to take his memory. They took my whole life from me, and now they want my soul. They want me to give up the one thing they couldn't take from me – my self-respect – my dignity. I would love to leave from this courtroom and never have to go back to prison.' I took a breath. 'It's not like I don't have a life, you know. I have a life in there. It's not the one I would have chosen, but it is a productive life nevertheless. And I feel good about myself. I teach people, I have friends, I am a respected member of my community. And besides I don't eat steak. I'm a vegetarian. Tell Mr Satz to put it up on the table because I'm gonna cut it off at trial.'

As we were talking, the assistant prosecutor came back in with the guard who had been stationed right outside.

'Are you ready?' José asked, placing a strong hand on my shoulder.

I told them to take me back to prison. The guard picked up his cue, unlocking the handcuffs from the chair and locking them around my wrists.

* * *

I don't remember the ride back to prison after turning down the deal. I felt good when I left the courtroom, clothed in righteous indignation. But afterwards, back in my chains and shackles, the consequences of what might have been a rash act began to seep in through my wrists and ankles. The waist chain to which my handcuffs were attached didn't allow my hands to reach my face and so the tears simply gathered at the point of my chin and fell to my lap. Did I do the right thing?

The van pulled into the prison through the rear gate. I felt the relief I always felt to be 'home' again. It was familiar and safe, no matter what else it was. Now I would have the chance to settle the churning in my guts and my head and figure out what I had really done.

That evening at dinnertime, I went out to the ball field to walk. It was the only place left where you could be alone. I walked out to the furthest end of the field and began to cry. Maria saw me and left the after-dinner strollers to see how things had gone for me that day in court. I was absorbed in my struggle and did not see her so she called my name as she approached. Maria's senses were fine-tuned and we had become as close as sisters. In a patois of English and Spanish, I explained what had happened as we walked slowly around the field. Maria stopped walking and turned to face me.

'Sonia, you know you did the right thing,' she said. 'There are miracles. People don't see them any more because they don't believe in them. But you know, Sonia, you don't have to sell your soul. Not now. Not after you have come so far. I love you, Sonia, and I wouldn't tell you this if I didn't believe it with my heart.' She placed her right hand over her left breast, patting it softly.

'But Maria, I could have been home tonight, free, with my children. I hope you're right, Mamita. I'll fast tomorrow, and pray and read the scriptures. It's Yom Kippur. I think Micki will be here to see me tomorrow too.'

Back in the dorm, I sat on my bed trying to switch tracks from secular to spiritual. It was Rosh Hashanah, the holiest time of the Jewish year, and tomorrow the holiest of days. At 11 p.m., count time, I got out a picture of my mom and dad. Did I do the right thing? Am I throwing my life away again?

Today I had felt I was being loyal to Jesse but really I was being loyal to myself – what I believed in. I put the prayer book and my parents' picture under my pillow and went to sleep.

I got up early the next morning to dress for the visit and went down to wait with Ms J. Usually she was like a little kid, clapping her hands and excitedly asking for all the details. These days she was more subdued. She hadn't been feeling well lately. She hadn't been well since her appendix burst a few years earlier.

'I don't know what I'll do when you leave.' Ms J was always sure I would get out. 'You are my whole life. I don't think I'll want to live any more.'

I had never heard Ms J sound depressed or hopeless before. She was a fighter, proud, full of sugar and spice and spit and vinegar.

'Ms J, I'll need your help more than ever if I get out. You have to call me every night, tell me what to wear, how to act. And anyway, you're going to be next. Remember, I told you I'd get you out too. Micki will help me. You have to come to live with me. What would I do without you?'

Ms J smiled, a bit watery but an improvement.

'And anyway,' I added quickly, 'I'm not going anywhere yet. I refused to leave! I like it here, right?'

'You could go to Kansas to see Ben, the guard from the jail I told you about. He knows I didn't kill my husband.'

'That's right.'

My name was announced on the PA system. 'Sonia Jacobs to the visiting park.'

'Have a good visit!' Ms J waved cheerily and I ran for the park.

Micki was sitting where she could watch the door. When she saw me she waved and talked to the people next to her who waved too. More supporters. Micki never rested. She was so passionate about what she believed in. She lived and breathed it. I could see how she had got into all those political demonstrations in the '60s. I wondered who she would have been friends with in prison ... Marti, the revolutionary, maybe? Mary Dalih, the crusader?

As I emerged from the strip-search room, Micki got up and came towards me and we hugged.

It was a serious visit. It was the first time I didn't eat in the visiting park. I was still fasting.

'Did I do the right thing, Mick?'

548

'Sunny, I want you to go to trial and be exonerated. Your children will understand what you did and be as proud of you as I am.'

We went on to talk about Tina and the situation with the school, how Eric was doing, how crazy Rhodes had acted on the stand, and how supportive Micki's mom and dad and sister had been. Micki told me how much support we had got from so many people. Christie had become part of the defence team, doing much of the research and helping Richard with the writing too. Micki seemed to attract extraordinary people.

The visit was over in the blink of an eye as always. I spent the rest of that day and the next doing my Yom Kippur thing, fasting and reading from the prayer book in Hebrew.

I prayed as hard as I could for guidance, for favour, for the strength to deal with the outcome of this new trial, whatever it would be. I said Kaddish for my parents, Uncle Joe, Jesse and Irish John, who had been killed in a fight over a woman a couple of years earlier. No matter what other paths I follow, Judaism echoes within the core of my being, like the hum in the universe left over from the Big Bang. I don't always practise it or follow its teachings, but it is always with me. Zen is my personal choice. It resonates with my nature. It was Zen that brought me through the Valley of the Shadow of Death; it was Judaism that held the Shadow at bay. And so, on this holiest of days, I pay my full respect to my ancestors and to my Creator, whom I now know I am in partnership with in creating my life and in the effects I have had on the lives

549

of others. I know my responsibility by now although I haven't yet acknowledged or accepted the full impact of what that means.

We broke the fast in the dining hall after dark – Cory, Donna and I. We each read a little from the prayer book and then we ate for the next hour until we were full as ticks. We were escorted back to our respective dorms. I was almost comatose and fell into my bunk and into a deep sleep.

42

THE NEXT DAY, Friday, I went to work as usual. I did my work as usual. But I was waiting for a sign I had been praying for, a call, a message. None came. I was in the bosses' office showing my supervisors how to use a program on the new computer system. It was almost 4 p.m. Recall would soon end my agonizing – the day would be done and nothing more would happen before the weekend, which I would have to spend in limbo. The phone rang. The supervisor answered. Probably her daughter who usually called around 3.30 p.m.

'Sonia, they want you at the dorm. You're going out to court.'

'Now?'

'They said to hurry because the van is waiting for you at the rear gate.'

I could feel myself hyperventilating. No one gets called to court at 4 p.m. on a Friday unless they are being released because the jails don't like to keep us 'convicts' over the weekend.

'Well, get going, Sonia. They're waiting for you. I'll write you a pass.'

'OK!' I grabbed my stuff – purse, coffee cup, pens.

'Hey, if I don't come back, give the rest of my stuff to the girls, OK?'

'Just go, Sonia. Don't worry about that. Everything will be fine. You're going home, you know that? I can feel it, and you know I can feel these things! Forget about this stupid shit! You're going home!'

'Thanks, Mrs George.' There are sparkling smiles, and shining tears, and hope in every eye as we all say our good-byes and good lucks.

As I turned the corner I could see the van waiting outside the rear gate. I speedwalked towards the dorm. A guard was waiting on the path, signalling to me to hurry up. I began to run. As I got to where she was standing, she joined me, running by my side.

'Pack up all your stuff and we'll have a couple of carts to load it in when you bring it out. Just hurry!'

We jogged up the front steps into the dorm.

'I'll need boxes,' I said as I kept on going down the hall towards my room. The officer stopped in the office to get the paperwork ready. They would have to inventory all my property. My roommate, Betty, was already there, separating things into piles – state stuff in one pile and everything else into the boxes to go with me.

'Hurry up, Sonia. You're going home, girl!'

I had to do my combination lock twice before I could get into my locker for the rest of my stuff. I had prepared a list of instructions just in case, which I now gave to Betty.

'Here's what to do with my things if I don't come back by Wednesday. You get most of my things. Don't pack my comforter or my pillow.'

'Thanks. I'll miss you.' We hugged.

'Take care of yourself and Ms J for me, will you?'

'You know I will. Get going!'

The officer was calling for me to start bringing down my boxes and finish the paperwork in the office.

Ms J came up to the office to say goodbye.

'Remember what I told you, Ms J, and don't forget to call Micki's number.'

She gave me a hug. I saw Annie McC, another of the lifers, in the doorway. She had come to see that Ms J would be OK.

'Here, Annie, you can have these cigarettes. I don't want them in my nice clean life!'

We push the cart along the street towards the rear gate. There are inmates lining the walkway, even though it is still work time. The word has spread and they are coming out to say goodbye. Someone is going home. People gather to participate in the miracle. A lifer is leaving. They are clapping, and some are crying, as we pass by. 'Go get 'em, Sonia!' 'Good luck, baby!' 'Go kiss your children!'

People touch me as I go by, as if by doing so whatever grace I have received will rub off on them. I am crying. It is so beautiful. Even women I don't get along with are there, wishing me well. It is a magical moment.

We reach the rear gate. There is a van with two uniformed officers from the Broward Sheriff's Office waiting for me. Bring on the chains! The BCI officers load my boxes on to the van while the BSO officers fit me with my travelling jewellery – waist chains with the black box and attached handcuffs, leg chains with the cuffs that lock around your ankles. I always wear socks for trips outside otherwise the cuffs eat up your ankles. They give me a hand up into the back of the van and close the doors behind me.

We are on the way. They are racing along the access road. I can see the prison through the dust behind the van. It is fading like some dusty dream. I know I will not see it again. I don't know what's happened but I know something has changed. I feel as if I am surrounded by spirits. I am not alone in the back of this van. My mother and father are with me. Jesse is with me. Uncle Joe and my grandparents are with me. They are all there, telling me it is safe. I will not be killed on the way. This is the end of it and I am going home now. But where, I wonder . . . but the moment is now. I have to keep my awareness on the moment. We make it to the courthouse in record time. I feel infused by love. As we pull into the parking lot of the courthouse, I feel the spirits withdraw. It is all right. They are not far. I can still feel their presence, like a warm cloud. I feel much more calm now.

The officers collect me from the back of the van, removing the shackles from my legs. 'We have to hurry. Your attorneys are waiting for you in the judge's chambers.' Well, OK! That sounds real good. We enter the building at a clip, heading for the elevators. We go up to the courtroom and I am taken to an anteroom. My attorneys are there. They thank the officers, who then leave, closing the door behind them.

'They've offered you what's called an Alford plea, a plea of convenience.'

'Whose convenience?'

'Theirs, of course. But listen and then tell me what you think . . .'

This time the deal is that they don't want me to say anything. In fact, I am not allowed to say anything during the proceeding. They will read into the record what they would have presented if we had gone back to trial. Also, I have to allow them to read an adjudication of guilt of a lesser degree into the record to prevent me from being able to sue for false imprisonment or whatever later. In effect, I am to sit there in silence while they cover their arses. It's all about money and not taking responsibility. I will end up as a convicted felon with a charge of second degree still on the books. I will be a free woman. Clean break. Free to go. I could be with my children again. I could be with my granddaughter. I would be free.

I am thinking about it. I am forty-five years old. I am a grandmother. I am tired of fighting. I can leave that to the younger ones whom I have taught to use the law library to fight the system. I am an old war horse and it is time to retire, as long as I can leave with my self-respect and dignity intact. That is how I feel. As far as a conviction remaining on the records, well, whoever believes I am innocent will continue to believe it and whoever believes I am guilty will continue to believe that. Even if I went back to a new trial, they would just say I had a good attorney who got me off. I want to be free . . .

'I'll do it. I'll take their deal. A plea of convenience – not mine. I'm tired and I want to be with my children and my grandchild.' I am firmly resolved, but I am waiting for the reaction of my dear friends. Their opinion matters to me but the decision is mine, as will be the consequences. Whoever is on the bus is on the bus. At least half of my life is over and my children haven't had a mother in a long time. They are adults now. I was robbed of their childhood. At least I can be there for them now.

We entered the courtroom. I saw Micki in her usual place. She looked so uptight. I had been worried about how she would take it if I ended up staying in prison. It would be almost worse for her than it would be for me. She had invested her entire being in championing my cause. She had nothing in reserve. I had a life to go back to if worst came to worst. I was a respected elder in my community. I had a position and a family of sorts. Life on the outside would go on as usual. But for Micki it would be devastating – not only to have been defeated by the evils of society but to have failed her friend. It is hard being a champion, a fighter for causes and hopeless 10,000-to-one cases like mine. It's hard investing your heart and soul. But that is what it takes to fight against those kinds of odds.

After the announcement that we were ready to accept the Alford plea, everybody came back into the courtroom and took their places. It was like a staged performance, an operetta. The prosecutor stood before the court and delivered his prepared speech, the litany of reasons, excuses, justifications – and all the while I sat there listening, I was trying to think of something I could get away with saying. I couldn't just let him off without making my feelings about it known somehow. And then it came to me . . .

'Your Honour!' I felt a severe warning pinch on my arm administered by a horrified Holly.

The judge acknowledged me, allowing me the rope with which to hang myself and the deal I rode in on.

'Your Honour, I have a bad taste in my mouth. Could I have a drink of water?'

He knew – I could see it in his face that he knew – but who could deny a person a sip of water at such a moment?

'Bailiff, bring Ms Jacobs a glass of water.'

The bailiff poured and I drank – just a sip – and thanked him prettily. I'd had my say and I felt content as the prosecutor continued on with his speech, and when he was through, the judge read back the plea we had agreed to accept.

He said I had done approximately 16 years 233 days and asked if that was correct. It sounded like an awfully long time. I started to cry, telling him that it seemed about right to me and I would take his word for it. Then he explained that he would read a charge of a lesser degree into the record and I would get time served and be free to go. That was all. I was free! The bailiff came over to undo my handcuff from the chair and I remember José's firm hand on my shoulder and looking up into his eyes to see the best grin I had ever seen on a grown man's face! And Micki was struggling with a matron to get past the barrier to reach me. It was pandemonium!

The bailiff said I would have to be fingerprinted, again, and that the process of my release would take a couple of hours so my friends might as well go to a bar nearby to wait. I was led to the front of the courtroom, feeling like a helium balloon, grinning my face off!

I was now carrying the piece of green paper that said I was a free woman. Clutching it to my chest, I held it like a talisman before me – against whatever evil forces might try to take it from me, or send me back, or kill me before I could step through the doors into the fourth dimension. Trust was something that would come much later, very gradually and in very limited circumstances.

After the ritual fingerprinting, we left the courtroom by a side door, only to be diverted to the property room. It was not the usual routine. Normally the prisoner is taken back to the holding cell while the paperwork is processed. But this time they were ready to release me without any further complications. They wanted me gone.

The matron joined us at the desk where we stopped to pick up my two boxes of personal property. They contained all I owned in the world – two white shirts, two pairs of jeans, six pairs of panties, four bras, six pairs of socks, two pairs of sneakers and a Walkman radio. I was given a paper to sign, saying that I had taken possession of the two boxes and releasing the county from responsibility for the contents. The bailiff and the matron each took one box and we proceeded towards the door. We crossed the large corridor and the bailiff held open the door for us. They piled the boxes into my arms and told me to 'Have a nice life!' The whole thing had taken fifteen minutes.

Freedom was right on the other side of the glass doors in front of which I was standing. I stepped out—

* * *

Freedom! Inhaling it into my nostrils. Filling myself with it. Letting it wash over me inside and out. It does smell different! I knew it would! Perhaps it is my nostrils that are different now. In any case, it is the freshest breath of air I have ever taken since the first moment of my birth.

I am all aglitter. My whole body is made of twinkling sparkles of light; my breath, swirls of bright colours. Heart singing, mind humming, vibrating the air around me, trying to keep my molecules from flying off in all directions.

The door closed behind me. I began to laugh. Yes! Yes! Free! I held the green paper that said I was 'free'. That was my passport, my lifeline, my 'right' to be here. But what did that mean? No one had told me what to do next. What did one do? I put the boxes down and looked around. I was in a large courtyard. There was a stairway leading down to somewhere. Two policemen were standing in the corner smoking. They didn't seem to notice me. A few people were sitting around on benches at the far end. There was a young couple with a child in diapers, a little boy. 'That feels like my speed right now, a child's speed. Let's see how I do.' I took two steps into my new world and paused. There was no shouting, no gunfire. No one seemed to care. I gave the green paper in my hand a quick squeeze and walked out into the courtyard. The parents gave me a cursory glance as I passed by, nothing more – still no shouting. I approached the boy. Wearing a disposable diaper and sucking his thumb, he raised his eyes to look into mine. I smiled. He did not move. I walked slowly up to him and waved in a small way. 'Hello.'

He did not run. I smiled again and this time he smiled back, grinning around his thumb. 'This is good. Doing OK so far.' I slowly brought up my hand to wave goodbye. He took off on his tiny, bare feet, running towards his parents. They were not paying attention. He stopped midway, turning to look back at me. I waved again. He waved back with his free hand, still sucking on the other.

Feeling a bit more solid now as a result of this brief but successful contact as a free person, I decided to see what was down the stairs, heading towards them slowly. My boxes were sitting by the door. I wondered if they would be safe there. Maybe the two policemen on break would be willing to keep an eye on them for me for a while. I dared to ask, but they were going right back inside, they said, and couldn't be responsible.

'Could you tell me what's down those stairs?'

They looked at each other, back at me and then at the boxes. I had called attention to my newly arrived status. I brought the paper to my chest, holding it close, hoping they would see it and know that I was allowed to be there.

'The parking lot is down there,' the first one said, flicking his cigarette away in a long arc towards the stairs.

'Thank you. Is it OK then to just leave the boxes here for a while?'

The other one shrugged and made a twisted face that said the question was irrelevant. No one cared. I liked that. No reaction to my leaving the pavilion. They must know what the green paper meant. I was allowed to decide to go down the stairs. I was allowed to decide to risk leaving my boxes. 'Thank you,' I repeated for good measure.

Poised at the top, like a high diver, preparing myself for the big leap, elation began to displace apprehension. And then I was running, flying down those stairs. I hit the street at a dead run, laughing and waving my green paper at the people coming and going. 'Hello! Isn't it a beautiful day!' I ran past them, out of the parking lot and on to the street.

The world opened up and I poured myself into it – the eclipse that had darkened my world had passed. The sun and the moon were both waiting there to greet me. Suspended at opposite ends of the horizon, like proud parents watching their newborn taking her first steps, smiling down upon me with great pride, sharing in my celebration!

So, the Universe has provided once again. I am never alone any more. This was another birth, with only mother Moon and father Sun in attendance. It was a private affair, set up by the Universe to be that way – no doctors, no lawyers, no media, no midwives, not even Micki. All the joy and adrenaline I had been keeping suppressed bubbled up and exploded outward. Laughing louder, running faster, feeling the wind caressing my face, making whistling sounds in my ears, I was rushing headlong into my new life in this bright and shining new world! I didn't know where everybody was, but this was my moment and, apparently, the Cosmic Humour in its infinite wisdom had planned for this moment to be mine and mine alone.

Epilogue

*I*N 1976, WHEN I WENT IN, *I was a young mother, a daughter and a wife. When I came out, in 1992, I was an orphan, a widow and a grandmother.*

I didn't do any of the things I thought I would when I left prison. Everyone has an agenda of what they're going to do when they get out but most of those things didn't happen until much later, except for my bubble bath.

I went to Holly and Richard's house in Coral Gables and ate Chinese food. I spent the night at the Fontainebleau Hotel on the ocean. All the girls were there – Colleen, Dottie Marie, Heidi, Micki and Kay Tafero. I didn't sleep a wink! Too stimulated.

In the morning I ran on the beach and then directly into the open sea, enveloped and washed and purified. Only the sea could be powerful enough to wash away the experience that seemed to shroud the very essence of my being. The sea, with its saline properties like tears, dissolved it and washed it away. A huge celebration party that night. Rabbi Richter and Rabbi Rocklin were there, Micki and her sister and parents, all the attorneys and loads of well-wishers. Linda came by briefly but she didn't come in.

* * *

Micki drove me to visit Naranda at her ashram in nearby Hallandale. She spent the day with us as we walked around the grounds, picked herbs from her garden and sat on the floor of her room, talking. She wore only orange, the colour of devotion. Her hair, long and pure white, was tied in a topknot with an orange cord. Something about being in her presence was both calming and exhilarating. For the first time since my release, I felt grounded in the familiar. She was my Universal Mother and I remembered who I was. I would return to spend weeks at a time with Naranda, sleeping at her feet and walking at her side, learning, observing, absorbing. She would give me teacher training instructions, and meditate with me and give me a spiritual name.

Before we left, Naranda gave me a necklace of wooden beads that she rubbed with special oil. As we drove away, Sri Naranda Devi stood in the driveway on one foot with one hand twined around the other in the Eagle pose, sending us a farewell blessing with her energy. I could feel her. Micki looked in the rear-view mirror and said she wished she had a camera. But I don't think a camera could have captured the aura of benevolent strength that issued forth from that little old woman wrapped in orange cloth and balanced on one foot. I love you, Naranda.

With Micki as guide, I began my journey up the eastern coast of the United States. First stop North Carolina, to be reunited with my son and his family and my brother and his family; then on to Maine, to try to reconnect with my daughter. I wasn't sure how I was going to do that – I would find a way. Now our plane was landing and my son was waiting for me at the gate.

'Mom! Mom!' he shouted and waved as we appeared. He put his head on my shoulder as we embraced.

'I'm so glad you're finally home, Mom.'

'So am I, Eric.'

And then I felt Claudia's little hand. 'Grandma!' I scooped my three-and-a-half-year-old granddaughter up in my arms and Deb, Eric's wife, joined in with a big welcoming hug and herded us out of the airport to the car.

Claudia said solemnly, 'Grandma, I know you couldn't come here before because you were lost. But now you're not lost any more.'

'Yes, Claudia, that's true – and I'll never be lost again.'

Underneath the waves of joy was an undercurrent of sorrow, always there to remind me of what was missing. My mother, my father, Jesse . . . and Tina. But I have always chosen to ride the waves rather than to dwell on the bottom, so I rode the next wave of joy that came over the horizon.

Claudia reminded me that I had promised to read to her and sleep with her in her bed. It was almost like starting over where I had left off, reading bedtime stories and singing lullabies. As we cuddled together in the warm darkness, I slept for the first time in the five days since my release.

From Eric's house we went to see my brother and his family. They met us at a restaurant. His children were grown up, like mine. It was amazing to be there with them, in a restaurant, eating together.

It would take many years for all the issues that had been growing up around our relationships to come to fruition. Each would ripen and manifest in its own time and in its own way.

Then we headed for Maine to try to see my daughter. There was snow on the ground when we arrived. It had been a long time since I had seen snow. I had the impulse to play in it but I wanted to get ready for my appointment at the school. They said I was to come alone – Micki wasn't to be allowed on the school grounds. I wore the light greenish-blue outfit that Kay had chosen for me and did my yoga breathing exercises on the way. The school was located in the woods. I was dropped off at the front gate and, after a silent prayer, I walked in to face whatever was waiting for me with open heart and open mind.

I was escorted to a room filled with people sitting around a long table. I was shown to the end seat. People were introduced – teachers, counsellors, administrators, etc. Then they explained that my daughter, Christina, would be brought in, with a friend of her choice, to speak to me. OK. I accepted this arrangement. One of them went to get my daughter. I sat in the chair trying not to hold my breath, watching for her to come through the door. I had no idea what she would look like. It had been a while since I had seen even a photograph. The door opened and I sat up straighter, holding the breath I had taken in antici-pation. She was beautiful. Shy, alert, nervous. She slid her eyes sideways for a brief glance before proceeding to the chair offered to her at the other end of the table. Her friend sat beside her. One of the moderators encouraged her to 'tell your mother why you are mad at her'. She hesitated and was encouraged further until finally she spoke.

'But I'm not mad at her any more. I was mad at her because I thought she lied to me. She always said she would come home – for my birthday, for Christmas, for my graduation – but she never did. So I thought she was lying to me. But now she's here – so I'm not mad at her any more.'

She asked if she could take me to her room. She wanted me to meet her friends. They gave permission and off we went, together. Her friend became very animated and Tina took charge, telling me about everything she wanted me to see. She introduced me to all her friends as her mother. At one point she clarified that I was her biological mother, as distinct from the mother who had raised her since Grandma and Grandpa died. Sherry and Bob, who had fostered her, were her mom and dad now. Jesse was gone, and I retained the title of biological mom. OK, for now. We were allowed to go for lunch under the supervision of one of the school employees. Tina chose an Italian restaurant. I smiled at that. It was a magical time and she slipped me a note during the meal. She called me 'Mom' and said she loved me. When we said goodbye back at the school, I knew in my heart and soul that we would find our way back to each other again, some day.

For me there was no home to go back to, though Eric had said there would always be a home for me with him. And I was supposed to be the elder now . . . matriarch of the family. Micki invited me to live in California. Before leaving for the West Coast, we went to New York City. I wanted to go to the bookstore that Jesse and I had talked about and Micki wanted me to meet some of the people whom she had enlisted for the Defense Fund. One of them, Rosie, became a lifelong friend and helped me through many of the healing crises of the psyche that I would face.

New York City is a big, fast-paced metropolis where a certain level of competence is expected. Yet there were so many things I wasn't used to doing for myself, simple things that most people wouldn't think about at all. Opening doors was one of them. We would get to a doorway and I would stop and wait for someone to open it. My hand would never move from my side. I would look to Micki, or whoever I was with, to open it so we could go inside, like a well-trained dog. I was aware that I was doing it, but I did not yet have the self-confidence to break the habit. That would pass in time. I would still hesitate and look, but then I would push the door open and go inside. Answering phones was another thing I wasn't comfortable with doing. Crossing streets was another. It is amazing what simple things we find difficult at first. I remembered hearing about a girl who got stuck halfway across a street and had to be led the rest of the way by a kind stranger. It was a problem for which I was prepared.

Coming from an environment where nothing moved at a pace faster than a walk, the rush of people and traffic on the streets of New York City was overwhelming. Cars going by at 40 mph were intimidating. Micki and I crossed one street after another until I finally felt I had mastered it.

That mindset, having to feel like I had 'permission' to go somewhere, stayed with me for a long time. I wouldn't dream of doing anything not exactly right. I still felt that somehow I could be sent back, like my freedom was a very tentative thing that could vanish like a dream. Being touched was something else I needed to work on. Even proper table manners were something I had to think about, having eaten with a large dessert spoon for so long.

There is a core experience in every life around which all else is based. For me, that experience has been being locked in a cell on death row for five years. It is like a logjam in the middle of the river of my life, over around and through which everything must flow. Everything is configured around its presence midstream. It changes the course of my life – sometimes opening up new paths, sometimes blocking old ones.

Having accomplished crossing streets, opening doors and table manners, we went on a day trip to Long Island to visit our childhood homes and the store that Micki's father used to own. We even went back to our old elementary school, which was much smaller than we had remembered. It was a trip down memory lane for Micki and me.

Back in the city, I went to the Japanese store and bought the book on Japanese gardens that Jesse and I had spoken about. I carried Jesse around with me for a long time.

ぞ California, mid-October 1992

*Once again, I come with all of my valuable posses-
sions. But this time they are almost all intangible. I
bring my virginity, sense of self, enthusiasm for life,
feeling of gratitude, dignity in the dirt, and a few
basic material items, including a portable radio
with headphones and a watch. I come with a fully
developed and tested set of values and principles
that I have worn for a long time and with which I
am very comfortable. Although my attitude is good
I am not sure of the rules. I am afraid of breaking
them inadvertently. Yet I know this time I will be
in charge of what happens. I will learn the rules of
my new world, like I have three times previously,
but this time I will be responsible consciously for
my own life. I am determined to do and not just be
done to. Each day in my life is a gift and I am
determined never to forget that.*

When we got to LA, I moved in with Micki and Christie.
There were two other women living upstairs. And they had
a cat named Rita. Six of us, all women. The Cosmic
Humour had done it again, putting me in with a bunch of
women just like I was used to in there.

I was fortunate in that a place was provided for me in
those first months of freedom. But it wasn't my space.
After all those years, I needed to take the next step towards
independence. So I went on to create my own space. It is
a process that continues to this day.

From the very first, I had been adopted by the

anti-death-penalty movement – sort of like the poster child, as Micki used to say. Micki and I went to Indiana to the Journey of Hope from Violence to Healing. That was great for me because I got to meet some of the other people who had been wrongly sentenced to death. I remained a member of the Journey of Hope – I liked that theme and it meshed with what I was trying to do myself. The work that had begun in my death row cell, which I had expanded into my everyday life in prison through yoga, meditation and prayer, now became a way of life and a paradigm for living in this world.

When Tina was released from the school, her curiosity led her to me. After Eric's divorce from Debbie, he and Claudia came to join us and we were a family again – all of us in my one-bedroom apartment. At first, everyone was content to let me be the mother, which meant I was the only one who worked, cooked, cleaned and paid bills. It took a few months for me to come to terms with the situation. When I decided I had done sufficient penance, I initiated changes which led to a responsibility-sharing arrangement that helped everyone to grow up and grow beyond the remnants of the past and into our new relationships to one another. There was no going back. These people who had started life as my children were adults now. We couldn't start from where we had left off but we could begin from where we were now, with a shared past and a common desire to know and love one another. It was good. And in the end, Tina – now known as Christina – found the nest too crowded, got a job and a boyfriend and moved out. Eric found love on the net – in an internet chat room – and eventually moved to Australia to be with his lady love. Claudia finished the school year living with me, giving us the opportunity to bond in a very special way. She is a survivor, like me, and landed on her feet in her new home in Australia just as she had done before.

And, after a couple of years, when the children had left the nest and found their own path, I met someone with whom I found the deep connection I had been seeking all my life. I hadn't been trying because I didn't think I could ever find anyone to live with again. And this time, everyone approved. Even Christina, who had never liked any man I had met since her father. I was fifty-one years old, in the sixth year of my new life, when I met the man with whom I would find the greatest happiness and peace I had ever known. I would love for you to meet him. I said goodbye to Los Angeles and the life I had known, packed two suitcases like my ancestors before me, and travelled back to Europe, to Ireland, to live with him in a little house by the sea. There I would find the dream I had left behind so long ago. And every day, when I walk through the garden where we grow our food, with the dogs and the cat, I look up at the sky and thank the Universe for this amazing life.

I LOVE LIFE
I LOVE MY LIFE
THANK YOU FOR THIS GIFT OF LIFE!

PUBLISHER'S
ACKNOWLEDGEMENTS

All the photographs were kindly supplied by the author except for the following:

Broward Correctional Institute for Women and Florida State Prison gateway: courtesy Florida Department of Corrections; death row, Florida State Prison: courtesy of the State Archives of Florida; Sunny in polytunnel: The Scotsman Publications.

The article entitled ''76 Murder Case Haunts State Attorney', from the *Miami Herald*, is by Tom Dubow and Scott Higham. Copyright 1992 by *Miami Herald*. Reproduced with permission of *Miami Herald* in the format Other Book via Copyright Clearance Center.